Middle East Authoritarianisms

Stanford Studies in Middle Eastern and Islamic Societies and Cultures

Middle East Authoritarianisms

GOVERNANCE, CONTESTATION, AND
REGIME RESILIENCE IN SYRIA AND IRAN

Edited by Steven Heydemann and Reinoud Leenders

Stanford University Press
Stanford, California

Stanford University Press
Stanford, California

Printed in the United States of America on acid-free, archival-quality paper

Library of Congress Cataloging-in-Publication Data
Middle East authoritarianisms : governance, contestation, and regime resilience in Syria and Iran / edited by Steven Heydemann and Reinoud Leenders.
    pages cm.—(Stanford studies in Middle Eastern and Islamic societies and cultures)
    Includes bibliographical references and index.
    ISBN 978-0-8047-8301-9 (cloth : alkaline paper)
    1. Authoritarianism—Syria. 2. Authoritarianism—Iran. 3. Syria—Politics and government. 4. Iran—Politics and government. I. Heydemann, Steven, editor of compilation. II. Leenders, Reinoud, editor of compilation.
    JQ1826.A91M53 2012
    320.955—dc23   2012024771

Typeset by Thompson Type in 10/14 Minion

CONTENTS

CONTRIBUTORS

Caroline Donati is a journalist and independent consultant specializing in the Middle East. A graduate of the Institut d'études politiques de Paris, she was Beirut correspondent for *La Croix* (1996–2000) and is the author of *L'Exception syrienne: entre modernisation et résistance* (La Découverte 2009). She writes for the online journal *Mediapart* (www.mediapart.fr).

Teije Hidde Donker is a PhD candidate at the European University Institute, department of political and social sciences, Florence, Italy. His research focuses on Islamist movements in the Arab world, with particular attention to the interaction between regimes and social movements in Syria and Tunisia.

Anoushiravan Ehteshami is professor of International Relations in the School of Government and International Affairs, University of Durham. His books include *Reform in the Middle East Oil Monarchies* (coeditor, Ithaca Press 2008); *Globalization and Geopolitics in the Middle East: Old Games, New Rules* (Routledge 2007); *Iran and the Rise of Its Neoconservatives* (coauthor, I. B. Tauris 2007); *Iran's Security Policy in the Post-Revolutionary Era* (coauthor, RAND 2001); *Syria and Iran: Middle Powers in a Penetrated Regional System* (coauthor, Routledge 1997); and *After Khomeini: The Iranian Second Republic* (Routledge, 1995).

Kevan Harris recently received a PhD in sociology at The Johns Hopkins University, where he completed a dissertation on the politics of social policy in postrevolutionary Iran. His research focuses on comparative and historical sociology of state and class formation in the Islamic Republic. He has written on labor unrest and the political economy of privatization in Iran, as well as an ethnographic study of the 2009 Green Movement. He conducted fieldwork in Iran on an International Dissertation Research Fellowship from the Social Science Research Council and was a U.S. Institute of Peace Jennings Randolph Peace Scholar. He is currently a research fellow in the Department of Near Eastern Studies at Princeton University.

Steven Heydemann serves as senior adviser for Middle East Initiatives at the U.S. Institute of Peace. From 2003 to 2007, Heydemann directed the Center for Democracy and Civil Society at Georgetown University. His books and articles include *Authoritarianism in Syria: Institutions and Social Conflict, 1946–1970* (Cornell University Press 1999); *War, Institutions and Social Change in the Middle East* (edited, University of California Press 2000); *Networks of Privilege in the Middle East: The Politics of Economic Reform Reconsidered* (edited, Palgrave Macmillan 2004); "Upgrading Authoritarianism in the Arab World" (2007); "Social Pacts and the Persistence of Authoritarianism in the Middle East" (2007); and "Authoritarian Learning and Authoritarian Resilience: Regime Responses to the 'Arab Awakening'" (with Reinoud Leenders, 2011).

Raymond Hinnebusch is professor of International Relations and Middle East Politics and director of the Centre for Syrian Studies at the University of St. Andrews. He is author of books and articles on the international politics of the Middle East and of studies on Syria and Egypt. His books include *Syria: Revolution from Above* (Routledge 2001); *Syria and the Middle East Peace Process* (coauthor, Council on Foreign Relations Press 1991); and *Authoritarian Power and State Formation in Ba'thist Syria: Army, Party and Peasant* (Westview Press 1990).

Heidi Huuhtanen holds a PhD in political science from the University of Durham. Her research has focused on the impact of war preparation on authoritarianism in Syria and the general nexus between security and governance. She currently guides conflict prevention and resolution related activities of the Crisis Management Initiative in the Middle East.

Reinoud Leenders is reader in international relations with a focus on Middle East Studies in the Department of War Studies at King's College, London. He formerly worked as Middle East analyst for the International Crisis Group based in Beirut (2002–2005). His research interests include Middle East politics generally and Syria, Lebanon, and Iraq in particular and focus on authoritarian governance, corruption, armed conflict, and refugee issues. He authored several articles in academic journals and edited volumes and *Spoils of Truce: Corruption and Institution-Building in Post-War Lebanon* (Cornell University Press 2012). His current research focuses on mobilization and the popular uprising in Syria.

Arzoo Osanloo is associate professor at the University of Washington in the Law, Societies, and Justice Program. Formerly an immigration and asylum/refugee attorney, Osanloo conducts research and teaches on the intersection of law and culture, including human rights, refugee rights and identity, and women's rights in Muslim societies. She has published in various academic journals. Her book *The Politics of Women's Rights in Iran* (Princeton 2009) analyzes the politicization of "rights talk" in postrevolutionary Iran. Her current project considers the Islamic mandate of forgiveness, compassion, and mercy in Iran's criminal sanctioning system; jurisprudential scholarship; and everyday acts among pious Muslims.

Thomas Pierret is a lecturer on contemporary Islam at the University of Edinburgh. He was a postdoctoral research associate at Princeton University, Department of Near Eastern Studies. In addition to articles in academic journals, he is the author of *Baas et islam en Syrie: La dynastie Asad face aux oulémas* (Presses universitaires de France 2011).

Paola Raunio is a PhD candidate in the School of International Relations at the University of St. Andrews. Her research title is "Saving Muslim Women in the Era of 'Axis of Evil'? Universal versus Local Understanding of Women's Rights in Iran." She graduated from the School of African and Oriental Studies, London University, in 2008.

Güneş Murat Tezcür is associate professor of political science at Loyola University, Chicago. He has published extensively on democratization, political violence, Muslim political attitudes, judicial activism, ethnic conflict, and electoral politics. He is also the author of *Muslim Reformers in Iran and Turkey: The Paradox of Moderation* (University of Texas Press 2010). His current project examines the conditions under which ordinary people take extraordinary risks and join insurgent movements.

Maaike Warnaar is a PhD candidate at the University of St Andrews and teaches international relations of the Middle East at the University of Amsterdam. Her doctoral research is on ideology and Iranian foreign policy under President Ahmadinejad.

Max Weiss is assistant professor of history and Near Eastern Studies at Princeton University. He is the author of *In the Shadow of Sectarianism: Law, Shi'ism and the Making of Modern Lebanon* (Harvard University Press, 2010) and the translator, most recently, of Hassouna Mosbahi, *A Tunisian Tale* (American University in Cairo Press, 2011), and Samar Yazbek, *A Woman in the Crossfire: Diaries of the Syrian Revolution* (London: Haus, 2012).

Tina Zintl is a PhD candidate at University of St Andrews (research project on "Syria's Modernization from Above: A Success-Story Unfolding Due to the Political Inclusion of Foreign-Educated Returnees and Expatriates under Bashar al-Asad?"). She holds a master's degree in political science, economics, and geography from University of Erlangen-Nuremberg.

ACKNOWLEDGMENTS

THE AUTHORS THANK the Dutch NGO Hivos, which made the research and workshops for this volume possible within the framework of its joint research program with the University of Amsterdam on Civil Society in West Asia. Juliette Verhoeven assisted our efforts as program coordinator at the University of Amsterdam. Kawa Hassan, Knowledge Officer for Hivos, was consistently supportive of our aims.

Our gratitude also goes to Sami Atallah, director of the Lebanese Center for Policy Studies, who helped organize a workshop at LCPS in Beirut held in May 2011 where Syrian, Iranian, and Lebanese researchers and writers provided valuable input in response to a presentation of selected papers of this volume. Audiences gathering in March 2011 at the Stimson Center, the National Democratic Institute, and the Center for Contemporary Arab Studies at Georgetown University similarly provided useful comments and critiques. Meir Walters provided invaluable help with the production of the manuscript.

Middle East Authoritarianisms

1 AUTHORITARIAN GOVERNANCE IN SYRIA AND IRAN

Challenged, Reconfiguring, and Resilient

Steven Heydemann and Reinoud Leenders

AFTER A DECADE of authoritarian renewal, nondemocratic regimes in the Middle East find themselves under stresses that only a short time ago were, if not unimaginable, then certainly unexpected. As the first decade of a new century ended, regimes that once seemed all but invulnerable found themselves on the defensive. In Tunisia, an entrenched authoritarian ruler collapsed under the weight of mass protests. By mid-January 2011, incumbent President Zine al-Abdin Ben Ali had taken refuge in Saudi Arabia and, together with his family, was the target of international arrest warrants. Also in January, mass protests led Jordan's King Abdullah to dismiss his government and initiate a process of limited constitutional reforms. In Egypt, protests on a scale unprecedented in the region forced the end of the Mubarak era in February 2011 and, as this is being written in early 2012, continue to pressure the Egyptian military to open the political system and permit a transition to real democracy. In October 2011, Muammar al-Qaddafi, Libya's ruler for over forty years, was killed following months of armed struggle against rebel forces backed by NATO air support. The following month, similar protests and the armed mobilization of regime opponents forced Yemen's President Ali Abdallah Salih out of office, bringing his forty-three-year tenure as Yemen's ruler to an end. Elsewhere in the Middle East, from Morocco to Bahrain, authoritarian regimes moved to shore up social policies that they felt would mitigate, at least temporarily, the economic and social pressures that contributed to popular uprisings.

The significance of these changes cannot be overestimated. At the start of December 2010 authoritarian regimes in the Middle East appeared more deeply consolidated than they had in the late 1980s, when the Third Wave of democratization broke against the southern and eastern shores of the Mediterranean and then receded. Despite two decades of Western support for democracy and civil society promotion, by late 2010 hopes for genuine and far-reaching democratic change in the Middle East seemed to have reached a dead end. Yet, only two months later, Arab citizens, acting spontaneously and outside any formal political framework, revitalized the possibility of Arab democracy. Through their sacrifice and commitment, they achieved more in a matter of weeks than Western democracy promoters had accomplished in two decades.

The protesters who have redefined politics in the Middle East also pose significant challenges to scholars of authoritarianism. Although it is too soon to know whether Tunisia, Egypt, Libya, and Yemen are on the path to genuine democracy, as opposed to the reconfiguring of authoritarian governance, their recent experiences will undoubtedly force a reassessment of arguments about authoritarian persistence and the durability of authoritarian systems of rule in the Middle East. Those who have developed arguments accounting for the success of authoritarianism in the region, including the editors of this volume, thus have a particular obligation to be clear about conditions under which their arguments might be falsified and will undoubtedly be among those who assess old arguments in the light of new facts.

What seems clear, however, even from a vantage point that is deeply enmeshed in the urgent struggles underway across the region, is that authoritarianism in the Middle East will survive this transformational moment. In Syria, one of the two cases on which this volume focuses, fear of civil war is deepening as a popular uprising begins to morph into armed resistance to a repressive regime. Syrians have joined their Tunisian, Egyptian, Yemeni, and Jordanian counterparts in taking to the streets to demand the end of a brutal authoritarian government. The Syrian regime responded with promises of reform but then, like its counterparts elsewhere, quickly resorted to large-scale repression. In Iran, the second case covered in this volume, the hard-liners of the Islamic Republic initially showed extraordinary audacity in claiming the Egyptian uprising as an omen that the region was tipping in their direction. However, supporters of Iran's failed "Green Movement" of 2009—the wave of protests and mass mobilization prompted by Iran's rigged elections that year—viewed events in Egypt very differently. They found the most important parallels to be between their own treatment at the hands of the Revolutionary Guard and the fate of Egyptian protesters or their Syrian counterparts, who have been attacked by regime thugs and state militias. Regardless, the relative success of the Arab uprisings thus far has failed to revitalize Iran's own protest movement or to force the Iranian regime into major concessions, let alone bring about its demise.

None of the key approaches to the study of Middle Eastern regimes saw the wave of protest coming. Yet far from contradicting recent work on authoritarianism in the Middle East, the response of many Arab regimes to mass pressures for change has been largely consistent with the expectations and frameworks developed in the research literature: surviving authoritarian regimes have learned from the experiences unfolding across the region and have adapted their strategies of governance in response (Heydemann and Leenders 2011). They have made concessions—more cosmetic than real in many cases; adopted policies intended to mitigate the economic and social drivers of conflict; sought to divide and fragment nascent oppositions; applied heavy repression when deemed necessary; imposed stricter controls over social media, the internet, and new communications technologies; and otherwise demonstrated the flexibility and adaptive capacity that have served them so well over the course of their many decades in power.

Whatever our own hopes for more widespread and deeper democratic transformations in the Middle East, therefore, the facts suggest that authoritarianism will remain a prominent and formidable presence in the lives of millions of citizens. The study of authoritarian governance therefore remains essential for our understanding of the political dynamics and inner workings of regimes across the region—even while recognizing that recent events demand renewed attention on our part to shifts and pressures that might drive cases such as Syria and Iran in directions that now, in the wake of Tunisia, Egypt, Libya, and Yemen, cannot be ruled out. Indeed, from March 2011, Syria too became engulfed in turmoil, its government struggling to contain protests demanding the fall of the regime, demands from which, as late as January 2011, Bashar al-Asad believed his regime to be insulated by virtue of its Arab nationalist credentials. Largely due to the regime's harsh and unremitting response to what began primarily as calls for reform, confrontations between the regime and protesters have become so violent that there appears to be no possibility for a return to the status quo ante. Regardless of what the future will bring—regime change or not—the protracted struggle now holding Syria in its grip speaks volumes about the Asad regime's willingness and capacity to press for its survival at any cost and by any means.

The developments of 2011 will leave the political landscape of the region changed but recognizable. Yet they also highlight concerns that have animated this volume since its inception in late 2009. Among the most important of these is the understanding that the Middle East is home to not one but to many forms of authoritarian governance. Differences among regimes were always present but have tended to be overshadowed by the use of "authoritarianism" as a generic descriptor awkwardly capturing a rich pallet of nondemocratic rule. In the aftermath of the successful popular uprisings in Tunisia, Egypt, Libya, and Yemen, however, it has become more important than ever to break this generic category apart and assess not only the attributes that regimes such as the Syrian and Iranian share—and, as we argue in what follows, they share more than might be evident at first glance—but what distinguishes them, as well. As the political trajectories of Middle Eastern states seem increasingly likely to diverge in years ahead, with some perhaps consolidating democratic gains while others remain under distinct and resilient forms of authoritarian rule, understanding variations in modes of authoritarian governance and linking these to varying degrees and forms of regime resilience become an increasingly urgent priority.

WHERE TO FROM HERE IN THE STUDY OF MIDDLE EAST AUTHORITARIANISM

For much of the past decade, research programs in political science, political economy, sociology, and anthropology have chronicled experiences of authoritarian regression across the Middle East, explored sources of authoritarian persistence, and developed explanations that account for authoritarian survival in an era of democratization (Brownlee 2002 and 2007; Lust-Okar 2005; Posusney and Angrist 2005; Pratt 2007; Schlumberger 2007). Setting aside not only the lingering essentialisms of previous research but also the more recent (and perhaps newly relevant) legacies of "transitology," these research programs have in large measure turned away from earlier efforts to understand failures of democratization. Instead, like the current volume, they assumed the viability of authoritarianism as a system of rule, not least because it has been around for over half a century, and directed their attention to understanding how authoritarian regimes in the Middle East govern. Individual rulers at times faced daunting challenges. They explored how authoritarian systems of rule managed the challenges they confronted and how, in doing so, they reconfigured existing institutions and practices, developing new configurations of both that equipped them to endure significant economic, social, and political stresses without breaking, even while societies in the Middle East were themselves adapting to new patterns of authoritarian governance (Heydemann 2007a).

The current volume is a contribution to this emerging and still relevant research program. In keeping with the assumptions that inform such approaches to the study of authoritarianism in the Middle East, the following chapters view authoritarian regimes in Iran and Syria as consolidated and viable systems of rule able to withstand significant, although by no means all, challenges. We do not presume that our two case countries are either stalled in transitions to democracy or exceptional in the challenges they face and the strategies they have developed to manage them. Nor do we rule out the possibility that significant political change can occur in the future, especially in Syria, where popular demands for an end to the regime have been so intense that it would be foolish to assume that the regime will succeed in its increasingly violent attempts to hang on. Instead, the chapters focus on understanding and explaining longstanding patterns that shed light on critical aspects of how these regimes govern, including at moments of crisis, and how the societies over which they rule have themselves adapted to their political environments.

While broadly situated within emergent research programs, however, this volume also seeks to stretch their boundaries by extending and refining assumptions about authoritarianism in the Middle East in at least four ways. First, our focus in this volume is not on the *persistence* of authoritarian regimes in Syria and Iran—a theme many of the authors have addressed in previous work—but their *resilience.*[1] To some, this may appear to be a minor distinction. We view it as consequential, however, both for how we conceptualize authoritarianism in the Middle East and for how we organize our research. Authoritarian persistence carries connotations of anachronistic, one-person dictatorships stubbornly clinging to power while falling increasingly out of touch with their societies and rapidly changing environments. Chehabi and Linz's "sultanistic regimes"—personalist rule resting on little more than sheer force and bribes, weakly institutionalized, and enjoying no social base to speak of—appear to be compatible with these conceptualizations (Chehabi and Linz 1998). By contrast, authoritarian resilience refers to the attributes, relational qualities, and institutional arrangements that have long given regimes in the Middle East, conceptualized as *institutionalized systems of rule,* the capacity to adapt governance strategies to changing domestic and international conditions. If questions of persistence draw our attention to explanations of *outcomes,* questions of resilience shift our focus to explanations of *processes* and in particular to the dynamic and complex interconnections between processes of authoritarian renewal, on one hand, and social adaptations to these processes, on the other. Questions of resilience thus require that we broaden our analytic focus beyond regime-level analysis—which remains relevant—to encompass the microlevel adaptations among social actors to new patterns of authoritarian governance.

Second, in contrast to some research on Middle East authoritarianism, which has implicitly viewed state and social actors as occupying discrete political spaces, the chapters here focus on the interconnections and overlap between the two. In particular, scholars who maintain normative expectations about the role that civil societies play as advocates of reform, democratization, or "development," or who assume that civic sectors provide an inherent counterweight to authoritarian states, tend to assume the separateness of "associative life" even if they acknowledge that reality is often far messier than these assumptions warrant and that civic sectors may even reinforce authoritarianism instead of posing a challenge to it (Jamal 2007). Without in any sense erasing the all-too-real disconnects between Middle East states and the societies they govern, the following chapters focus instead on the political effects of this distance: how gaps between ruler and ruled are themselves productive of certain kinds of social adaptations to authoritarian rule, how social actors exploit these gaps in unintended ways, and how their shape and boundaries (whether viewed as constructed or not) are in turn affected by regime-level efforts to contain and manage Middle Eastern societies. Thus, in making authoritarian governance central to the analysis of Syrian and Iranian politics, we have not discarded the significance and role of nonstate actors but have instead set aside the expectation that nonstate actors effectively organize in spheres independent from or (only) in opposition to the state, thereby generating a platform for liberal-democratic change. In the current volume this interactive conception of state–society relations is evident in Güneş Murat Tezcür's analysis of Iran as a competitive authoritarian regime and in Arzoo Osanloo's chapter on the strategies developed by Iranian women to seize the regime's focus on women's rights as the basis for expanding their legal autonomy in ways that have challenged the regime's intent. In Max Weiss's chapter, we see these interconnections reflected in contemporary Syrian literature and the quietly subversive strategies that novelists adopt to convey the effects of life under authoritarianism for their protagonists.

Third, building on research that Heydemann (2007a and 2007b) and others have pursued over the past decade on authoritarian upgrading, our focus on resilience extends and deepens how we conceptualize the *adaptive capacities* of regimes and societies in both Syria and Iran. Unlike much of the more recent work on authoritarian modernization, we do not view the adaptive attributes evident in these two cases as limited in scope to "defensive" responses to political and economic challenges. They are not episodic features that emerge during moments of crisis only to fade back once the crisis recedes. Thus, we do not conceptualize this capacity in terms of "survival strategies" (Brumberg 2003). Instead, we define regimes in Syria and Iran in terms of what we call *recombinant authoritarianism*: systems of rule that possess the capacity to reorder and reconfigure instruments and strategies of governance, to reshape and recombine existing institutional, discursive, and regulatory arrangements to create recognizable but nonetheless distinctive solutions to shifting configurations of challenges (Stark 1996).[2]

This recombinant quality is critical for understanding the sources of regime resilience in Syria and Iran. It creates possibilities for incumbents to amend and modify the arrangements, both formal and informal, through which they manage the distribution of power and resources, the production of legitimacy, and the maintenance of their authority. It is manifest in the processes of authoritarian upgrading that reshaped strategies of governance in the Middle East over the past decade. We see it at work, as Thomas Pierret's chapter shows, in the expansion of state regulatory authority over religious affairs in Syria since 2008 and the resulting transformation of a critical domain of state–society relations along lines that mark a sharp break with the past experience of the Syrian Ba'thist regime. The picture emerging from Pierret's chapter is more complex and fluid than is suggested by frequent references to the Syrian regime's uncompromising "secularism." We can find it in the capacity of the Syrian regime to adjust the roles allocated to judicial institutions as circumstances and regime requirements change, as Reinoud Leenders demonstrates in his chapter. It is also evident, as Kevan Harris's chapter attests, in the multiple and competing institutional frameworks the Iranian regime maintains to manage social policy in the Islamic Republic. In other words, recombinant authoritarianism is not simply a defensive reaction to threats, though the plasticity of some Middle East regimes at such crucial moments is certainly essential to their survival. Rather, these two regimes, and perhaps others as well, are exhibiting something deeper: an *institutionalized flexibility* that is characteristic not only of reactions to threat but also of everyday governance. Recombinant authoritarianism, as the following chapters show, is as much a feature of normal politics as it is of regime responses to moments of exceptional stress.

Fourth, our conception of Middle East regimes leads us to take seriously the question of *authoritarian legitimacy* along several dimensions: the strategies regimes use to secure domestic support; the institutional arrangements—judicial and redistributive arrangements in particular—that regimes construct both to support legitimacy claims at home and to consolidate claims to sovereignty in the international system; and the capacity of regimes to exploit external threats to reinforce domestic legitimacy. Though legitimacy is often viewed as a secondary consideration for regimes that rely heavily on coercion to secure their citizens' compliance, the following chapters not only reinforce the importance that Middle East regimes attach to legitimacy, importance that seems likely to be amplified as a result of regime collapse in Tunisia, Egypt, and Libya; they also explore strategies of legitimation as an arena within which the Syrian and Iranian regimes demonstrate their recombinant capacities. This is not to say, of course, that such strategies are necessarily successful; the Syrian regime has undoubtedly lost much of its legitimacy through its repression of largely unarmed protesters. Yet the chapters in this volume underscore the flexibility with which such regimes respond to legitimacy challenges and thus push our understanding of authoritarian legitimacy and regime resilience well beyond the truism that high legitimacy is equated with survival and low legitimacy with potential regime breakdown. Instead, as seen in the chapters by Anoushiravan Ehteshami, Raymond Hinnebusch, and their coauthors; Leenders; Tezcür; and Harris, legitimacy has a far more dynamic quality than might be assumed given the strict ideological orientations commonly attributed to the Syrian and Iranian regimes.

The emphasis of the chapters in this volume on the dynamic and adaptive qualities of governance and of state–society relations thus underscores the importance of exploring processes of political change within consolidated authoritarian regimes. Yet it also acknowledges that, even in the wake of regime collapse in Tunisia, Libya, Yemen, and Egypt, political change in the Middle East may in some instances become regime reinforcing and will not necessarily be of a liberal-democratic nature or evolve toward preconceived frameworks of authoritarian breakdown or democratic transition.

SYRIA AND IRAN AS RECOMBINANT AUTHORITARIAN REGIMES

The following chapters engage these issues through a focus on two very differently organized authoritarian regimes, Syria and Iran. Syria is emblematic of the region's secular autocracies, dominated by a single-party regime since 1963, when the Ba'th Party seized power and distinctive in the limited extent to which it has participated in broader trends toward political openings and selective economic reform in the Middle East. It occupies a position as one of the more intensely authoritarian regimes in the Arab world. Iran, on the other hand, stands out not only for its character as a theocratic regime, an avowedly Islamic republic since its revolution in 1979, but until recently for its relatively soft form of authoritarian rule. Prior to June 2009, when mass protests broke out over an unprecedented degree of election rigging, Iran combined theocratic rule supported by a repressive state apparatus with meaningful electoral competition and limited space for political mobilization. Even following the June 2009 elections and a sharp increase in regime repression in response to the Green Movement, politics and governance in Iran have exhibited a degree of institutional fragmentation, decentralization of decision making, and sustained levels of social mobilization that continue to distinguish the Islamic Republic from most of its Arab neighbors.

Indeed, setting aside their shared reliance on anti-Americanism and anti-Westernism as sources of legitimacy and the basis of their strategic alliance, Syria and Iran are such strikingly divergent regime types that for many purposes they would serve well as "least similar" cases, useful primarily to illustrate variation in modes of authoritarian governance. We selected these cases, however, not to highlight their self-evident differences but to underscore the ways in which, despite these differences, Syria and Iran display significant elements of comparability across two divergent models of authoritarian rule. Most important from our perspective is that both exhibit the recombinant attributes that we view as central for explaining regime resilience in these cases. What the following chapters demonstrate, across domains that range from strategies of economic governance, to the roles and functions of the judiciary, to the management of state relations with key organized interests (such as women in the Iranian case and Islamists in the Syrian case), is the degree to which these two very different authoritarian regime types share the capacity to reconfigure and adapt strategies of governance to accommodate a changing political, economic, and social landscape, even if this by no means guarantees regime survival into the indefinite future.

When seen through the lens of recombinant authoritarianism, in other words, important similarities between Syria and Iran move to the fore. At a macrolevel, both are cases in which regimes that rely heavily on clientalist networks and the use of patronage to exploit and manipulate formal institutional frameworks, alter organizational roles and functions among state agencies, and deploy state regulatory authority to give a legalistic appearance to the arbitrary exercise of political power. In both cases, regimes promote the proliferation of "rules of the game," adding and combining modes of governance with considerable flexibility. In recombinant authoritarian regimes, multiplicity prevails. Indeed, it is a defining element of regime resilience, as it allows incumbents to juggle their options, constituencies, and resources without being beholden to any of them or being irreparably undercut by the unintended consequences of their choices. Multiple modes of economic governance overlap and coexist: market-based, clientalist, and state-directed strategies provide a wealth of opportunities for the management of regime constituencies—even if, at times, shifts in the balance of opportunities may lead to tensions between competing constituencies of a regime or, as in the Syrian case, to widespread discontent. This is especially evident in Caroline Donati's account of the emergence of new cohorts of politically influential business cronies in Syria who have exploited economic liberalization to capture the benefits of deregulated economic sectors, while an older generation of regime beneficiaries within state and party institutions perceived that they were losing ground. In Iran, as Harris shows, multiple institutional networks oversee complementary systems of redistribution, each of which generates loyalty and legitimacy among the particular social sectors they serve. Similarly, in both cases, we find multiple judicial systems operating under distinctive rules and procedures, including, in Syria, an entirely distinct set of courts created to handle security-related matters.

In both cases, moreover, the demands of regime legitimation required important shifts in strategies of governance, leading the Iranian and Syrian regimes to reconfigure relationships with key domestic constituencies in the process. As Ehteshami and Hinnebusch and their coauthors demonstrate in their chapter, the erosion of domestic support for the Iranian and Syrian regime at moments of significant external pressure made foreign policy an especially attractive domain for their efforts to renew and revitalize their legitimacy at home, although in the Syrian case insufficiently so to have prevented the current uprising. Yet if both exploited external threats for domestic purposes, the effects of these efforts moved the Iranian and Syrian regimes in opposing directions—creating incentives to broaden political inclusion in the Syrian case while undermining such incentives in the Iranian case, producing a narrowing and hardening of the Iranian regime's ruling coalition in recent years.

The following chapters elaborate on these elements of recombinant authoritarianism from a variety of disciplinary and thematic perspectives. In identifying participants for this project, we attached a high priority to scholars who have spent significant time on the ground in either Syria or Iran, countries that do not offer welcoming conditions to researchers. We brought together authors whose work was based on original, primary-source material and whose research interests and approaches, however diverse, provide insight into the dynamic qualities of authoritarian governance in Syria and Iran through detailed attention to specific empirical cases. We were less concerned with achieving symmetry in our coverage of each case than in bringing core aspects of recombinant authoritarianism to the fore in both cases. Nonetheless, several unifying themes emerged in the course of the project, and in the remaining sections of this introduction we summarize the findings of our authors in four key areas that we also use to organize the presentation of chapters in the volume: (1) economic governance and recombinant authoritarian rule; (2) authoritarian resilience and the management of religious affairs; (3) social and literary responses to authoritarian resilience; and (4) strategies of authoritarian legitimation. In all these respects, a comparison of the two countries—using single-case chapters to shed light on both similarities and differences—will enhance an understanding of the resilience and the recombinant quality of authoritarianism in both Iran and Syria. And if findings from two cases may not be sufficient to satisfy claims about the generalizability of recombinant authoritarianism in the Middle East at large, its presence in two such divergent regimes gives us a useful starting point for further comparative research.

ECONOMIC GOVERNANCE AND RECOMBINANT
AUTHORITARIAN RULE

In both Syria and Iran, authoritarian regimes have constructed systems of economic governance that express distinctive political logics yet provide incumbents with extraordinary flexibility in managing access to and the allocation of economic resources and opportunities. In both cases, these systems provide vivid examples of how seemingly discordant economic and political goals can be accommodated through the proliferation of economic institutions, the appropriation of formal institutional frameworks by informal predatory networks, and the use of social policy to reward some constituencies and marginalize others. They highlight the extent to which rules of the game proliferate, as new institutions, new policies, and new informal networks are layered onto those already in place. Yet they also demonstrate the frictions and challenges incumbents face as they restructure systems of economic governance to adapt to changing circumstances. Real resources are at stake when recombinant authoritarian regimes realign the flow of economic benefits and opportunities. The shift from state to market in Syria, however selective and limited it might be, changed patterns of corruption and clientelism, privileging some regime loyalists over others. The use of social policy as an instrument of political competition in Iran created competing welfare systems offering varied levels of benefits and support. In both cases, those who lose out in the process can become a potential threat to regimes, in turn prompting new adjustments and adaptations to contain potential challenges.

Donati's chapter on authoritarian renewal in Syria situates economic policy change in the context of broader processes of regime restructuring that followed the rise to power of Bashar al-Asad as his father's successor in July 2000. Even as the second President al-Asad consolidated his control over critical instruments of regime authority, placing his own loyalists in positions of power in the security services and the Ba'th Party apparatus, he was also reconfiguring frameworks of economic governance to redirect rent-seeking opportunities toward new elements of his ruling coalition. As Donati writes, Hafiz al-Asad's generation "got rich through the state sector," while Bashar al-Asad's networks of supporters "monopolized the private sector and prospered, to the detriment of economic growth." In effect, a system of market-based cronyism emerged alongside of, and at times at the expense of, a longstanding system of state-based cronyism. This process of privatizing the state, as Donati notes, "creates new players and new forms of political, economic and social regulation, which transforms authoritarian rule." It also transforms the organization of Syria's political economy.

For Bashar al-Asad and those in his immediate circles, economic liberalization created new domains of rent seeking, permitting him both to increase the scale of economic resources at the regime's disposal and to manage access to these economic opportunities in ways that enhanced the president's authority; sustained the loyalty of those on whose support he depended, especially in the security services; and thus buttressed the security of his regime. This took place through a variety of means, as Donati details based on her extended periods of fieldwork and interviews in Syria. These include the controlled privatization of public sector assets that were delivered into the hands of regime cronies; the liberalization of previously regulated sectors such as banking, with highly politicized criteria used in determining who would receive permission to establish private banks; loosening of controls on foreign investment while directing investment flows through regime loyalists; and the development of new markets in areas such as telecoms that were similarly allocated to individuals close to the president.

In addition, however, the shift from state-based to market-based modes of rent seeking also permitted the regime to broaden its support among certain segments of Syrian society. Economic reforms fueled a real estate boom in and around Damascus. The withdrawal of Syrian forces from Lebanon in early 2005, although certainly constituting a setback in foreign policy terms, created opportunities for commercial development in Damascus and elsewhere, with the shift to Syria of all kinds of routine economic activities that were no longer so easily conducted in Beirut. Many Syrians gained access to new communications technologies. Private universities were established. Western-style shopping malls proliferated. Despite the regional and international turmoil roiling Syria's foreign policy, daily life within Syria became more comfortable for the well-to-do, and the regime received credit from the few who benefited from its economic "modernization."

During 2005, these trends were formalized in what the regime came to define as a new development strategy: the "social market economy." This phrase was intended to capture and reconcile divergent and frequently contradictory frameworks of economic governance that had emerged under Bashar al-Asad. In this neatly packaged formulation, the regime would preserve its commitment to the populist and redistributive social policies that defined state–society relations under the Ba'th (Hinnebusch 2002) and retain the public institutions that such policies required but would complement these elements with newer, market-oriented policies and regulatory frameworks that would overcome the dysfunctions and inefficiencies associated with the public sector and give Syria the foundations for improved economic performance.

Beyond this attempt to brand Syria's economy in terms that would make it palatable to international financial institutions and foreign investors, however, the move toward a social market economy both depended on and reflected the kinds of adaptive flexibility that we associate with recombinant authoritarian regimes. The capacity of Bashar al-Asad and his inner circle to reconfigure Syria's economy, create new sources of rents, and generate the resources needed to manage new networks of patronage and clientalism is, as Donati affirms, central to the resilience of the regime.

Yet this process of authoritarian renewal, as Donati calls it, should not be seen as an unmitigated success or, indeed, a guarantee for regime survival.

In providing the most detailed picture yet available of how authoritarian renewal has unfolded in Syria, she is also keenly attentive to the effects of this process, both on the segments of society that have fueled Syria's uprising and on those who were the principal beneficiaries of previous frameworks of economic governance, especially those who relied on their positions within the Ba'th Party and the public sector to generate economic resources, political power, and social status. Under Syria's new economic dispensation, all of these groups found themselves falling behind and, increasingly, disgruntled about their decline. At the same time, the social groups that have benefited from economic liberalization are not yet tightly bound to the regime: their loyalty is far less secure than was that of their Ba'thist predecessors. Reconfiguring the economic and social bases of the regime thus carried considerable risks. It has helped Bashar al-Asad to consolidate his authority in the short term, while creating new political and economic tensions that placed his regime under strain. Indeed, in hindsight one could view such tensions as key to the background that made many Syrians responsive to the massive outpouring of popular discontent elsewhere in the region, especially in Egypt. Donati does not imply that sustaining Hafiz al-Asad's approach to economic governance was a feasible option for his son. Nor does she predict how the regime of Bashar al-Asad will cope with emergent strains among or within an increasingly discordant ruling coalition. Yet it is possible to glimpse in her analysis, and its focus on the capacity of Bashar al-Asad's regime to adapt its strategies of economic governance to changing conditions, that it will need these capacities as much in the future (should it have a future) as it did in the past. Accordingly, much of the regime's response to the current uprising consists of a careful balancing act, juggling economic and financial measures simultaneously to appease the country's business community, its still sizeable public sector constituency, and the takers of subsidies on essential items.

In the Iranian case, questions of economic governance and the organization of social policy have often been overshadowed by attention to conflicts among contending factions of the political elite. Yet, as Harris shows in his chapter on welfare provision and social policy in Iran, these domains offer important insight into the resilience of the Islamic Republic and underscore the adaptive flexibility it has displayed since its founding in 1979. Harris traces the emergence and effects of a mixed welfare regime in Iran that operates through two largely separate sets of institutions, "each with its own historical lineage and constituencies." One, inherited from the Pahlavi monarchy (1925–1979) but preserved under the Islamic Republic since 1979, Harris characterizes as a "corporatist welfare regime," providing economic benefits directed largely at the urban working and middle classes. The other, which directs social welfare benefits to Iran's least-well-off social strata, is described as a "revolutionary welfare regime." It traces its origins to the postrevolutionary formation of endowed foundations (bonyads), the Imam Khomeini Relief Committee (IKRC), and the creation of a network of rural health facilities that served segments of Iranian society, especially the rural poor, which had been largely excluded from Pahlavi-era welfare programs.

Not surprisingly, postrevolutionary social policy in Iran and the institutions created to support it reflect the ideological ambitions of Iran's newly empowered clerical leaders to mobilize and integrate segments of Iranian society that had been excluded under the Shah. Despite the ideological fervor of the early postrevolutionary period, however, Pahlavi-era frameworks of social provision were not dismantled. Rather, a parallel system of social welfare took shape alongside them. This parallel system responded to real and urgent social needs among Iran's poor and veterans of its eight-year war with Iraq but also generated significant legitimacy and political capital for the new revolutionary regime. By preserving the corporatist welfare regime it inherited, the Islamic Republic retained enormous capacity to deliver social welfare to social groups that did not constitute the core social bases of the regime but could have become a significant source of social discontent had it sought to exclude and marginalize them on ideological grounds. Moreover, corporatist welfare frameworks did not merely survive, they prospered, growing to oversee massive social security programs such as the Civil Society Retirement Organization and the Social Security Organization that manage pension benefits for tens of millions of Iranians. As a result, as Harris points out, the Islamic Republic

> developed a dual set of institutional apparatuses for administering social policy. One part was technocratic, well-trained, and possessed experience administering services to a portion of the population. The other part was unplanned in structure, ideological in rhetoric, and saw itself as the real social auxiliary of the new regime. Unusually, what did not subsequently occur was the fusion of these institutions.

Drawing on data collected through fieldwork in Iran, Harris illustrates the inner workings of social welfare institutions that have contributed significantly to the consolidation and resilience of the Islamic Republic. By maintaining social safety nets that reach large segments of Iran's poor and middle classes, the regime has sustained a broad base of popular support even as it faces increasing international pressures. Indeed, Harris's chapter shows the extent to which the regime has insulated social welfare programs from austerity measures taken in response to economic sanctions imposed on the country in recent years. Even as subsidies are cut, the regime has largely protected its social (and political) safety nets. Yet, as in the Syrian case, the presence of multiple, sometimes overlapping modes of economic governance—in this case the flexible management of social provision—carries with it new political and economic tensions. In Iran, ideological justifications for access to social benefits have weakened over time: "'legitimate' welfare given to war veterans in the 1980s and 1990s," Harris states, had "morphed into 'undeserved' benefits for a group too young to have fought in the war, and in some cases (such as the Basij), for youth actively engaged in preventing the middle class from enjoying autonomy from the hated paternalistic intrusions by the state." Adding to middle-class concerns about the privileges provided to social groups favored by the regime, it also confronts declining economic mobility as it is superseded in status and access to the regime by those with stronger revolutionary credentials. If the clients of the revolutionary welfare regime view their economic security as having been enhanced by the social policies of the Islamic Republic, their middle-class counterparts feel increasing economic vulnerability. It is not surprising, then, that the Green Movement included strong representation from precisely those segments of the middle class that felt themselves to be losers in the Islamic Republic's efforts to construct an economic order consistent with its revolutionary theocratic identity.

In their own ways, and consistent with the broader political, social, economic contexts in which they took shape, systems of economic governance in both Syria and Iran provide insights into the recombinant qualities that have contributed to regime resilience. Despite its historical origins in a radically populist, redistributive, and egalitarian ideology, the Ba'thist regime under Bashar al-Asad was able to reorient Syria's political economy around a mix of state and market that generated the resources needed to consolidate the regime's authority within emergent clientalist networks. Despite its origins in a radical conception of clerical authority linked to a redemptive and egalitarian vision of Iranian society, Iran's theocratic regime was able to sustain social welfare systems created under the Shah during a period of revolutionary state consolidation, mitigating potential social pressures that might have proven deeply disruptive had they not been addressed through the creative use of social policy.

AUTHORITARIAN RESILIENCE AND THE MANAGEMENT
OF RELIGIOUS AFFAIRS

To assess strategies of authoritarian governance in the management of religious affairs, the volume includes two chapters that focus on different aspects of the relationship between regime and religious actors in Syria. For the ruling Ba'th Party, with its roots in secular-nationalist ideologies of the 1930s and 1940s and its long history of conflict with Syrian Islamist movements—culminating in the massacre of February 1982 in which some 10,000 to 20,000 residents of Hama were killed by Syrian armed forces—this relationship has been especially fraught. The regime's engagement with religious affairs became even more volatile with the rise to power of an Alawite minority faction within the Ba'th Party in the period preceding Hafiz al-Asad's "Corrective Movement" in 1970. Although the regime has continued to articulate a nationalist and pan-Arab identity that transcends sectarian differences, it has at various points in its history struggled to contend not only with armed resistance from Syrian Islamist movements but with the challenge of preserving its secularism amid the growing popular appeal of political Islam across the Arab world in the 1980s and beyond, a trend that has had considerable resonance within Syria over the past twenty years.

Despite the centrality that relations with Islamist actors has occupied in the experience of the Ba'thist regime, however, there is a striking absence of research about the place of religious affairs in the Ba'th Party's approach to state building and to governance or on the ways in which its management of religious affairs has changed over time. Until recently, research focused heavily on the confrontation between Syrian Islamists and the regime, especially the Syrian Muslim Brotherhood. Far less attention was directed toward understanding state strategies for the regulation of religious affairs or the informal networks that Islamist actors and their regime counterparts developed over the years to provide each with instruments for managing a relationship that extended well beyond the formal hostility between the two.[3] Pierret's chapter addresses the first of these issues; Teije Donker's chapter focuses on the second. In both cases, what becomes clear is that, even in a domain in which we might anticipate rigidity and a reluctance to accommodate changing conditions, we find, instead, that the Syrian regime has shown itself capable of modifying and reconfiguring its approach to the management of religious affairs over time, both in terms of formal regulatory oversight and in terms of its informal ties with key Islamist actors. As broader political contexts changed, as the regime calibrated and recalibrated the calculus of its own survival, the Syrian regime's strategies for managing the religious sector also underwent significant modifications.

Pierret's chapter identifies the summer of 2008 as one such turning point in the regime's management of religion, highlighting the introduction of new regulatory instruments that brought the state much more centrally into the regulation of religious affairs than had been the case at any previous time in the forty-eight-year history of Ba'thist rule. Characterizing this as signaling the possible end of the regime's "indirect" approach to the management of religious affairs—an effort to "nationalize" Islam—Pierret situates this move in longer-term and often ad hoc strategies of upgrading and adaptation that have contributed to the Syrian regime's resilience yet have also generated potential new sources of political and social conflict.

To reinforce the scale and significance of the changes introduced in mid-2008, Pierret reviews the contemporary history of efforts to manage religion in Syria dating back to the immediate postindependence era. During the brief republican phase of Syrian history, 1946 to 1963, national leaders adopted a modernizing approach to the governance of religious affairs, creating new regulatory frameworks in the hope of "rationalizing" and institutionalizing religious practices. *Waqfs*, or religious endowments, were nationalized. Clerics were required to pass exams, after which they would be permitted to wear clothing approved by the state as appropriate for religious leaders. With the initial Ba'thist coup in 1963, however, this modernizing approach à la Ataturk (the staunchly secularist founder of the modern Turkish state) was abandoned. Although the Ba'th oversaw the massive expansion of the Syrian state in virtually every area, it adopted an indirect, hands-off approach to the management of religious affairs. For ideological reasons, and in response to opposition movements that were framed in religious terms, Ba'thist regimes sought to neutralize religious institutions, not rationalize them, and to suppress and marginalize leading religious figures. The Ministry of Religious Endowments remained small, its functions and personnel limited. Instead, the regime cultivated individual religious personalities whom it trusted to oversee religious affairs in major urban centers. In Pierret's terms, the regime adopted a policy of "malevolent limited interventionism" in its handling of religious affairs.

Following Bashar al-Asad's rise to power, however, the escalation of regional and international threats led the regime to modify its strategy. With the U.S. invasion of Iraq in March 2003 and the assassination of Lebanon's former

Prime Minister Rafiq al-Hariri in February 2005 in Beirut, the Syrian regime came under extraordinary pressure. In response, it took measures to shore up its domestic support, including by appropriating and exploiting Islamist trends that had taken hold within Syrian society and increasing state support for religious affairs. As part of this effort, the regime sought to strengthen its ties with organized Islamic actors, including charitable societies controlled by informal educational movements that had previously been engaged in anti-regime activities. It adopted a more permissive attitude toward Islamist activities, expanded the space available for Islamists in Syria's public sphere, and generally sought to align itself with moderate Islamist actors.

This rapprochement, however, was to be short lived. As Islamist activists became a more visible and more vocal presence in Syrian society, and as external threats receded following the Israel–Lebanon war of June 2006, the Syrian regime changed course yet again. It reimposed tighter controls on religious affairs and curtailed the autonomy it had briefly extended to Islamist actors. Yet the regime did not simply revert to its early policy of malign neglect. Instead, it moved far more assertively than it had in the past to institutionalize the management of religious affairs, to bring religious activities under tighter state control rather than to push them to the margins of Syrian political life. It expanded the role of the state as an actor in the religious sphere. Given the history of the Ba'th's tense relationship with religious affairs, these measures represented an unprecedented shift in the overall orientation of the regime toward the management of religious affairs. As we have seen in other domains, these adaptations delivered significant immediate benefits to the regime—another instance in which adaptive flexibility has served the ends of regime resilience—yet created new challenges for the regime in the longer term. Indeed, these challenges too help to understand the backdrop against which mass popular mobilization against the regime became possible in 2011. As Pierret makes clear, by inserting itself more directly into the management of religious affairs the regime became far more vulnerable to criticism from observant Sunnis within Syrian society. The impression that a minority Alawite regime, one bound strategically to the Shi'ite government of Iran, is now directly controlling the religious affairs of a Sunni majority population has the potential to exacerbate sectarian tensions—and to do so at a moment when Arab regimes are already feeling exceptionally vulnerable.

If Pierret focuses on the recombinant qualities of formal state policies toward the management of religious affairs, Donker sheds light on how regime relations with religious actors unfolded at the level of informal network ties between regime elites and their Islamist counterparts. Starting with Pierret's account of the regime's long-standing preference for an arms-length approach to the management of religious affairs, Donker traces how shifts in regime strategy looked from the perspective of Islamist elites, first during the brief era of rapprochement between the regime and Islamist actors and subsequently during the more recent phase in which the regime expanded its role in the direct management of the religious sphere. For Donker, the regime's strategy of managing religious affairs, not through incorporation and close regulation of Islamic elites but by their marginalization from formal institutions and the state apparatus permitted Islamist actors to retain a measure of autonomy in the governance of religious affairs, even while lacking formal channels through which to mediate their relationship with the regime. As a result, "brokerage" became an important means for negotiating the relationship between the regime and Islamist actors, with critical religious figures taking on the role of brokers who would mediate with the regime on behalf of their constituencies, with these informal ties substituting for more institutionalized frameworks through which the regime could regulate religious affairs.

As Donker observes, these informal ties exhibit precisely the recombinant qualities that we associate with resilient authoritarian regimes. Regime elites played a dominant role in relationships with Islamic brokers and could adjust the degree of space accorded to Islamic actors with tremendous flexibility. During the period from 2003 to 2006 or 2007, when the Syrian regime felt it would benefit from greater inclusion of Islamic actors, it exploited informal channels of communication and exchange to permit Islamic elites greater discretion in their role as religious leaders. These efforts worked hand-in-hand with shifts in the formal regulation of religious affairs described by Pierret. And, as noted earlier, during the post-2007 period up through 2011, when the regime felt itself to be on a stronger domestic footing, informal channels were tightened, the regime inserted itself more directly into the management of religious affairs, and the discretionary authority of Islamic elites was curtailed.

Moreover, Donker finds that informal ties between Islamist actors and the regime had significant deterrent effects on the prospects for collective action among Syrian Islamists. Informal channels not only permitted information about religious groups to flow to the regime but also provided a means for the regime to deliver selective benefits to Islamic elites it regarded as reliable. Faced with the prospect of severe sanctions in the event they pursued collective strategies of religious mobilization, Islamist elites in Syria preferred to maintain informal channels of brokerage and exchange with the regime, even if doing so consolidated their subordination to the regime.

SOCIAL AND LITERARY RESPONSES
TO AUTHORITARIAN RESILIENCE

If authoritarian regimes in the Middle East do not simply persist, but adapt and reconfigure themselves as circumstances change, so too do the societies they govern. In many respects, these societies exhibit recombinant attributes that are similar to, and develop in close relationship with, those exhibited by regimes. Despite the constraints that life under authoritarian rule imposes on individuals, not only in their roles as citizens but in virtually every other domain of individual expression, the subjects of authoritarian regimes have preserved degrees of agency. They have developed repertoires both for collective action and for preserving some autonomy of self-expression. They have been adept at exploiting strategies of authoritarian governance to pry open space within which they can advance collective and individual agendas at odds with those articulated by regimes.

To be sure, Syria and Iran represent sharply contrasting cases in this regard. The fragmentation and decentralization of political power in Iran; its "competitive authoritarian" system of rule in which electoral competition, though highly restricted, remains relevant; and the enduring tensions that exist between the Islamic and the republican aspects of the regime's identity all contribute to a context in which social actors have relatively greater scope for sustained collective action, even if such scope is narrower today than it was a decade ago. In Syria, on the other hand, until the uprising broke out in March 2011, the scope for social mobilization was far more tightly constrained by the omnipresent security apparatus of the regime and by a system of rule that is organized to manage and contain any kind of collective dissent, as well as individual forms of expression that do not fall within limits defined and policed by the regime. These differences are apparent in two chapters in this volume, one by Osanloo that focuses on social mobilization in the area of women's rights in Iran and the other by Weiss on individual expression and the "literary transformation" of authoritarianism in contemporary Syria.

Osanloo focuses on the relationship between an evolving "state form" in Iran—one in which strategies of governance have undergone considerable change over time—and efforts to secure recognition of women's rights under the Islamic Republic. The success with which Iranian women have advanced claims on the state to recognize their rights in such areas as family law might appear counterintuitive given the Islamic identity of the regime. Yet, as Osanloo argues, the "unusual fusion between Islamic principles and republican institutions has allowed a novel state form to cultivate its repressive and nonrepressive practices, permitting greater control over the population, yet increasing its participatory elements, thus giving rise to greater calls for individual rights and liberties."

As postrevolutionary processes of state building unfolded, clerical elites used women's status as a defining element of what made the new regime distinctively Islamic. Contrasting the conditions and status of women in the West and challenging the secular-Westernized conceptions of Muslim women associated with the Pahlavi regime, clerical elites valorized Iranian women as symbols of the regime's Islamic authenticity. At the same time, however, and also in direct contrast to the modernizing authoritarianism of the Shah's regime, Iran's new political order included the participatory, electoral, legal-constitutional, and legislative institutions consistent with its identity as a republic. If the relationship between its theocratic and its republican aspects has been an enduring source of tension and political conflict in Iran, the combination of the two—the "blended legal system," as Osanloo calls it, together with the conflicts that accompanied struggles to secure the primacy of one over the other—created both the political space and the institutional means for women to advance collective claims about their rights and status in the Islamic Republic. In some instances, these struggles produced legislative or legal outcomes that were more progressive than those that had existed under the Shah.

Osanloo traces the politicization of "rights talk" within the Islamic Republic over time and draws on fieldwork and interviews to shed light on how this process played out. In addition, however, she notes that since 2005 the tensions between the Islamic and republican aspects of the Iranian regime have been overcome, often coercively, as hard-line clerical figures have weakened legal-constitutional and participatory institutions and imposed a more unified and more repressive system of rule. As in other domains, what we see in this instance is another case in which an authoritarian regime exploits the presence of multiple, divergent rules of the game to gain the flexibility to respond adaptively to a changing configuration of challenges. What we also see in this instance, however, is the extent to which such arrangements lend themselves to political possibilities on the part of social actors that regimes in all likelihood did not anticipate or appreciate. As the space for social mobilization has narrowed since 2005 and become even more constrained after June 2009, the gains women achieved in earlier periods may themselves be subjected to modifications and adaptations. As the regime's clerical attributes assert themselves, its republican identity becomes secondary, and its recombinant qualities manifest themselves more in coercive than in participatory ways, women's rights may be reconfigured in more socially conservative terms.

In the Syrian case, our focus on social responses to the reconfiguring of authoritarian governance enters relatively uncharted waters with Weiss's chapter on literary transformations of Syrian authoritarianism. As Weiss notes, scholars of Arab literature have devoted relatively little attention to modern Syrian authors. The intersection of cultural production and authoritarian governance is perhaps less neglected (Wedeen 1999) but remains thinly studied. Weiss's chapter illustrates what has been lost as a result. Unlike human rights activists or democratic reformers, who are routinely and brutally silenced by the regime, Syrian novelists who address controversial topics have benefited from "benign neglect." Their books may be banned after the fact, but authors whose work touches on sensitive themes are able to publish, though perhaps not with Syrian publishers, and to continue working with relatively little interference from the regime. Compared to other forms of expression, therefore, Syrian literature has undergone a modest revival, "tentatively emerging from the shadows and hesitantly stepping into the limelight."

This is not to suggest that Syrian writers are in any sense insulated from their political environment; quite the contrary. The space afforded to writers is always contingent, intentionally ambiguous, and routinely redefined as the regime draws and redraws the red lines that demarcate forbidden territory. Writers, like other artists, struggle to navigate the tensions between self-expression and authoritarianism. In this respect, the transition from Hafiz to Bashar al-Asad marked a significant turning point. After 2000, the regime recalibrated its orientation toward the arts and culture to better reflect the self-image that Bashar and Asma al-Asad cultivated of cosmopolitanism and cultural sophistication. Syrian literature entered a period of "efflorescence." As in other social domains, shifts in patterns of authoritarian governance, in this case a process of limited cultural liberalization, were exploited by writers who seized the opportunity to expand the thematic boundaries of their work. Issues that had been forbidden under Hafiz al-Asad were now tolerated. Syrian literature thrived as a result.

Yet this "moderate shift toward greater cultural opening," as Weiss describes it, aligned only briefly with an equally moderate shift toward greater political opening. Within eighteen months of Bashar al-Asad's rise to power, the "Damascus Spring"—a brief episode of reform promises and bounded regime tolerance for expressing dissent that he inaugurated in July 2000—had been shut down. A renewed but even more modest political opening overlapped with a period of intense international pressure on Syria, beginning with the U.S. invasion of Iraq in 2003 and extending through the aftermath of the assassination of Rafiq al-Hariri in February 2005 and the subsequent anti-Syrian protests in Lebanon. By early 2006, however, the regime entered a phase of authoritarian regression. Political space became significantly more constrained as the regime adopted a much tougher line toward all forms of political dissent. Nor was the transition to Bashar al-Asad's presidency accompanied by the renewal of Syrian "official culture," which remained "moribund." The disconnects that Syria under Bashar came to reflect between a modest tolerance of critical cultural expression, the increasingly repressive practices of the regime in the political sphere, and continued official neglect of public culture, more broadly, created an especially difficult terrain for Syrian writers over the course of the 2000s.

Thus, even as Syrian writers explored themes that included imprisonment and torture, state repression of Islamists, and the omnipresence of the state security apparatus, Weiss's chapter underscores the marginalization and subordination of cultural production by a resilient authoritarian system of rule. Authors publish, yet their books are banned. Novels may have a local audience, but their social resonance, whether in terms of public culture, popular discourse, or a broader revitalization of Syrian cultural life, is inevitably constrained. They reflect an important social response to shifts in patterns of authoritarian governance. Yet, ultimately, they cannot escape the limits that authoritarianism imposes on cultural production.

THE QUEST FOR AUTHORITARIAN LEGITIMACY

At few moments in the modern history of the Middle East has authoritarian legitimacy seemed more tenuous than in 2011. Mass uprisings swept across the region, overthrowing four authoritarian incumbents as of the end of the year, while their surviving counterparts struggled, largely in vain, to defuse popular anger and buttress the loyalty of citizens through modest political concessions and economic incentives. As has been widely noted, these protests had little to do with the issues on which Middle East regimes themselves hoped to focus the attention of their citizens, such as the Arab–Israeli conflict or the imperial designs of Western powers. Nor did they validate the scare tactics that regimes had long used to fend off Western pressures for political reform, notably the threat of radical Islam. Islamists participated in protests, along with others, but these mass uprisings were animated by severe and persistent failures of governance, popular demands for accountability and representation, and a deep conviction throughout Middle Eastern societies of the illegitimacy of their leaders and the repressive, authoritarian systems of rule over which they presided. What these uprisings have done, as a result, is to force the question of authoritarian legitimacy to the forefront of Middle Eastern politics. Not surprisingly, those regimes that, as of this writing, had not succumbed to mass demands for democratic change were desperately if unconvincingly struggling to adapt and reconfigure their strategies of governance to demonstrate their responsiveness to the concerns of protesters. In Jordan, Iraq, Algeria, Morocco, Saudi Arabia, and the Gulf, governments hoped to recapture some measure of legitimacy through means that ranged from changes of government, to shifts in social policy, to commitments from long-serving rulers that neither they nor their sons would seek election in the future.

Among the states of the Middle East, Syria initially seemed virtually immune to the wave of protests sweeping the region. However, in mid-March 2011, it witnessed its own outbreak of mass uprisings, which were met with stiff repression. In Iran, developments in Arab states generated a struggle between the regime and supporters of the Green Movement, who both sought to appropriate the Arab revolutions for their own purposes. Yet these efforts did not seriously shift the post-2009 balance of forces in Iran. Although both countries exhibit similar demographic, socioeconomic, and political pressures to those driving mass movements in other parts of the region, the balance of fear in Syria and Iran continued to favor regimes. Ironically, however, this has not prevented leaders in either country from explaining the limited effectiveness of protests in terms of regime legitimacy. Bashar al-Asad told a journalist that Syria was different because his government pursued policies that were popular with the people (*Wall Street Journal* January 13, 2011). Only weeks later these remarks were contradicted by mass protests. Mahmoud Ahmedinejad made similar claims and went so far as to criticize the repression of protests by regime forces in the Arab world, even as his own Basij militants and security agents were muzzling critics and beating back protesters on the streets of Iranian cities (*Washington Times* February 23, 2011).

If the uprisings of early 2011 have given new prominence to questions of political legitimacy in the Middle East, it would be a mistake to assume that authoritarian regimes, especially those most likely to survive, were not previously attentive to the importance of legitimacy or the need to develop tools and instruments for securing popular support among at least some segments of their societies and beyond. Yet the targeted audiences and persuasiveness of such strategies stand out as major concerns of research. The final section of this volume presents chapters that address the challenges of authoritarian legitimacy from a variety of perspectives.

The first of these chapters, by coeditor Leenders, addresses the question of why the Syrian regime came, at least until recently, to rely on judicial instruments to manage some instances of dissent and opposition, rather than more directly repressive means. Leenders notes that "resilience cannot be explained solely in reference to coercive mechanisms" but points out that it is not self-evident why a repressive regime, one that ultimately rests on the use or threat of force to secure compliance, would develop an extensive and highly articulated set of judicial and legal-constitutional mechanisms as instruments of authoritarian governance. Nor, he adds, is it clear how such mechanisms contributed to regime resilience or why a regime might vary in the ways it deploys them over time. While linking his research on the judicialization of repression in Syria to an emerging literature on the role of law in authoritarian regimes, Leenders views the apparatus of legalism that Syrian leaders have constructed as posing several distinctive analytic challenges.

With respect to the question of legitimacy, for instance, the literature tends to view legal institutions as a means by which authoritarian regimes can enhance their domestic legitimacy in the absence of other "credible mechanisms of public accountability." Yet in the Syrian case, so much of what the judiciary does happens behind the veil of state security rather than in public that this argument does not seem to apply. More persuasive, he argues, is the connection between the presence of a legal-judicial apparatus and the interests of the regime in presenting itself to the international system as a fully sovereign entity, one that possess the institutional attributes and features that mark it as a equal member of the community of states with all that this implies about its sovereign rights and prerogatives. These include, among others, the right to assert noninterference in Syria's domestic affairs by foreign actors. In this sense, judicialization advances Syrian claims to "juridical statehood" and thus contributes to the regime's sense of security and legitimacy as an international actor.

Yet the judicial system in Syria is not simply decorative, an ornament of sovereignty that serves no function. It plays a significant role in support of the Syrian regime's efforts to maintain social control, repress dissent, and punish those who transgress against the regime. How it advances this function, moreover, sheds important light on the dynamics of authoritarian resilience. As Leenders documents, Syria possess multiple, sometimes overlapping, sets of judicial institutions—another instance of the multiplicity and proliferation of rules of the game that are shared features of recombinant authoritarian regimes. These range from ordinary civilian courts to military tribunals to the Supreme State Security Courts (SSSC) to military field courts. This dense field of judicial institutions creates flexibilities that permit Syria's leaders valuable leeway in how they allocate cases to specific institutions under specific circumstances.

Over time, Leenders finds, the regime has varied in the handling of similar kinds of political crimes. In some instances, it has moved such cases through ordinary civilian courts; in others through SSSC or military field courts. And in some instances, it has marginalized the judiciary altogether and resolved political cases through extrajudicial means. These cycles in the judicialization of repression do not follow a neat pattern, although the general trend since Bashar al-Asad's rise to power until recently had been toward greater use of civilian courts rather than the SSSC in dealing with cases of political dissent. As he notes, "Compared to the 1980s, courts seemed to be winning terrain from extrajudicial means in their designated task to punish, curb, or prevent political dissent." What Leenders observes more broadly, however, is that judicialization is not entirely arbitrary but can be linked to regime perceptions of threat and how these vary over time. Perhaps not surprisingly, extrajudicial tactics have tended to dominate during period when threats were perceived to be high, such as the low-level insurgency waged against the regime by the Syrian Muslim Brotherhood in the 1970s and early 1980s and indeed during the uprisings of 2011. On the other hand, judicialization tends to dominate during periods when the regime feels less deeply threatened. Despite these trends, however, the regime maintains a diverse arsenal of judicial institutions and thus reserves for itself the authority to manage political dissent in highly flexible ways.

Shifting to the Iranian case, Tezcür amplifies themes that both Leenders and Osanloo address in their chapters. Focusing on the period from 1997 to 2009, Tezcür asks how it was possible for hard-liners within the Iranian regime to roll back a reformist movement after 2004 and how their success contributed to the emergence of the Green Movement in 2009. Like Leenders, he directs his attention to how authoritarian elites appropriate and adapt an institutional domain that is often associated with accountability, in Tezcür's case electoral frameworks, to enhance regime resilience. Like Osanloo, he views the interactive relationship between state and society, or regime and society, as essential for understanding patterns of social mobilization around the expansion of rights. As he notes,

> Contemporary political struggles do not take place between two opposing and monolithic societal and statist sides with well-ordered preferences. Societal actors confront state authorities on certain issues and negotiate and collaborate on others. . . . Consequently, democratization in Iran can be conceptualized as a dynamic but reversible struggle that involves cross-cutting alliances among state and societal actors.

Challenging structural arguments that focus on the state's coercive capacity, economic endowments, or geopolitics to explain the rise of hardliners in Iran, Tezcür goes on to argue that elections serve as critical moments in struggles between hard-line and reformist coalitions—groupings that cut across regime and society—to define the boundaries of political contestation and democratic rights. Echoing claims advanced by other authors in this volume, Tezcür argues that authoritarian resilience is rendered contingent by the uncertainties associated with electoral competition. Uncertainty creates powerful incentives for political mobilization among both hardliners and reformers; it ensures that the boundaries of political contestation and political inclusion come to the fore as core issues around which political struggles are organized. Seen through this lens, the political defeat of reformers after the 1997 election of Mohammed Khatami as Iran's president is explained in part as a result of an authoritarian backlash engineered by regime hardliners but also and more significantly as a popular response to the flawed performance of the Khatami administration by large segments of Iranian society, linked politically to hardline factions among the ruling elite: "Elections that had earlier served the reformist goals of broadening the scope of liberties now became the primary mechanisms through which the ruling regime demonstrated its resilience" with the electoral victory of Mahmoud Ahmedinejad in 2005. Despite widespread concerns about the undemocratic character of Iran's elections, victory at the polls reinforced the legitimacy of regime hard-liners and reinvigorated the social networks they rely on for popular support. It provided the political capital that permitted hard-liners to move decisively in subsequent years to marginalize reformers situated within state institutions and to undertake a radical process of dedemocratization, rolling back the expansion of rights and liberties that had been achieved under Khatami. In turn, this backlash revitalized the reformist opposition, setting the stage for the hotly contested elections of June 2009 and the rise of the Green Movement, which ultimately failed to defeat Ahmedinejad or to mobilize the broad-based cross-class and cross-sectoral coalitions that might have forced the regime to accept reformist demands for political liberalization.

The final contribution to this volume, by Ehteshami, Hinnebusch, and their coauthors, shifts from a focus on domestic institutions such as the judiciary or elections to explore linkages between external threats and the strategies developed by the Syrian and Iranian regimes to manage popular demands while securing mass compliance. As they note, "To assess authoritarian resilience, we must start with basic notions of how such regimes exercise power and manage pressures for political participation." To address these issues, the chapter builds an analytic framework around two core variables: levels of elite contestation and levels of inclusion of social forces. Exploring how regime strategies vary across these two dimensions over time and what the drivers are that lead regimes to recalibrate their strategies is central for understanding the dynamics of authoritarian adaptation in these two cases, which could take the form of "widening or narrowing on both dimensions, or widening of one and contraction of the other, or sequences of widening and narrowing."

Real or perceived external threats loom especially large in explaining how regimes position themselves along both the contestation and inclusion variables, reinforcing Leenders's point about the importance of the international context in explaining regime strategies. For Ehteshami, Hinnebusch, and their coauthors, however, what matters is not only the presence or absence of external threats but the capacities and resources that structure regime responses in ways that can either enhance or erode their legitimacy. They focus on three key resources in particular: political capital, financial capital, and human capital. They also take into account the historical processes through which each regime was formed and the role of ideology in defining elite preferences with respect to contestation and inclusion. Thus, in the Syrian case, tracing the origins of the current regime to its roots as a populist, inclusionary revolution from above, and one in which elite fragmentation represented a serious threat, the regime has tended to exhibit greater willingness to adjust the boundaries of inclusion than it has to widening the scope of elite contestation. The Iranian regime, with its origins in a mass revolution from below, has tended to move in the opposite direction, contracting the scope of political inclusion over time while exhibiting greater tolerance for elite contestation. In each case, moreover, the discursive strategies and policy tools through which these regimes have shifted their positions along these two dimensions have reflected the mix of resources that each has at its disposal.

Through detailed case studies of each country, Ehteshami, Hinnebusch, and their coauthors provide important empirical support for claims about the linkages between external threats and resources, on the one hand, and the strategies adopted by the Syrian and Iranian regimes to expand or contract the boundaries of inclusion and contestation, on the other. In both cases, moreover, they map the capacity of these regimes to adapt their strategies of rule, exploiting external threats in ways that not only consume political, economic, or human capital but generate it, as well. What matters most for the purposes of this introduction, however, is the contribution of Ehteshami, Hinnebusch, and their coauthors to our understanding of the mechanics of recombinant authoritarianism: how the adaptive capacities of the Syrian and Iranian regimes enhance their resilience not merely by reinforcing existing strategies and practices but by modifying frameworks of governance as conditions warrant, in this case as the profile of external threats that confront these regimes changes over time.

CONCLUSION

As the Third Wave of democratization unfolded in the 1970s and 1980s, research programs in the social sciences turned away from the study of authoritarian governance to focus on processes of democratic change. It took more than a decade before the limits of democratization and the persistence of authoritarian systems of rule sparked a new generation of "posttransitology" research (Valbjørn and Bank 2010), this time with an interest in variation among authoritarian regime types (Brownlee 2007; King 2009; Lust-Okar 2005; Posusney and Angrist 2005; Pratt 2007; Schlumberger 2007), and in the causes and effects of authoritarian persistence. For scholars of the Middle East, this renewed interest in authoritarianism offered important opportunities to reconnect to broader comparative debates in the disciplines and, as we showed earlier in this chapter, to develop important insights into the political, economic, and social dynamics of persistent authoritarian regimes.

Now, as transitology may acquire relevance for the Middle East for the first time, it will be important for scholars of the region to avoid repeating the experiences of their colleagues who focus on other regions and to dismiss the study of authoritarian governance as no longer relevant to the Middle

East. What is needed, instead, and what we view this volume as a contribution toward, is a reframing of research agendas on authoritarianism in the Middle East to focus on what we have defined as recombinant authoritarian regimes, with particular attention to the causes and effects of regime resilience, rather than regime persistence.

We argue that this research agenda on authoritarian resilience throughout the region ought to include four main foci. First, even where important changes have been set in motion by mass unrest, the capacity of authoritarian regimes to learn and adapt, with the effect of constantly reinventing themselves, needs to be fully appreciated and integrated into research programs on authoritarian resilience. Indeed, protesters in Tunis and Cairo have realized this all along, as their calls for *isqat an-nizam* (the downfall of the regime) continued even after Mubarak and Ben Ali left the stage. Second, researchers should pay attention to the capacity of authoritarian regimes to appropriate and exploit institutional arrangements often associated with democracies, such as judiciaries and elections, to generate regime legitimacy. Even in circumstances where such institutions appear to be bolstered, chances are that not democracy but regime transformation will be served most. Third, overlapping and interconnected sets of institutions of authoritarian governance, associated with multiple and often competing sets of rules, should not be written off as merely paradoxical or bound to whither but as critical to the adaptive capacity and thus the resilience of authoritarian regimes. Fourth, social actors are no less adept than regimes in managing their own relationships to authoritarian systems of rule, for purposes of their own survival, accessing resources and contesting authoritarian governance. Their success in doing so may not necessarily contribute to processes of political opening or liberalization. Yet the complex interactions such maneuvering contains may nonetheless hold out important clues to when and how the few gains that they make may swell into mass demands for change.

ECONOMIC GOVERNANCE AND RECOMBINANT AUTHORITARIAN RULE

Part I

2 THE ECONOMICS OF AUTHORITARIAN UPGRADING IN SYRIA

Liberalization and the Reconfiguration
of Economic Networks

Caroline Donati

FOR DECADES PRIOR TO THE UPRISING that began in March 2011, the "Syria of the Asads" overcame and endured, offering a remarkable example of authoritarian longevity. Far from opening up the political system and beginning the transition to democracy, Bashar al-Asad has perpetuated the authoritarian framework put in place since 1970s by his father, Hafiz al-Asad: a presidential authoritarian regime that combines repression with co-optation. This is not to suggest, however, that Bashar has simply reproduced the authoritarian schema he inherited. Instead, he has rejuvenated the regime's political formula, reconfiguring critical patronage networks that are central to its survival (Camau and Geisser 2003, 31–38). Without underestimating the effects of the Syrian uprising on the dynamics of authoritarian governance in Syria, this chapter explores how the regime of Bashar al-Asad responded to changing economic and political conditions of the 2000s. It highlights the regime's recombinant capacity as a critical attribute in accounting for its resilience and illustrates how processes of authoritarian upgrading affected the distribution of political and economic power in Syria.

Since his rise to power the summer of 2000, Bashar al-Asad has worked to integrate into his system of rule shifts in internal, regional, and international dynamics and to insulate the regime from their destabilizing repercussions. He and other "heirs" of the earlier Asad regime live in a globalized, near-unipolar world, at the heart of which the market economy has imposed itself. Prior to the uprising of 2011 and the introduction of diplomatic and economic sanctions that have left Syria profoundly isolated, Syria's ruling elite recognized that the Ba'thist regime could no longer live reclusively inside its own borders. It began a process of normalization with its regional and international environment. This authoritarian reconfiguration is taking place according to market criteria: on emerging from a state-controlled economy, Syria's leaders have chosen the model of the "social market economy," a strategy that conveys the impression of openness but in reality penalizes reformist aspirations that are viewed as a threat by the ruling coalition. This choice is in part dictated by strong international pressure, which has had an impact on the regime's strategic resources, ranging from the "loss" of Lebanon to the isolation of the Syrian regime from 2003 through 2006. It is also a function of transformations within Syrian society: half of Syria's population is under twenty years old, and economic performance has not been sufficient to absorb large numbers of young job seekers; inequality has increased, and the redistributive capacity of the state has declined.

In response, Syria, like other Arab authoritarian regimes from Egypt to Morocco, undertook a process of selective economic reform intended, in large part, to ensure the regime's access to resources in the form of rents that it could extract from newly liberalized sectors of the economy. Yet the move toward a social market economy beginning in the mid-2000s was not simply an effort to reanimate Syria's private sector as a way to address failures of economic performance within the public sector. Rather, as Syria's rulers have long understood, Syrian authoritarianism rests on patronage networks established throughout the different institutions of the Ba'thist state. It is these clientalist links and personal allegiances, and not the coercive apparatus alone, that have secured for the Asad regimes their exceptional longevity. This type of governance presupposes access to rents, or else to external resources, which allow the state, as a leading source of employment, to clientalize its elites and to gain the support of the population through redistributive social policies. The economics of upgrading Syrian authoritarianism draw our attention to these extracommunity networks within the various institutions of the Ba'thist state. As a hybrid authoritarian regime, Syria blends personalism and clientalism within a flexible institutional framework. How institutions are configured determines the way in which those involved in politics define their interests and structure their relationships of power with other groups.

During Bashar al-Asad's term in office, these relationships of power have been affected both by dynastic transition and the privatization of the state that was set in motion to free up the resources necessary to perpetuate the regime. Authoritarian governance changes as a result of liberalization. Drawing on empirical data gathered through investigative work as well as written sources, this chapter examines the logic and strategies that are revealed in this process of renewal. Privatizing the state creates new players and new modes of political, economic, and social regulation that transform authoritarian rule. The chapter will also address the emergent stresses and tensions that have accompanied this process of market-oriented restructuring of authoritarian practices in Syria, including those that affect the regime's coercive capacity and factor into the eruption of the Syrian uprising in March 2011.

UPGRADING THE MILITARY-COMMERCIAL COALITION AND NEOPATRIMONIALISM

The liberalizing trend experienced by Syria from 2004–2005 onward confirmed the importance of selective economic reforms for the process of authoritarian upgrading. The reforms generated resources that helped to enlarge the ruling coalition, which had been facing a loss of rents and external pressure: "Regime elites and their allies use[d] their political privileges to capture the resources generated by economic openings." (Heydemann 2007b, 15)

THE "SOCIAL MARKET" AND THE "PRIVATIZATION" OF THE RENTIER ECONOMY

Syria's new economic direction consisted in large part of liberalizing the banking sector and external trade. While the Ba'th Party had approved the creation of private banks as early as December 2000, it was not until the end of 2004 and the summer of 2005 that such banks became active, owing to a relaxation of the banking laws and rules governing bank lending. From then on, banks were able to finance imports that had previously been financed by the black market and by Lebanese banks. Islamic finance was allowed, and the insurance market was liberalized at the same time. The opening up of external trade took the form of lifting import restrictions, reducing customs barriers, relaxing exchange controls, and standardizing exchange rates (as well as legalizing currency exchange offices). Syria was able to join the Greater Arab Free Trade Area (which had entered into effect on January 1, 2005) and to multiply its free trade agreements with regional partners. Friendly countries such as Iran and Turkey thus compensated for the isolation that the Americans and Europeans had imposed on Syria, providing it with new forms of external support that generated new economic and political resources (Ehteshami and Hinnebusch et al., Chapter 10 in this volume).

This opening up followed the same logic as its predecessors: it was dictated by a political regime experiencing difficulties in securing new rents, a new base of support, and new allies (Donati 2009). The main liberalizing measures were taken after the spring of 2005, meaning after the withdrawal of Syrian troops from Lebanon, which had deprived the regime of the rents that had sustained its ruling coalition. They were further motivated by a continuing decline in oil revenues: Syria, a semirentier state, was faced with the looming exhaustion of its oil resources. Liberalization along these lines was also necessary to circumvent American sanctions, which impeded the ability of the Commercial Bank of Syria (CBS) to finance the import of goods and services. In this context, liberalizing external trade was a response to the challenge of renewing rents within the framework of a globalized economy, by a regime subject to significant economic sanctions by Western governments. The opening-up of the banking sector to private investors not only reinvigorated the Syrian economy, which began to experience higher levels of economic performance at the macrolevel; it also enhanced the regime's access to growing pools of investment capital in the Gulf that were generated by the rise in world oil prices.

This liberalization was necessarily incomplete and selective and did not create the conditions for a fully market-regulated economy. It aimed instead to renew the rentier economy. Thus the liberalization of the banking and financial sector was not accompanied by in-depth reforms that might, for example, have restructured state banks or brought about the prerequisite for this to occur, namely an audit of state-owned companies. Private banks, lacking financial instruments such as treasury bonds, were faced with the problem of how to use their capital because opportunities for lending remained very limited. The regime appeared unwilling to put an end to the special financial facilities granted to state companies and the agricultural sector, at the cost of creating state-bank debt. The regime was careful not to offend patronage networks that might cause the Ba'th Party to intervene, preferring instead to let state banks get by on the interest they earned from agricultural and housing loans, while private banks focused on meeting the very modest capital requirements of Syria's tightly regulated (and small) private sector though the provision of financial services and investment activities that became a new source of rents for the regime.[1]

The privatization of part of the state's resources thus secured replacement rents to support the ruling coalition. "The plunder economy first takes the form of nationalization, then of privatization" (Hibou 1998, 167). The heirs to the old generation in power, especially those who were initiated into capitalist practices in Lebanon, took control of sectors that would guarantee them exceptional profits. Their predecessors got rich through the state sector; they themselves monopolized the private sector and prospered, to the detriment of economic growth. Liberalization—meaning the privatization of the authoritarian state economy and its penetration by external trade—increasingly blurred the line between private and public.

The trajectory of the president's cousin on his mother's side, Rami Makhlouf, who became the country's chief "private" investor, illustrates this privatization of the plunder economy. His father, Mohammed Makhlouf, had controlled the management of oil resources and other prebends derived from overseeing state-owned companies, the National Tobacco Board, and the Syrian Land Bank during Hafiz al-Asad's reign.[2] His son took up the torch by cornering the income derived from the high-tech sector, the media, and other lucrative niches. His empire ranges from mobile communications and the media to duty free, from oil to air transport, from real estate to the banking sector and tourism. Using his closeness to the regime, he has freed himself of all restrictions and exploits his allies in the security apparatus to neutralize competitors unceremoniously. Those allies connive closely with the head of state, whose capitalist accumulation strategy they share (Picard 2008, 325).

The regime has thus expanded its predatory activities from the control over "rents derived from the state" to a position that permits it to dominate "private rents" without any transparency. As in Morocco (Catusse 2009, 8), this privatization takes the form of licensing or concessions, through delegated management or concessions mainly in the public services. Profitable state-owned companies are managed by "wheeler-dealers" on build-operate-transfer (BOT) contracts, thus renewing the ruling elites' strategy of appropriating economic resources (Hibou 1998, 160). The illicit practices of the socialist and state capitalist eras have been adapted to the new economy: bribes have become real investments; rigged calls for tender have been transformed into commercial contracts; companies and holding companies have been created to seize new riches; the stock market, opened in March 2009, offered further opportunities to these same players, united by a solidarity based on capital.

In this new economy, oligopolies tended to replace monopolies, and import-export, which had been a source of wealth for Syria's rulers, was supplanted by private industry. In the booming construction sector, former cement importers who had prospered under a state monopoly now got rich by becoming cement manufacturers in a market without competition. Moreover, their association with foreign investors illustrates what Hibou (1998, 161) calls "the displacement of external rents." The "good" governance provided by foreign capitalists associated with projects ensures that the ruling elites obtain financial and relationship resources, thus strengthening the regime through new incomes and connections. A part of the capital of such projects is in fact reserved for national shareholders or even for the state itself. Foreign participation in raising capital for private banks follows the same logic.[3] The benefits of these new incomes are considerable. After oil, license fees from the mobile phone sector are said to be the state's second largest resource, ensuring plentiful revenues to the licensees, who pay half of their profits to the state. Private banks posting record profits and rivalling (in terms of deposits) the public-sector giants such as the Syria Commercial Bank and the Land Bank secure their shareholders real dividends.

These new incomes also enable ruling elites to establish a network of associates, whose loyalty they buy with market shares and protection. Mohammed Saber Hamcho, who comes from a family of industrialists and was among the prominent Syrian businessmen sanctioned by the U.S. government in August 2011, had in the space of three years become a powerful figure owing to his association with Maher al-Asad: the activities of the Hamcho Group extend from IT equipment to tourist infrastructure. With an Alawite mother and Sunni father, Hamcho first joined the "*asabiyyat* Asad" through his marriage to the sister of Maher's wife. That was the start of his rise. Politically ambitious, he was elected a member of Parliament for Damascus in 2003 and 2007 with the support of a security executive who sold him protection. Hamcho is also on the board of directors of the Syrian Computer Society, which allows him access to markets in new communications fields.

RENEWING THE ENTREPRENEURIAL CLIENTELE

Selective liberalization makes it possible to renew the "military-commercial coalition" (Picard 2008) which unites high-ranking officers and private-sector entrepreneurs; it seals long-term alliances between regime elites and business elites (Heydemann, 2007b), while encouraging some renewal of this entrepreneurial clientele, which is more in tune with the new economic trends. The regime, having put in place a new team in the military and security apparatus, as well as in government, tried to set up a circle of businessmen who might serve as a counterweight to the former allies, in particular the directors of Chambers of Commerce, who were preventing a new class of entrepreneurs from asserting itself because newcomers might eventually disrupt established business elites in their industrial activities. The creation of Chambers of Industry, and in 2006 a national federation uniting various local branches, illustrates this development. Its leadership was handed to the entrepreneur Imad Greiwati, a figure of the new entrepreneurial class that emerged under Bashar and that asserted itself during the elections to the Chambers of Industry in 2006. Greiwati, who was placed under sanction by the European Union in September 2011 due to his close ties to the regime, is known as Syria's "Mr. Electricity"—the Greiwati Group's primary business has been the manufacture of electric and telephone cables—and became a major player in just eighteen months. An importer of steel cables and a representative for nine makes of imported cars, he subsequently invested in Rami Makhlouf's cement works. The 2009 Chambers of Commerce elections consecrated the victory of this renewed clientele, a victory symbolized by the presidential appointment (and not the election) of the Damascene Bassam Ghrawi, a man in his fifties who was close to the president and had successfully taken over the family chocolate company.[4] As secretary-general of the Damascus Chamber of Commerce, he similarly became secretary-general of the Federation of Syrian Chambers of Commerce, a post occupied for over two decades by Ratib Challah, a key figure among the shopkeepers of the Damascus souk and thus a regime partner.

The creation of two holding companies constituted another step in the renewal of the regime's networks in the business world. Anxious to consolidate its base amid a context of international tensions, the regime encouraged the principal figures of Syria's and Aleppo's business communities to join the two holding companies founded by the "new wheeler-dealers" in 2007. Al-Cham, which is controlled by Rami Makhlouf, has seventy members (entrepreneurs close to the regime and families of the Syrian business bourgeoisie) and a capital of $350 million. Al-Sourya, the second holding company, has a capital of $80 million and includes young entrepreneurs (a total of twenty-five), particularly the "sons of," grouped around Issam Joud, the nephew of a successful Sunni entrepreneur from the coastal town of Latakia who was associated with the regime in Hafiz al-Asad's day. In a way, the pact that already existed between the regime and a section of the business community has been extended and formalized: the members of al-Cham and al-Sourya procure capital, networks, and political support for the regime. In return, they are offered a share in the dividends that result from the expansion of market-oriented economic sectors, as well as the confidence that their business interests enjoy the protection of powerful regime elites. The old guard who resisted these initiatives lost their protection. In some cases, their licences were not renewed. In others they found themselves subject to accusations that they had committed various offences—some of which are almost impossible to avoid in the normal conduct of business. "Adversaries" are thus punished and "friends" rewarded.

Businesses that are members of the two holding companies take the most profitable projects, benefiting from regulations that are tailor made for their interests. Joining al-Cham or al-Sourya opens the doors to ministries and contracts. For example, al-Cham obtained a forty-year licence to exploit the site of the former Hijaz railway station in Damascus for a project to build a mall and an airport and railway service. In 2007, with the president's personal support, al-Sourya was granted a seventy-five-year BOT contract by the tourism minister for operating the very-well-located site of the Baramké bus station in Damascus. The "heirs" grouped in al-Sourya have also been authorized to set up the Syrian Business Council, a network of 280 businessmen who use their privileged positions to develop links with the expatriate Syrian and Arab business communities—typically enjoying more success in these efforts than do other, less-well-connected businessmen. The participation in Syria's economy of these foreign players strengthens the regime's position, while the line between public and private players is blurred by the regime's manipulation. Being close to the security-political establishment is still a prerequisite for prosperity in the framework set by the "first wheeler-dealers" who are predominant in the regime. The president himself seems to be the arbitrator of last resort in the nonegalitarian redistribution of the dividends of liberalization among the oligarchs.

On the margins of this entrepreneurial clientele, other businessmen who are not involved with the regime also try to profit from the expansion of the market. They are tolerated because of the investments they make in the less lucrative sectors and because they bring in foreign partners whose capital is sought after by the regime. However, they have to avoid upsetting the interests of the oligarchy and its partners. There is therefore a limit as to how much their companies can grow, and they are not allowed to form groups with other independent Syrian merchants.

A NEW, MORE LIBERAL BASE

In fact, selective liberalization offers opportunities for larger networks, made up of entrepreneurs who are on the margins of traditional figures and their allies. These entrepreneurs are less visible, but just as important politically, and they constitute a basic component of the regime (Heydemann, 2007b). The liberalization of the banking system and the real-estate sector has created the conditions for a speculative economy that offers considerable opportunities to the upper middle class, the Syrian bourgeoisie, and the bourgeoisie of the Gulf Diaspora, which has been deprived of its traditional outlets since September 11, 2001.[5] Some of the entrepreneurial bourgeoisie who left the country after the nationalizations of the 1960s have come back, as have the émigrés who founded Lebanese banks. Besides, the business bourgeoisie channels elements of the educated upper middle class into its projects, providing an outlet for its skills and resources in the new social market economy. The regime is also looking to renew its support base among shopkeepers and "market people" (Rabo 2006, 45–47).[6] Islamic banks invest capital coming from the Gulf and would like to attract this entrepreneurial world made up of thousands of family-run firms, a world that is mainly Sunni and conservative. Import-export traders and distributors have also profited from the liberalization of foreign exchange and from tax reductions.

This "crony capitalism," together with the persistence of authoritarianism, seals the renewal of the military-commercial coalition and represents the transformation of the Ba'thist regime into a form of neopatrimonial rule. As in Egypt and Indonesia, a new generation of leaders invests in the private sector, thus giving a regime kept in authoritarian shackles a liberal tint. However, and this supports Hibou's work (1998), privatization does not mean a retreat by the state but rather its redeployment in ways that modify authoritarian rule. Exercising its recombinant attributes, the state off-loads particular functions, in this case the generation of foreign exchange, onto "private" intermediaries. This increasingly indirect rule has been favorably received by the prevailing liberal discourse and helps to procure the authoritarian regime the resources needed to sustain itself in an era of globalized, market-oriented democracy.

NEW AUTHORITARIAN RULE: PRIVATIZATION
AND THE REDEPLOYMENT OF THE STATE

As is the case with other authoritarian regimes that have embarked on this process, Syria's political authorities have decided to privatize the development sector, regulatory functions, and a part of the ruler's regalian function—the right of monarchs to the income of certain estates (Hibou 1998). This privatization aims to create new sources of rents in a context of budget constraints, but it is also guided by a concern about speed and results. It is therefore imperative to have access to modern techniques for circumventing the inertia of the state apparatus. Redistribution and development no longer exclusively go through Ba'thist structures, which have become anachronistic in the eyes of Syria's post-2000 ruling elites.

THE PRIVATIZATION OF DEVELOPMENT: RECONFIGURING THE NGO SECTOR

Syria's entry into the "liberal era" resulted in the emergence of new development nongovernmental organizations (NGOs), whose creation was encouraged by the Tenth Five-Year Plan (2005–2010). The opening up of Syria's community-based associations, which happened late compared to other authoritarian regimes, was part of the same strategy of upgrading authoritarianism in the global era. The Syrian regime "exploit[s] the rhetoric and organizational frameworks of civil society to generate political resources": these bodies contribute to enhancing the image of a regime seeking legitimacy and undermine the emergence of a truly civic life (Heydemann 2007b, 8). In reality these development organizations, which claim to have the status and properties of an NGO, are closely linked to the regime and have more in common with governmental NGOs, or GONGOs. Far from contributing to the spread of a civic democratic culture (*thaqafa madani*), they in fact block the emergence of an autonomous civil society. The rapid growth in the number of development GONGOs has gone hand-in-hand with the repression of activists, politically oriented (and often unregistered and thus illegal) NGOs, or other independent forms of engagement in public life. The activists of the "Damascus Spring," who initiated public debate about civil society as early as 2000 and tried to mobilize a population that had been cut off from res publica for over two decades, were repressed. The rare associations working exclusively on human rights issues that appeared at about the same time were tightly controlled and subject to similar repression. The generation that has emerged from the educated upper middle classes, as well as segments of the intellectual community, have been co-opted into controlled bodies by those who come from or are close to the regime. More autonomous associations, meanwhile, are forced to operate in a gray zone of restrictive legislation and ambiguous legal standing. The emergence of GONGOs is part of the process of privatizing regulatory functions, as described by Hibou, where "the definition and the terms of development are themselves privatized" (Hibou 1998, 158). The state, losing resources, "off-loads" functions related to, for instance, rural development or women's empowerment onto these GONGOs, which make it possible to tap into private funds as well as the grant-making programs of international donor organizations whose resources then flow to well-connected heads of these "civil society" organizations as a form of "associational rents."

The Syria Trust for Development (STFD),[7] the umbrella association set up under the sponsorship of the first lady, Asma al-Asad, has helped to gain the support of local populations. Asma al-Asad's direct involvement in the activities of the Fund for Rural Development of Syria (FIRDOS), and media coverage of her commitment to its work, demonstrated the regime's renewed interest in the countryside. FIRDOS, which grants microcredits and conducts training and education activities, serves to extend the regime's reach into rural areas but does so by reproducing clientist arrangements that help broaden the regime's social base. FIRDOS is active in sixty villages and six governorates (Aleppo, Idlib, Latakia, Homs, Hama, Quneitra), where it has established a parallel structure, the "rural community," made up of several villages and run by a committee of volunteers. These committees decide who will be granted a microcredit loan and stand as guarantor for its reimbursement, making them important as instruments of social control and co-optation. The lack of transparency that has been observed in their work, particularly in the granting of microcredits, highlights the extent to which clientalism shapes their operations.

The new NGOs sponsored or supported by the first lady are also in tune with the regime's efforts to broaden popular support for the move toward a more liberal, social market economy. From the countryside to young entrepreneurs, from young children to thirty-somethings, all segments of society are affected by these efforts. FIRDOS is aimed at the rural environment, Massar at children, Shabab at youth, and Rawafed at the world of culture. In their own spheres, all of these GONGOs place their clientele in a private network that runs parallel to the traditional Ba'thist (state) network. The Syrian Young Entrepreneur (SYE) is a FIRDOS partner supported by Asma al-Asad and has the mission of spreading business culture and helping young entrepreneurs. Owing to the positions of its directors in the private sector, it is able to offer these young entrepreneurs privileged services, such as expertise, contacts with private banks, and access to the market. These new "private" players have been called on to take their place in local development in a partnership model that links NGOs directly to government or council entities. This model is meant

to make up for the failures of state and local administrations, circumvent bureaucratic deadlocks, and offer access to modern technologies at a lower price
than is available to the public at large.

These NGOs, created with the support of the regime, meet the stringent criteria imposed on sponsors—namely a well-developed structure and endorse-
ment by the administration—unlike independent NGOs. As already noted,
foreign funding for civil society development has become a new rent that
can be tapped by the regime via these organizations. For instance, European
Union aid granted as part of its civil society development programme makes
up 75 percent of FIRDOS's funds. In addition, however, the creation of these
GONGOs creates new channels for the extraction of resources from politically
connected businessmen anxious to demonstrate their support for the regime.
FIRDOS and other NGOs sponsored by Asma al-Asad have benefited from significant contributions from businessmen and private firms close to the regime,
who use these donations to signal their allegiance to the Asads and to position
themselves to obtain contracts generated by STFD and other NGO projects.

Such contracting opportunities have expanded through other means, as
well, notably the introduction of public-private partnerships (PPPs) as the
framework for the renovation of worn-down public infrastructure that the
state cannot otherwise afford to repair. As Khaled Yacoub Oweis noted in a
Daily Star article on November 3, 2009, the construction of the first private
power station in Syria was entrusted to Marafeq, a joint venture of the al-
Cham Holding Company and Kuwaiti partners. At the end of the twenty-five-
year BOT contract that it signed with Marafeq, the Syrian government has
committed to supplying free fuel to run the plant and to buy and distribute
the electricity that it generates.[8] Prior to the start of the Syrian uprising in
spring 2011, investments in rehabilitating infrastructure as part of PPPs were
estimated at $50 billion over the next five years. In addition to the new oppor-
tunities such partnerships offer for predatory forms of rent seeking by regime
elites, they also generate real political benefits for the regime, which takes
credit for the modernization of infrastructure, depicting it as an expression
of the state's continued commitment to its a social pact that had broken down
with the retreat of the welfare state. In the final analysis, the privatization of a
part of the Syrian state's regalian functions, which has seen new intermediaries emerge parallel to formal state structures, has modified modes of regulation and the extraction of rents in both the social and the political arena.

NEW METHODS OF POLITICAL AND SOCIAL CONTROL

The Ba'th Party, symptomatic of the technocratization and even the "growing economicization of both political elites and policies" (Albrecht and Schlumberger 2004, 379), is no longer the only body that co-opts and reproduces elites. NGOs and GONGOs have also imposed themselves as locations par excellence for reproducing elites and reclientalizing regime networks. Their personnel is made up of sons of leaders, ministers, or officers and of entrepreneurs: members of the former educated middle class are co-opted and thus dissuaded from using their abilities in the political arena. For example, the president has depended on the Syrian Computer Society (SCS) to enhance his legitimacy as a leader who is in tune with society and open to the world and to expand his networks throughout Syria. The *Maaloumatiyya*, as it is called by Syrians, is present in the country's twelve governorates and is brought in as a consultant to public bodies on equipment and new technology purchases in IT and telecommunications. The SCS is a breeding ground for young scientists, academics, and entrepreneurs, whether Ba'thist or independent, to whom it offers prospects of social advancement in the Syrian state, thus renewing the president's loyalty networks at the same time. Behind its facade of modernity, the SCS also symbolizes the pursuit of control by the security forces, by enhancing the technological capacities of the intelligence services—capacities the regime has deployed extensively since March 2011. This privatization of the state, resulting in a new form of off-loading, allows leaders to meet the challenges of globalization and technological innovation and to circumvent formal political institutions or arenas that might be threatening or deficient. The policy of encouraging expatriates to return is part of this same logic of trying to attract a skilled workforce.

The new private intermediaries also get involved in political mobilization. On their return from Lebanon in 2005, Syrian military personnel were received not by Party executives but by the CEO of a private press consortium. Demonstrations in support of the regime have also been privatized. The campaign for the 2007 presidential referendum showed the extent to which Rami Makhlouf's group could mobilize regime supporters, in contrast to the Ba'th Party's pitiful performance in the parliamentary elections. Thanks to a voluntary fundraiser organized among his allies in the business world, the president's cousin covered the costs of all meeting venues in the country. The same networks were active in organizing and financing demonstrations in favor of the regime during the uprising of 2011. Such activities can be seen as a more elaborate form of "privatizing the tax system as an instrument for extracting and redistributing resources" (Hibou 1998, 153). Private companies finance local development, law and order services, and political mobilization all at once so as to be politically accepted and in return receive favors granted by the state. Even so, this delegation of functions does not imply the retreat of the state or the emergence of new contrastate forces. Instead, new players strengthen a state that no longer has the financial, political, or symbolic resources to guarantee social and political control. One can thus assert with Hibou (1998, 167) that these processes contribute to the upgrading of the authoritarian state to the extent that they renew and revitalize the informal integration of public actors and public institutions with private individuals and firms.

The Ba'th Party remains an important cog of Bashar al-Asad's regime, but its central position has been eroded. It is thwarted by a structural and ideological crisis and lacks executives capable of managing the challenges associated with the shift toward a liberal Syria that is open to the globalized world. It has thus lost part of its capacity to produce social discourse, as well as its monopoly on social control. This is evident in a number of areas in which the Ba'th Party previously had an exclusive presence. The Ba'thist youth organization, *shabibat al-Ba'th*, used to offer children traditional holiday camps; today, the NGO Massar, which works with youth, raises awareness of environmental issues among them by sending teams out into the field and to schools and cultural centers in the various governorates. In practice, the programs focusing on citizenship issues provided by the presidential NGO are avowedly patriotic, taking over from the Ba'th Party's civic education classes. Private entrepreneurs also led the mobilization against the Israeli offensive in Gaza in 2008–2009, thus appropriating a role in the production of Pan-Arab legitimacy that used to be the Party's reserve.

Privatization also encompasses the cultural domain, which has led to the emergence of an alternative cultural scene on the margins of the fossilized cultural system (Weiss, Chapter 7 in this volume). The regime profits from this politically. Artists are directed and paid by well-known personalities who are part of the regime or close to it and can create original art that corresponds to Western norms and helps to convey a positive image of Syria. New cultural entrepreneurs, characterized by their closeness to personalities who are part of the regime or one of its support groups, have revived a certain way of co-opting the artistic and intellectual community. The organization Echo-Sada, created in November 2008 to support the artistic development of the music scene, enjoys the active support of Talah Khair, the wife of Manaf Tlass, the son of the former defense minister and colonel of the Presidential Guard, and other representatives of the Sunni bourgeoisie. Moreover, her involvement in the cultural domain perpetuates a tradition of cultural elitism among the Sunni bourgeoisie, as well as a form of co-opting. The first lady's umbrella association has also been asserting itself in cultural domains. In 2008, Syria Trust financed the Third International Jazz Festival, and Asma al-Asad also sponsored the organization of Damascus, Arab Cultural Capital 2008, which brought together renowned artists who enjoy a degree of autonomy with respect to the regime. They were being offered a relatively open space for their creativity, something that neither the traditional structures, infested with rivalry and clientalism, nor the more autonomous structures (whose development is controlled and even blocked because of a lack of political and financial support) can provide.

As has been shown, liberalization and privatization release resources that are likely to work as instruments for co-opting and reorganizing networks of allegiance. But the Syrian example also demonstrates the limits of these adjustments: this type of privatization of patronage and allegiances produces new imbalances. Because Syria's experience reflects an incomplete and often informal mode of privatization, it involves a continuous reworking of the relationships of power.

COMPETING PATRONAGE NETWORKS: WHEELER-DEALERS VERSUS BA'THISTS

Reorganizing patronage networks weakens the consensus that welds the ruling elites and their traditional clients together by modifying the conditions for redistributing resources. The issue of institutionalizing new authoritarian governance also arises. The increase in power of wheeler-dealer types within the ruling coalition—powerful individuals who form predatory networks to extract resources from liberalized sectors of the economy—has an effect on the regime's internal cohesion. They are challenging the Ba'th Party's monopoly on political and social control, all the while consolidating their position in the Syrian economy. However, they are not in a position to equal either the Party's rallying or clientalizing capacity or the resources it garners through ordinary corruption. The Ba'thists' power of patronage is being eroded in the "New Syria," but they nonetheless remain at the head of well-established networks that generate considerable economic benefits. The Ba'th Party remains influential because of the positions it occupies at all levels of the administration and public sector, which enable it to redistribute privileges and build up the loyalty of a much more considerable clientele than new structures can, whether they are the wheeler-dealers' private companies or the first lady's umbrella association. The company Syriatel, dedicated to gathering financial resources, can tap into a clientele because of the high level of remuneration and other advantages that it offers its employees, but that clientele still remains numerically relatively small. Even if the presidential NGOs gain in power and visibility—a development that has been severely set back by the 2011 uprising—they will still have a limited impact on the local population compared to Ba'thist structures.[9] They must count on Ba'thist hostility and the suspicion of the security forces, who hamper their activities in the field. The privileges granted to the STFD's NGOs, which enjoy the president's support, create dissatisfaction that generates tensions within the Party. Finally, the new patronage networks set up by the rulers find themselves in competition with the old networks overseen by the Ba'th Party, which has resisted the erosion of its influence.

The result is additional deadlock in a system that is already paralyzed by the dysfunction of the state apparatus. Wheeler-dealers often find that implementation of major initiatives is delayed because of obstruction from an administration that does not back projects that are detrimental to the apparatchiks' interests. The privatization of certain activities in Latakia's port illustrates these tensions, which pitted contradictory interests against one another. The Latakia Maritime Transport Trade Union, with the support and backing of the General Federation of Trade Unions (controlled by the Party), opposed handing over the management of the container terminal to a private French-Syrian company, leading to intervention by the security forces. While the private entrepreneurs gained the upper hand in the end, managing to obtain rulings from the relevant bureaucracy that meant they could carry out the transfer, they nevertheless had to absorb the port personnel, who had gone on strike for three weeks. The state thus imposed terms and conditions on private entrepreneurs to protect the interests of dominant public players, who make up its social base.

The public sector remains an important patronage instrument for the regime, as well as an essential source of jobs. In fact, positions within it, and related privileges, are threatened more by the vague impulse to institutionalize this new private governance, which portends further social and political tension, than they are by their internal inefficiencies and dysfunctions.

In an attempt to strengthen their position in the system and institutionalize their patronage networks, the wheeler-dealers aspire to mould the institutions of the Ba'thist Republic further. As the 2010 Party Congress approached—though the Congress ultimately was not held—they were determined to circumvent the Party by obtaining political representation, either within a Ba'th Party that would abandon references to its role as the defender of working class interests, thus clearing the way for the wheeler-dealers to join the Central Committee, or in parliament as part of new parties created with the help of a new law relaxing restrictions on political party formation. These new parties, running on an economic platform, would bring together private entrepreneurs who are regime clients and already co-opted into politically connected holding companies and would facilitate the implementation of their projects through new patronage networks that would be established within the bureaucracy. This vague impulse to institutionalize aroused strong resistance, which was openly expressed by Party loyalists, and contributed to the postponement of the Tenth Party Congress to a date that has yet to be set.[10]

THE IMPACT OF RECONFIGURATION:
A POTENTIAL REVOLT AMONG NEW ELITES?

The increase in power of the wheeler-dealer class has also restructured the economy in ways that underline how risky their position really is. Alawites are increasingly numerous in business circles. Unlike Sunnis, who need an Alawite partner to free themselves of the rules and prosper, Alawites are given preferential treatment from the start. But they owe their position in the business world exclusively to their closeness to the regime and their alliances with the security forces and therefore do not constitute an entrepreneurial class proper. Resorting to foreign associates increases their leverage vis-à-vis both potential competitors and Syrian society more broadly, which makes up for their loss of legitimacy. Foreign entrepreneurs, who are mostly from the Gulf and Europe, supply the Alawites with capital and know-how, but these new networks cannot compare in size or resources with those that make up the core of the Syrian commercial system, which remains in the hands of the Sunni and Christian bourgeoisie.

The renewed alliance between the regime and the world of business is fragile and volatile because it has been established under pressure and because it is a function of each side's interests. Thus businessmen risk only a small share of their capital in these partnerships with the regime. As in the past, the type of agreement concluded between the state and private individuals is kept deliberately unstable, secret, and continuously up for renegotiation. In this way, the regime reserves the right to spontaneously sideline any entrepreneur who has lost his usefulness or shown too much ambition. The conditions for privatizing the tax system have not been brought together: out of prudence, private entrepreneurs refuse to declare the totality of their revenues to the regime, and the regime still tolerates tax evasion because it "legitimates" future coercive measures (Donati 2009, 238). Authoritarian logic contradicts the logic of privatization. As a result, the regime has to count on the "old hands." It is forced to handle Ratib Challah carefully because he still commands the respect of the traders of the Damascus souk, a commercial world dominated by Sunnis.[11] His successor, Ghrawi, cannot yet boast of having so much influence because he owes his position exclusively to his closeness to Bashar al-Asad. Besides, the new economic activism of Alawite leaders is creating some discontent among Sunni entrepreneurs.

These tensions, and the double-edged quality of the regime's attempts to expand opportunities for predation in liberalized sectors of the economy, is also evident in the emergence of an Islamic economic sector in Syria over the past decade. Private Islamic finance is a particular example of the challenges that the liberalization process poses to the regime. Establishing Islamic banks that mobilize players from the Gulf—in terms of investments and executives recruited from among the Diaspora—is supposed to attract religious entrepreneurs, who see these banks as opportunities for investments that conform to their ethics. But the regime, anxious to control the expansion of the private sector and the autonomy of participants from "at-risk" social categories, checks the growth of Islamic finance.[12] Islamic banks are intended to tap into the savings of that part of the population, especially Aleppo's small and medium enterprises (SMEs), which forego conventional banks for religious reasons or out of mistrust of public institutions (Thépault 2010).[13] This category of small traders, small urban industrialists, and small agricultural entrepreneurs has to be included in the economic system so as to support business activity and job creation. Syria's leaders need a private sector that delivers, both to even up a trade balance that has been affected by the decline of oil exports and competition from Turkish and Chinese products and to sustain growth capable of absorbing job seekers. Yet they do not wish to encourage its expansion at the expense of their own financial and political interests or those of the new wheeler-dealers who surround them. This suspiciousness is reciprocal: the SMEs refuse to grow out of prudence and so as not to excite the covetousness of the wheeler-dealers; they still resort to the cash economy to finance their activities. The regime accepts the lost opportunities for rent seeking that a more fully developed Islamic financial sector might create to avoid facilitating the emergence of autonomous domains of economic activity.

Reorganizing patronage networks under the impact of privatization, together with the Ba'thist backlash against this trend, affects the countryside, as well, which is a supply base for the Ba'thist regime. Rural workers (farmers, workers on former state farms and in cooperatives) have been affected by the agrarian counterreform at work since 2000 (Ababsa 2006) and the "return" of the landlords. Large estates financed by private investments have been created in the east of the country and have helped a rich entrepreneurial class to emerge, made up of former landlords and new agricultural entrepreneurs. This is a source of social tensions and at times gives rise to violent clashes because at the same time the tribalized state no longer has the resources to build up loyalty among its traditional local clients. The clashes between tribes from the north of Raqqa province and tribes from its south during the 2007 parliamentary elections demonstrated the extent to which the state had lost its hold over rural social dynamics, as well as a failure of the political system.[14] It is also significant that the Hauran, the province where Syria's uprising first took hold, is representative of those rural zones which have been marginalized by economic liberalization and the reconfiguring of authoritarian practices. Hauran has lost its access to public services, social promotion, and political resources through the Ba'ath Party that it enjoyed during the tenure of Hafiz al-Asad. As this suggests, Syria's entry into a deregulated economy has aggravated socioeconomic imbalances and deepened the cleavages between, on the one hand, a privileged group from the upper middle classes and the bourgeoisie and on the other hand a large part of the population excluded from new patterns of predation and redistribution, including the lower middle class. While the end of the welfare state two decades ago already had weakened the "social pact" that previously served as a guarantor of stability, liberal Syria is faced with the emergence of a social problem.

THE BREAKDOWN OF THE "SOCIAL PACT" AND THE EROSION OF SOCIAL POLICY

Both the shrinking of economic resources and the new economic direction have led the regime to do away with the social protections that were the cornerstone of the Ba'thist state. The erosion of social policy has involved reducing consumer subsidies, abandoning the protection model of state employment, and privatizing basic services such as health and education. If the intent of these shifts is to break "the tacit pact of state clientelism" and to push issues of inequality and social justice off the political agenda (Camau and Geisser 2003, 188), they nonetheless deprive the regime of important political resources.

The public sector has long been considered the natural outlet for the ever-growing numbers of job seekers; job security has traditionally been high, and the low salaries paid by the state can be complemented by other sources of income. Yet the political problems posed by state employees are thornier than those of employees in private sector companies because so many of them have been recruited through clientelist connections.[15] Inadequately trained, they cannot find equivalent posts in the private sector. State-sector employment is therefore still preferred over those private-sector jobs that do not offer comparable benefits: despite legislation requiring that private sector employees be covered by social security, only some 14 percent are in fact enrolled. Half of the people taken on by the private sector work informally, without access to employment benefits (Aïta 2007, 576). Moreover, the private job market is not dynamic enough to compensate for declining public sector employment: while the number of new state employees dropped by half in 2005, the private sector only contributed 35 to 40 percent of new job offers.[16] In practice, economic liberalization is generating few opportunities for the 300,000 new job seekers who enter the labor market every year. The services sector, which is expanding rapidly, offers few places and those only to a privileged minority who typically acquire positions through networks of family, clan, and community alliances.

The regime's efforts to reduce social and political employment have not gone unchallenged. In 2004 the sudden and radical decision by the state no longer automatically to employ all engineering graduates caused unprecedented demonstrations in Aleppo and Damascus. The movement of the "unemployed graduates," which rallied hundreds of students, ended only when it was repressed by security forces. It also coincided with the establishment of a counterglobalization movement in Syria, which demonstrated that social problems might impose themselves as first-class collective causes. Moreover, the basic components of the popular uprising in 2011 are unemployed graduates and the "rurbains," elements among the rural population who have migrated to the peripheries of the cities to find work. Until the rise of mass protests across the region in early 2011, fear made the possibility of riots against increasing economic vulnerability in the countryside and ex-urban peripheries remote. Yet, even prior to the uprising, deepening inequality and growing social cleavages gave rise to increased levels of violence in Syria, whether in the form of clashes between identity-based groups or as rising criminality, especially in large cities. The excesses that have marked the regime's forced evacuation of unplanned settlements over the last few years were an obvious sign of deepening tension between the winners and losers of Syria's move toward a social market economy and the reconfiguring of economic and political networks that it produced. No less troubling given Syria's ethnic and sectarian diversity, social and economic stresses can be expressed in terms of identity politics. Acts of violence involving the Kurdish community, which is the victim of discriminatory policies, are due to the systematic economic exclusion of Kurdish youth. In 2004 young Kurds played a unifying role in the attempt to set up a student movement in the wings of the "unemployed graduates' rally." Often the poverty map is superimposed on the communitarian map: the country's margins are inhabited by Kurds and proletarianized Bedouins, and it is these vulnerable populations, dependent on state services, who crowd into overpopulated urban peripheries, most frequently along communal lines.

The exacerbation of social risks through privatization and more generally through liberalization, has pushed social issues onto the leaders' agendas, forcing them to reformulate their social policies. This reformulation consists first of all of drawing up a social discourse: the recognition that underdevelopment and poverty exist, together with the establishment of state bodies dedicated to finding solutions to these problems, is meant to show that social issues feature on the state's agenda.[17] Official declarations assuring the population that the state will not go back on its commitment to helping those who need it most are intended to emphasize that the highest levels of the regime, including the president, are involved in making "the perception of inequalities" intolerable. Without modifying the drift toward economic liberalization, Syria's rulers content themselves with redirecting social policy toward the provision of welfare, even charity. The implementation of a reconfigured social safety net has also been planned. Financial grants are intended to replace the subsidies of the socialist period, a social security system and unemployment benefits to replace social employment, and a pension fund to be created for state employees. But the state has neither the political nor the financial means to implement these measures. Nor are such resources readily available, given the state of Syria's system of tax collection. Only civil servants pay their taxes, which are deducted at the source. Yet the regime lacks the political will to tax private entrepreneurs and risk undermining the pact that links them with the state. Not surprisingly, the private sector on its own is neither able nor willing to bear the costs of a social policy that, as designed, is as generous as the one implemented by the public sector. Thus, for want of global administrative reforms, social policy initiatives collide with the lack of skills, institutional capacity, and the inertia of a system that resists orders given from on high.

THE PRIVATIZATION OF SOCIAL SERVICES AND THE AUTONOMIZATION OF "ENLIGHTENED ENTREPRENEURS"

For over a decade, the deterioration and cost of public social services have pushed the state to shift responsibility for well-defined welfare tasks (medical care and food for the population) to religious or civil associations (the latter being called *ahliyé*). At this liberal turning point, those NGOs and associations profit further from the redeployment of the state, which increases their leverage. This is especially the case with the network of development agencies of the Aga Khan, the head of the Ismaili Muslim community. The Aga Khan Development Network (AKDN), already present in the cultural domain and especially in restoring heritage sites, advocates for a partnership model between public and private sectors to raise the quality of social services and shift welfare provision from charity to forms that will promote sustainable local development. This type of partnership is particularly significant in the countryside, where the agency presents itself as an intermediary between farmers and the agricultural administration. This type of cooperation between public authorities and nonstate actors, particularly foreigners, constitutes "new terms for regulating social risks" (Catusse 2009, 208). However, this delegation of social services to a nonstate actor is slower and less advanced in Syria, both because of the obstacles put up by the bureaucracy and because of the regime's determination to ensure that the activities of such groups do not come to constitute a threat to its authority. Private development agencies are certainly instrumentalized by a retreating state, which sees in them a means of appeasing social discontent, "offloading traditional responsibilities," and even "displacing social issues outside of the traditional institutional arenas" (Catusse 2009, 208).[18] However, the agencies end up filling a vacuum and become the population's negotiating partner, creating an alternative framework to the structures of the Ba'thist state. Eventually, this position enables them to extend their leverage vis-à-vis the authorities. Or, as Catusse puts it, "a range of actors, having flexible relations with the political and with the administration, find niches for their aspirations—their appetite for power, their desire for action or, in certain cases, their search for social recognition" (Catusse 2009, 208).

The communities that dominate associations no longer limit themselves to charity: they have tended to expand the services they bring to the population and diversify their activities, becoming true private entrepreneurs. They have thus created a social base that increases their negotiating power with the state regarding their role and status within the system. Christian communities are linked to the regime by minority solidarity, and yet their demands can induce exaggerated identity politics on the part of the religious majority.[19] As the work of Thomas Pierret and Kjetil Selvik shows, the development of the Islamic charity sector, which dominates associations and in which a cooperation between ulemas and entrepreneurial circles is taking place, is distinctly more problematic: within a decade, the Jama'at Zayd has created for itself an unequalled popular and economic base within the Sunni religious majority, from the underprivileged to young middle-class graduates (Pierret and Selvik 2009). The security response is indicative of the stakes: in 2008 the regime banned leading religious sheikhs from combining their functions as directors of private religious education establishments with those of presidents of one or several charities, before revising its religious policy, as Thomas Pierret highlights in his contribution in Chapter 4 of this volume.

The state's new partners who have emerged with the help of privatization are forcing the regime to rewrite the rules of the game. The central role of coercion in upgrading authoritarianism according to market criteria is at the same time confirmed, as much for containing social tensions as for "regulating" the aspirations of private entrepreneurs. But these social tensions can also thwart the coercive apparatus, whose cohesion might eventually be affected by the shrinking of the army's communal base due to a certain degree of disaffection with military careers among Alawites. Originally from the marginalized rural zones of Deir ez-Zor, Qamichli, or Raqqa, the Sunnis who make up the majority of the troops are Bedouins, whom the regime is leaving in a position of subordination so as to be able to clientalize them. Yet in a context of rampant sectarianism and internal troubles or unrest, their loyalty is not secure. By 2011, it was regular soldiers from these regions who made up the bulk of those who had defected and joined the Free Syrian Army to defend civilians from regime violence. The contingent loyalty of the army's rank-and-file has led the regime to resort to elite units mainly composed of Alawites to repress protests. Elements of the Republican Guard were sent to quell the Kurdish riots in the spring of 2004 and have been deeply involved in crushing the uprising in the city of Homs in 2011 and 2012.

CONCLUSION

This chapter has outlined a process of upgrading authoritarianism on which the post-2000 leadership of Syria embarked. For more than a decade, before it was confronted by massive protests from below, this process consisted of renewing and enlarging the ruling coalition, developing new streams of rents to sustain a reconfigured military–commercial coalition, the backbone of the Syrian authoritarian regime. Before it was hit by the intense sanctions that followed the regime's brutal response to the uprising of 2011, opening up the market and privatizing the state provided essential resources for reforming the patrimonial regime. Liberalization served as an instrument for co-opting and reorganizing networks of allegiance while making it possible to circumvent traditional players and institutions that viewed economic opening as a challenge to their own privileges.

What resulted was, in effect, a new mode of authoritarian governance in Syria, highlighting the Asad regime's recombinant capacity. This new mode of governance reflected the intent of regime elites to off-load some of its regalian, predatory functions onto private players. Yet off-loading and the privatization of key state functions came at a price in terms of the resistance of those who perceived themselves to be losers in the emergent order of the Asad regime and in terms of the increasing sense of economic marginality among Syrians in general, conditions that provided fertile ground once the spark of uprising was lit in Tunisia and Egypt in early 2011. The inclinations of some within Syria's ruling circles to push off-loading further were constrained, as well, because of the inherent tensions that exist between privatization and control. Upgrading through off-loading has progressed in fits and starts over the past decade because it so often collided with authoritarian logic and constraints that are specific to the Syrian framework. Syrian authoritarianism progresses by jolts and adjustments because the Mukhabarat state intends to keep strict control over its clients and society in general. The privatization of the tax system has been unsuccessful, too, and, generally speaking, new modes of regulation are struggling to be institutionalized. The resistance coming from former leading figures in the public sector has to be taken into account as much as the new aspirations generated by an increasingly indirect type of governance.

These new imbalances are evident in the Syrian uprising but exist in a number of other domains at the same time. First of all, the renewal of the ruling coalition changes the regime's internal cohesion because it modifies the redistribution of rents among leading public and private players. Newly constituted patronage networks compete with older networks without being able to equal their resources, either material or political. Before they were eclipsed by the Syrian uprising, the clashes and tensions that expressed this competition bore witness to the dysfunction of the political system. The Ba'th Party had seen patronage power erode away in the "New Syria"; however, it retained influence because it occupied a central position within the system and slowed the institutionalization of new governance. At the same time, its incapacity to evolve so as to confront the global market economy makes resorting to new private intermediaries essential, and these, in turn, reinforce the off-loading impulses of a regime whose resources are shrinking.

Second, the wheeler-dealers who dominate the liberalized sectors of the Syrian economy do not yet constitute an entrepreneurial class proper and must still rely on allies within the business world, an urban environment that is mostly Sunni and has uncertain relations with the regime. Nonetheless, the emergence of new clientele networks in both towns and the countryside (which is affecting the regime's support base) has modified the internal "predatory pluralism" that has been a defining element of Syrian authoritarianism. This has created new sources of friction within the regime, while exacerbating the economic vulnerability of Syrians more broadly, including many whom privatization has pushed outside of the Ba'th's longstanding redistributive and social policy frameworks, because newly empowered private actors were neither able nor willing to bear the costs of the previous social policy.

Thus, privatization and more generally liberalization have lead to a reconfiguration of the Syrian economy and created new challenges with which the regime might contend, such as the emergence of an Islamicized middle class and enlightened entrepreneurs, whose ambitions must be simultaneously encouraged but also contained. This imbalance has led the regime to supply permanent arbitration to satisfy the interests of the wheeler-dealers and its new base (middle and upper bourgeoisie) and to look after the interests of the Ba'th Party and its traditional base (workers and the rural populations).

Syrian authoritarian corporatism, which rests on a strategy of counterbalancing, has always produced corporatist frustrations and demands, which necessitate permanent negotiations. Privatization introduces new domains of negotiation because it continuously reformulates relationships of power, using as criteria the often contradictory strategies and interests of the dominant players. This is not about simply identifying the "winners" and "losers" of this upgrading but about measuring the reconfiguration induced by the regime's strategy and its impact on authoritarian governance. At the time of this writing, these effects appear muted. "Routine" tensions and conflicts have been pushed into the background by the regime's ruthless response to the mass demands for economic and political change that have sustained Syria's uprising since March 2011. Thus, the 2011 uprising can be understood, in part, as the ultimate expression of resistance by Syrians to the economic and social costs of reconfiguring authoritarian governance in Syria: it has involved populations that have been excluded from new patterns of predation and redistribution. What we are also seeing is an attempt to redefine or to overthrow, from below, a ruling coalition that has became a minority.

3 A MARTYRS' WELFARE STATE AND ITS CONTRADICTIONS

Regime Resilience and Limits through the Lens of Social Policy in Iran

Kevan Harris

IN A RECENT INTERVIEW, Ahmad Batebi, the young man who ended up on the cover of *The Economist* magazine in 1999 holding up a bloody T-shirt during university student protests, languished in prison as a result, and finally escaped to the United States in 2008, gave a rather concise version of what most people think of when they hear the term "Iranian welfare state":

> In Iran, there are two groups of people with connections to the government: those who ideologically believe in the system and those who receive benefits and monetary compensation. The former group, who is either brainwashed or is a supporter through family ties, would not join the Green Movement even if they were dissatisfied with the government. They would rather opt for political apathy and inaction. The latter group, however, will join the movement, if their funding is cut.[1]

This conception of social policy in Iran is quite common, not just among activists and pundits but also within scholarship. Welfare policy in Iran is formulated as a hegemonic project of ideological exhortation coupled with a crass political machine where public goods are narrowly targeted at poorer strata to secure mobilization or, at least, complacency (Dorraj and Dodson 2009). Certainly, the state itself, as self-appointed protector of the *mostazafan* (dispossessed), would like us to believe that it devotes itself to servicing the least fortunate in society. Semipublic endowed foundations known as *bonyads* (Maloney 2004) and paramilitary apparatuses such as the Basij (Thaler et al. 2010) elicit much of the scholarly attention when it comes to social policy, with the policies themselves often seen as residual to more pressing concerns of factional competition, state exigency, or patron–client networks.

A closer examination of the social policy of the Islamic Republic of Iran (IRI), however, reveals a rather surprising picture. Instead of a single welfare apparatus that targets the poorest strata, Iran contains two distinct "welfare regimes," each with its own historical lineage and constituencies. A *revolutionary* welfare regime, partly consisting of the aforementioned *bonyads*, the Imam Khomeini Relief Committee (IKRC), and the rural village health system, undoubtedly targets the lower strata. This regime is what the historian Ervand Abrahamian once labeled the "martyrs' welfare state" (1989, 70). It took shape in the postrevolutionary period, especially during the long war with Iraq (1980–1988) and subsequent reconstruction era. Yet, by far the largest expenses for the state, and the most beneficiaries for any social policies in Iran, are for the pensions and health care that are maintained by such institutions as the Social Security Organization (SSO), the Civil Service Retirement Organization (CSRO), and the subsidies of staple goods, energy, and medical services. To compare, the IKRC claims 6 to 7 million beneficiaries and dependents out of a population of over 70 million; the SSO claims 27 million. These public goods target the working and middle classes of Iran by design, while the urban subproletariat (around 30 percent of the urban population) suffers from severe problems of access. This *corporatist* welfare regime originated long before the 1979 revolution and has its roots in the state-building efforts of the Pahlavi monarchy. The presence of these two welfare regimes, and the capacity they provide the Iranian government to adapt flexibly as patterns of social demand and the broader political environment change, are important elements in understanding its resilience over the course of three decades.

As a result of perennial factionalism within the political field and lack of a forceful state apparatus from which to carry out bureaucratization schemes effectively, these two welfare regimes remain mostly autonomous from each other as distinct institutional clusters. This rather byzantine structure also presents a curious puzzle for analyzing the resilience of the postrevolutionary Iranian government. For if it is the case that Iranians support the regime because they are "bought off" by the state through welfare policies, then why are the main sites of public contestation to the regime centered around those social classes seemingly best protected from economic risk and embedded in the larger of the two welfare regimes? Is welfare patronage a mechanism of regime rule, or does it empower new social actors and give force to new demands? For the Iranian case, to paraphrase Claus Offe (1984), I will argue that the answer is: both.

Given social characteristics common to other middle-income countries in the world economy, the IRI is constantly "running fast to stay in place" (Silver 1990). In other words, state policies recurrently generate a variety of expectations from various social classes and status groups, which often include protecting the populace from social and economic risks, "catching up" to the wealthy North via development, maintaining the status and prestige of the "nation," and constructing social and/or political rights, to which it can respond either through available institutions or the creation of new ones. But, in the course of doing so, it partially fails to deliver on existing expectations as well as generating new grievances. In this chapter, I first explain why two welfare regimes exist in the IRI, not one, each reflecting a particular logic of governance and historical origin. Then, I discuss some of the most important institutions in each welfare regime as well as perceptions among Iranians concerning them and why comments such as the one from Ahmad Batebi are prevalent in public discourse. Lastly, I outline the sociopolitical implications of the Iranian welfare system and how it generated mechanisms for regime resilience yet also helped to produce new challenges to its rule—the strongest of which is the Green Movement itself.

CONCEPTUALIZING THE IRANIAN WELFARE STATE

"Iran has a welfare state, but not a welfare state discourse," an Iranian sociologist once told me.[2] He was referring to the fact that while a large array of social welfare institutions existed in both the Islamic Republic as well as its predecessor, the Pahlavi monarchy, a discourse of social rights had not developed in tandem. Hidden behind this statement lurked the ghost of T. H. Marshall (1964) and his archetype of the linear development of citizenship rights in European states. Yet Iran is not alone. Once we look outside Europe, social policies enacted by various states in the former Third World were rarely based on citizenship rights.

A "welfare regime" is an analytic conceptualization of how state institutions interact with market and household activities in processes of social reproduction. Scholars originally focused on wealthy Western European and Anglo-American states, with the emergence of a comparative typology that sought to explain the observable "worlds" of welfare under capitalism (Esping-Anderson 1990). When the global South is included in this "world," the variety of the institutional mix expands, but a clustering of welfare regime types grouped around region and income level can still be detected (Wood and Gough 2006). Recent studies have moved from descriptive groupings of states based on policy outcomes toward theorization of the origins and consolidation of different welfare regimes outside of the global North (Haggard and Kaufman 2008). In nonsocialist East Asia, welfare policy was seen as an instrumental input for the purpose of economic development, embedded in nationalist Cold War policies (Castells 1992; Gough 2004). In Latin America, social protections enacted for formal sector workers, due to high rates of proletarianization as well as the developmental models in vogue at the time, seldom extended to the larger and growing portion of the population in the informal sector (Segura-Ubiergo 2007). For countries in the Middle East and North Africa, it has been argued that social welfare was directly tied to postcolonial efforts of building and legitimizing new nation-states (Karshenas and Moghadam 2006). Yet, as with Latin America, large segments of the population in agricultural and informal sectors, as well as the majority of females not in the labor market, were left out of the policies' targets. Up until the 1979 revolution, Iran's welfare policy easily fell into this latter category, reflecting the Pahlavi monarchy's emphasis on "modernization" of the sort understood in the post-1945 era (Gilman 2003). While it often emulated the Egyptian and Turkish republics to its west, each of which had constructed popular regimes with efficient military apparatuses out of the breakdown of nineteenth-century colonial order, the monarchy under the Shah was never able to create similar bases of mass support with welfare policy.

While he may not have been fully aware of it, the Shah's plan to implement a "revolution from above" originated not with Ataturk but with Bismarck. Like the Prussian chancellor, the Shah's social reforms came only after pressure from nationalist and socialist movements pushed his hand. The diffusion of European models for social welfare and educational institutions arrived in the country and were put forward during brief periods of Iranian parliamentary rule (1906–1911, 1943–1946, 1951–1953). Yet these proposals, often radical in the region for their time, were reformulated and directed toward building up the military and industrial capacity of the state under Reza Shah and then later under Mohammad Reza Shah's own reign after 1947 (Messkoub 2006). Educational expansion occurred to create a technocratic class to fill the burgeoning state sector, both civilian and military. Social insurance widened from covering only government sector employees in the 1920s to targeting large industrial enterprises' employees by the 1940s. A 1953 bill passed in the parliament headed by Prime Minister Mohammad Mossadeq created an Organization of Workers' Social Insurance, centralizing existing social insurance funds under the management of a single state bureaucracy. The subsequent removal of Mossadeq and the reassertion of the Shah's authority in all state matters limited the full implementation of the law, but the organization survived the 1953 coup d'état. Still, it covered no more than 180,000 workers and their dependents throughout the 1950s—around 4 percent of the population (Schayegh 2006).

The introduction in the 1960s of the Shah's "White Revolution" aimed to legitimize the state in the eyes of the growing professional middle classes, remove its alliance with the landowning class via land redistribution to a segment of the peasantry, ameliorate the conditions of rural life, and centralize state control over the development process (Abrahamian 2008, chapter 5). The overall revenues of the government rapidly increased due to economic growth through import substitution and rising prices of oil, and the state ramped up absolute spending on social affairs. However, while the White Revolution saw the formation of a Health and Literacy Corps specifically for rural villages, the emphasis on urban expansion and industrial modernization remained at the center of social policy. These programs did send youthful and energetic individuals with a high esprit de corps out to rural regions (Sabahi 2002), but the welfare effects on villages were disjointedly uneven at best. As Grace Goodell detailed in her ethnographic study of Iranian villages under the White Revolution's policies, the imposition of technocratic administrations of hygiene and literacy from afar could produce results as absurd as any found in Joseph Heller's *Catch-22*. For instance, corpsmen who improved their assigned villages along particular indicators the most were offered scholarships in college. At Goodell's village field site, a bright yellow mailbox was installed by the young corpsman on the main road, and his corps supervisor came to appear next to it in photographs, proclaiming the young man a national patriot. The problems were that "few in this largely illiterate village had ever seen a postage stamp or . . . the fact that no rural postal service existed" (1986, 150). Not surprisingly, even while health and literacy indicators improved across the country, the gap between rural and urban Iran in those indicators did not. Overall life expectancy rose from forty-eight years in 1960 to fifty-five years in 1972

(World Bank 2011). But in 1973, while male urban life expectancy stood at 60.7 years, for rural males it was 50.7 years; for urban females life expectancy was 62 years, while for rural females it was 51.4 years (Messkoub 2006, 234).

A national health system was formally enacted in 1976 and was administered under a newly merged Ministry of Health and Social Welfare. This did expand the provision of basic vaccination throughout the country and capped the prices of certain pharmaceuticals and medical services. But while some Iranian public health administrators were urging a switch to a primary care approach aimed at preventive medicine and community-based service delivery, and even began a pilot project in West Azerbaijan to demonstrate its effects, no rural infrastructure was created to administer any such plans beyond the Army-administered Health Corps (Moore 2007; Newell 1975). Furthermore, there was fierce resistance by the private medical establishment, which preferred to manage high-technology-dependent hospitals in urban centers that emulated the latest Western advances (Underwood 2004).[3]

The result was a social and health insurance system similar to many middle-income countries in the postwar era with an increasing urban and formal labor force that relied on import substitution industrialization. In such an environment, heavy industry and public sector workers benefited most from the modernization drive (Haggard and Kaufman 2008). The Shah was concerned, as were many states in the 1970s, about the increasing demands of urban working classes located in key industries. This fact, combined with the inspiration from modernization theory that the joint development of industrialization and oil would result in a "withering away" of Iran's traditional merchant and peasant classes, oriented social policy toward urban formal workers both professional and proletarian. As the Shah reiterated in his exile-penned book, *Answer to History* (1980), his policies were meant to speed that expected transformation.[4] Yet, instead of commanding a revolution from above, the monarchy called into being a revolution from below. Land reform and rapid growth had dislocated many in the rural sector, boosted migration to cities, and agitated the large petty merchant class and the informal labor force it relied on. When the Pahlavi regime collapsed amid the urban demonstrations of 1978–1979, it left the coalescing revolutionary state a set of social welfare institutions that reflected the previous modernization paradigm.

Given the paternalistic and conservative origins of these policies in the prototypical "late developer" of Bismarckian Germany (Steinmetz 1993), and the adoption of such policies in Iran at the same time as other middle-income countries in Latin America and East Asia, I categorize this set of institutions in Iran as a *corporatist welfare regime*. This does not refer to the tripartite concertation in Western Europe among labor, capital, and government that Schmitter (1974) deemed an inclusionary "social corporatism." Instead, the Pahlavi state structured the population into interest groups that it then claimed to represent through a variety of social and political institutions imposed from above (Akhavi 1992; Stepan 1978). This exclusionary corporatism was common to state-building projects among authoritarian regimes in the Third World that felt more threatened from external social forces than weak internal configurations of labor and capital, and it disciplined the latter in an attempt to build state capacity and catch up to wealthy Northern countries (Cox 1987).

During the initial months after the 1979 Iranian revolution, a major consequence of the distrust of the existing bureaucracy was the creation of parallel organizations for almost all of the requirements of governance in the new regime. From local committees of Khomeini-supporting militants rose the Revolutionary Guard Corps, who, in Napoleonic fashion, refused to use the officer ranking system of the existing armed forces. Ad hoc courts for punishing Pahlavi officials with "Islamic justice" were haphazardly organized under a revolutionary tribunal system, which often clashed in jurisprudence with existing civil courts. The 1979 constitution itself combined the Fifth Republic–inspired structures of Parliament and president with separate bodies of Islamic "guidance" overseen by the quite unorthodox Shi'a position of Guardianship of Jurisprudence that Khomeini occupied. And, in social policy, a wide range of revolutionary organizations were either created or recognized ex post facto and given authority.

The large amount of property and assets that belonged to the Pahlavi monarchy (including its Pahlavi Foundation charity) turned into the Foundation for the Oppressed, which was supposed to manage the assets as a trust for the benefit of those who made the revolution. A state-mandated freeze on property prices in Tehran from 1980 to 1982—the only period out of the entire latter half of the twentieth century that property values did not increase in Tehran—brought into being the Islamic Housing Foundation, which was to provide interest-free loans and develop new properties for the homeless (Amouee 2003, chapter 1). A volunteer aid organization centered in Iran's large bazaars during the revolution became the Imam Khomeini Relief Committee, which was mandated with alleviating poverty in urban and rural areas. Young revolutionaries who had travelled back to their villages were called to participate in the Construction Jihad to aid in the creation of basic rural infrastructure. All of these institutions were paragovernmental and actively competed against preexisting social welfare institutions in both the implementation of policy and in the ideological field (Moslem 2002).

Throughout the war period in the 1980s, nationalized industry and paragovernmental agencies acted not only as producers and as procurers in the war economy but also as job retention and hiring programs. The state reached deeper into Iranian society on its war footing than the Pahlavi regime had ever done, but it also had to meet the heightened expectations of newly mobilized social groups that anticipated and demanded a redistribution of goods, resources, and prestige under the new Islamic Republic. New organizations specifically focusing on social policy for war veterans such as the Martyrs' Foundation were established, and existing welfare institutions began to include veterans' needs in their own policies. These forms of social policy proved effective in the legitimation of the state during wartime, and, while the preexisting corporatist welfare regime was never dismantled, the revolutionary welfare institutions took precedence as evidence of a new social contract. As mentioned, by the late 1980s Ervand Abrahamian could analyze the postrevolutionary regime on the eve of Khomeini's demise as a "huge martyrs' welfare state," which, unlike its predecessor, presided over a solid social base (1989, 70).

These policies were justified with Islamic conceptions of charity, but the state's intensive role in supporting and directing these institutions illustrates that they go well beyond the traditional forms of *vaqf* that existed in Iran previously. Furthermore, while the rhetoric of many of these organizations espoused "protecting soldiers and mothers," these institutions did not arise from the loose, decentralized political process that Theda Skocpol (1992) analyzed for late-nineteenth-century social policy in the United States. Instead, these policies emulated other major revolutions in the Third World associated with the emblematic year of 1968, including the Cuban and Chinese revolutions. The policies were not directed toward any single class or occupational category but focused on incorporating segments of society excluded by the former regime into social bases of the postrevolutionary state. I categorize this set of institutions as a *revolutionary welfare regime*.

In sum, the IRI developed a dual set of institutional apparatuses for administering social policy. One part was technocratic, well trained, and experienced in administering services to a portion of the population. The other part was unplanned in structure and ideological in rhetoric and saw itself as the real social auxiliary of the new regime. Unusually, what did not subsequently occur was the fusion of these institutions into a single social welfare apparatus under an administrative or ministerial authority. The revolutionary welfare regime, instead of withering away, expanded in conjunction with the corporatist social insurance and pension programs that had been reactivated after the revolutionary turmoil (Saeidi 2004). In this way, the Iran–Iraq war effectively locked in place a dual institutionalization of welfare organizations as social regulatory structures in the Iranian state. Postrevolutionary welfare policy often seemed ad hoc and was not directed toward a long-term developmental strategy, but it contributed to the state and war-making capacity of the Islamic Republic as a key nexus of social inclusion for the new regime.

OUTCOMES VERSUS PERCEPTIONS OF WELFARE POLICY

The welfare state does not simply reinforce ongoing processes of social reproduction. It also actively draws boundaries in society. The effects of social policy, intended or otherwise, include not only a set of path-dependent welfare institutions but also a symbolic ordering of individuals (Clarke 2004). Conflicting accounts and perceptions of the role of social policy can therefore illustrate larger schisms, negotiated settlements, and unspoken assumptions within the social order. With this in mind, each of the two welfare regimes in Iran presents significant insights into mechanisms of regime resilience as well as challenges generated to state rule.

Among the revolutionary foundations, arguably the most effective as well as the largest is the Imam Khomeini Relief Committee (IKRC). With an annual budget of $2 billion (less than 1 percent of Iran's GDP), it provides a range of services, including financial aid to low- or no-income families, health insurance, interest-free loans for housing, scholarships, and stipends for the elderly poor in rural areas. The IKRC headquarters, once nestled in grimy downtown Tehran, now sit in northeast Tehran in a lavish multiple-building compound. The organization boasts that nearly 7 million Iranians received some type of monetary or in-kind benefit in 2009. However, of that number, 4.5 million, or 6 to 7 percent of the population, get month-to-month aid.[5] The bureaucratic habitus of the IKRC is unmistakably "revolutionary." Its managers wear the oversized suit, visible beard, and personal religious accoutrements that became popularized via the particular revolutionary "counterculture" that was spawned in the public sector after 1979. Not only are photographed visits from Hezbollah leader Hassan Nasrallah and various Hamas dignitaries visible in the entryway, but the IKRC itself also has branches in Lebanon, Syria, the Palestinian Territories, Afghanistan, and Tajikistan. Its blue-colored street donation boxes, with a pair of yellow hands cradling a cartoon family, are ubiquitous not just in every Iranian city but also in Beirut's Shi'a neighborhoods and businesses. The crumpled currency shoved into these boxes is emptied in local offices around the country and added to IKRC coffers, though the organization admits that most of its budget comes from the government.

A visit to one such local office in Tabriz in February 2010 revealed at least five individuals sorting piles of thousands of Iranian notes, each worth one to fifty cents. This illustrated that an organization wholly identified with the regime (even though they at times are presented as a nongovernmental body) can benefit from Iranian traditions of *zakat* and *nazr*. I witnessed hundreds of middle-class Iranians dump their small bills or change from a restaurant or grocery into these boxes in Tehran and other cities, even while most of them would express disgust at the regime if queried. This testified to the permanence of certain revolutionary organizations and policy in the social imagination—this particular stream of revolutionary social policy had acquired an aura of "common sense," as Gramsci would put it.

The IKRC frequently publicizes its welfare efforts, even though it is beholden only to the office of the supreme leader and rarely undergoes scrutiny by other branches of the government. For example, one learns from the IKRC's website that, during three months in the spring of 2010 in the town of Shahr Babak, in Kerman province, with a population just over 50,000, monetary allowances of $20 to $30 per month were given to 3,800 families, nearly 700 students received some form of stipend, $300,000 in microloans were given to forty-six borrowers, 120 food baskets were delivered, twenty-two cases of rent arrears were covered, $1,000 in medical bills were paid, food and energy coupons worth $500,000 were distributed to 4,000 families, dowry and funeral costs were financed for tens of families, and $64,000 in donations were collected.[6]

Discussions on the political impact of IKRC policies tend toward caricature. Critics argue it is a bastion of regime "soft power" masquerading as an "ordinary charity" (Majidyar and Alfoneh 2010). The IRI itself is responsible for a fair amount of this perception because IKRC charity events are often shown on television or described in large banners unfurled near town bazaars. The current head of the IKRC, Hossein Anvari, even claimed that none of the families helped by the organization took part in the Green Movement protests in June of 2009, which he said was "natural because [these families] have touched the warmth of people's donations" (*Financial Times*, June 30, 2009). While a statement like this is taken at face value by opposition activists, who often similarly claim a correspondence between state largesse and political co-optation, a more nuanced reading is needed. My interviews with IKRC managers revealed that the organization not only emphasizes "charity" but also conceives of itself as actively *competing* with the corporatist welfare regime. These officials portrayed the social insurance provided by the large Social Security Organization (SSO) as passive and unable to reach everyone in society. The bureaucratic cadres of the IKRC, even if they disagreed with some of the current regime's politics, are still believers in the mission of the state to reorient social policy in a "revolutionary" fashion. I was told that attempts by some politicians to "scientifically" establish an absolute poverty line did not take into account the security given by a "comfortable" life—a veiled critique of President Khatami's attempt to enact such a poverty line during his administration (1997–2005). Instead of an absolute poverty line, where one is entitled to particular benefits if income dips below that level, the IKRC and similar organizations administer benefits based on criteria of status and life history as well as income.[7]

Looking outside Iran, the IKRC's methods are compatible with a recent trend in the development field: "Just give money to the poor" (Hanlon, Barrientos, and Hulme 2010). From Indonesia and South Africa to Mexico and Brazil, small but reoccurring cash transfers to segments of the poorest strata of these countries have resulted in lower absolute poverty levels and increased basic welfare outcomes such as literacy and infant survival. In the Iranian case, no one has attempted to measure the IKRC's individual effects on alleviating poverty on a national scale, but its presence in the smaller cities and towns in every province assuredly plays a role.[8] We do know that while the IRI exhibited high absolute poverty levels during the 1980s war, over the past two decades this has starkly declined in both rural and urban areas no matter which poverty line is used (Salehi-Isfahani 2009). Of course, from the mid-1990s onward, the slow rise in global oil prices and bouts of economic growth in Iran provided the framework for such poverty reduction, but there is no guarantee that oil revenues will generate decreased inequality. Indeed, in many cases historically, increased oil revenues produce exactly the opposite outcome. But, according to the World Bank's PPP-based "$2 a day" measurement of global absolute poverty, Iran has remained at single-digit levels since the mid-1990s (World Bank 2011).

The IKRC's presence is centered in urban areas, including small towns, even though it does deliver services to rural villages. However, in the poorest neighborhoods of southern Tehran, northeast Ahvaz, or northern Tabriz— sites of major migration influx from both rural areas as well as Afghan or Arab communities—there is no sign of the organization.[9] Instead, applicants must go to the IKRC offices in other neighborhoods and put in requests for aid. Still, when I did observe individuals attempting to sign up for IKRC aid, the process was hardly one of ideological exhortation by revolutionary charity agents. Instead, what I witnessed was a combination of supplication and negotiation, almost always by female members of households. In some cases, women demanded to see managers higher up in the organization for particular complaints or requests. The process was bureaucratic in appearance, with forms, account numbers, and queues, but individuals frequently went beyond these Weberian avenues because it was clear that personal communication could deliver services if phrased in the appropriate way.

A fact of life among the poorer strata in Iran is that, for better or worse, they have to interact with various state apparatuses on a much more frequent basis than Iranians located in the formal professional and working classes. The poor possess a discourse of "revolutionary" rights that can be used in engagement with state officials, similar to "rights talk" in other postrevolutionary regimes (Lee 2008), but they are also at the mercy of the state for a portion of their livelihood. Moreover, the politics of the "informal sector" can tend toward active avoidance of state encroachment, especially when issues of commerce or housing are at stake (Bayat 1997; Lomnitz 1988). Even so, the permanence and flexibility of an institution like the IKRC illustrates that the regime possesses some means to channel social and economic grievances held by poorer strata into a set of routine everyday interactions with the state.[10]

Without question, the most successful segment of the revolutionary welfare regime is the rural health house system (Mehryar 2004; Shadpour 2000). Indirectly based on Cuban and Chinese revolutionary models of primary health care that became popularized in the 1970s by global public health professionals, today 95 percent of Iran's villages are no more than an a hour away from a station staffed by two trained health workers. Not only are all services free at these stations, but health workers also monitor individuals as long as they reside nearby. Local data on births, deaths, disease outbreaks, vaccinations, and contraception use are collected by the staff and centralized upward. Doctors visit each health house at least one day a week, and referrals for advanced treatment in major cities and transportation can be obtained. Furthermore, because multiple welfare organizations have extended services to rural areas, no less than three insurance programs are available for villagers to enroll in if they qualify. The most common is known as "rural insurance," which was amended and expanded in 2006 to allow rural residents to more easily receive care in urban hospitals. As long as an individual is counted present in the village at the time of the annual survey, he or she is eligible for free health care in the rural network. Because this survey takes place at the time of the Persian New Year, when many urban migrants return to their villages to visit their close and extended families, the social safety net is cast more widely into the networks of migrant labor that travel between urban and rural areas.[11]

Begun in the mid-1980s, the health house program continues to expand today and is partly responsible for the large reduction in infant mortality and Iran's total fertility rate (TFR). In 1980, Iran had a TFR of nearly seven births per female. Only twenty years later, Iran's TFR stood at two births per female— a figure under the population replacement rate. Remarkably, this rapid drop occurred even after a slight *increase* in the birth rate in the early 1980s, partly due to a rise in the marriage rate as well as the introduction of pronatalist policies by the state. Public health experts and more pragmatic politicians realized that this would lead to disastrous effects on developmental prospects after the war had ended, and attempts began to reverse this policy (Hoodfar 2008).

Among countries in the Middle East and North Africa region, Iran's "demographic transition" was startlingly rapid and mostly occurred in the 1990s. Given that top-down exhortations to decrease family size are rarely successful by themselves, the reasons for Iran's transition are still debated. When urban, middle-class Iranians are asked why the birth rate in Iran is so low, one often hears the reason "poverty." However, even at similar levels of urbanization, other middle-income countries, especially in the Middle East and North Africa (MENA) region, possess higher birth rates than Iran, and poorer countries such as India are still struggling with reducing rural birth rates. This popular misconception in Iran about its own demographic transition is so frequently heard that health house workers I interviewed were eager to provide alternative explanations. Most believed that the demographic transition was due to family planning instructions given by the state to rural families who were previously *bifarhang*—uncultured. These health workers told me that, in the initial years of the plan, older villagers were harder to convince to have fewer children and had to be repeatedly instructed on the benefits and Islamic appropriateness of such a lifestyle, but now it is rare that anyone produces more than two offspring. Even more important to the successful implementation of rural health care, however, seemed to be the permanence of the institutions in these areas. Almost every one of the health workers I interviewed had been in her or his position in the same village for over a decade—some for almost two decades. The system is designed to train local individuals, and the villagers are therefore already familiar with the health workers and their families. Qualitatively, this is in stark contrast to the Shah's attempts at family planning administered by the Army Health Corps in the 1970s, where health workers lived outside the village, stayed no longer than one to two years, and were often from an entirely different province of Iran.

However, the decline in fertility began *before* the full launch of family planning policies in 1989 (Abbasi-Shavazi, McDonald, and Hosseini-Chavoshi 2009), which implies additional causal mechanisms of demographic change other than a direct link between the family planning espoused by health houses and reduction in the birth rate. For a household to decide to produce fewer children, its members must trust that the social welfare provisions the state supplies in the present will be continued for at least a whole generation; otherwise the incentives to reduce family size will not change. In other words, the replacement of *kin*-based networks of social protection with *state*-based networks is not only a top-down process. It requires an extension of a household's time horizon related to how its members perceive the state's role in their lives, or what Arthur Stinchcombe calls the "solidity of institutional futures" (1997, 391). Arguably, the revolutionary welfare regime's social policies generated this shift in opinion. As a group of economists who looked at the causes of the demographic transition in Iran wrote,

> The new family planning program . . . was built on an existing and rapidly expanding rural health infrastructure, known as the rural Health Network System (HNS), that focused on mothers and child health to the exclusion of family planning and was very popular with rural families. As a result, when family planning was added to the HNS services, they had reason to view it as part of a rural development program rather than merely intended to control their numbers. (Salehi-Isfahani, Abbasi-Shavazi, and Hosseini-Chavoshi 2010, 162)

In retrospect, then, the establishment of a revolutionary welfare regime in rural areas *before* state exhortations for changes in reproductive behavior may have generated the trust necessary to make these policies successful. A disconnect between this transformation in the rural sector and city centers was intriguingly telling. Most urban middle-class Iranians I spoke to—usually those individuals who had no ties to any village residents in their age cohort—were completely unaware of the existence of the rural health system.

The large institutions that comprise the corporatist welfare regime have not simply plodded on after 1979 but instead engaged themselves in the task of social policy as developmental strategy. The bureaucratic *habitus* at the Social Security Organization (SSO), for instance, is distinctly different from its revolutionary competitors. It is filled with technocrats who keep abreast of the latest social science and international developments in welfare policy. The SSO publishes far more data on its own operations, including the investment of its pension funds in management consortiums that own sizable portions of the economy.[12] When a sociologist like myself showed up at the SSO, I was treated as a bearer of scientific knowledge and practices, while at the IKRC I was regarded with half-joking suspicions of being a spy. During the Khatami administration, the SSO came under the supervision of the newly created Ministry of Welfare and Social Affairs, in an attempt to corral all of the welfare organizations into one managerial agency. This attempt failed, and even the SSO retains some residual autonomy from the ministry. However, the 1990s saw a period of major expansion of the corporatist welfare regime that continues to this day.

In Iran, civil servants belong to a separate pension fund, the Civil Service Retirement Organization (CSRO), while workers for state-owned enterprises belong to the SSO, which includes both public and private sector workers. In addition, the SSO attempts to enroll self-employed, part-time workers and agricultural workers, who have to pay a lower monthly contribution but receive benefits equal to other pensioners.[13] SSO and CSRO pensions cover over 40 percent of the labor force, a high figure for the MENA region. Even more surprising is that the gross income replacement rate for these pensions in the IRI—the share of total gross income that is replaced or reserved at retirement—is the one of the *highest*, not just in the MENA region, but in the *world*. With an average income replacement rate of 116 percent in the SSO, Iran's largest pension fund is more generous than the regional average in MENA states (78 percent), Latin America (57 percent), and the OECD and Eastern Europe (56 percent) (Robalino 2005). The minimum benefit in Iranian pension schemes is also quite high, as well as the maximum benefit—close to eight times the average wage. Oddly for a region so well known for large public sectors, the SSO (which covers private industry as well) is slightly more generous than the CSRO in its benefits.[14]

The SSO and CSRO go beyond American-centric notions of a "social security" agency because, as "Bismarckian" bodies of social insurance, they are also responsible for offering and administering health insurance to many of their beneficiaries. In 2007, the SSO claimed that nearly 41 percent of the labor force was covered by its health insurance plan, while the CSRO covered around an additional 10 percent (Statistical Center of Iran [SCI] 2009). Health insurance in Iran varies widely in its reimbursement schemes, and some are quite meager, but they are supplemented by deep government-mandated price cuts in pharmaceuticals and medical services. These form part of the large subsidy system in the IRI, which included basic foods such as bread and milk, cooking oil, and energy such as gasoline and electricity up until 2011. Tellingly, while the Ahmadinejad administration reduced the subsidies for gasoline and food in that year, it did not touch the health-related subsidies at all (Harris 2010). The subsidies for medical and health services are substantial. By an odd but opportune chance in mid-2010, I needed a trip to the hospital emergency room in Shiraz in the middle of the night for a severe back muscle spasm. My total cost—*without* insurance—for an emergency room visit, doctor examination, and administered shots amounted to roughly $6 U.S.

Yet while the poor benefit from universal subsidies at the point of consumption, the largest portion of the subsidies—and the largest cost to the state—goes to those very classes who are targeted by the corporatist welfare regime (Iqbal 2006). If we include a large public sector in the list of policies that forge social insurance against economic risk (Rodrik 2000), then it seems that the IRI still expends a significant amount of resources attempting to protect and decommodify the formal proletarian and professional middle classes from market risk through this welfare regime. Certainly, to the extent that employees contribute some percentage of their income to pension schemes, they are likely to consider these benefits as entitlements instead of government charity. Yet as we know from experiences with welfare policy in wealthy countries, the division between those segments of the population "entitled" to social policy and those who are "undeserving" is a political construct that itself deserves analysis (Schneider and Ingram 2005). Indeed, the same rhetoric one hears about the "dependency" of the "underclass" in the United States on its welfare system is frequently used in Iran, in addition to the stigma attached to such social policies by their beneficiaries. For example, a University of Tehran student I interviewed registered complaints about quotas of admission to poor and/or religious applicants, while at the same time she enjoyed free health care and did not consider herself beholden to the state at all.[15] A taxi driver in Tabriz, whose pension fund is contributed to by the government and whose income is dependent on energy subsidies, grumbled to me about provincial visits by President Ahmadinejad where those in the crowd are given ten to twenty dollars.[16]

This is partly a function of how social policy is differentiated between the two welfare regimes. Corporatist pensions are "universal" public goods, hypothetically available to all. Of course, in reality, Iran is a conventional middle-income country with large swaths of structural unemployment, underemployment, and an informal sector, so any welfare provision tied to formal work is out of range for a substantial portion of the population. Conversely, "particularistic" public goods that not only target the poor but also are main fronts of state self-promotion tend to generate discontent among social classes who see themselves as exempt from these forms of social protection, even while some stigmatize the beneficiaries of those policies. Still, if one purpose of social policy is to bind important social groups whose support is needed to the state (Skocpol 1992), there is a curious puzzle in Iran. Why are main sites of public contestation against IRI policies centered within those social classes seemingly best protected from economic risk and embedded in the larger of the two welfare regimes?

SOCIAL AND POLITICAL LIMITS
OF THE IRANIAN WELFARE STATE

In discussing welfare policy and its mediating role between the state and various social classes and status groups in Iran, I am not discounting other sites of political contestation or legitimation within the IRI (see Osanloo, Chapter 6 in this volume). However, by attending to the political elements of distribution—their forms of institutionalization as well as their effects on social change—we can gain insights into the contested terrain of middle-income countries that exhibit authoritarian forms of rule. From a wider perspective, popular perceptions of the Iranian welfare state whereby social policy is seen as a mechanism of control or "soft" coercion echo the analysis of European and U.S. welfare states in the 1960s by Herbert Marcuse, who decried the "pacifying" effects of welfare benefits on the political potential of subaltern classes in works such as *One Dimensional Man* (2002 [1964]). Alasdair MacIntyre's response to Marcuse is therefore instructive:

> The notion of [the welfare state] as simply handed down from above, as nothing but an administrative device of the rulers to subordinate the ruled, is historically absurd—and that it is not necessarily a source of political or social stability. For the institutionalization of welfare, like all other rises in the standard of living, alters the horizons of possibility for different social groups and alters too the standards by which they assess their deserts and their rights. Not absolute but relative deprivation becomes crucially important. (2008 [1967], 346)

How does this relate to the Iranian case? Compared to other middle-income countries, the IRI's revolutionary welfare regime has registered success at reducing absolute poverty, lessening rural–urban gaps, and stabilizing population growth. This was part of the postrevolutionary push to incorporate poorer social classes during wartime, and the institutional flexibility it retains still plays a role in channeling popular grievances into more manageable forms of interaction with the state. There is scant rhetoric within these institutions of the "withering away" of Iran's large informal, semiproletarian class through economic modernization. There is little chance that this segment of the population will transform into a fully proletarianized workforce, in Iran or any middle-income country, because this is a result of a global division of labor that these states can only slightly affect through development policy (Amin and van der Linden 1997; also see Portes and Hoffman 2003 on the persistence of the informal sector in Latin America for a point of comparison). Instead, even with its many faults, the revolutionary welfare regime in Iran targets some of the gaps in social policy that earlier corporatist welfare regimes across the Third World failed to address. This should be seen as a major institutional innovation by the IRI compared to its predecessor, one that features recombinant elements of resilience and flexibility that have allowed for the IRI to head off large-scale unrest at times of economic crisis.

However, the developmental prerogatives of the IRI, especially after the war with Iraq, demanded a project of state building that in many ways mirrored the Pahlavi state's "big push" of the 1960s. A series of five-year plans were instituted that, while never reaching the lofty goals of economic takeoff, did expand the middle class over the subsequent two decades as a percentage of the population (see Behdad and Nomani 2009 for measurements of class structure in Iran). Social policy, including higher education, in the corporatist welfare regime was widened in an endeavor to incorporate these individuals in the developmental project, create a technocratic class that would fill the cadres of the postrevolutionary bureaucracies, and form a nascent domestic capitalist class to spur the private sector. This was an attempt by a segment of the IRI political elite to carve out a new social compact that would, it was hoped, help to craft a developmental state that could legitimate the revolutionary project in the postwar period. In fusing the nationalist aspirations of Iranian elites with the language of independence and autonomy, it was surely a bold attempt at recombinant state formation. Resistance to this effort by the conservative political faction in the 1990s was a major factor in fashioning the bureaucratic gridlock that characterized the state under the Rafsanjani and Khatami administrations. Even yet, during this period, the social policies enacted by the IRI over the previous years were having profound effects.

While poorer Iranians struggled to gain access to the new state-generated flows of prestige and status that would insure better livelihoods, such as "martyr" or veteran affiliation for admission to educational institutions or jobs in provincial government offices, the target population of the corporatist welfare regime was demanding access to the political and cultural capital that would allow for the creation and maintenance of middle-class lifestyles free from the bureaucratic authoritarianism of a postrevolutionary state. In this social landscape, "legitimate" welfare given to war veterans in the 1980s and 1990s morphed into "undeserved" benefits for a group too young to have fought in the war and, in some cases (such as the Basij), for youth actively engaged in preventing the middle class from enjoying autonomy from the hated paternalistic intrusions by the state. Meanwhile, it became glaringly apparent that political elites and officials possessed the means of protecting their own networks from downward mobility, while the new professional and formal working classes' "fear of falling" became manifest. Hence it was easy for political entrepreneurs to create a social consensus that middle-class exclusion by the state was occurring. This, however, has little to do with the sort of politics of absolute poverty that proved important during the 1979 revolution and its populist consolidation. Instead, as MacIntyre recognized in an earlier era of global protest, relative scarcity became the predominant factor in determining social grievances in the IRI. This includes not only the relative scarcity of political and cultural capital needed for upward mobility within Iranian society but also the relative position of Iran in the world economy that generates the discontents of economic "backwardness" and sentiments of national malaise among the middle class. By the 2000s, it looked to many middle-class Iranians that their country was indeed "running fast to stay in place," or worse, falling behind relative to other states (Turkey is usually the imagined "other" in this sort of comparison). In other words, the democratization and widening of social policy that occurred through the innovations of a "dual" welfare regime proved limiting partly because the "horizons of possibility" had been altered within key segments of the population by the regime's own welfare policies.

To conclude briefly, while there have of course been critics of the IRI since its beginnings, the millions-strong popular demonstrations of 2009 for civil-political rights are a reflection of middle-class *empowerment* in Iran. This could not have transpired without earlier regime efforts at legitimation and state building through recombinant practices of social and economic policy that had proved a force for regime resilience when they were first implemented. It is no coincidence that the parents of many of the young protestors I met in Iran during the summer of 2009 were active or retired government employees whose grandparents had been born in villages. The onset of democratic challenge by social groups empowered through earlier rounds of state-led development is not exclusive to Iranian history. It is perhaps the overarching characteristic of the "Third Wave" era of democratization, which took place mostly within middle-income countries in the world economy (Arrighi 1990). The Green Movement of 2009, therefore, is not a "nation" or a "civil society" positioned against a state, even though this sort of rhetoric is powerfully effective for opposition politics in Iran. Rather, it is an outcome of the various and conflicting lineages of state-building efforts by the IRI, and the response to those efforts by newly empowered social classes.

AUTHORITARIAN RESILIENCE AND THE MANAGEMENT OF RELIGIOUS AFFAIRS

Part II

4 THE STATE MANAGEMENT OF RELIGION IN SYRIA

The End of "Indirect Rule"?

Thomas Pierret

IN 2010, FOR THE FIRST TIME since the early 1970s, the Syrian president did not invite leading ulema to break the fast of Ramadan.[1] The regime's relations with the Sunni clergy had started to deteriorate in the summer of 2008 following a sudden repressive turn in the regime's management of religion. After almost a decade of limited decompression, the state was tightening its control over private religious schools and charities, prominent Islamic figures were jailed or silenced, and measures were taken to curb so-called extremist manifestations of religiosity such as the face veil.

There was more in this shift than a mere stiffening: it was in fact the most profound change in the religious policy of the Syrian state in half a century. Indeed, the Ba'th had always opted for a strategy of "indirect rule" in its management of the Sunni religious field. Although the latter was tightly controlled through the security apparatus, it retained a wide autonomy in terms of financing and training structures, while state-run Islamic institutions always remained embryonic. Since 2008, on the contrary, ambitious reforms aimed at curtailing this autonomy and expanding direct state control over the clergy: the staff of the Ministry of Religious Endowments (*awqaf*) grew exponentially, private Islamic schools were partially nationalized, and new state institutes destined to train the country's men of religion were created.

The first aim of this chapter is to provide an innovative analysis of the management of religion by a Middle Eastern regime—a key aspect of authoritarian recombination. Although there are studies of the institutionalization of Islam by Middle Eastern states (Böttcher 1998; Erdem 2008; Zeghal 1996), very few of them assess the actual extent of this process, which has often been hindered by the weakness of the state or, as will be suggested for the Syrian case, by deliberate self-restraint (Antoun 2006; Gaffney 2004).

Second, by identifying the factors that provoked the shifts from one particular pattern of state management of Islam to another, this chapter stresses the fundamentally unstable character of authoritarian upgrading or recombination. As users of the most popular operating system for personal computers know well, if software has to be updated, it is not only to become more efficient but also to get rid of the bugs and security flaws of the previous updates. Likewise, I will show that the various changes in the religious policy of the Syrian regime since the 1960s were responses to the unexpected outcomes and shortcomings of previous strategies. Indeed, authoritarian regimes do not act in a void but face vibrant societies that seize the opportunities left by the readjustments of the state.

My third and last point consists in calling into question the reliability and durability of a widespread pattern of authoritarian recombination, that is, the "redeployment of the state." The latter is the fact that the retreat of formal state institutions from certain arenas of social life is combined with continued effective control, in particular through the selection of the "private" actors in charge of responsibilities that are not or no longer borne by the public sector (Hibou 2004). Such a strategy is not always efficient in the long term: the Syrian regime, which "tried" the policy of outsourcing in religious matters during more than four decades, eventually came to the conclusion that "indirect rule" through informal support to private actors does not offer the same level of control as does "direct rule" through bureaucratic structures. In Michael Mann's terms, the reforms launched in 2008 aimed at building a "strong state" that relies more on "infrastructural power" and less on "despotic power" (Ayubi 1995, 449).

Syria is not the only example of such a trend in the recent period: during the turbulent 1990s, the Egyptian regime—which, unlike its Syrian counterpart, could already rely on a massive religious bureaucracy—decided to nationalize thousands of private mosques and to require that preacher-educators be licensed by the state (Mahmood 2005, 75). Likewise, the Moroccan monarchy reacted to the Casablanca bombing of 2003 by establishing national, local, and even overseas councils for the supervision of religious affairs, as well as by tightening its grip over the training of clerics (Maghraoui 2009).

BEFORE THE BA'TH: INSTITUTION BUILDING
AND KEMALIST-INSPIRED MODERNIZATION

The best way to understand the management of religion by the Syrian Ba'th is to contrast it with the approach of the first regimes of the postindependence era. This approach was oriented toward formal regulation and institution building and was driven by the need to set up the structures of the newborn Syrian Republic, as well as by a particular brand of modernism inspired from Turkish Kemalism.

Attempts at building official Islamic institutions had been very limited under Ottoman and French authorities, with the result that postindependence Syrian regimes had to start almost from scratch in that realm (Böttcher 2008; Pierret 2011a, 34). Local muftis were placed under the authority of a "Grand Mufti of the Syrian Republic" in 1947. The first law defining the status of the mosque personnel was issued in 1949. The same law established a Directorate of Religious Endowments within the Ministry of Interior, two councils composed of senior Muslim scholars (the "Higher Council of Religious Endowments" and the "Higher *Ifta*' Council"), as well as local Councils of Religious Endowments. During the short-lived union with Egypt (1958–1961), governmental control over the religious sphere was strengthened through the creation of two new directorates, one for Orientation and Guidance and another for Religious Education. After the secession, an elected parliament completed the law of 1949 with a new one that set up the current Ministry of Religious Endowments (Böttcher 1998, 18–24, 63–65).

From the mandate on, the state was also directly involved in the development of religious education. Public Islamic seminaries were established in Aleppo (1922) and Damascus (1942), and in the 1950s these were reorganized and standardized to become what is known today as "sharia high schools" (*thanawiyyat shar'iyya*) (Pierret 2011a, 56–60). From 1954 on, their graduates were given the opportunity to continue their studies at the Faculty of Sharia that was created that year within the state-run University of Damascus (Botiveau 1986).

Besides institution building, the young Syrian Republic was also concerned with social modernization, a project that was chiefly promoted by the military rulers of the time. The latter's vision of modernization was inspired by Turkish Kemalism, which was itself a descendant of Josephism (after Emperor Joseph II of Austria), a policy based on the idea that the state has the mission to uproot "backward" traditions and rationalize social life through the regulation of its most trivial details. Following Ataturk's model, Syria's first military ruler Husni al-Za'im (1949) not only nationalized religious endowments and established a secular legal code (except for personal status) but also encouraged Syrians to give up their "traditional" Arab clothing (Seale 1965, 58). The latter project was upheld by Colonel Adib al-Shishakli, who toppled al-Za'im's successor Sami al-Hinawi in December 1949. Under al-Shishakli, official newspapers "requested" the standardization of clothing for the whole population because "this modern and civilized nation needs a unified fashion that abolishes the Eastern colors of old" (OFA, January 16, 1952).[2] This project was never implemented, but a uniform was imposed on the men of religion, which they were allowed to wear only after passing an exam at the local committee of religious endowments (OFA, August 1, 1951). Al-Shishakli's Josephist zeal was nowhere as evident as in the meticulous description of the clerical uniform:

> The ulema must wear a white turban . . . These turbans must be worn on white hats, not on tarbushes. The habit of the ulema consists of a long, open tunic worn on trousers and a vest of the same color. The tunic is black during official ceremonies and navy blue, brown or grey in ordinary times depending on the season. A hard white collar is worn under the tunic and must be visible. Shoes and socks are exclusively black. (OFA, March 12, 1952)

The struggle against "backwardness" also targeted religious institutions that were seen as anachronistic like the permanent residences of the Mawlawi Sufi order and the *tekkiye,* that is, almshouses for students in religion and poor people (OFA, June 14, 1952). Such measures were purely ideological in the sense that they were not driven by security concerns. Indeed, they were not aimed at weakening the power base of the potentially threatening urban clergy, but at destroying politically inoffensive structures that were already being undermined by social change. In 1950s Syria, many "backward" religious customs were disappearing by themselves, such as the celebration known in Homs as the "Thursday of the Sheikhs," whose end is—wrongly but tellingly—attributed to al-Shishakli by popular memory (Gillon 1993, 69–71).

BA'THIST REVOLUTION AND THE END
OF INSTITUTION BUILDING (1963–1980)

By contrast with the regimes that preceded the "revolution" of March 8, 1963, the Ba'th displayed striking neglect for the development of the religious bureaucracy and was concerned only with neutralizing it politically. The laws of 1949 and 1961 theoretically remained in force, a situation that reflected the new authorities' disregard for legal reform in general (Ghazzal, Dupret, and Belhadj 2009). Ba'thists did not content themselves with subduing official Islam by replacing the independent-minded Grand Mufti Abu al-Yusr 'Abidin (1955–1963) with the compliant Ahmad Kaftaru. The new rulers of Syria also debased the position of Grand Mufti, which no longer consisted in the issuance of fatwas but rather in mere protocol and public relations. Tellingly, when the regime was in dire need of religious legitimization to face the Islamic uprising that erupted in the late 1970s, it did not find it among its—discredited—religious bureaucrats but in the vocal support of the popular Islamic writer and academic Sa'id Ramadan al-Buti (Pierret 2011a, 99–105).

The Ba'thist regime also moved to deprive the ulema of most of their influence over religious administration. Although Kaftaru was formally elected by a committee of peers, considerable pressure was exerted on the voters to prevent them from choosing their favorite Hasan Habannaka (Böttcher 1998, 54–58). When Kaftaru died forty years later, his successor Ahmad Hasun was simply appointed through presidential decree (Pierret 2011a, 107–110). In 1965, the appointment of mosque personnel, which until then was a prerogative of the clerical councils, was entrusted to the Presidency Council (Rabinovich 1972, 143).

By depriving most senior ulema from any responsibility within the state apparatus, this decision brought their bureaucratization to an end. It must also be noted here that men of religion were not affected by the unions and syndicates that were set up by the regime in the 1960s to supervise social groups such as peasants, workers, women, teachers, artists, writers, and students.

The only employees of the Ministry of Religious Endowments who ever benefited from the full status of state functionaries (*muwazzafi al-dawla*) were a limited number of high-ranking clerics (muftis, "fatwa lecturers") as well as a small cadre of administrators that grew by only one-third (from 200 to 300) during the two first decades of Ba'thist rule (see Figure 4.1) (Central Bureau of Statistics 1962–1978). As for mosque personnel, which always constituted at least 90 percent of the ministry's employees, they remained consigned to a financially disadvantageous special status. In any case, many men of religion continued to depend heavily on the resources of the private sector, thus remaining autonomous from the state in economic terms (Batatu 1982, 14; Pierret and Selvik 2009, 599).

Likewise, the reluctance of the regime to involve itself in the development of specialized Islamic education allowed the ulema to retain wide autonomy

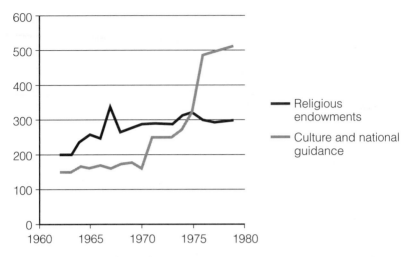

Figure 4.1. Number of state functionaries in two Syrian ministries, 1960–1980.
Source: Central Bureau of Statistics.

in the training of young clerics. Syria was not home to anything comparable to the prestigious and state-controlled al-Azhar in Egypt. Moreover, the recently created Faculty of Sharia at the University of Damascus was deeply distrusted by the Ba'thists because it had been founded by the Muslim Brothers and remained under their influence well after 1963. Despite this, not only did the authorities abstain from creating new institutions, they also excluded private sharia institutes—which had multiplied in the 1950s and 1960s—from the school nationalizations of September 1967.[3] In the following decades, therefore, only a minority of the Syrian ulema graduated from state-owned religious schools (Pierret 2011a).

How can we make sense of the Ba'thist regime's reluctance to expand the institutions of official Islam? Why did it refrain from trying to subdue the clergy by "nationalizing" it? The most probable explanation is that Ba'thists had neither the means nor the will to pursue such a strategy. As far as means were concerned, the regime had limited economic resources and commanded little popular support in the cities. The lack of will resulted from the ideology of the Ba'th and more particularly from its radicalized, Marxist version, which inspired the "Neo-Ba'thists" who ran Syria between Salah Jadid's coup in 1966 and Hafiz al-Asad's in 1970 (Ben-Tzur 1968).

The modernism of the Ba'thists was different from that of their predecessors. As "conservative modernists," al-Za'im and al-Shishakli were chiefly concerned with order. Their goal was not to turn society upside down but to rationalize it. Neo-Ba'thists, on the contrary, were "structural" modernists: they saw socialist reform of the economy, not Josephist regulation, as the key to modernization. Transforming the infrastructure—that is, the relations of production—would necessarily entail the emergence of a new superstructure. In the new social order there would be no place for "reactionary groups" such as the ulema.

In a remarkable illustration of the confidence that characterized the Neo-Ba'thists' vision of the future in the late 1960s, Minister of Education Suleiman al-Hass told a French researcher, "Backward preachers and other men of religion can say whatever they want, it will not catch on, and we are not worried about it" (Carré 1979, 31). According to the most secularist wing of the party, religion itself was doomed to go with the wind of revolution. The best-known illustration of this idea was the famous article published by the intellectual Ibrahim Khalas in the magazine of the army in 1967, which said:

> The New Man believes that God, religions, feudalism, capitalism, imperialism and all the values that govern the ancient society are mummies that are just worth being put away in the museum of History. . . . We don't need a man who prays and kneels, who bows his head with baseness and begs God for pity and mercy. The New Man is a socialist, a revolutionary. (Petran 1972, 178)

Although Khalas was disowned by the government and jailed, briefly, to calm the rage of the ulema, atheism was well and truly widespread among the ranks of the ruling party. As early as 1948, Fadil Jamali, the leader of the Damascene section of the Ba'th in the mid-1950s, was teaching his students at university that religions were on their way to collapse because of their incompatibility with progress (OFA, February 28, 1955). For Khalas, Jamali, and others like them, religion was not a legitimate dimension of social life that had to be meticulously regulated by a transformative state: it was the foremost symbol of "reaction" that had to be knocked down to allow for the emergence of a new world. In such an ideological context, the idea of a clerical uniform, for instance, had become entirely irrelevant.

Despite the Islamic "awakening" observed within Arab societies after the defeat of 1967, the religious policy of the Syrian regime did not fundamentally change during the first ten years that followed the "Corrective Movement" launched by Hafiz al-Asad in 1970. The new president initiated a détente with the Islamic trend by showing outward signs of piety, raising the salaries of mosque personnel, and providing grants to mosques and Islamic schools

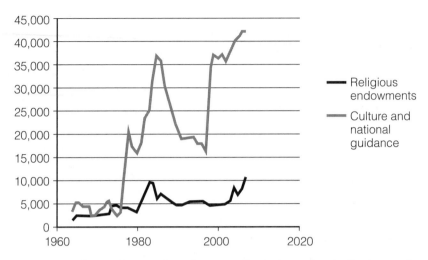

Figure 4.2. Real expenditures of two Syrian ministries in 1964 units (in thousands of SYP), 1960–2010.
Source: Central Bureau of Statistics.

(Batatu 1999, 260). As a result of the two latter moves, the expenditures of the Ministry of Religious Endowments grew by 71 percent in real terms between 1970 and 1975.[4] This trend did not last, however, because these expenditures dropped by 30 percent during the second half of the decade. Such a figure is all the more striking given that at the same time other state agencies—and in particular those that had the mission to promote the secular worldview of the Ba'th—thrived as a result of the tremendous economic growth that followed the 1973 oil boom: for instance, the real expenditures of the Ministry of Culture and National Guidance were multiplied by almost *seven* during the last five years of the 1970s. Whereas in the Ministry of Religious Endowments, the number of statutory functionaries stagnated, in the Ministry of Culture, it was multiplied by three (see Figure 4.1). Likewise, whereas in 1974 the real expenditures of the Ministry of Religious Endowments were superior to those of the Ministry of Culture, the former amounted to only one-fifth of the latter by 1979 (see Figure 4.2) (Central Bureau of Statistics 1970–1980). The same period also witnessed a considerable expansion of Ba'thist youth movements inspired from Eastern European communist countries (Seale 1989, 175). What the post-1973 windfall revived, then, was not the buildup of official religious institutions but rather the regime's ambitions for secular social transformation.

As in the 1960s, the regime's religious policy was almost entirely focused on the neutralization of direct political threats. Accordingly, waves of arrests continued to target the Muslim Brothers and their radical offspring, but the authorities turned a blind eye to the considerable growth of education-oriented Islamic movements. Such "lenience" almost proved fatal to the rule of the Ba'th because educational movements ended up playing a key role in the Islamic uprising that started in 1979. Indeed, by providing the initially small militant groups with thousands of new recruits, they considerably widened the scale of the insurgency, which was brought to an end only after three years of ruthless repression and thousands of casualties (Pierret 2011a, 86–89).

OUTSOURCING AND THE WITHERING AWAY OF THE RELIGIOUS BUREAUCRACY (1980–2000)

The failed Islamist uprising constituted the most serious domestic threat the Ba'thist regime ever faced. As such, it entailed unprecedented budgetary efforts on the part of the Ministry of Religious Endowments, which tripled its real expenditures between 1980 and 1984 (look again at Figure 4.2) (Central Bureau of Statistics, 1980–1990). The significance of this figure should not be overstated, however, not only because these expenditures were subsequently cut in half as a result of the dire fiscal crisis of the mid-1980s but also because the new financial resources were used to increase the meager salaries of mosque personnel as well as to support mosque construction and restoration (Batatu 1999, 260), not to develop a genuine religious bureaucracy.

Apart from a quarterly journal, *Nahj al-Islam* ("The Way of Islam"), which was launched by the Ministry of Religious Endowments in 1980, the only state-owned religious structures that appeared at that time were the Hafiz al-Asad Institutes for the Memorization of the Koran, which were established the same year (Böttcher 1998, 117–120). This decision was far from a significant step toward further bureaucratization of the religious field. Indeed, the "institutes" were nothing but memorization circles held in mosques under the supervision of volunteers, the director of the institute (generally the imam or preacher of the mosque) being the only one to receive remuneration (Böttcher 1998, 117–119).

An even more striking illustration of the regime's continued reluctance to expand the human resources of the Ministry of Religious Endowments in spite of the bloody warning of 1979–1982—or, more probably, *because* of it—was the fact that its administrative staff actually *declined* in number after 1980: from 296 statutory functionaries in 1978, it had fallen to 237 in 1984

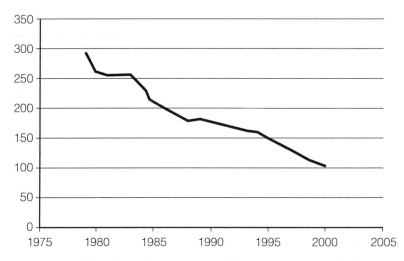

Figure 4.3. Number of state functionaries in the Syrian Ministry of Religious Endowments, 1970s–2000s.
Source: Central Bureau of Statistics up to 1985; various sources for further years.

(Central Bureau of Statistics 1979, 1985) and to 103 in 2000 (see Figure 4.3).[5] In other words, this staff was reduced by *almost two-thirds* in the twenty years that followed the uprising, mainly as a result of cuts carried out in the central administration as well as in Aleppo. Internal records of the Ministry show that during that period, departments often had to use temporary transfers to make up for their understaffing. From the 1980s to this day, ministers of Religious Endowments have regularly denounced the fact that their ministry was "neglected" (Böttcher 1998, 60–84).[6]

This situation, which contrasted with the continued growth or at least stagnation of the other ministries, was likely related to the regime's lack of trust in its religious functionaries. Throughout the 1970s, suspensions, dismissals, and repeated transfers of senior civil servants had been frequent within the ministry (Böttcher 1998, 80–83), and several cases of defection had been witnessed during the uprising. In March 1980, an arrest warrant was issued against the director of Aleppo's state-run sharia high school, Sheikh Abu al-Nasr al-Bayanuni (the brother of Ali Sadr al-Din al-Bayanuni, a well-known figure of the local Muslim Brothers), because of his collusion with militant Islamic groups. A few months after he fled the country, al-Bayanuni became the head of the Saudi-based oppositional Islamic Front. In the same city, the Director of Religious Endowments Abdallah al-Salqini, the son of a prestigious family of scholars whose appointment in 1980 was intended as a conciliatory move on the part of the authorities, went into exile less than two years later (Pierret 2011a, 95).

Lacking symbolic and economic resources, the postuprising Ba'thist state had limited transformative capabilities and consequently was less able than ever to bring about the emergence of a disciplined religious administration obediently promoting a Ba'thist version of Islam. In such circumstances, any strengthening of the staff of the Ministry of Religious Endowments would instead have led to a situation similar to that in Egypt, that is, the development of a powerful conservative Sunni lobby within the state apparatus. Of course, such a phenomenon would have been much more destabilizing in a political configuration dominated by an Alawite, secular-minded military elite.

Thus, instead of measures of "nationalization" in the religious field, the regime's reaction to the events of 1979–1982 took the form of a twofold strategy of repression and outsourcing. On the one hand, the role played by seemingly apolitical movements in the insurgency convinced the authorities that the activities of most of these groups should be much more severely limited than in the past. On the other hand, the Syrian leadership could not shrug off society's increasing religiosity, which among other things implied a tremendous growth in the demand for religious education. To solve this puzzle, the authorities selected a number of "subcontractors" among the clerical factions that had demonstrated their loyalty during the uprising. At a time when many places of worship remained closed between the five daily prayers, these factions were reserved the right to organize mosque lessons, Koran memorization circles, and celebrations such as that of the Prophet's birthday (*mawlid*).

In Aleppo, the local religious administration was literally handed over to a single man, Sheikh Suhayb al-Shami, whose father had been assassinated in 1980 by militant Islamists because of his close ties with the regime. During the twenty-three (lucrative) years he spent as the director of the city's religious endowments (1982–2005), al-Shami gave the leading administrative positions as well as the largest mosques to his clientele and in particular to members of the Sufi network to which he belongs, the Nabhaniyya. In 1964, the latter had founded a private Islamic institute known as "al-Kiltawiyya," which became the main provider of personnel for the mosques of Aleppo thanks to al-Shami's favorable appointment policy (Pierret 2011a, 69–72, 106–109).

In Damascus, the two main religious subcontractors, that is, the Sufi brotherhood of Grand Mufti Ahmad Kaftaru, known as the "Kaftariyya," as well as the sons and disciples of Sheikh Salih al-Farfur (1901–1986), were entrusted with the development of higher Islamic education. Thanks to the financial help of their merchant supporters these groups founded two post–high school private institutes, respectively, the Abu al-Nur Islamic Center (1982) (Böttcher 1998, 154–163) and the "Section of Specialization" of the al-Fath Institute (1991). At the same time, no attempt was made to strengthen the Faculty of Sharia at the University of Damascus, which the security services prevented from awarding doctorates until 1998. Moreover, it remained the sole structure of its kind in Syria until the opening of a sister faculty at the University of Aleppo in 2006. The institution was still distrusted because it had managed to preserve relative autonomy (the last notoriously Muslim Brothers–affiliated professors were excluded only in the late 1970s), just as it successfully resisted the regime's attempts to fill its ranks with Ba'thist students in the early 1980s. As for the lasting refusal to open a similar faculty in Aleppo, it was due to the regime's lack of trust in the religious elite of the Northern metropolis (Böttcher 1998, 131–143; Pierret 2011a, 56–60, 176–182).

In view of what has been said here, subcontracting was a relatively obvious solution for the regime in the aftermath of the uprising: it was safer than institution building, which would have led to the inclusion of a growing number of conservative elements within the state apparatus, and it was more economical because the new institutes for higher Islamic educations were private and, as such, financed by the merchant community. Nevertheless, this "weak state strategy" had drawbacks, and at the turn of the twenty-first century its unexpected outcomes would force the regime to reconsider its religious policy twice in less than a decade.

FOREIGN THREATS AND NEW DOMESTIC PARTNERSHIPS (2000–2008)

The first half of the last decade was a difficult period for the Syrian leadership, as Syria was faced with an increasingly aggressive U.S.–Israeli axis, especially after the invasion of Iraq in 2003. Starting in 2004, the Lebanese crisis also badly damaged Syria's relations with European countries as well as with Saudi Arabia and Egypt.

In such circumstances, the young president was in need of additional domestic support. Given the increasingly visible presence of Islam in Syrian everyday life and the rise of Islamist parties in neighboring countries, Asad unsurprisingly turned toward the religious trend. He raised the salaries of clerics by 50 percent and expanded the policy of relaxation on religious ac-

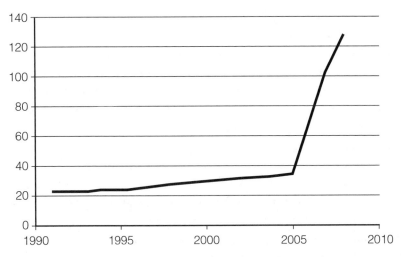

Figure 4.4. Number of sharia high schools in Syria, 1990s–2000s.
Source: Central Bureau of Statistics.

tivities that had been initiated by his father in the early 1990s: the ban on the
wearing of headscarves in public schools was lifted; prayer halls were opened
in universities; the number of (both private and state-run) sharia high schools
multiplied almost by four (from thirty-five to 129) between 2005 and 2008,
whereas it had increased by only 45 percent during the previous fifteen years
(see Figure 4.4); the number of charitable associations (a majority of which
had a religious orientation) also skyrocketed during that period, perhaps even
doubling between 2004 and 2006. As a result of these policies, the real expenditures of the Ministry of Religious Endowments doubled between 2002 and
2007, even exceeding their record level of 1984 (Figure 4.2) (Pierret 2011a, 110,
257; Pierret and Selvik 2009, 601; Zisser 2005, 43).[7]

On the other hand, Bashar al-Asad reconfigured his alliances within the
clergy and reached out to religious actors other than the traditional partners of
his father. Through both symbolic gestures and concrete measures of liberalization, the head of the state tried to win over former enemies of the regime such
as the leaders of Jama'at Zayd, one of the educational movements that had been
involved in the uprising (Pierret and Selvik 2009, 608). In early 2006, liberalization also benefited the Qubaysiat, an influential, upper-class female sisterhood
whose (previously underground) study groups were now allowed in mosques.
In Aleppo, the notoriously independent-minded and highly respected Sheikh

Ibrahim al-Salqini was appointed as mufti in 2005, and the opening of a Faculty of Sharia was scheduled for September 2006 (Pierret 2011a, 257).

Courting clerics proved to be a clever move because it helped stabilize the regime in a period of crisis: while the political opposition was asking for democratic reforms, extremely popular Muslim scholars lent Asad their support by publicly stating that the real priority was to defeat foreign enemies (Pierret 2011a, 252–261).

At the same time, the new policy was tantamount to an acknowledgment of the limits of the strategy of subcontracting followed since the 1980s. Despite the backing they had received from the state, and despite the repression exerted against rival networks, loyal clerics had not managed to dominate the religious field. In their quest for domestic support, therefore, the authorities had no choice but to establish partnerships with groups they had tried to marginalize until then but who retained more prestige (and often more economic resources because prestige entails donations) than regime-friendly sheikhs.

To some extent, the limited transformative capabilities of the Syrian state over the religious field constituted an asset during the first half of the 2000s. Indeed, it is precisely because they were largely perceived as independent that groups like Jama'at Zayd commanded such prestige and that a rapprochement with them was so beneficial for the regime's legitimacy. Yet this strategy would soon prove to be risky, the new atmosphere of relative freedom resulting in a slackening of the clergy's discipline.

First, the ulema's rapprochement with the regime made them increasingly confident in their attacks against secularists, including members of the state apparatus. In June 2006, for instance, the first petition of senior clerics since 1973 was sent to the president to protest against the Ministry of Education's decision to close religious junior high schools, which the petition described as "a conspiracy aimed at destroying religion" (Pierret 2011a, 261–265). Second, prominent scholars publicly denounced purported Iranian-backed Shi'ite missionary activities in the country. By doing this, they were expressing fears that had become widespread among the Sunni religious elite due to the regionwide rise of sectarian tensions that followed the U.S. invasion of Iraq. These sentiments, of course, were deeply embarrassing for a regime that is dominated by a Shi'ite sect, the Alawites, and whose main strategic ally is Iran (Pierret 2012). Third, although their attitude had been rather positive during the 2005–2006 crisis, the new religious partners of the regime had not turned into genuine allies, and distrust persisted on both sides. Members of Jama'at

Zayd were anxious about the fact that they had no guarantee that the policy of liberalization would last;[8] as for security officials, they took umbrage at the abrasive statements of Sheikh Usama al-Rifaʿi, who warned Syrian leaders that God would "replace them with better people" if they did not "raise the flag of Islam" and privately accused the movement of spreading "extremist ideas" in its mosques (Pierret and Selvik 2009, 609).[9]

A fourth problem was that the climate of détente had led even traditional clients such as Kaftaru's children and disciples to adopt a more independent stance. In 2004–2005, Kaftaru's son Salah al-Din, the director of the Kaftaru Academy (formerly the Abu al-Nur Islamic Center), and his grandson-in-law Muhammad Habash, an "Islamo-liberal" member of Parliament, emerged as vocal proponents of democratic reforms, the former even developing personal ties with leading dissident Riad Seif after the latter's release from jail in 2006. Kaftaru also distinguished himself by calling for the dismissal of the secular-minded minister of media during a Friday sermon, as well as by "privately" formulating criticisms of Shi'ite proselytizing that soon became an open secret (*Syria News*, June 8, 2007).[10] That one of the main pillars of the subcontracting strategy had become a troublemaker was the best possible demonstration of the regime's failure to turn the religious elite into a stable and reliable partner. A new approach was needed, and, by the end of the decade, new circumstances would provide the Syrian leadership with the opportunity to shift away from its long-standing policy of "indirect rule."

U-TURN: BRINGING THE STATE BACK IN (2008–2011)

In December 2007, Asad replaced the minister of Religious Endowments, Ziyad al-Ayyubi, with his assistant Muhammad al-Sayyid, the former mufti of Tartus, whose own father had headed the same ministry in the 1970s. During the next summer, al-Sayyid initiated a sudden authoritarian turn on the order of his supervision officer, Hisham Ikhtiyar, the head of the Ba'th's National Security Bureau.[11] The minister vowed to reestablish the authority of the state over the religious field through a set of measures targeting private sharia institutes, charities, and female preachers.

As far as sharia institutes were concerned, the minister promised "the end of the era of anarchy" where "each institute was a state within the state."[12] To change this situation, which he portrayed as conducive to the spread of extremism, he created a position of vice minister for religious education and announced the impending standardization of religious syllabi. In the realm of charitable projects, the former mufti of Tartus decided that the *mawa'id al-rahman* ("tables of the Merciful," that is, public distribution of food in mosques) would be forbidden during the month of Ramadan that was about to start to avoid the "exploitation" of mosques "as a means of advertising." The third target of the reforms was female preaching, which in Damascus is carried out for the most part by the Qubaysiat. Here also, al-Sayyid aimed at unifying the content of religious teachings, creating a new department within the ministry with this purpose (Pierret and Selvik 2009, 609).[13]

Such a U-turn in the religious policy of the regime after the more hands-off approach of the previous years was made possible by the considerable improvement in the country's international position, which lessened the importance of domestic support. In May 2008, Syria won a major indirect victory in Lebanon through the takeover of West Beirut by militias of the 8th of March coalition and the subsequent Doha agreement. In July, Bashar al-Asad's presence at the official celebration of the French national day in Paris symbolically marked his comeback as a respectable partner for Europe, at a moment the Bush administration was about to leave the White House. Just as foreign pressures had entailed a more lenient religious policy on the part of the regime in previous years, favorable strategic and diplomatic developments now paved the way for a tougher approach.

In September, a tragic event further strengthened the position of the regime and gave him the opportunity to widen the scope of the reforms: on the 27th, a car bomb exploded close to a building of the intelligence services in Sidi Qazzaz, a suburb of Damascus. Seventeen civilians were killed in the attack, the worst of its kind since the 1980s. The authorities quickly arrested purported members of the Tripoli-based jihadi movement Fath al-Islam, whose confessions were broadcast on national television. Their "revelations" were, unsurprisingly, compromising for the anti-Syrian Lebanese Sunni leader Sa'd al-Hariri, who was said to have funded Fath al-Islam, but also for the Syrian clergy. One of the prisoners asserted that his studies at the al-Fath institute in Damascus had played an important role in his adoption of jihadi ideology because of the number of "radical Arab [that is, non-Syrian] students" he had met there. He also mentioned that his organization had been raising funds "under the cover of charitable associations" (*al-Thawra*, November 7, 2008). Islamic institutes and charities were already the main targets of the reforms announced by the minister before the bombing. Following these revelations, they would again be at the center of new measures presented by al-Sayyid as a way to "purify Islamic thought from the stains of Wahhabism and Takfirism."[14]

The government was very quick to react. Only three days after the attack, it was decided that from then on private religious institutes would depend on the Ministry of Religious Endowments "from the administrative, scientific, educational, and financial points of view."[15] In other words, they were partially nationalized. They would still benefit from private funding, but they would no longer receive the money directly: donations would be registered by a committee of clerics headed by the Grand Mufti, which would transfer them to the institute and control their use. As the director of religious education in the Ministry of Religious Endowments stated, "We want to know where the money comes from, as well as where and when it is spent." Moreover, the professors of the institutes would become state employees, with the result that the government had the power, the official insisted, to "hire and fire any of them" (*Syria Today*, March 2008).

During a meeting with the ulema organized a few days after the bombing of September 2008, al-Sayyid justified this measure by arguing that clerics had failed to fight extremism.[16] The next year, however, the minister would explain that the reform had a more ambitious, long-term goal: the government was working according to a "strategic plan for the next fifty or sixty years" to turn clerics into genuine functionaries. "The people who officiate in mosques," he said, "consider that they are not related to any institution . . . That is why we have decided to take over the institutes [where they are trained]." As for the standardization of the syllabi, which had already been decided prior to the September bloodbath, it was now explicitly presented as a way to expurgate "sectarian"—that is, anti-Shi'ite—content.[17]

An even more telling illustration of the state's renunciation of the strategy of "indirect rule" was the decision to open two state-run Islamic institutes that were the first post–high school religious institutions to be created by the government since the Faculty of Sharia in 1954: the Middle Institute for Religious and Arab Sciences, which was dedicated to graduates of Syrian secondary schools; and the International Institute for Religious and Arab Sciences, which would cater to foreign students who previously were scattered between different private schools. The ministry also announced the forthcoming creation of a Higher Institute for Islamic Studies. In November 2009, the Ministry of Religious Endowments established a training center intended to inculcate in clerics the principles of "moderation" as well as the "thought and action in the framework of the institutions" (*fikr al-mu'assasatiyya wa-l-'amal al-mu'assasi*) (*Nahj al-Islam* May 2009, 81–87, and March 2010, 81).

Thus the term *institution* had become the watchword of the ministry, which as mentioned previously wanted clerics to feel that they "belonged" to one. To make clear that he had heard the message, the director of the (private) al-Fath Institute, Sheikh Husam al-Din al-Farfur, stressed twice that his school was "part of the Ministry of Religious Endowments" during a speech he gave on the occasion of an official visit by the minister.[18] Bashar al-Asad himself insisted that "working within the institutions [*al-'amal al-mu'assasati*] is the best way to spread the message of Islam" while he was breaking the fast of Ramadan in presence of Muslim scholars (*Nahj al-Islam*, December 2009, 85).

In the meantime, the ministry itself was becoming, in the words of Salah al-Din Kaftaru, a "ministry of institutions."[19] Besides the measures already mentioned (creation of a position of vice minister for religious education and of a department for female preaching) and the establishment of permanent supervision committees for the teaching of the Koran and the Pilgrimage, presidential decree no. 180 of April 2009 provided for a massive increase in the ministry's staff of statutory functionaries, which was about to be brought up to 1,500 people—a 1,500 percent increase as compared with the year 2000 (*al-Thawra*, February 6, 2009; *Nahj al-Islam*, August 2009, 82). The minister also announced that he was preparing a new law on the organization of his ministry to replace the outdated frameworks of 1949 and 1961. Interestingly, the projected new law provided for renaming the ministry, which would become the "Ministry of *Religious Affairs* and Endowments"—an obvious reference to the executive's growing ambitions of social control (*Nahj al-Islam*, May 2009, 86).

Of course, institutionalization was not the only pillar of the new religious policy of the regime, which also resorted to repression against both "conservative" and "liberal" representatives of the Islamic trend. To reduce the ulema's influence over private welfare, clerics sitting in the boards of charities were ordered to resign from such positions (Pierret and Selvik 2009, 609). Men of religion were also banned from leaving the country without an authorization issued by the Ministry of Religious Endowments (Maleh 2008).

In 2009, the regime took advantage of the political capital it had acquired by siding with Hamas during the Gaza war to push repressive measures forward. In early 2009, Islamic TV channel *al-Da'wa*, which had recently been launched by Jama'at Zayd, was closed by the police.[20] A similar fate befell the

Center for Islamic Studies, the think tank of Muhammad Habash, who was subsequently dismissed from his Friday pulpit.[21] Prominent figures even ended up in jail. Islamic-leaning Human Rights activist Haytham al-Maleh was condemned to three years in prison; ʿAbd al-Rahman al-Kawki, a junior scholar of Jamaʿat Zayd, was imprisoned for several weeks following a debate on al-Jazeera where he denounced the anti–face veil position of Sheikh al-Azhar, Ali Tantawi. Perhaps most significant, the late Grand Mufti's son, Salah al-Din Kaftaru, spent one year behind bars beginning in July 2009 following accusations of embezzlement, abuse of company assets, and "incitement of sectarian strife."[22]

By arresting the son of the late Grand Mufti and the head of the Kaftaru Academy, the authorities not only got rid of an undisciplined cleric but also achieved direct control over Syria's largest Islamic institute. In blatant disregard for the academy's private character, the Ministry of Religious Endowments took it upon itself to appoint a new board of administrators headed by Sharif al-Sawwaf, a disciple of the late Ahmad Kaftaru but first and foremost an executive in the ministry.[23] In Aleppo, too, the regime was turning against one of its former subcontractors, although in a less dramatic way. During a speech he gave in front of the city's ulema, Minister al-Sayyid stated that the struggle against extremism implied keeping close watch on the graduates of the Kiltawiyya institute, which until then had been a privileged partner of the authorities.[24]

In parallel to the bringing to heel of the religious elite, measures were taken to roll back the influence of the Islamic trend in the broader public sphere. During a meeting of the Damascene branch of the Baʾth party in December 2009, the president's political and media counselor Buthayna Shaʿban warned against a "wave of religious fanaticism" that had "spread over the country . . . as result of the (party's) failure" at the ideological level.[25] In following May, the president himself told a U.S. journalist—in English—that "the biggest challenge (we face) is how can we keep our society as secular as it is today."[26] Although such an unusually forthright statement was obviously designed for foreign consumption, it was matched by practical steps with that intent. Prayer rooms in shopping centers and restaurants were closed.[27] The widespread display of religious signs on cars (Koranic excerpts and invocations for Sunni Muslims, the two-pronged sword of Imam Ali for Alawis, the Holy Cross or a fish for Christians) was banned as a means to curb the expression of sectarian identities (al-Quds al-Arabi, October 13, 2010). In June 2010, ten elected deputies of the Damascus Governorate Council—including no fewer than three of the ten members of the council's Executive Bureau—were dismissed by presidential decree because they were considered too close to the ulema.[28] Indeed, as had previously been the case in the early 1970s (Seale 1989, 176), the political decompression of the last decade had allowed for the inclusion of a significant proportion of conservative elements within local representative institutions.

At the same moment, the National Security Bureau ordered that veiled students were barred from entering university campuses and transferred more than 1,000 veiled schoolteachers to administrative positions in the state administration. The minister of education justified this decision by the need to ensure the "secular character of teaching,"[29] but a security official declared that it was more specifically part of a move aimed at curbing the influence of female Islamic movements like the Qubaysiyat, whose followers constitute a large proportion of face-veiled women. These movements, the security source added, were playing a leading role in the recent development of private schools, which had multiplied to the extent that at the primary level, they were teaching an estimated 25 to 30 percent of Damascus's children.[30]

Although the opening of private schools (either through denationalization of public institutions or through the creation of new ones) was theoretically made difficult by the law, it had become straightforward for female preachers. Many of them were the spouses of businessmen and officials and relied on their wealth and political acquaintances, in particular among Ba'th members from old urban families like the former head of the Damascene branch of the party 'Ala' al-Din 'Abidin (d. 2007) to influence the authorities. For the same reasons, these preachers had been able to choose the state-appointed directors of their schools and/or to ensure their silence about the illegal addition of religious content to the curricula established by the Ministry of Education. Money had also allowed them to neutralize the inspectors sent by the ministry and even to fend off intelligence officers. Such widespread corruption explained the intervention of the higher level of the security apparatus (the National Security Bureau), which had set up a "gradual plan to fight fundamentalism and extremism in numerous places like schools, universities, Sharia institutes," but also in "the Ministry of Religious Endowments."[31] In other words, the policy shift was directed not only against social actors but also against the "enemy within," that is, the myriad of state employees who were facilitating the spread of "fundamentalism" out of sympathy or venality.

The buildup of official Islamic institutions, on the one hand, and the reassertion of secular values, on the other hand, were obviously contradictory goals. For instance, to boost the credibility of his reforms, the minister of religious endowments relied heavily on the figure of the aforementioned Sa'id Ramadan al-Buti, who was regularly seated next to him during the numerous meetings with men of religion he organized across the country. The eighty-year-old scholar was appointed as the scientific supervisor of the new state-owned sharia institutes and as the head of the committee in charge of unifying the curricula of the country's religious schools.[32] Yet al-Buti is an archtraditionalist well known for his fierce denunciation of Islamic modernism, as well as for conservative fatwas such as one that stipulates the compulsory character of the . . . face-veil (Buti 1973, 49). Al-Sayyid's own discourse is not liberal by any standard. To mitigate the unpopularity of his authoritarian policies among clergymen, the minister adopted a strongly conservative stance. For instance, he repeatedly reviled calls for a renewal (tajdid) of Islamic thought as part of a project aimed at "eliminating our roots, our culture, and our identity, which were built on the Law of the Lord" (Nahj al-Islam, May 2009, 85). According to him, "the principle (to follow) is moderation, not renewal, contrary to what some people pretend; we do not believe in renewal . . . but in Islam as it was revealed."[33] Such statements were clearly directed at MP Muhammad Habash, the most vocal proponent of Islamic "renewal" in Syria. Using his spouse's name as a cover, the latter responded by expressing fierce criticism of the minister's "fundamentalist" posture and was eventually dismissed from his mosque position in 2010 (Kaftaru 2010a and 2010b).[34]

Regardless of the ministry's doctrinal orientation, the expansion of the religious administration was bound to strengthen the Islamic trend within the state apparatus. Indeed, speaking of a "secular" religious administration would be an oxymoron because such a functional bureaucracy is necessarily composed of a majority of people endowed with minimal competence (and, generally, interest) in religious issues. As was suggested earlier, concerns about such an outcome are a credible explanation for the Syrian religious administration remaining embryonic until the late 2000s.

The problem posed by the growth of a conservative lobby was not that the latter would directly challenge the legitimacy of the regime but rather that it was likely to conflict with secular-minded state elites. On several occasions during the years that preceded the 2011 uprising, the Syrian leadership had to arbitrate between the two. In 2009, for instance, a fierce debate opposed the supporters and detractors of a project of reform of the law on personal status. The latter had been drafted by a secret commission composed of conservative judges and Muslim scholars, with the result that it was even more religious-minded than the sharia-inspired law of 1949. Within state institutions, the project was supported by the Ministries of Justice and—of course—Religious Endowments, whereas it was chiefly opposed by the secular-dominated Committee for Family Affairs, several members of which were dismissed for their lack of discipline (*All4Syria*, August 2, 2009; Aws 2010). The presidency managed to avoid arbitrating the conflict but only by purely and simply freezing the planned reform.

CONCLUSION

The shifts that occurred in the religious policy of the Syrian Ba'thist regime underline both the regime's strength because they demonstrate its ability to undertake the major revisions it deemed necessary to its survival, but also its weakness, which resides in its inability to stabilize its relations with the religious elite in the long term.

In the aftermath of independence, the need to build the structures of the young Syrian Republic and the influence of Kemalist-inspired modernism pushed the country's leaders to adopt an approach to the management of religion that focused on institution building and formal regulation. In 1963, however, the Ba'thist takeover put an end to this approach. Whereas previous regimes had dreamed of modernizing society, Marxist-leaning Ba'thists aimed to overturn its very foundations. Therefore, they had no intention of further integrating the "reactionary" clergy into the state apparatus. Instead, Islam was dealt with as a threat that had to be contained through the use of force. Although he initially aimed to mend fences with the religious trend, Hafiz al-Asad did not fundamentally depart from this model. He approved significant increases in the expenditures of the Ministry of Religious Endowments when he was in need of support from the clergy (after his takeover in 1970, and during the Islamic uprising ten years later), but he never opted for a policy of institution-building in the regulation of religious affairs.

Even after the large-scale Islamic revolt that shook the foundations of his regime, he did not try to curb the relative autonomy of the ulema in terms of funding and training. Instead, his management of Islam relied on a combination of repression and outsourcing: apparently, exploiting existing social resources was safer, cheaper, and more efficient than direct state involvement in the institutionalization of religion. While the religious bureaucracy was severely downsized, privately funded Islamic institutes owned by "subcontractors" were entrusted with an increasing role in religious education.

Although the "weak state strategy" paid off in the medium term—if only because it prevented the "infection" of the state by an increasingly religious society—it limited the ability of the regime to influence the allocation of economic and symbolic resources within the religious field. This limitation clearly appeared when the regime's attempts to widen its support during the regional crisis of the 2000s led Bashar al-Asad to allow for the comeback and successful involvement in private welfare of Jama'at Zayd, a movement that had retained most of its prestige and consequent fund-raising ability despite the repression of the 1980s. Once again, the immediate results of the policy shift were satisfactory in terms of domestic political stability, but the growing outspokenness of the ulema—whether among recent partners whose loyalty had remained dubious or long-standing religious clients of the state—was seen as a worrying development. Moreover, the softening of the regime's posture, as well as the intimate connections between religious leaders, on the one hand, and the Sunni bourgeoisie and political elite, on the other hand, had allowed the Islamic trend to expand its influence over private schools and even local representative councils. In such circumstances, the secular (and dominant) wing of the Syrian leadership decided that it was necessary to change course as soon as the improvement of the international context allowed it.

After 2008, the Syrian government not only cracked down on the Islamic trend but also undertook a spectacular expansion of the official religious bureaucracy and of the state-owned structures dedicated to the training of clerics. Through this reorientation, the regime did more than reassert its authority over a social sector that was deemed too autonomous: it gave back the role of religious entrepreneur to a state that had reduced itself to the function of policeman during almost half a century.

EPILOGUE: FACING THE 2011 UPRISING

When demonstrations started in Tunisia in December 2010, the relations between the regime and the ulema had deteriorated to an unprecedented extent. Long-standing loyalist Dr. al-Buti openly defied the government when the latter called for a rogation prayer—a traditional prayer of supplication (*salat al-istisqa'*)—to put an end to a winter drought. According to the scholar, God would not accept such prayer because of the "injustices" the country had recently witnessed, such as the measures against veiled women as well as the national television station's refusal to censor a series that was deemed offensive to observant Muslims (Pierret 2011a, 277–78).

When demonstrations erupted in Syria in March 2011, the regime unsurprisingly took a set of measures aimed at appeasing the ulema. Not only did it backtrack on its policies of "resecularization" (veiled teachers and observant members of the governorate council were reinstated), but it agreed to close the recently opened casino of Damascus. More important for this account, new state-run religious institutions were created: an Islamic satellite channel called Nur al-Sham ("the Light of Syria") and a higher institute for religious studies, al-Sham. Through the establishment of the latter, the state was completing the nationalization of specialized Islamic education. Indeed, the new structure was a federation of three "colleges," that is, the—until then private—Kaftaru Academy, the al-Fath Institute, and the Shi'ite Hawza of Sayyida Ruqqaya. The former managers of these schools would remain in command, but under direct state supervision. They were thus losing what was left of their autonomy, but by granting official recognition to the diplomas delivered by their institutes the regime satisfied one of their long-standing demands (Pierret 2011a, 281–82).

By addressing key concerns of the ulema, the regime managed to ensure the loyalty of its traditional religious allies, such as the aforementioned "subcontractors" as well as al-Buti, who vehemently criticized demonstrators as agents of foreign conspiracies. It was not enough, however, to prevent more independent scholars of Damascus, such as Jama'at Zayd's spiritual leader, Usama al-Rifa'i, from overtly condemning the ruthless repression of the uprising. Al-Rifa'i and other rebellious clerics were banned from preaching in August 2011, a move that sparked little reaction among their (predominantly middle- and upper-class) following. This passivity had obviously much less to do with religion than with the fact that many well-off Syrian Sunnis were not entirely enthusiastic about a predominantly peasant and working-class movement (Pierret 2011b).

The severe deterioration of the situation in the country, which by the autumn of 2011 included a looming armed insurgency in Homs, combined with the relative quiescence of the Damascene and Aleppian ulema, made religious issues a third-tier priority for the regime. Likewise, with the gradual strengthening of international economic sanctions against the regime, the Ministry of Religious Endowments was very likely to suffer from major budget cuts in the short run, forcing it to renounce most of its ambitious projects. In any case, with the prospect of civil war drawing closer, what was really at stake in late 2011 was no longer the situation of official religious institutions, but the fate of the Syrian state itself.

5 ISLAMIC SOCIAL MOVEMENTS AND THE SYRIAN AUTHORITARIAN REGIME

Shifting Patterns of Control and Accommodation

Teije Hidde Donker

AT FIRST SIGHT, Syria is an "ideal type" authoritarian regime. By any standard it has a closed political system, and social activism is harshly repressed, as was shown in 2011. Freedom House ranks the Syrian regime at the very bottom of its political rights score and very near the bottom with respect to civil liberties.[1] It can safely be stated that all Syrians are affected by repression in one fashion or another. This is especially the case for Syrians who engage in forms of Islamic activism, whether political or social. Historically Islamist activists were the main challengers of the Ba'thist regime—and, perhaps unsurprisingly, the main targets of state repression (Lobmayer 1995). They currently constitute the largest group of political prisoners in Syrian prisons.[2]

Nonetheless, the conventional conception of relations between the Ba'thist regime and Syrian Islamists does not reflect the complexity or fluidity that have often defined interactions between the two. Despite strict regime repression, Islamic movements have always been among the most active and resilient frameworks for sociopolitical activism in Syria. Certain Islamic groups have occasionally received a surprising degree of freedom and organizational capacity (Selvik and Pierret 2009). Repressive measures seem to be applied unevenly, and groups sometimes appear to have political leverage over regime actors. This is not to suggest that repression is either absent or ineffective; quite the contrary. Yet within this generalized environment of repression, Islamist political opposition exists, both inside and outside the regime.[3] At the same time, this opposition has clear limits. Its presence expresses a more complex relationship between Islamist forces and the regime than is often assumed, but Islamic activism is nonetheless constrained. In particular, it has largely failed to provide a framework for collective antiregime mobilization over the past several decades. The question this leaves us with is: why not? Why, if Islamist modes of social and political engagement continue to operate in Syria, have they not emerged as compelling or widely embraced modes of collective opposition to the regime? Why, if Islamist actors are occasionally able to expand their autonomy and the scope of their activities, have they largely failed to capitalize on such moments to reinvigorate more enduring forms of Islamist mobilization on a large scale?

The answer to these questions lies in the organization of Syrian authoritarianism and how this organization affects the dynamics of state–society relations. Authoritarianism is not only a political phenomenon, and the effectiveness of repression is not only dependent on the strength of the state and its executive bodies. Social dynamics also play a key role in the resilience of authoritarian regimes (O'Donnell 1999, 5). Despite increasing attention to state–society interaction in authoritarian regimes (see Cavatorta 2008; Tuğal 2009; Wiktorowicz 2004), the influence of social processes on authoritarian regimes has been understudied. I address these lacunae through a focus on the scope and limits of Islamist activism in a secular authoritarian context. More specifically, I argue that:

- Multiple Islamic movements exist within Syria. Within these Islamic movements we can see a number of "elite" actors, including the best-known Syrian sheikhs, muftis, and *ulema*.[4] Though very much part of Islamic movements, these religious elites often also belong to networks of economic and political significance.
- The specific Syrian political context encourages the existence of constantly shifting informal relations between regime actors and their Islamist counterparts, permitting religious elites to extend their influence beyond the religious sphere to become critical brokers in the mediation of relations between the regime and Islamic movements.
- The concept of brokerage can describe how the regime and religious movements are bound together; this could explain the pervasiveness of private (as opposed to public) forms of contentious mobilization, in addition to sustaining the perception among religious actors of their vulnerability to regime repression.

The argument made in this chapter builds on fieldwork conducted during the period February through May 2009 and a short follow-up fieldwork period in July 2010. During these periods, I conducted approximately sixty interviews with secular and Islamic activists as well as with a small number of foreign observers and diplomats. In addition to interviews, primary sources relating to elite religious figures are used in the analysis.[5] Mostly due to constraints inherent to conducting research in authoritarian settings like Syria, the research focuses exclusively on the Syrian capital, Damascus. Therefore, the analysis presented in this chapter constitutes an initial exploration of an observed phenomenon that no doubt extends beyond the spheres in which it is covered here. That said, I am convinced of the added value of describing relations between movements and authoritarian regimes through the concept of brokerage, and I invite the reader to apply and test the hypotheses presented in this chapter in Syria and other authoritarian contexts.

The chapter is structured as follows. After a brief introduction to social movement studies, I explore Syrian Islamic movements and the political context in which they are active. I then link these two explorations through the mechanism of "brokerage" and analyze its implications for the resilience of the authoritarian regime. In the conclusion, I provide a short outline of insights gained using social movement studies and discuss possible future developments regarding Islamic movements in Syria.

SOCIAL MOVEMENTS AND ISLAMISM

Why do people mobilize? What can explain the time, the mode, and outcomes of specific episodes of mobilization? These are central questions in the study of social movements. Over the years, these questions have been addressed from multiple vantage points. Traditionally, social movement research started out as critique of psychological or relative deprivation explanations for mobilization that argue, for example, that people mobilize out of personal frustration (Klandermans 1984). As the field developed, social movement scholars have explored the influence of previous social contacts with "mobilizers" in the spread of mobilization;[6] how social movement actors gain access to and use symbolic, economic, and political resources;[7] how certain issues are strategically described (or "framed") by actors as normative problems to mobilize bystanders;[8] and what the influence of the political context is on mobilization form and success.[9] Increasingly, social movement scholars have appreciated the interdependent nature of these various explanations and the cross-fertilizations that have emerged among them (Della Porta and Diani 2006).

This chapter explores how types of mobilization can be influenced by a political context. In social movement research, the concept of political opportunity structures (POS) has been dominant in exploring the influence of a political context on social movement mobilization (Kriesi 1995; McAdam, McCarthy, and Zald 1996). This approach theoretically links the formation, modes of mobilization, and eventual outcome of social movement mobilization to specificities of a political context (Della Porta and Diani 2006, 196–221).

Despite renewed appreciation for the importance of context in understanding mobilization dynamics, the conceptualization of political opportunity structures has suffered from a "dichotomy" bias. This is a direct result of the historical development of social movement studies (SMS). These studies emerged as a counterweight to the focus on formal institutions in studies on interest representation in liberal democracies. Therefore, social movements are often seen as "politics by unusual means" (Armstrong and Bernstein 2008). This, in turn, implies that social movements are detached from formal political and state institutions. As such, the traditional view is that political regimes (and their formal institutions) implement strict rules concerning what (forms of) institutions and repertoires are prescribed, tolerated, or forbidden. Noninstitutionalized social movements within society react, which in return elicits a reaction from the side of the regime (Tilly 2006). Thereby a dichotomy between formal and informal politics, and state and society, became ingrained in this field of SMS research (Tarrow, Tilly, and McAdam 2001, 7). As will be shown in the following discussion, however, in authoritarian settings, where informal political rules and ambiguous regime-movement relations dominate, this dichotomy is unsustainable. To understand how social movements emerge in authoritarian regimes, we need to acknowledge the ambiguous nature of state–society boundaries and the prevalence of informal forms of interest representation. We also need to acknowledge that these have a profound impact on how mobilization strategies evolve within such contexts.

A related point can be made about social movements and the basis for their mobilization. An analytical dichotomy has emerged in the literature between mobilization focusing on distributive grievances aimed at political elites and mobilization around social issues aimed at changing norms and values in society. Various social movement scholars have pointed to the changing basis for mobilization within social movements since the 1990s: from mobilization around material and distributive challenges to mobilization around issues of norms and values. A few examples are the ecology movement, the peace movement, and the women's movement (Kriesi 1995, xviii). These movements were dubbed "new social movements" as they aimed at changing perceptions and behaviors in society rather than addressing material grievances vis-à-vis political elites. The argument has been made, however, that the "newness" is analytical rather then empirical (Melucci 1996). Most movements incorporate both "new" and "old" elements, in the sense that their "social" project was often intrinsically linked to political aims.

In the discussion on Islamic and Islamist movements a similar dynamic is taking place. From a conceptualization of Islamism as an explicit political (revolutionary) project aimed at creating an Islamic state (Roy 2006), it has evolved to incorporate bottom-up *dawa'* movements aimed at the Islamization of society. The traditional Islamist project has increasingly been marginalized due to repression and a failure to achieve practical results: no Arab regime has ever been brought down by Islamist mobilization (Roy 1996). This failure reverberates within academic discussions. Though in many academic fields Islamism in the narrow political sense is still very much at the center of debate (for an elaborate discussion, see Volpi 2010), other fields have been open to the recognition that the political impact of Islamic movements in the Middle East is not only a result of their direct political ambitions but also in its intent to change norms and values in society is in accordance with a conservative interpretation of Islam. Tuğal has shown the political impact of restructuring daily routines through an Islamist project in a neighborhood of Istanbul (Tuğal 2009). Saba Mahmood (2005) has made a similar claim concerning the Egyptian piety movement. She states:

> If we examine . . . the piety movement, it is quite apparent that this particular strand of the Islamist movement is only marginally organized around questions of rights, recognition, and political representation. . . . It is not toward *recognition* that the activities of the mosque or the piety movement are oriented but rather toward *retraining* of ethical sensibilities so as to create a new social and moral order. . . . It would therefore be a mistake to assume that all contemporary social movements . . . should be analyzed as responses to the judicial language of rights, recognition, and distributive justice. (Mahmood 2005, 193)

The definition used here of a social movement recognizes the insights from the works previously cited. A social movement is defined, following Della Porta and Diani, as social processes consisting of "mechanisms, through which actors engaged in collective actions [1] are involved in conflictual relations with clearly identified opponents; [2] are linked by dense informal networks and [3] share a distinct collective identity" (2006, 20). In Islamist movements the "collective identity" around which mobilization occurs is an Islamic one. Note that "conflictual relations" does not imply an a priori interaction with a state, nor a language of rights or distributive justice: mobilization can be aimed at Islamisizing society in direct opposition to secular trends.

Prior to the uprising of 2011, most Syrians would never openly state that *social* movements exist in their country—let alone that they are active in one. In the traditional, material, understanding of social movements, they are correct. The most obvious example of political Islamist mobilization in Syria was the Islamic uprising in the late 1970s and early 1980s, in which the Syrian Muslim Brotherhood played a central role. Consequently, the Syrian Muslim Brothers were harshly repressed, crushed in the city of Hama, and banished from the country (Lobmayer 1995). Today, people fear even mentioning the name *al-Ikhwan al-Muslimun* (the Muslim Brotherhood) in public. Yet, in the wider conceptualization of a social movement, contemporary examples do exist.

ISLAMIC MOVEMENTS IN SYRIA

Various Islamic movements are present in Syria. The collective identity at the base of these movements can be built around preexisting forms of religious organization. For instance, we can state that a movement can emerge around a sheikh (as is the case with the Qubaysiat, following Munira al-Qubaysi) or around a specific religious school (such is the case with the Naqshbandi school at the Abu Nour Institute). Collective movements can also emerge along more general religious cleavages, for instance belonging to or following a specific religious ideology (for example, Salafism) or divisions between adherents of "liberal" or "conservative" modes of Islamic observance. All these movements aim to defend the implementation of Islamic norms and values in society. But they all defend and spread *specific* interpretations of Islam that can be, and often are, at odds with each other. The result is a constant struggle between Islamic movements, even within a broader Syrian context that is distinctly hostile toward politicized forms of religious mobilization.

An example of an Islamic social movement emerging around a sheikh is the women's movement around Munira al-Qubaysi, the so-called Qubaysiat. The movement is specifically aimed at empowering women in a conservative Islamic framework, for instance by emphasizing the importance of women's roles in the home.[10] The explicit religious conviction of followers is strengthened through education and informal discussion groups. Though they publicly state that they are aimed solely at the religiosity of the individual, public displays are a key part of their repertoire and thereby express the collective commitment of group members to a specific set of Islamic norms and values. In effect, the movement is aimed at increasing religiosity among Syrian women in general and is part of a broader Syrian religious revival. In 2006 the movement apparently had tens of thousands of followers, mainly in Syria but also abroad (Hamidi 2006a, 2006b).

An example of Islamist movements forming around more general religious cleavages is the mobilization of both conservative and liberal Islamic movements around the position of religion in formal state law. A specific example of this is mobilization around the drafting of a new personal status, or family, law. The current personal status law was drafted in 1956 and outlines, for instance, parental recognition of children, inheritance matters, and intersectarian marriages. It is a law that draws on religious jurisprudence. In early 2009, a reform of the law was initiated. When the first draft was leaked it proved to be very conservative, much more so than the 1956 version it was intended to replace. An outcry from more liberal elements in society, including some Islamic activists, was the result (Haysu 2010). A more liberal draft of the new law was then created, with state officials concurrently stating that any further public discussion of the status law was out of the question.[11] Indeed, the new draft was met with an utter silence. Nonetheless, as of mid-2010 a new law had yet to be implemented. A more liberal Damascus-based sheikh openly shared his frustration over a regime that in his view had grown afraid of conservative movements in the religious sphere: "When opposition mounts among conservative currents against a specific issue, let's say the family law, the state is wary to really do something about it. They just take their hands off and let it be. We [the sheikhs in parliament] try to influence Islamic issues. But we are powerless."[12] The very cautious reaction from the regime seems to imply that regime elites were convinced they were not dealing with a small number of individual sheikhs but rather a broad based movement, not public but still very real, within Syrian society opposing a more liberal personal status law.

Concerning institutionalization, most of the movements discussed here build on Sufi-inspired notions of informal organization. They define their organizations as *jama'at,* signifying an informal socialized congregation, though their level of practical formal institutionalization on the ground differs immensely, ranging from informal groups to large religious institutes (Pinto 2006). A number of the leading sheikhs have a well-developed structure of informal home-teaching circles, headed by teachers, that are linked to larger circles headed by subleaders and eventually combine as the informally institutionalized following of a specific sheikh. The home-teaching circles are illegal but widespread. Around these informal *jamia'at,* various formal institutions can exist: for instance mosques, charitable associations, religious schools, and universities.[13] Currently, Islamism in Syria revolves around a small number of elite Sunni activists and related large Islamic institutes (though whether the current uprising will affect the standing of these individuals remains to be seen). Within these constellations of actors, the relevant figures for this chapter are:

- Ahmad Kaftaru (1912–2004) is the late Grand Mufti of Syria. Under his leadership, the Abu Nour Institute in Damascus grew from a modest mosque to a large institute containing a charitable association (*al-Ansar*), and "Islamic" education on the primary, secondary, and university level. The growth of the institute was built on the combination of religious authority and close regime relations that Ahmad Kaftaru possessed. After he died in 2004, the daily management of the Institute transferred to his son Salah al-Din.[14]

- Hisaam al-Din Farfur and the al-Fatah al-Islami Institute. As in the case of the Abu Nour Institute, the al-Fath Institute incorporates a charitable association and an educational institute. The main sheikh related to the Institute is the late Saleh Farfur (1901–1986). Currently one of his sons, Hisam al-Din Farfur, is among the main sheikhs of the institute.[15]

- Muhamad Said Ramadan al-Buti, former head of the sharia faculty of the University of Damascus and a renowned Muslim scholar. He is one of the main advisors to the president on religious affairs. Al-Buti has a large following, mostly among intellectuals of conservative classes.[16] He is also well known regionally.[17]

- Ratib al-Nabulsi is a preacher who broadcast four times daily on Syrian radio.[18] He is mostly popular with conservative working-class Syrians.[19] He has been member of various councils at the Ministry of *Awqaf* (Religious Endowments).

- Muhammad Habash, preacher at the al-Rahma mosque in the Damascus upper-middle-class suburb of Mezze. He is also a member of Parliament. He does not have a following comparable to the above sheikhs but is (in)famous for his liberal reform approach to Islamic speech that attracts sizable audiences to his sermons.[20]

Somewhat simplistically, it can be stated that the al-Fatah al-Islam Institute belongs to the more conservative Islamic movements and its Kaftaru counterpart to the more liberal, while al-Buti is more conservative than "liberal outliers" such as Sheikh Habash. Despite these various differences, Islamic activists share a common identity of being part of one "Islamic sphere" and therefore belong to a single broader family of Islamic (Sunni) movements.

THE MOBILIZATION CONTEXT

Within authoritarian Syria, access to political power is by nature highly restrictive and ambiguous. Power is concentrated around individuals and groups close to the president and other political elites. Important individuals are, for instance, Rami Makhlouf, cousin of President al-Asad and one of the most powerful Syrian businessman, at least until the spring of 2011; and Assef Shawkat, brother-in-law of President Asad and deputy chief of staff of the Syrian Army. Another important individual is Major General Hisham Bakhtiar, a former director of the General Security Directorate and current national security advisor to Bashar al-Asad.[21] These individuals are the top of a political elite that exists within opaque informal networks of individual relations closely related to various state institutions (Lust-Okar 2006, 4; Perthes 1997, 135–202).[22] Between the president and his close army and security advisers, main policy issues are decided and eventually disseminated through the state apparatus (Perthes 2004b).

The political regime is fragmented along various groups of influence. Different groups (and families) within Syrian political elites have dynamic and diverging interests and opinions. As such, political elites are in constant struggle over decision-making power (ICG 2009, 3–4; Perthes 2004b). Additionally, social conflicts in general, and intra-Islamic movements' struggles specifically, tend to reverberate in the political regime and state organizations. Individual ministers are often dubbed to be "with" or "against" the "Islamists." The current minister of *Awqaf*, Mohammed Abdul Sattar, is known as pro "conservative" Islam, the former minister pro "liberal" Islam. The current minister of culture, Riad Nasaan Agha, is accused by seculars of being an "Islamist"—as is the entire Damascus municipality.[23] As such, the mobilizing context is not marked by a unified regime; nor do state organizations repress (Islamic) activism uniformly. Rather, socioreligious struggles influence the state, and the state concurrently influences these struggles (Migdal 2001).

Despite such varying attitudes toward the Islamic movements, Bashar al-Asad's regime has inherited, and further developed, an extensive formal and outwardly less ambivalent institutional structure for managing religious (and Islamic) activism. Through various state agencies, it has an effective veto over any Islamic organization or initiative.[24] State authorities control the appointments of formal mufti positions, appointments of imams, and financial flows through (Islamic) charitable associations: the Ministry of *Awqaf* directs all religious activities (for instance assigning Imams to mosques and managing local and national mufti positions); the Ministry of Social Affairs and Labor controls all financial flows to charitable associations; and the ministries of Education and Higher Education are mostly concerned with the accreditation of Islamic teaching institutes (see also Ziadeh 2008, 68–70).[25]

Apart from attempts to suppress contentious and more explicitly political forms of Islamic mobilization, this institutional framework is aimed at supporting "state-sanctioned" Islamic interpretations that focus on individual piety as the accepted mode of religious expression. At the same time, though, formal state Islam has never gained the dominant position that it has in, for instance, Egypt. Historically, Syrian religious movements have always had a measure of independence vis-à-vis the Ba'th regime, and religious actors have never been completely incorporated into regime structures.[26] A few of the larger institutes in Damascus for instance, most notably al-Fath al-Islam and the Abu Nur Institute, have their own financial resources and initiatives that provide them with a level of independence. But the preceding implies that the formal institutional structure ensures continued close contact, for better or worse, between the state and Islamic movements by providing a state-sanctioned religious arena through which brokerage can occur.

This political context has very practical effects for grassroots religious activists. The lack of transparency renders repression seemingly random—but not less severe. Islamic activists can be subject to harsh repression over seemingly small offenses. In a telling example, an Islamic bookstore owner from the al-Tel region was arrested for possessing a "jihadi CD." Ironically, possessing a jihadi CD isn't prohibited, and, additionally, the store owner was able to say where he had bought the CD in Syria. He was still incarcerated more than a year after his arrest, at the time of the interview in April 2009 (see also Human Rights Watch 2009a, 5).[27] On December 27, 2008, the corpse of Yusif Jabuli, civil servant and graduate of the sharia faculty of Damascus University, was returned to his family after his arrest a week earlier. Authorities prohibited the family from publishing an obituary and, even more troublesome, opening the coffin to look at the body. Death due to torture was suspected.[28] These are two examples, but stories like these abound.[29] In practice, the boundaries between what is prohibited and permitted are not clear-cut. Complicating matters further, these boundaries constantly change by being hardened or softened or by being applied in a highly selective fashion. When asked why some Islamic activists are arrested (and others not) a human rights activist noted that it was just a matter of being lucky—or not; "The unpredictability is the power of the system."[30]

In a context where political power is concentrated in informal spheres, it is not surprising that regime and movement elites are deeply intertwined. At the same time, religious movements in Syria have a certain level of independence and are not powerless. The political regime is shown to be very careful, up to the point of seeming to be unable to act, when contention mounted within conservative Islamic movements in the country. Though activists themselves often describe their situation as vulnerable to the whims of a cruel, random, repressive state—this suggests that religious movements have real power. Then why have religious movements remained so quiet on the more (public) contentious front? To find an explanation, I argue, we need to look at the concept of brokerage, apply it to elites in Syrian religious movements, and see how this role influences grassroots activism.

BROKERS AND BROKERAGE

With brokerage I denote the "linking of two or more previously unconnected social sites by a unit that mediates their relations with one another and/or with yet other sites" (following Tarrow, Tilly, and McAdam 2001, 26). Brokerage often involves relation building between various groups within social movements.[31] It is closely related to, or results in, relations between the parties involved and has been predominantly used in conjunction with diffusion of information within and between social movements. I prefer to use the concept of brokerage rather than other related concepts (such as alliances) as it denotes a process and thereby provides a better appreciation of the dynamic nature of relations between actors in the regime and Islamic movements in a context where boundaries between the two are often ambiguous.

I argue that brokerage can effectively be used in analyzing mobilization in a context where state–society boundaries are blurred. Specifically the multiplicity ("two or more sites") and absence of a built in (implicit) polity–movement dichotomy renders the concept perfect for the analysis at hand. The multiplicity makes it possible to analyze the importance of actors' concurrent participation in multiple networks; the absence of a regime–movement dichotomy makes it possible to show that these networks can exist in various spheres: social, economic, or political. The concept has mostly been used in analyzing contacts between different movements, not between a political regime and mobilizers. As such, the influence of brokers' positions between multiple social, economic, and political networks on mobilization strategies has so far received little scholarly attention. This is what I attempt here: to describe how religious elites navigate their positions in both regime and society by using the concept of brokerage and subsequently analyze how this enables or constrains strategies for collective action.

ISLAMIC ELITES AS BROKERS

The specific position of religious elites means that they can be described as a type of broker between elites in the political regime and Islamic movements. These brokerage roles can exist on both a formal and informal level. I demonstrate this here by providing a few examples on both formal and informal levels, outlining why brokerage is a useful concept to describe the position of elites in Islamic movements, and assessing what the implications can be for collective mobilization.

Many religious elites have had some formal position in either a ministry, state organization, or political body that is, strictly speaking, not directly related to their religious project. Muhammad Habash, for instance, is a member of parliament. Sheikh Farfur is a special advisor to the Ministry of *Awqaf*. And Sheikh Nabulsi has been member of various councils at the Ministry of *Awqaf*.[32] These types of positions are readily available because of the extensive institutional framework that exists for managing religious affairs. Additionally, the majority of these religious elites combine their formal religious positions with other jobs—for instance, trading. Nabulsi is one example. Alongside his position as mufti and sheikh he is an international trader in agricultural goods.[33] This also holds for informal positions. A prime example is al-Buti. He is currently an informal advisor to the president and has recently been appointed khatib (preacher) at Damascus's Umayad Mosque, an especially significant position. He has been one of the most prominent conservative religious figures in Syria for decades, though for much of his career he has not held an official religious position, even though he was the head of the sharia faculty of the University of Damascus. These elite actors are not only the leaders of religious movements; they are also economic elites and embedded in networks of political elites. I contend that the use of this multiplicity of positions is crucial to the advancement of their religious projects.[34]

Part of this behavior can be explained as a form of rent seeking. Though not necessarily focused on securing financial resources, cultivating ties to officials can directly aid religious projects through the resources they control. The positive implications of the positions mentioned in the preceding paragraphs are obvious. That an informal "deal" has been made between al-Buti and the regime—concerning what al-Buti can say and do publicly–is widely accepted. Al-Buti has been one of the only major writers of the contemporary Islamic revival in Syria whose books were available in Syrian bookshops (Pierret 2009). In return for this preferential treatment, he provides the regime with a level of religious legitimacy. The same is true for some other elite sheikhs. It is widely accepted that elite Islamic activists have close relations with regime elites. An employee of the Abu Nour Institute stated openly that "the friendly relations between Sheikh Ahmad Kaftaru and [former] President Hafiz have really helped the Sheikh, our projects, and the Institute. Without it we would not be where we are now." He added that other sheikhs have accepted this strategy and all try to engage as much as possible with the regime.[35] That something had to be given in return is clear. As the late Ahmad Kaftaru once strikingly remarked:

> Islam and the Regime's power ... are twin brothers. It is impossible to think of one without the other. Islam is the base, and the Regime's power of rule is the protector; after all a thing without a base is destined to collapse and fall, and a thing without a protector will end in extinction. (Ahmad Kaftaru in Zisser 2005, 51)

What is important to note here is that elite religious actors can have formal positions that bring them close to or render them part of other spheres in society and the political regime. It is also clear that their religious influence on Syrian society has grown because of these various other activities. Some go even further and argue that this is a necessity and state that any Islamic activist needs to acquire some form of regime relations to be able to acquire the resources needed to set up noncontentious social activities.[36] "All you need is contacts [with regime actors], money, and information."[37] It is what local Syrians call "*wasta*" (see also Selvik and Pierret 2009).[38]

Yet I argue that these strategies go beyond rent-seeking behavior and beyond a so-called co-optation of specific religious elite actors into the regime. These actors do not just idly act as mouthpieces of the regime so as to remain in good standing. Nor are they rendered incapable of contentious mobilization through endemic clientelism (for a similar example concerning Palestinian civic associations, see Jamal 2007). There is popular mobilization at the grassroots level, and religious elites function as go-betweens between movements and regime elites. They provide influence. In a situation where public displays of contestation are prohibited, existing informal relations between Islamic actors and elite political actors gain importance as conduits for interest representation. For instance, secular activists noted that, within the capital, it has become increasingly difficult to open bars that serve alcohol outside the Christian quarter (Bab Tuma) and that bars have been closed following Islamic-based mobilization. The interviewees attributed this shift to informal pressure on the regime by conservative Islamic groups.[39]

Another example is the already mentioned personal status law. The (closed) council that had written the initial draft was largely composed of people from the sharia faculty of the University of Damascus, which is close to Syrian conservative movements and Sheikh al-Buti. When asked who produced the first draft of the personal status law, the regime or conservative Islamic movements, a secular activist said, "It is impossible for me to tell, maybe both. Seen from my side, they're so close together . . . you can say it is as if they are married."[40] When a second, more liberal, draft was proposed, the whole reform process stalled—and without one person going into the streets. Apparently the regime had grown wary of antagonizing conservative religious movements. Therefore, elite actors seem to be more than mere puppets of the regime and seem to act as a key conduit for popular discontent that exists within religious movements.

I argue that the relations between regime actors and religious elites are not just about rents but also about a form of religious interest representation at elite regime levels. I also argue that it is not just financial benefits that convinced most sheikhs that engagement is the way to go; it was also the opportunity to be effective brokers.

IMPLICATIONS FOR SOCIAL MOVEMENT ACTIVISTS AND REGIME RESILIENCE

The accepted position of elite Islamic actors between movements and regime has consequences for the position of Islamic movements vis-à-vis the Syrian state and authoritarian regime—and it has an influence on what mode of contentious mobilization occurs. I argue that this context inhibits both the formation and spread of polarized mobilization repertoires to larger audiences. Continuing with the concept of brokerage, these types of roles tie together movements and regime and promote informal modes of interest representation. They thereby tacitly acknowledge the supreme power of the state and its authority over Syrian society and prevent the wider dissemination of public modes of contentious mobilization. As such, brokerage can feed into regime resilience. In essence, pervasive brokerage by movement elites promotes non-

antagonistic state–movement interactions, thereby inhibiting direct opposition and contributing to the resilience of the Syrian regime.

More contentious opinions do exist among actors in Syrian religious movements, but they are not expressed in public. When talking to activists in private
they express (material) grievances, directly related to state policies or related
to the position of Islam in contemporary Syria, that they would not articulate
in public. A secular interviewee noted that "many activists feel they are active
on the basis of exceptions and therefore do not want to cross any lines. . . .
Everyone has a *mukhabaraat* in himself."[41] The perpetual uncertainty of repression in the Syrian case makes Islamic activists extremely cautious about
undertaking public activism. On the question of whether there have been open
discussions about the personal status law, a young Muslim activist answered:

> No . . . there were no open discussions, about five interviews—that was it.
> This is because the topic is close to sectarianism. Everything that smells like
> sectarianism is repressed. So stating openly that there are multiple currents on
> this issue is very dangerous. But one-on-one, informally, of course there have
> been discussions.[42]

Another young activist noted that in relation to home teachings:

> In these groups we don't discuss politics. We focus on practical issues of being
> Muslim: how often you have to pray, how you have to pray, other questions that
> they [the students] have. We don't discuss politics or other sensitive issues. The
> teachers are too scared that something will happen. But it is the place where
> you meet each other . . . So yes, we do discuss these things amongst each other.[43]

As is clear from the preceding quotations, people do discuss contentious
issues but in an extremely private manner. They are constantly scared. The
intensity of regime repression can be only part of the story: public contentious mobilization has occurred in regimes with a comparable amount of repression, including Egypt and Tunisia. Rather, perceptions among religious
activists of the threats and opportunities they face are not directly linked to
a political context or objective amount of repression but are just as much the
result of an interpretive process (Tarrow, Tilly, and McAdam 2001, 70). One
can argue that wide acceptance of regime–movement elite brokerage implies
a subservience of religious movements to the regime and thereby sustains a
perception of threat that reinforces the resilience of Syrian authoritarianism.

The fact that these opinions exist but are not brought out in public gives an
implicit recognition to the regime's power to determine what is kept private or

can be discussed publicly (Donker 2010; Wedeen 1999). Therefore, the mode in which mobilization takes place can imply a subservient position of activists toward the existing regime—a relationship that may well undergo significant change following the 2011 uprising. When asked why they were so lenient toward engagement with regime actors, the remembrance of 1982—Hama and its bloody aftermath—was recounted time and again.[44] It might be that every time activists act on this remembrance, even implicitly, they actually keep it alive. They sustain the image of the broad-based all-encompassing repression of almost thirty years ago and thus participate in sustaining the perception of a regime that will stop at nothing to defend itself.

As long as the formal politically quiescent "shell" is respected, contentious mobilization by Islamic social movement activists is likely to remain limited. For mobilization to threaten regime stability, it needs to shift in scale: a larger number of people have to collectively show their contention in the public sphere—as has occurred, though without an explicitly religious cast, from March 2011 onward. As long as diffusion of more contentious polarizing frames remain in the informal private realm, it is unlikely that the coordination necessary for these types of mobilization can be met. In other words, many activists, in their aim to defend the implementation of Islamic values in Syrian society, agree that state power should be challenged. But, at the same time, at least prior to March 2011, they also implicitly acknowledged that brokerage is necessary for religious movements and often accepted the ambiguous state–movement position that religious elites have. Again, this is not to say Islamic activists were powerless before the start of the uprising: they exerted pressure through personal, informal, relations. It is to say that in general Islamic activists seem to have accepted the brokerage function of religious elites instead of retreating and taking a principled stance against the political regime. As such, existing brokerage strategies end up contributing to the resilience of the authoritarian regime.

From the perspective of movement elites, there is no reason for them to have grassroots participants in religious movements overcome this constant perception of threat; quite the contrary. The position of regime elites is built on the existence and informal mobilization of religious movements, as it provides them with authority at regime levels. Public displays of discontent will probably, in contrast, threaten this position. This is also true of various (nonreligious) roles they have: they can be fired from state positions, lose business opportunities, and the like. For much of the preuprising period, movement elites seem to have been best served by Islamic social movements that focused publicly on norms and values and served as informal arena for contention, permitting religious elites to position themselves as key brokers for interest representation between grassroots movements and regime elites.

Using the concept of brokerage, I have shown that Islamic mobilization in authoritarian regimes does not have to be a priori completely antagonistic to the regime against which it takes place. Rather, the political context is such that boundaries between movements and political regime are diffuse—and this ambiguity is capitalized on by elites in these movements. Islamic elites sense they have to be pragmatic, and Muslim activists on the grassroots level seem to concur. More can be gained by working with regime actors than working directly against them through a nonpolarized strategy instead of a more antagonistic one. As consequence though, they participate in keeping the regime alive. In essence it is the rule of pragmatism: if you feel you need to be pragmatic, then pragmatism will rule—and the status quo will be sustained.

CONCLUSION

I have argued in the preceding pages that multiple Islamic movements exist within Syria. Within these Islamic movements we can see a number of "elite" actors: the best-known sheikhs, suftis, and *ulema*. Though very much part of Islamic movements, these elites often also belong to elite networks of economic and political relevance. Secondly, I have argued that the specific, preuprising Syrian political context encouraged the existence of constantly shifting informal relations between regime actors and their Islamist counterparts permitting religious elites to extend their influence beyond the religious sphere to become, what can be called critical brokers in the mediation of relations between the regime and Islamic movements. Finally, I argued that brokerage positions of the elites in religious movements tie together movements and the regime and promote informal modes of interest representation. It thereby prevents the wider dissemination of public modes of contentious mobilization, sustains the political status quo, and becomes part and parcel of mechanisms supporting the resilience of Syrian authoritarianism.

What I also showed is that SMS provides a useful conceptual framework to analyze interaction between a macro political context and the microlevel of perceived opportunity and threat. Through this chapter I provided a sketch of how such an analysis might evolve, demonstrating that insights from social movements do clarify specific mechanisms at work in enhancing the resilience of authoritarian systems of rule and help to analyze interactions between them. This is possible even if the case at hand is not "perfect": in Syria no religious-based public protest has emerged in perhaps twenty-five years. Additionally, the often naturally assumed difference between state and society does not capture Syrian reality sufficiently. Despite its limits, however, SMS helps to provide useful insights into how actors interact in a specific context and how this eventually influences the mode in which mobilization emerges.

Nothing lasts. The year 2011 would prove to be a turning point in the history of the MENA region, with three revolutions in North Africa and widespread unrest and uprisings throughout the Middle East. Syria was no exception. Strikingly, Islamist movements were not at the basis of mobilization, not in Syria, and not in many other countries. The initial uprising was marked by its noninstitutionalized and nonreligious character. This is not surprising in light of the analysis presented here.

In light of this analysis, it will be interesting to observe how regime–movement boundaries change during the current uprising and how this influences brokerage. The polarization of boundaries between political regime and Islamic movements might imply that the context needed for brokers to emerge ceases to exist: elite religious actors are either with the regime—and lose popular support—or with mobilizing, largely Sunni masses—implying an antagonistic relationship with the regime. At the same time, it might also be that broker positions are sufficiently flexible, and vested interests so well entrenched, that religious elites will find a way to remain brokers between movements and regime, even under conditions of increased polarization. It could be that regime elites are counting on their religious counterparts to provide a conduit for popular discontent among Islamic movements while keeping these movements domesticated.

Whatever the outcome, it is important to realize that, without exception, the current uprising has compelled religious elites to reevaluate their previous choices concerning engagement with the regime. These reevaluations will undoubtedly influence how the uprising will unfold. Therefore, the position of religious elites between regime and society is directly linked with the dynamics of the uprising itself. I hope to have shown that SMS provides a good conceptual framework for analyzing the actors and processes that are central in influencing these current and future dynamics. They are, in the end, a result of the interaction between a changing political context, elite brokerage, and the perception of threat and opportunity among grassroot mobilizers.

SOCIAL AND LITERARY RESPONSES TO AUTHORITARIAN RESILIENCE

Part III

6 CONTESTING GOVERNANCE
Authority, Protest, and Rights Talk
in Postrepublican Iran

Arzoo Osanloo

IN THE AFTERMATH of the June 2009 elections, Iranian dissenters and detractors forged a new social and political movement that challenges the legitimacy of their leaders. Members of the Green Movement for Freedom referred to the Iranian regime as a "coup d'état government." Commentators both inside and outside of the country increasingly characterized the Iranian government as authoritarian, dictatorial, and even fascist.

Soon after the 1979 revolution that was followed by a consolidation of power by Islamists led by Ayatollah Khomeini, Muslim leaders moved to set into motion a new kind of governance, an Islamic government or *hookoomat-e Islami*. This form of government, led by a guardian of Islamic jurisprudence, or *Vali-e Faqih*, would ascertain that the social order was maintained in accordance with Islamic principles.

Today's protestors, including former leaders of the 1979 revolution and dissident members of the *ulema* (community of Islamic legal scholars), fashion their grievances in terms of rights, especially human rights, not solely Islamic values. This chapter ties together current calls for rights with the often overlooked aspects of the Iranian government's "republic," noting that, up to now, Khomeini's vision of a so-called pure Islamic government has been overshadowed by the compromise formation of an Islamic Republic. The struggles in Iran must be understood, thus, in the context of an ongoing contest over the form of governance still taking shape there today, thirty years on. They illustrate the fluidity of governance and the capacity of an ideologically laden government as the one established following the revolution to engage in "recombinant" behaviors (see Heydemann and Leenders, Chapter 1 in this volume), as it consolidates itself and adapts to changing configurations of pressures from Iranian society.

In this chapter, I explore how the institutions of the state produce both systematic repression and, at the same time, a strong protest movement with considerable consciousness of individual rights and democratic principles. In doing so, I move beyond speculative arguments that prerevolutionary state building or outside pressures influenced the protestors. Notwithstanding international pressure, including from the Iranian diasporic community, the leaders of the Green Movement have emerged from "inside" the Islamic Republic. It is this production of defiance from within that I analyze here.

Thus, in what follows, I show how protests, like those in 1999 and 2009, are the products of the form of government, an Islamic Republic. I do this by exploring how the institutions of the Islamic Republic have taken shape and operate, and by examining the special emphasis on women's status in post-revolutionary Iran. This is not an arbitrary selection; women's status has been and continues to be a legitimating theme for the Islamic Republic. The manner in which key officials and institutions define issues surrounding women's status sheds light on governmental authority, the limits of protest, and indeed, individual rights.

That is, while the issue of improving women's status continues to be an important vehicle of legitimacy for the Islamic Republic today, the way the issue is framed shifts with the different administrations of the Islamic Republic. This in turn tells us something about the different agendas of various state institutions and officials, and the extent to which the malleability of governing institutions contributes to ongoing attempts to reframe issues such as women's status. Not only are these administrations not monolithic, but as they consist of multiple institutions, texts (laws and regulations), and individuals, they produce multiple and sometimes conflicting discourses and, in turn, have real, material effects. The focus on women's status will serve as a lens through which I explore the contradictory effects of the state-form and thus address the question posed in this volume: in the face of such apparent dissatisfaction, how do we understand the seemingly resilient nature of the Islamic Republic today? To this question, I suggest, first, that the Islamic Republic is a novel enterprise still taking form through the efforts of multiple stakeholders. Grounded in discourses of freedom from oppression, the Iranian revolution easily harnessed the sentiments of a wide range of groups from Shi'i ulema to leftist intellectuals. Since the elections that brought Mahmoud

Ahmadinejad to the presidency in 2005, however, the state's repressive forces have appeared more unified and emboldened. Certainly repression by state authorities existed before but was limited to specific populations and distinct branches of the government. Thus, it was more predictable. Now attacks by repressive forces seem perverse and capricious, but they are also more reactive to multiple and shifting challenges. Today, this includes the increasing alienation of Ahmadinejad's executive branch, and, at the same time, the impending criminal charges against his challengers, Mehdi Karrubi and Mir-Hossein Mousavi, currently under house arrest.

Second, the Islamic Republic is not and has never been one monolithic entity. Like other modern nation-states, it takes shape through the "effects" that render it legible (Mitchell 1999). What we see as a resilient state is rather an arrangement of a number of processes that produce an effect of the state. Mitchell suggests we analyze the state "as an effect of mundane processes of spatial organization, temporal arrangement, functional specification, supervision and surveillance, and representation" (1999, 96). These processes might create the illusion that a whole or coherent state exists as an entity apart from these practices, but it takes form through the accumulation of such practices. With the understanding that the state is the accretion of effects, the shifts in its makeup and structure are not beyond it but are parts of the whole. For instance, the state is not visible just through its boundary with society. Rather, its ability to order and control society through nonrepressive forms, such as legal regulation, is a central component of state power and thus its resilience. Mitchell argues that the institutions of the state wield power through processes of regulation, which not only create laws that order and normalize society but also inflect subjectivity and personhood. Thus the state also takes form in shaping its citizens through its power to regulate subjects using law (Mitchell 1999, 84).

In the Islamic Republic, one of the most significant effects of its state formation is the assemblage of select readings and sources of Shi'i Islamic jurisprudence to form a juridico-legal authority. This authority passes laws to allow the state to maintain its monopoly on "legitimate" violence (Benjamin 1978), an effect of all modern nation-states. In Iran, however, the state's monopoly on defining legitimate violence extends beyond civil and constitutional laws to a monopoly on the interpretation of the sharia, as well. This effect of power allows an additional source of control over the lives of the population, who are now guided by a regulatory authority through civil laws as well as religious principles.[1] This is significant in the context of Shi'i Islam because, until this point, Shi'i Islam, unlike Sunni Islam, did not provide a theory for the administration of a polity.[2] Indeed some theologians argue that political administration is inimical to the role of the Shi'i ulema.[3]

In other words, the unusual fusion between Islamic principles and republican institutions has allowed a novel state form to cultivate its repressive and nonrepressive institutions, permitting greater control over the population. Yet by increasing its participatory republican elements, the state simultaneously gives rise to the language of individual rights and liberties.

While a rendering of past events permit us to explore a seemingly coherent picture of institutional authority, one of the more significant features of the postrevolutionary state is that, for years after the revolution, what the Islamic Republic was or would be was not clear to anyone. As one Iran scholar, Richard Cottam, observed of the Islamic Republic early on, "After several years of revolution, there is still no accepted developmental strategy for achieving this esoteric end" (Cottam 1986, 71).

In what follows, I introduce a discussion of the novel state, with specific attention to its discourse on women's status. Next, I explore the consequences this new state form has had not only for normalization and regulation of Iranians but also their subject formation—as rights-endowed individuals, despite the revolutionary discourse against individualism. Finally, I highlight some of the changes in this discourse during the presidency of Mohammad Khatami, noting the consequences for the state form, particularly the cultivation of its participatory elements.

THE "ISLAMIC REPUBLIC": COMPROMISE AND ENTERPRISE

In the years since its formation, the uncertainty that characterized the Islamic Republic has led to certain confusion. At times, this confusion has created struggles for power, has yielded to the participatory elements of the state, and has led to the reinstitution of infrastructure from the previous era, even as the religious elite attempted just the opposite.

The emergence of the state as an Islamic republic was drawn from Islamic and French republican principles in 1979. At that time, various revolutionary groups, who had come together to overthrow the monarchy, disagreed on the composition of the new government. Disparate factions, including nationalists and secularists, envisioned a power-sharing arrangement with the *ulema*. Nationalists and intellectuals who had joined the clerical ranks to overthrow the Shah argued for a democratic republic with multiple parties, as did Islamic reformists.[4] Ayatollah Khomeini and his supporters, however, were adamant that Islamic principles define the state; he even rejected the use of the word *democracy* in the name of the new state (Arjomand 1988). When an Islamist student group took over the U.S. Embassy on November 4, 1979, the shared power arrangement fell. Khomeini shored up his authority by exploiting the widespread anti-Americanism and associating it with other groups, especially the left. Khomeini secured ratification of several articles in the Constitution that granted extensive governmental powers to the highest Islamic authority in the state, the Guardianship of the Jurist (*Velayat-e Faqih*). The *Velayat-e Faqih* consists of a set of state institutions led by the leader (*Rahbar*) who is the *Vali-e Faqih*.

The result was a state formation that emphasized two main factors leading to the revolution: Islam and popular consensus. As an Islamic Republic, Iran has a constitution, which promises equal protection of the laws to citizens and offers universal suffrage.[5] The current republic consists of three branches: the executive, the legislative, and the judiciary. The administration of Iran's judiciary, however, departs from other republics in that in Iran this branch of government is supervised by the leader. Thus, Iran's republic has an overriding religio-legal power that is the highest authority on Islamic jurisprudence. All governance operates in accordance with the sacred laws of Islam as interpreted by this authority.

The contemporary expression of *Velayat-e Faqih* was proposed by Khomeini as an alternative to Iran's monarchy.[6] The theory was novel in Shi'i Islam because it rejected the long-standing principle of separation between political and religious life and delegated the authority of state leadership solely to qualified Islamic jurists. This new form of state power was authorized by the people through a referendum passed by 98 percent of the polity in 1979 and set the groundwork for debates about the role of Islam in governance. Its ratification was not the end of the discussion about the meaning of *Veylat-e Faqih* in governance, but the beginning.

Iran's current leader, Ayatollah Khamenei'i, has the final word on all questions that concern the state, particularly whether actions on behalf of the state conform to Islam and the goals of the Islamic revolution. The leader can make statements or issue legal opinions (fatwa, pl. fatavi) that enter into numerous domains of everyday life. Among his powers, the leader controls the military and selects the highest-ranking members of Iran's judiciary, its national security council, and state-owned radio and television. The position of the leader places a limit on popular governance because the elected president and parliament cannot easily check his power.

After thirty years, the Islamic Republic continues to take shape and is made legible for Iranians and outside observers through the actions of those who test its limits, its reach, its capacity, and its effects. The preceding discussion lays the foundation for understanding that the state's institutions provide spaces for Iranians to explore avenues for social, political, and legal expression. The dynamism of this seemingly austere religious state is significant.

FROM ISLAMIC GOVERNMENT TO ISLAMIC REPUBLIC

"The Glorious Koran and the Sunna contain all the laws and ordinances man needs in order to achieve happiness and the perfection of his state" (Khomeini 1981,17). One significant change Khomeini sought for his vision of a pure Islamic government was the dissolution of the legislative branch of government. There was no need for "man-made laws." Only God's law would matter (Khomeini 1981). In attempting to give Khomeini's vision a tangible form, the provisional government of the Islamic Republic repealed some legislation and accompanying legal codes in the early 1980s. Among these was the Family Protection Law of 1967 (rev. 1975), which gave women some legal rights in marriage dissolution and child custody. It was not just the substance of the law that Khomeini opposed, but also its form. Code law gave too much authority to state functionaries who were not qualified to act as exegetes of the sacred texts. Thus, one of his first acts as the *Vali-e Faqih* was to suspend this law and the civil courts it had created. The confusion over how to adjudicate the laws of God, however, caused such severe outcry that over time many similar laws were reinstated, but only after their conformity with Islamic principles was verified by the vetting branch of the Islamic Republic, the Council of Guardians. Legislative authority, too, was slowly reinstated; no longer could the legislature be a simple planning body as Khomeini has envisioned it (Khomeini 1981, 28). The esoteric aims of the Islamic state were in need of practical governing tools. The state needed bureaucratic arms to translate and implement Islamic principles into statutes and regulations to guide social, economic, and political life. This became most evident in the arenas of marriage and family and penal laws.[7]

Despite an anti-Western revolution that initially led to dissolving the legislative body, civil codes, and courts, the Islamic Republic has today reattained civil courts as a venue for adjudication and reinstated civil codes as the formal expression of the law through a legal hybridization. The civil laws have been authenticated by Islamic jurists. Such verification notwithstanding, civil codes, as the expression of a value system, have their own effects. Codification disrupts the historical power of Islamic jurists—who are not simply judges—to use a certain level of discretion in assessing the cases before them. These factors in the legal system have tangible consequences on rights and legal claims, and they came into being even after Khomeini had nullified and invalidated the code law. The legal blending also interrupted a conventional symmetry between the sharia and the state-administered law that had existed for many years. And, for the first time ever, codification gave the sharia unambiguous legal force.

A blended legal system grew through struggles to determine how to put into operation a new system consisting of Islamic principles and republican institutions and procedures. If the combining of sharia and civil law was a reflection of the compromises among these disparate groups, it was also an effect of the final outcome of the revolution: that the entity that came to fruition after the revolution was neither a pure expression of Islam nor a copy of the European state model, but something different.

Public debates about the relationship between Islamic principles, law, and contemporary concerns, such as gender equality and human rights, reveal dynamism in exegesis and offer at least the possibility of achieving practical solutions to current issues, even among the ulema. These debates are interesting not only because they illuminate the pragmatic possibilities within Islamic jurisprudence (*fiqh*) but for other reasons as well. First, implicit in the debates about current problems is the idea that sharia, while perhaps providing a basis for finding solutions, is not in practice a limited canon and allows for new developments consistent with a principle of public interest.[8] Second, the debates are increasingly carried out by laypersons, not only those trained in the specific methodologies of Shi'i explication.

An increase in scholarship by lay persons not trained in Islamic jurisprudence on issues such as women's legal rights and the role of women in Islamic societies evidences this point. Among the women I interviewed, publications such as the women's magazine *Zanan* guided their thinking on issues ranging from teenage runaways to women serving in parliament.[9] Given that a significant portion of the sharia guidelines deal with the relationships between individuals in familial matters, religious guidelines also played a crucial role in demarcating women's roles in the Islamic Republic. Because the personal status laws reemerged through a centralized legal system that draws from civil law both in its material form, as in codes, and in procedures, new implications about women's legal status and rights also emerged. Women's scriptural reading groups, which I attended during fieldwork in 1999–2000 and again during annual research trips between 2003 and 2010, were notably different from such gatherings prior to the revolution. Women in the postrevolutionary reading groups chose to read and interpret the sacred texts on their own, in Persian language versions, without a member of the *ulema* to guide them on the "correct" understandings. Instead, the women I interviewed told me that it was their duty to read and understand the Qur'an themselves and to be able to apply it to their lives in the present. This, one of the meeting's hosts told me, was a big difference with how they understood their religious obligations from before the revolution. During these meeting, moreover, the women invited experts on family law and psychology, as well as candidates running for public office, to enlighten them on current social concerns. Women discussed legal issues associated with marriage dissolution, child custody, and elections. Important in this context is the fact that the women understand that social changes would occur within a civil legal framework system.

Scholars who refer to sharia as "law" conflate a modern legal infrastructure with Shi'i principles and thus fail to consider the implications of this hybrid legal formation, particularly with regard to the impact of civil legal process and its relationship to subject making. Notwithstanding problems of implementation and enforcement, the significance of the hybrid legal system is at the juncture of Islamic principles and the republican state. Women's claims for improvements in their status are articulated through discursive practices premised on the autonomous individual endowed with rights, a discourse that was considered to be redolent of the Western-inspired individualism just after the revolution.

With the systematic codification of the Islamic law, the weight of the authority of the judge is now compromised by the law's own transparency and accessibility by anyone who can read, for the codification has also rendered the law in written form. Pocket-sized copies of legal codes covering areas of law anywhere from property to family law are readily available for mass consumption. They can be found in local bookstores, universities, and even sidewalk bazaars. Weber's oft-quoted notion of "qadi-justice," marking the absence of judicial formalism, is now undone by the rationalization of Islamic law through its codification based on civil legal formalism. Legal formalism offers avenues for lay people to assert their rights in an Islamico-civil legal framework. This is a postrevolutionary formalism with which a whole generation of Iran's population has grown up.

As we have seen in other societies, greater social individuation is a consequence that accompanies bureaucratization (Fitzpatrick 1992). In Iran, the bringing together of Islamic principles with republican ideals to create a blended state and legal system brings about a rationalization of the religious domains of life as well. In this way, even areas of religious life, which appear to be set apart from the rationalized politico-legal order, also bring about greater individualization.

Today, the increased social rationalization of the ritualized religious spaces has also led to recognition of women as autonomous subjects. Of course as long as they were properly attired in *hejab,* women were invited, even called upon, to participate in most every segment of society, including public office.[10] As a result, the *hejab* has become every bit a marker of the Islamic autonomous individual woman as it is the international symbol of Islamic piety and homogeneity. And it starts with the training of schoolgirls. As Adelkhah notes, at school, the ritual celebrations of girls' initiation into prayer at age nine stresses their independence (Adelkhah 2000, 120).[11] While state forces may have expected that greater daily engagements with Islamic values would push people to further integrate its teachings into their daily lives, the consequences of such engagement produced some inadvertent results.

In the end, Islamic principles were interpreted and given materiality through the framework of the republican state. As they were, they produced and reauthenticated liberal subjects in various segments of society. The institutions of the state comprise the tangible apparatus of everyday life and shape the patterns of practice of its citizens, even if the content of practice is premised on Islamic principles. The state institutions of a republic require or "hail" subjects as liberal actors, especially when they interact with those institutions (Althusser 1970).

One arena in which the apparatus of the state calls on subjects to inhabit or perform a liberal subjectivity is Iran's family courts. Here, even though the laws are presumably principles derived from the sharia, women and men, judges and adversarial parties alike, make rights claims premised on codified civil laws. The effects of the reinstitutionalization of civil law become apparent through the hybrid discourse about rights that exist today.

WOMEN AND THE POLITICIZATION OF RIGHTS

While the revolution is sometimes called "Islamic," this is a misnomer that leaves out an important component of the revolution: that secular nationalists joined religious groups to overthrow a monarchy and establish a representative government. What ultimately became an Islamic Republic was the result of a compromise whose effects continue today. Among those effects was the politicization of "rights talk." In March of 1979, activists by the tens of thousands flooded urban centers to protest the suspension of a Shah-era law, the Family Protection Law, which had given women some rights in marriage dissolution and child custody, and the issuance of directives, including mandatory veiling, which did happen, and revocation of suffrage, which did not. The protestors, who held up signs favoring "equality" and "women's rights," were dubbed Western puppets and attacked. The attacks showed the early fissures within the popular struggle to remove a monarch. It was also here that we began to see the association of a language of rights with Western excesses and a threat of imperialism. That threat was in part characterized as a cultural one in which Western individualism, with its self-referential and gender-neutral discourse of rights, undermined a healthy social order by destabilizing the family (Mutahhari 1981). Supporters of the new government singled out women's status for improvement because women were seen as the kernel of the family unit and, therefore, a healthy social order (Paidar 1995). The rehabilitation of women, thus, was a key discourse of the new state (Khomeini 1981).

Revolutionary discourse mobilized an image of Iranian woman as a foil to the "Western woman," who, as objectified, commodified, and hypersexualized, was unemancipated and oppressed. The 1983 Veiling Act was legislated in tandem with a discourse of rehabilitating the Iranian woman and restoring her to a place of respect. The chador[12] was symbolic not just of the renewed piety of the Iranian woman, but also of a collective shift depicted by women, on behalf of the country—a political shift toward an Islamic-nationalist vision of Iran that represented the triumph of the revolution over Western values so symbolized by the fall of the Pahlavi monarchy. Many are already familiar with this story, and it is not my aim simply to repeat it.

Instead, I consider the meaning of improving women's status symbolically and materially as a primary revolutionary aim. By placing women's issues in central focus, the resulting government could now be held accountable for promises to improve women's status and rehabilitate women (of course rightly or wrongly much of the criticism of this project to rehabilitate women, both outside and inside of Iran, has been the excess focus on the dress code).

Indeed soon after the Iranian revolution, scholars were noting that women's roles were changing—away from the status initially prescribed by the religious elite, as financially maintained mothers and wives. The scholarship and some journalistic essays on this topic reflected the material changes and conditions but, by and large, revealed them as a change in women's status brought on by new readings of the Islamic texts, even as Islamic feminism. Others would attribute the shifts in status to the successes women had achieved before the revolution.

Something else was also happening. A certain legal infrastructure was being put into place, one in which actors came before state institutions as individual rights-bearers to make legally prescribed appeals to the state. After the suspension of the Family Protection Law, laws guiding family relations and marriage dissolution favored males, but the family court allowed women a space to come before a judge to file a complaint for legal protection. I have argued elsewhere that because the discriminatory laws of the state delegate greater control and ownership over family matters to males, these laws, thus, require women to become legal actors in marriage dissolution, custody, and other family law issues (Osanloo 2006). As a result, women have become increasingly savvy civil actors who have not only learned how to make use of their none-too-explicit or broad civil and family rights but have, through necessity, paved the paths for reform.

For instance, despite the initial suspension of the Family Protection Law, women's rights activists in the postrevolutionary era have managed to reachieve the rights afforded in the earlier law and, in some cases, have gone beyond them. Important among these changes are payment of dower or bride price, the right to financial maintenance after the marriage, and an expanded notion of child custody. Activists achieved important changes in legal procedures and in material terms with regard to marriage dissolution, despite the official position that Islamic jurisprudence permits males a unilateral and unqualified right to dissolve a marriage.[13] This unilateral right of males to dissolve marriage has been reined in by numerous legal qualifications, including marriage counseling, payment of bride price or dower, mandatory arbitration, and provisions for postdissolution financial support, all of which were earlier deemed to be inimical to Islamic values and did not exist in the previous era. Most recently, the unilateral right of husbands to end a marriage has been further limited by the requirement for husbands to appear in court and show cause for dissolution, as well. In fact, women's rights activists have used the sharia to put into place legal processes that guarantee certain protections for women, who, as mothers and wives, have earned an elevated status under Iran's constitution. This is not to say that the discriminatory laws have been invalidated. Instead, on the one hand, the status of women as mothers and wives has provided them with a legal strategy to demand state protections, with a specific appeal to Islamic values. On the other hand, the civil legal infrastructure of the courts requires women to make claims as individual rights bearers, with reference to the civil laws.

In marriage dissolution, for example, while men's right to dissolve a marriage without cause has been codified in Article 1133 of the civil code of marriage and family, women still need to show cause. By being required to articulate a legal basis for dissolution, build a case, offer evidence, and state a claim in legal terms, women have been forced to have greater interaction with the civil legal system and its infrastructure of positive rights. Activists have managed to increase the number of stipulations that would trigger the court's review of a complaint filed by women. They have also attended to the legal education of women would-be plaintiffs and the judges presiding over these courts to make sure that rulings are executed. Activists alongside of women plaintiffs have worked with the legislative branch of government and the civil courts to build legal infrastructure necessary to carry out certain decisions. These include providing legal consequences to oblige husbands to respond to complaints and court summons. At the same time, they have successfully circumscribed men's ostensibly unilateral right of marriage dissolution with qualifications, such as payment of dower before dissolution and obligatory marriage counseling. This is not to suggest that increasing the rate of divorce in a country is a sign of achievement toward women's rights. There is, however, a suggestion that the discourse of protecting and elevating women's status since the revolution has taken a surprisingly civil and legal turn, spurred by the cultivation of civil legal instruments for helping women gain their "protected status" as the kernel of the family and basis of social order. This legalistic turn with its individualizing effects was one of the aims of the Khatami presidency.

KHATAMI ERA REFORMS AND "FAILURES"

There are a number of circumstances that come together to produce the conditions in which Iranians are again couching their claims in a legalistic discourse of rights and making calls on state institutions for civil liberties and equal protection of the law. One important circumstance is the memory of the eight-year war with Iraq. Another issue revolves around the roughly two-thirds of Iran's 70 million people who are below the age of thirty, with universal suffrage beginning at eighteen. The power of this group does not come from their numbers alone. The conservative ulema have more difficulty discrediting the rights talk of young people whose claims are based on constitutional promises legitimized by the religious authorities themselves. This is also why it is hardly surprising that today's most vocal critics of the Islamic government are themselves members of the ulema and former revolutionaries. Most importantly, however, it is the election of Mohammad Khatami that ushered in the changes in attitude and made state practices more legible to the population.

The features of this curious state system began to come into view more clearly after the 1997 election of Khatami to Iran's presidency because they showed both possibilities and limits but, more importantly, revealed the unfixed and changeable nature of the new governing institutions of the Islamic Republic. During the Khatami presidency, debates about the status of women and women's rights and human rights took shape through the religio-political tensions concerning the kind of governance, the forms of the institutions, and the integration and interpretation of Islamic principles (Osanloo 2009). This confluence between Islamic guidelines and republican forms allowed for new formations and articulations, of, among other issues, the position of women, women's rights, and human rights. New possibilities and alliances were made available at the conjuncture of Islamic values and republican institutions, and now it is this space that permits some Iranian people, women among them, to recast their arguments for redress or government entitlements in those same apparently liberal terms, when just after the revolution they could not. Of course the 2009 protests show us that this process is not a smooth one. But since the Khatami period, it has become more evident that disputes about rights must be understood through the conflicts engendered in the larger debates about the nature of governance and the place of Islamic guidelines in governing over the population. Because it was state actors who deployed women's status as a trope to advance the cause of the revolution, the status of women's rights later became real recourse for women to make claims on state officials and institutions.

This new state form, Islamic Republic, challenged contemporary notions of rights steeped in Western ideals with political and social entitlements vested in Lockean possessive individualism. The ulema appeared to base their conception of rights on their interpretations of the sharia, calling for clearly defined gender roles amid clearly delineated divisions between public (read social) and private (read familial) arenas of life, claiming these were the foundations for building a "true" Islamic society. Presumably, the ulema defined rights in gendered harmony with their obligations as revealed by God to the Prophet

(Qur'an) and the Prophet's example (Sunna) and spoke in terms of women's status or roles in society and family more so than in terms of individual rights.

The productive effects of the Islamic Republic challenged the ways of thinking about the state—as either a secular or theocratic formation—and were allowing new conceptions that ultimately resulted in new knowledge and ideas about social harmony. The circulating ideas play out and are even reconfigured in local contexts. The new combinations that are emerging ultimately require a rethinking of state models, their political and legal institutions, and their on-the-ground effects. Iran's complex political system combines elements of a modern Islamic theocracy with republican democracy. The system operates under a leader who is, in theory, appointed by an elected body but, in practice, answers to no one and is, of course, inspired by the divine scriptures, even if he is not divinely inspired. One key question, then, is how this system develops amid the ongoing struggles between reformists and hardliners. As the formation of the Islamic Republic is the result of compromises, the tensions that emerge result from those trade-offs, but the tensions also create spaces for dialogue and the development of an innovative religio-republic body politic. The struggles for democracy in Iran today are in large part due to the consciousness-raising that Khatami's presidency, even through its failures, engendered due to his emphasis on the rule of law and the lawmaking branch of government.

By the latter half of President Khatami's first term in office, his constituents still had not seen the promised improvements that caused them to vote for him. After the student riots in July 1999, some of the president's constituents began to recognize the limits on the republican state system through its Islamic branding, which until then had not been so apparent.

Relative relaxations of social restrictions accompanied a resurgence of public gatherings and are effects of the complex negotiations that social actors were undergoing with heterogeneous and disordered state actors.[14] The intended subjects of the Islamic Republic's disciplining initiatives can also push back against state powers, assert their own power, and indeed collaborate with statist projects. State disciplinary power has allowed for significant productions of knowledge from nonstate actors. Within new productions of knowledge, statist discourses of rights are always present, even insofar as they are discourses against which nonstate actors, including women, shape their visions of rights.

Attempts by conservative factions to discipline subjects failed, as state forces were met with rebelling students and protestors, some of whom were calling for reform through institutional processes, such as the electorate. The electoral process, however, was not the only means through which resistance incarnated productive action. A tide of newspapers and meetings held by intellectuals and religio-political scholars, as well as impromptu gatherings in homes or even the sex-segregated beauty salons and health clubs, were the sites in which ideas could be shared and exchanged. People were coming together in assorted meeting groups, newspapers, journals, internet cafes, coffee shops, and workplaces to discuss government forces and their effects on the liberties of individuals in urban, rural, and lower-, working-, and middle-class regions at this specific historical moment. Televisions were often tuned to governmental debates and news analyses. Thus Iranians' contemporary experiences emerge through a new legal and political moment as the Shi'i Islamic republican state comes into view. The conduct of Iran's ulema and its government officials takes place in the context of an ideological power play that has emerged in earnest since the election of President Khatami in 1997. Encouragement of greater participation in one site should be considered in tandem with attempts by conservative government factions to clamp down on meager social liberties afforded to some when Khatami came into office.[15]

Today, while we find Iranians again employing discourses of rights, such discourses increasingly carry with them grave consequences amid fraught and often volatile political situations. Indeed the effects of contemporary discourses of "regime change" that highlight women's and human rights in their aims are used by Iran's increasingly authoritarian leaders against what are, on the one hand, domestic, internal reform movements, such as the One Million Signatures Campaign, or, on the other, international calls for Iran to abide by treaties that it has signed and ratified, even post-1979, such as the Convention on the Rights of the Child. This is because as the attacks are framed increasingly in ideological terms; the response is to further determine and restrict the field of possibility for activists, one that is also ideological and binary, and thus not only occludes, but even shifts, the possibilities for advocacy. And thus we have seen a backlash against rights groups. Post–June 12, 2009, rights groups and again (as in 1979) the very discourse itself are being blamed by state forces for fomenting a velvet type of revolution. For instance, in the indictments issued against some key protestors, the prosecutor alleged that some of the accused engaged in human rights and women's rights activism. In the following academic year, 2009–2010, several universities cancelled the human rights master's degree and retired the women's studies major.

CONCLUSION

The tensions that exist in Iran do so at the intersection of two primary state ideologies: Islam and republicanism. The laws are a new cultural production to which I have referred as "Islamico-civil." Understanding how the laws operate helps us to better appreciate the basis of current tensions and possibilities within Iran. And it also leaves us with some new perhaps a bit strange results. On the one hand, women are at the vanguard of reform: there are more women attending university than men, and more women in the workforce occupy roles in higher governmental and administrative positions. Some of this, I have argued, has resulted from the discourse of improvement of the status of women as an important revolutionary aim but emerges from the form of state institutions, where, by some measure, women have been active in producing change, as in cases of marriage dissolution and child custody. To be more precise, I return to my initial interest, in the resilience of the state. The seeming lasting nature of the state in the face of teeming dissatisfaction rests in the small but not insignificant possibilities found in the institutions of the Islamic Republic; they are often procedural, located in the operations of law or government regulations, where legal challenges to state promises, such as improving women's lives, can be mounted.

What I hope to have demonstrated in this chapter is that the backlash to reformists, their rights talk, and these social movements for Islamic Republic reforms emerged well before the June 12, 2009, elections. The world, however, came to see the factors limiting reform in the government's violent crackdowns after the June 2009 elections. Criticisms of rights discourses have again emerged at the forefront of the threat that has now been rescripted from imperialism to "regime change" or "velvet revolution." The indictments against persons said to be active in fomenting the velvet revolution are substantiated through claims that such persons are involved in women's rights and human rights campaigns. The deeper issue is an increasingly violent battle over the nature of governance today: Islamic government (*hookoomat-e Islamic*) or Islamic Republic (*jomhuri-e Islami*). This exploration of how state institutions reemerge, adapt, and then rescript the possibilities for protest also gives us a sense of how this form of state, an Islamic Republic, seems to remain resilient while growing increasingly repressive.

7 WHO LAUGHS LAST
Literary Transformations of Syrian Authoritarianism

Max Weiss

IN AN INTERVIEW with the *Wall Street Journal* in late January 2011, Bashar al-Asad discussed a range of political, social, economic, and even intellectual issues confronting the Syrian regime. In response to questions about the abysmal pace of "reform" in Syria, Asad identified some "internal" political, economic, and administrative changes that were of particular interest. "These are the changes that we need," he said,

> But at the same time you have to upgrade the society and this does not mean to upgrade it technically by upgrading qualifications. It means to open up the minds . . . You cannot reform your society or institution without opening your mind. So the core issue is how to open the mind, the whole society, and this means everybody in society including everyone. I am not talking about the state or average or common people. I am talking about everybody; because when you close your mind as an official you cannot upgrade and vice versa.[1]

Bashar al-Asad and his advisors appear to have been reading the most current scholarly literature on authoritarianism. Although this cagy response does not directly tackle the persistence of more brutal techniques employed in perpetuating the status quo in Syria, Asad suggests how "successful" regimes must retain all practical options open, especially when their authority and legitimacy are called into question or even opposed by more forceful and committed means. Meanwhile, Syrian writers had also been concerned with opening their minds for decades, often simultaneously attempting to open the minds of their compatriots and leaders, although to relatively little avail.

In spite of the voluminous and rapidly expanding literature on the problem of authoritarianism in the contemporary Middle East, however, surprisingly little has been written on the connections linking authoritarianism with the cultural field. Scholarly work on the history, nature, and potential futures of authoritarianism remains mired in the morass of politics—parties, elections, the behavior of regimes and affiliated institutions, issues of governance and the rule of law, and, to a somewhat lesser extent, ideological transformation (Crystal 1994; Gandhi and Lust-Okar 2009; King 2009; Posusney and Angrist 2005; Pratt 2007). Many of those studies, of authoritarian politics and polities, are exceedingly valuable. Be that as it may, other scholars (Brownlee 2007; Schlumberger 2007) have begun to jettison such restrictive frameworks for understanding authoritarianism as merely the persistent absence of democracy, taking into account as well the particular yet various structures, practices, and discourses that authoritarian regimes both depend on and manipulate to endure.

In one of the most comprehensive studies of mid-twentieth-century Syrian authoritarianism, Steven Heydemann (1999) argues that the successful co-optation of compliance by various postindependence regimes in Syria hinged on the production and maintenance of certain corporatist "social pacts" between the state and the populace, mediated most notably by certain state and parastate institutions. A growing body of research offers insights into historical (Hinnebusch 1990; Perthes 1995) and ongoing contemporary developments in Syria (Abboud and Arslanian 2009; Büchs 2009; Ghadbian 2001, 2006; Heydemann 2007b; Hinnebusch and Schmidt 2009; Lawson 2009; Perthes 2004b; Pierret and Selvik 2009; and Sottimano and Selvik 2008)— from the accelerated pace of economic opening (*infitah*) to infrastructural modernization as well as the gradual transformation of the political system. To be sure, there are scholars of Syrian authoritarianism who have grappled with the implications of autocratic rule and corporatist social policy for the realm of culture. In her important "political ethnography of power" in late-twentieth-century Syria, Lisa Wedeen (1998) convincingly demonstrates how Syrian citizens regularly engaged in a politics of "as if," simultaneously appearing to comply with ideological hegemony while also critically engaging with politically sensitive topics in both public and private settings. Her analysis (Wedeen 1999) of jokes and films, everyday life, and state spectacle underlines how the "cult" of Hafiz al-Asad was perpetually in flux and, therefore, subject to subversion, inversion, or, at the very least, informal critique. Scholar Miriam Cooke (2007) looks at the ways in which "official" state culture and "dissident" cultures coexisted and cross-pollinated in 1990s Syria. She shows how the plastic arts, cinema, theater, and literature are interwoven and inter-dependent as well as how the cultural field in contemporary Syria is both reg-ulated by and filtered through the hegemonic ideology of the state.

But in the wake of Hafiz al-Asad's death in 2000 and the coming to power of his son Bashar, the relative liberalization of cultural life under the Syrian Ba'thist authoritarian state has not yet attracted as much attention as it de-serves. The Syrian scene was transformed—gradual financial liberalization; further economic integration into global trade networks; subterranean, yet tentatively noticeable, political-institutional change; and the Damascus Spring, which was soon and swiftly extirpated by the regime. The Syrian regime proved exceptionally adept at managing, muffling, and ultimately absorbing political and social as well as cultural challenges. The passing of ten years since the transfer of power to Bashar has already occasioned a range of perspectives on the transformation of Syrian society and culture, on Syrian history in the mak-ing. This is an exceedingly opportune moment, therefore, to take stock of the variety of social, political, and cultural transformations the Syria has under-gone over the past decade but also to start interrogating the discursive, insti-tutional, and material ways in which the regime engages in both the politics of legitimacy and the practices of legitimation. If the political, institutional, and military foundations of authoritarianism contribute to the creative production of certain cultural formations, it should also be emphasized that those cultural worlds are invented, sustained, and nurtured under and through authoritarian circumstances but also, perhaps even more importantly, curtailed by coercive processes of state control, surveillance and repression.[2]

Critical studies of Spanish and Brazilian authoritarianism (Baden 1999; Ilie 1980; Johnson and Vieira 1989; and Martín-Estudillo and Ampuero 2008), for example, have innovated the notion of "inner exile" as one way to make sense of how writers continue living, working, and even thriving under au-thoritarian conditions. *Inner exile* refers to a state in which an author, intel-lectual, or critic both remains somehow within or inside the regime while simultaneously experiencing abject alienation from the system, often conse-quently finding him- or herself unable to engage in any meaningful political, social, or cultural activity. Such an optic of analysis has the advantage of clari-fying from among more radical forms of alienation, separation, or repression; that is, arbitrary rule, imprisonment, torture, and the like can more precisely be distinguished from, say, physical exile or "geographical relocation," or what might be termed landscapes of interior exilic identity. There are certainly Syrian writers who would recognize something of their own experience in terms of such sustained periods of "inner exile."

But a great deal of creative work and cultural production coming out of Syria is condemned to literally live in exile as well, whether as a consequence of being officially banned or simply poorly circulated at home. Meanwhile, structural obstacles to crafting ideas, writing, and publishing inside Syria are often surmounted through the forging of regional and international connections, and, perhaps most importantly, by exporting "Syrian culture" abroad. Building on one Syrian woman writer's claim in the mid-1990s that "our literature never leaves the country," Cooke (2007, 40–41) argues that foreign ignorance of Syrian culture has resulted in the cynical perspective "that Syrian literature is all the same, just one nightmare response to undifferentiated oppression. Such an attitude implied that it is all cathartic, not worth studying." It is no doubt the case that the volume of Syrian literature translated into European languages continues to lag behind even the admittedly dismal cases of Egypt or Lebanon. Be that as it may, any list of the most conspicuous and remarkable processes currently affecting Syrian writers would have to include both growing global interest in Syrian literature and the latter's halting but gradual internationalization. An adequate analysis of both literary and nonliterary responses to the highly differentiated ideological and political field of authoritarian rule in Syria would require deeper engagement with a broader range of material on the part of literary critics and social scientists, a task that remains incomplete.

The Syrian regime has practiced a kind of benign neglect, or at least adhered to a relatively laissez-faire position, vis-à-vis novelists and other writers in recent years, which might be attributed to the minor and marginal role literature plays in contemporary Syria. Without ranging too far into the reception history of literary works in late-twentieth and early-twenty-first century Syria, it is sufficient to point out that Syrian novelists at this particular historical conjuncture must directly confront both endemic structural obstacles to their literary endeavors and sizable aesthetic challenges presented by the dogged persistence of authoritarian rule. The remainder of this chapter will offer some preliminary reflections on the contemporary state of novel writing in Syria as it relates to the persistence of authoritarian rule, focusing in particular on two novels that raise critical questions and exemplify the limits of such critiques for challenging the ideological and political hegemony of the regime. Before turning to those works, however, I will first describe some of the necessary literary historical background for these more recent developments.

A NEW SYRIAN LITERATURE?

In a sense, the aesthetic and political challenges confronting Syrian intellectuals remain similar to those faced by previous generations of writers. Over the past decade or so, however, Syrian literary writing has undergone a period of creative efflorescence amid the gradual shift toward cultural liberalization. Nevertheless, structures of censorship and repression remain well in place; writing under such authoritarian conditions remains dangerous, to say the least. Article 1 of the General Law of Printed Matter (1949), which is still in force, established that "presses, bookshops and publications of all kinds are free and nothing limits their freedom except this law" (cited in Saqr 1998, 17). The Arab Writers' Union—a state-subsidized institution established in 1969—and other less public agencies, including the Regional Command of the Ba'th Party (*al-qiyada al-qutriyya*), are responsible for regulating the publication and sale of printed materials in Syria. Although Article 38 of the Syrian constitution protects the "right" of every "citizen" to "express his opinion freely and publicly in speech and writing and every other means of expression," Article 24.2 prescribes state protection for the "rights of authors and inventors who serve the interests of the people." The ambiguity of this phrasing introduces substantial potential for arbitrary state and parastate interference into matters of individual or collective speech. Many Syrian writers will sidestep local problems of literary production, circulation, and consumption by simply publishing their work abroad, typically in Beirut and increasingly with one of two publishers: Dar al-Adab or Riyad el-Rayyes. Intriguingly, the Syrian regime under Bashar al-Asad does not generally seem inclined to retaliate against writers who publish highly critical or controversial works but, rather, permits them to proceed, although their works may be officially banned. Instead, and particularly following the clampdown in the wake of the so-called Damascus Spring of 2001 and even more tragically since the Syrian uprising of 2011, the regime tightens the screws on political dissidents and human rights activists much more than it monitors or prosecutes novelists.

Whereas there had been a certain amount of formal and generic consistency covering the landscape of late-twentieth-century Syrian writing (historical novels and socialist realism were mainstays), scholars (Chehayed and Toelle 2001; Firat 2010; Halwani 1998; Meyer 2001; Vauthier 2007; and Wattar 2000) have helped to show how contemporary Syrian literary culture is increasingly characterized by striking diversity in terms of content, orientation, technique, and formal styles of expression. Be that as it may, an adequate critical reading of recent novels would have to be contextualized in light of longer-term transformations in Syrian literary culture and intellectual life. Syrian writers experimented with the novel as a literary genre as early as the first half of the twentieth century. Syrian intellectuals such as Faris al-Zarzur, Walid Ikhlasi, 'Abd al-Salam al-'Ujayli, Hani al-Rahib, Nabil Sulayman, Khayri al-Dhahabi, and others would go on to pioneer the Syrian novel form. Mid- to late-twentieth-century Syrian writing evinced a particular focus on the alienated condition of the intellectual; the fundamental transformations in society and economy spanning industrialization, urbanization, and rural–urban migration; the spread and radicalization of various ideologies; changing mores in Syrian society; and the ethics of political commitment and engagement. Among the scant extant scholarship that deals with literature in contemporary Syria, most of it focuses on the "generation of the sixties," on prison literature and commitment literature, the rise and fall of Arab nationalism, and the broader renovation of Arab intellectual culture in the wake of the 1967 war.

If 1967 was the touchstone for late-twentieth-century Arabic culture writ large, however, Syrian intellectuals, particularly novelists, were also deeply influenced by—and ultimately lashed to—the events and repercussions the Ba'thist coup and the so-called corrective moment that brought Hafiz al-Asad to power, respectively. The complex interplay of the Ba'thist state, which may be considered "fierce" without necessarily being "strong," with Syrian society—ranging from deep engagement to co-optation and even open armed conflict—has structured the conditions of possibility for fictional and nonfictional writing in Syria. Considering the substantial constraints on intellectual life in Syria under Hafiz al-Asad, which had often been perceived as a kind of evisceration of society and culture, it is remarkable to witness Syrian literary culture tentatively emerging from out of the shadows and hesitantly stepping into the limelight. Perhaps in response to the apparently growing global interest in the Arabic novel, some critics may have been too hasty in identifying something altogether new emerging in Syrian literary culture. Heightened interest in Syrian culture might ultimately redound to the deepening integration of Syrian intellectuals into the international literary scene. Be that as it may, literary critics should exercise some caution in examining and analyzing more recent novels in light of the fact that there has been some dispute regarding the extent to which there is something categorically new happening in the Syrian novel (Hamza 2009; Qaddur 2009).[3]

Nearly a decade ago, even as Syrian culture and society started to grapple with the implications of hereditary succession, novelist and literary critic

Mohja Kahf (2001) argued that state crackdowns on the Muslim Brotherhood and its allies in Hama and elsewhere, in addition to the low-intensity warfare conducted by the regime against its own people throughout the 1970s and 1980s, constituted a blind spot in Syrian cultural memory. Over the next ten years, there was indeed a steady trickle, if not a veritable torrent, of controversial novels and other writings that deal directly with those themes, which rendered Kahf's judgment both incredibly prescient and seemingly obsolete.

One recent novel to stir up this debate in both Syrian and global settings is *In Praise of Hatred* (*Madih al-Karahiyya*) by Khaled Khalifa (2008), which tackles head-on the matter of state repression of Islamism in Syria. In the novel, a young woman from Aleppo, which metonymically appears to stand in for Hama and all those places where opposition to Ba'thist rule in Syria was concentrated during this period of armed insurrection (if not full-blown civil war), finds her way into a radical Islamist milieu before going through a process of transformation in prison that leads her to espouse liberalism, tolerance, and, in somewhat stilted language, a rejection of all kinds of hatred. The protagonist acquires embittering and enlightening experiences in women's prison, which ultimately denude her of any Islamist tendencies, leaving her reformed and reconstituted. Although some readers have criticized this dimension, the novel boasts an international cast of characters who take part in a drama of nearly cinematic scope that extends beyond Syria to the United Kingdom, Afghanistan, and beyond. *In Praise of Hatred* acquired some notoriety for having been banned in Syria and getting short-listed for the Annual Prize for Arab Fiction, otherwise known as the "Arabic Booker" (Worth 2008). Novelist and literary critic 'Umar Qaddur (2009) insisted that the splash made by *Madih al-Karahiyya* and other such controversial novels had less to do with their content or with a new phase in Syrian cultural production than with the exigencies of the media, celebrity, and international politics. Whether or not one should identify a "new" Syrian novel emerging, literature remained a venue for the discussion of ideas that were rarely discussed in the open.

AUTHORITARIAN TRANSFORMATIONS

Any assessment of the limitations that continue to restrict Syrian writers needs to be separated from the overblown case that has been made previously about the totalitarian nature of social control and political repression in early-twenty-first-century Syria. Official state cultural policy hardly resembles a coherent or systematically applied set of principles. As many people in Syria are quick to point out, the official organs of the cultural establishment employ no consistent or discernible strategy. Many writers decry the utter bankruptcy and moribund state of "official culture," occasionally going so far as to rue the loss of any meaningful public culture in Syria altogether, which they understand as one direct consequence of the demand for intellectual conformity in consonance with Ba'thist principles. Indeed, much as the political realm is governed by a logic of irrationality, arbitrary detention, arrest, and disappearing that might be triggered by a simple personal dispute or indicate a broader attempt to spread fear and dissension within the Syrian body social (to say nothing of the dramatic events still unfolding in Syria as of this writing in October 2011), the Syrian *Kulturkampf* also relies on policies that might be ironically described as "creative destruction." The Syrian regime remains as keen on promoting itself as a cultural vanguard as it does in the sphere of politics and economy.

Contemporary novels confront the obfuscation, the arbitrariness, and the sheer violence of the regime—of Syrian life more generally, perhaps—through a range of literary devices, ranging from avoidance and detachment to plain talk, discursive intellectualizing, irony, and occasionally even droll humor. In addition, Syrian literature in the twentieth and early twenty-first centuries has been characterized by a pronounced dialectic that both joins and polarizes realism and allegory. Meanwhile, a number of recent Syrian novels follow plots that revolve around themes of conspiracy and state control, and they ultimately purport to pierce the veil of ideology and obscurity that surrounds the practice of politics, which in recent years has come to be described as the functioning of a "*mukhābarāt* state." The Lebanese poet and critic Abbas Beydoun (2009) identifies the emergence of a "*mukhābarāt* novel" in Arabic literary culture, a novel in which the security apparatus (*al-mukhābarāt*) may play an integral part in the setting, plot, and characterization. In the Syrian case, according to Beydoun, the narrative "becomes a quasi-police novel but without the structure, techniques or formula of a police novel."

Syrian writers have certainly taken risks before by critically engaging with themes or tropes of politics in fiction. But more recent writing extends that criticism of arbitrary arrest, detention, torture, and the general climate of fear in the country into new territory. The novels examined in this essay—*The Silence and the Roar* by Nihad Sirees and *The Treasonous Translator* and *Solo Piano Music* by Fawwaz Haddad—openly engage with the problem of authoritarianism in multiple, complicated ways. Beyond the dynamic dialectic established between mimesis—the visceral depiction of reality—and allegory—simplified moral judgments of an existential condition—do these novels open up a space for interrogating the place and the politics of humor and laughter, of silence and sound, of repression and freedom in contemporary Syrian fiction? To be sure, such broader philosophical or political engagements with the concepts and practices of freedom remain more or less sequestered within the realms of prose, poetry, and human rights discourse, all of which remain subject to the capricious regime of censorship that remains firmly in place. The greater irony, though, may reside in the fact that these novels wind up at common sorts of existential conundrums: how one can or ought to revive moral agency under conditions in which it has been evacuated from the modern Syrian subject. In response, some of the burning questions for writers (and their readers) might (have to) become: who gets to have the last laugh? And how, when, or why does one get to do so?

PULLING BACK THE CURTAIN:
FAWWAZ HADDAD'S *SOLO PIANO MUSIC*

Fawwaz Haddad was born in Damascus in 1947 and studied law at Damascus University before going to work for many years in the private sector. Although he always maintained a personal interest in writing fiction, for a long time he had no public profile, and he didn't publish his first novel until 1991. His early writings consisted primarily of historical fiction, evoking an exceptionally rich attention to Damascene urban detail. His *The Treasonous Translator* (*al-Mutarjim al-khā'in*) was short-listed for the Arabic Booker in 2009, and his more recent *God's Soldiers* (*Junūd Allah*) was long-listed for the prize in 2011.[4] In more recent novels, his work has sharply veered toward a kind of hard-boiled realism. Mainly solitary male figures, Haddad's protagonists get swept up in unexpected tales of intrigue and deception. The plot is ultimately revealed at the end to convey some sort of moral or to call into question some piece of news or history.

Such is the case in *The Treasonous Translator* (Haddad 2008), in which the protagonist Hamid Salim is an aspiring intellectual whom the reader first encounters just after he has published an Arabic translation of an African novel originally written in English. His translation ends with a slight twist; Hamid has modified the ending to suit his particular ideological taste.[5] When Sharif Husni, a towering local cultural figure, gets wind of this, he tries to expose Hamid and ruin his career before it can even start. Consequently, Hamid is battered by the cultural establishment and soon finds his life to be endangered by unseen forces. As a result, Hamid retreats into a series of assumed identities—taking on no less than three different pseudonyms—to continue writing without being identified. Along the way, even as he dissolves himself (and his identity) into this string of pseudonyms and fake lives, Hamid finds his reputation increasingly impugned and his life at greater and greater risk. Despite the relative freedom with which Haddad and his characters pontificate on matters of profound intellectual, philosophical, and cultural significance, the setting for all his novels is bathed in an icy solution of liquid fear. In the end, though, and in spite of an almost laughably formulaic moment of potential vengeance or revenge on his previous tormentors, Hamid chooses the way of moderation, forgiveness, and, ultimately, social peace. I prefer to conceive of the novel in terms of "treason" rather than "treachery" or "traitorousness" for both the term's connection with the classical double entendre of "traduttore, traditore" ("translator, traitor") and also for its semantic connections with notions of betrayal and, in particular, sedition or betrayal of country. The act of translation—simultaneously the professional identity of the novel's protagonist as well as Fawwaz Haddad's structural role within the global political economy of writing and publishing—is always already suspect in the eyes of the gatekeepers of the nation and their conception of national security and is regularly subjected to scrutiny and misunderstanding, if not outright affront.

In a conversation I had with him about a wide range of literary, cultural, and political issues in October 2009, Haddad claimed that he can talk about more or less anything he chooses, that he can write about anything he likes in his novels, and that the novel form can be populated with whatever events, characters, and stories he desires. Perhaps unsurprisingly, given the relatively limited range of personal freedoms in contemporary Syria, Haddad even went so far as to say that he is freer inside the novel than he is outside of it. Curiously, though, when I pressed him on whether he was any freer than other citizens because of this ability to imagine, invent, and inhabit stories, he demurred, saying that he considered himself less free for being confronted by certain boundaries as a writer and public intellectual. Be that as it may, he repeatedly indicated how his writing and his novels have allowed him (perhaps even obliged him) to exceed the limitations of the culture he lives within, to walk back and forth, as he put it, across a red line until it no longer appears to be red.[6]

These themes crop up again in Haddad's following novel, *Solo Piano Music* (*'Azf munfarid 'ala al-biyanu*) (Haddad 2009), the tale of Fateh al-Qalaj, an unsuspecting secular intellectual who gets mugged in the stairwell of his own apartment building by an unknown assailant in the opening scene.[7] Saleem, the street name for a savvy young investigator from the so-called terrorism affairs bureau, begins to piece together the case, discovering along the way certain inconsistencies in Fateh's public secularist identity even as Fateh comes to believe that he is being targeted for his outspoken views on, among other things, religion and the separation of mosque and state. Saleem soon discovers that Fateh had gone through a brief period in which he was a practicing believer, precisely at the moment in which his wife was in the hospital suffering from a terminal illness. In the wake of her death, Fateh increasingly turned to rely on his wife's old friend, Haifa, whose character and personality remain relatively undeveloped and who more or less functions as a source of comfort and guidance for Fateh.

Fateh and his controversial rhetoric acquire even greater significance both in the public view and in the perspective of the state authorities, amid ongoing negotiations between the government and representatives of Islamist forces found inside the country and abroad. After one relatively inflammatory public lecture—provocatively entitled "A School without Religion, a School without Sex"—Fateh begins to receive anonymous threats, becoming even more disconcerted when he learns that there are now larger organizations than the terrorism affairs bureau involved, including an International Agency for Combating Terrorism; protection from this agency, which can be provided by the local terrorism affairs bureau, appears to be his only hope for survival. His fear starts to become irrational and overtakes him even as he accepts this offer for protection from Saleem. Fateh lays out for Haifa some of his concerns, which seem anything but outlandish to him at the time: "A man overtaken by the idea of killing me as a means of getting closer to God, who has no connection to any Islamist organization or movement, who doesn't have any need of funding or matériel, who needs nothing more than a simple metal implement, a kitchen knife for example. If one isn't available he'd tear me to shreds with his fingernails and his teeth" (Haddad 2009, 199). After all, the narrator goes on, speculating on behalf of Fateh, "If the state itself isn't concerned with its own reputation, why would it be concerned with his?" (Haddad 2009, 200). Here is one instance of Fateh seeking to distance himself from both the regime and the Islamist opposition, which is, perhaps, how Fawwaz Haddad accomplishes something quite similar.

Meanwhile, Fateh has become reacquainted with an old childhood friend who is deeply religious and appears to be mixed up with illegal Islamist political activities. By the end of the novel, the pas de deux between "the investigator" and "the secularist"—as those two characters are often rendered generic—turns out to be mirrored by a similarly shadowy relationship between "the secularist" and "the fundamentalist." Fateh confides his incredulousness in this old friend at the fact that he might be at the center of such high-stakes political intrigue, involving the regime, the Islamists, international agencies:

> "What have I got to do with what you're talking about?!"
> "It's the script you're living in."
> Noticing that he was serious, Fateh shouted back at him: "You must be joking."
> He wasn't joking.
> "Know then, that the international secret apparatus for combating terror-ism is behind everything from beginning to end."
> Oh my God . . . if he knows about the international apparatus, he must know everything!! (Haddad 2009, 253)

Haddad employs free indirect style here as in much of his writing, shifting back and forth between third-person omniscient narration and internal con-sciousness. This passage also indexes the recurring theme to which Fateh repeatedly returns, namely that he is locked into some movielike script that reinforces a certain sense of ineluctable fate but also activates his feeling of paranoia. There is a hint of irony here that might be interpreted as poking fun at the extent to which conspiracy theory rules the day in so much Syrian political discourse, although Fateh's general state paranoia is more or less nor-malized if not explicitly confirmed through the course of the novel.

In a jarring and violent conclusion, the regime successfully stamps out what it had labeled and perceived to be a terrorist threat, with Fateh the secularist/ ex-secularist figure literally caught in the crossfire; in the end he is left speech-less, absolutely dumbfounded. Moreover, Fateh is left with a vague sense of shame and remorse for having been played, but he resignedly accepts (not only) his difficult situation—unending conflict and contestation between the regime and its opponents. There is no clear or easily discernible moral mes-sage. Regardless of whether the international agency for combating terror-ism is to blame, whether the Islamists whom Fateh knows personally or those whom he has never met deserve such a brutal fate, whether Saleem even works for the Syrian government, or whether the two agencies are working hand-in-glove, Fateh can do no more than come to the cynically apathetic conclusion that there is little difference between truth and its absence, between good and evil, affirming in this way that all conflicts are futile, and, in the end, that one can only but learn to rely on oneself. In some ways, the total atomization of

Syrian society is fully accomplished here despite, or perhaps even as a result of, Fateh's unsuccessful attempts to claw his way to the truth.

The novel ends without passing judgment on either the regime or the Islamists, perhaps suggesting the impossibility of distributive justice in contemporary Syria. In *Solo Piano Music* the climax signifies an almost inevitable moment of regime violence. But the individual experience of authoritarianism here entails not only the state. Impersonal forces not always traceable to particular individuals or local institutions weigh heavily on the lives and fates of these characters; generalized fear is an everyday reality. Danger, violence, and repression might come from anywhere, from next door, from a casual acquaintance, from an old friend. More often than not, they originate with individuals who have ties to the system or from unknown shadowy figures inhabiting the shady underworld of spies, secret agents, and international intrigue. Agents of the *mukhabarat* and the state end up looking like, at worst, nefarious manipulators, or, at best, bumbling yet well-intentioned functionaries caught up in an impersonal apparatus or regime. Be that as it may, characters in Haddad's novels are tragic and alienated, and they wield precious little power. Social relationships are confused, obscured behind a veil of uncertainty and relative anxiety. But unlike traditional police procedurals or crime novels, Haddad's more recent hard-boiled novels don't fully resolve in any cut-and-dried manner; they seem to end with no small measure of apathy or despair rather than a call to action or a clear didactic message. The curtain may be pulled back, but there is no wizard to be found.

POKING FUN AT THE PARTY:
NIHAD SIREES'S *THE SILENCE AND THE ROAR*

The gradual transformation of Syrian authoritarian culture has allowed for the emergence and coalescence of literary forms that take greater liberties in criticizing the regime through the use of irony and occasionally explicit humorous styles. Given the rich history of irony, obfuscation, and dissimulation in Syrian political culture and cultural politics over the past forty years, it would be instructive to analyze and critique the ways in which humor has been put to certain uses in the Syrian novel, a task that extends far beyond the scope of this paper. Syrian writing has often been identified with socialist realism, ideological conformity, and humorless seriousness. I would therefore like to conclude this essay by considering how a certain sense of playfulness expressed in one recent novel produces an entirely different perspective on the Syrian regime and potentially would have very different effects in terms of conceptualizing and actually living relationships to it on the part of Syrian intellectuals.

In contradistinction to the placid veneer and literary formality of *Solo Piano Music*, and certainly in more explicit terms than the jokes, comedic narratives, and film plots described by Wedeen and others, an altogether different tone of allegorical moralizing can be found in *al-Samt wa-l-sakhab* (*The Silence and the Roar*), undoubtedly the most politically charged novel to date by Nihad Sirees. Sirees was born in Aleppo in 1950 and, like many of his generation, traveled abroad to study civil engineering, eventually going on to earn a master's degree in 1976. Although he continues working part-time as a licensed engineer, Sirees has also written successful television serials, including the commercially successful *Thuraya*, as well as plays, children's drama, and historical novels set in Aleppo, such as *Khan al-Harir* and *Riyah al-Shamal 1917*. In an earlier novel, *al-Kumidiya al-fallahiyya* (*The Peasant Comedy*) (Sirees 1996), Sirees tackled taboo topics in Syrian society, history, and culture head-on, lampooning how tribal and ethnic groups from northeastern Syria encountered "national" life in the big city. At the same time, this biting satire of a world turned upside down as a trickling migration of villagers and nomads from the Jazeera region to Aleppo became a flood shows his willingness to subvert another powerful myth in twentieth-century Syrian politics and history, namely the seamless substitution of the urban(e) for the rural through rural–urban migration. Conversely, one might read into this critique a subtler dig against the dispersal of Party officials and bureaucrats—some of whom still had little to no technical expertise on such matters—out into the countryside both to promote developmentalist aims of the state and also to command loyalty to the ruling ideology of the Party. So just as intellectuals and politically connected figures were literally farmed out to the rural regions to promote Ba'thist-style agricultural modernization, an unprecedented and unanticipated deluge of rural–urban migrants also ensued, which provided the fodder for Sirees's savvy social criticism.[8]

The Silence and the Roar (Sirees 2004) takes a more universal predicament as its object, confronting directly, if allegorically, the problem of the individual in a society dominated and disciplined by a dictator, a repressive state apparatus, and "The Party."[9] The time frame of the novel is one twenty-four-hour period, in an unnamed Arab city that bears a striking resemblance to Sirees's native Aleppo, on a day in which yet another state-sponsored march is being held. This first-person narrative is related from the perspective of Fathi Sheen, a hapless writer and intellectual who is unemployed and generally down on his luck after unwisely deciding to cross the dictates of the cultural establishment, much like Hamid Salim in *The Treacherous Translator* but with no more dire consequences than Fathi's apparent consignment to oblivion and social death. Following a brief run-in at the march with security goons whom Fathi tries to fight off a young man they are arbitrarily beating up, the agents proceed to confiscate his ID and inform him that he must now pay a visit to *mukhābarāt* headquarters to pick it up.

Meanwhile, Fathi has been involved with a woman named Lama, whom he has continued seeing but has failed to marry, for both personal and financial reasons. Perhaps adding insult to injury, Fathi's widowed mother is romantically pursued by the nefarious Party functionary Ha'el 'Ali Hassan, a man who owes his meteoric rise to power to a single stroke of dumb luck; at a public event in the small, remote town where he once lived, Ha'el instinctively reached out his hands to prevent "the Leader" from falling, earning his place as part of the intimate coterie of advisers surrounding the dictator. But Ha'el 'Ali Hassan has an ulterior motive for marrying Fathi's mother, which is to bring Fathi back inside the ideological fold, to convince him to start writing once again in the service of the regime. Moreover, this metanarrative of intellectual co-optation by the regime—the literal union of the regime man with his mother—is reinforced further still by the parallel story of Fathi seeking to reclaim his ID, his very physical identity, from the *mukhabarat*. Amid the clamorous noise all around him in the city on this demonstration day, and throughout the persistent uncertainty surrounding his life, Fathi must determine both the practical matter of how best to recover his ID—again, in perhaps a relatively simplistic reference to how personal identities are stolen by the regime—and the thornier existential matter of whether it would be better for him to collaborate or resist, compounded by the emotional strain of what to do about his mother's prospective relationship with Mr. Ha'el.

The silence and the roar of the title index Fathi's extreme sensitivity to sound. The roar (*ṣakhab*) schematically stands in for the incoherent blathering of an authoritarian regime with little to no credibility in the eyes of its citizenry. Indeed, some of the most beautiful passages have to do with the ways in which Fathi conceives of both the deeply personal but also potentially political nature of sound itself: "I wished that all the man-made sounds would fall silent, leaving only the soft sounds of nature, like those made by the breeze when it blows through trees with hardy dusty leaves" (Sirees 2004: 156). But Fathi is not simply a radical pastoralist. "I'm not talking about absolute silence," he continues:

That's impossible anyway, and I'm not asking for it. What I mean though is the silence that allows for those gentle sounds that are all around us to actually reach our ears. Noise prevents them from doing so; it kills them . . . I was imagining how many beautiful and tender sounds are lost to us because of the noise made by our noble politicians, their vehicles and their ways of exporting the revolution . . . The most beautiful thing in the entire universe is the silence that allows us to hear soft and distant sounds. (Sirees 2004, 156–157)

In the end, the dialectic between silence and roar comes to represent the binary logic through which the regime frames the world. Silence becomes a politicized habit, as Lama reminds Fathi in one of their discussions regarding the ethics of his option to write on behalf of the regime. Although silence is not always an expedient choice when one's life is at stake, Fathi manages to find the space to valorize silence—at least theoretically—as a virtue. Moreover, Fathi resents the fact that Ha'el Ali Hassan has forced him to choose between "the silence of prison" and the "roar of the regime"; in response he is admonished to be careful, lest he find himself confronted with "the silence of the grave." In the end, Fathi subverts this false choice between the silence and the roar by embracing (and perhaps unwittingly fetishizing) laughter.

The liberal use of irony and other forms of humorous discourse stands out among the range of tactics and techniques available to critics and opponents of autocratic regimes. Both Fawwaz Haddad and Nihad Sirees use slightly different kinds of humor to poke fun at the Party, and yet, interestingly, both ascribe similar political and cultural valences to the distinction between prose and poetry, essentially valorizing the former over the latter as one means of underlining the intellectual and moral bankruptcy of the Party. In *The Treasonous Translator,* Hamid Saleem is convinced that the well-known writer Sharif Husni is making both real and rhetorical attacks against him. While trying to come up with a strategy to defend himself, he bumps into a journalist who writes about economics for the same paper where Husni works, who tells Hamid all about how Husni is responsible for having sent other people to jail and that the same fate could very well await him:

"Is [Husni] the one who sent him there?"
"Who else? He wrote a report to the *mukhābarāt* in which he accused him of writing stories filled with antigovernment and anti-Party references. Tell me, who would dare to ask about this, the Writer's Union, his friends, his family?!"
"The Party wouldn't allow that to happen."

"What do you know about what the Party would or wouldn't allow?"

"Don't tell me Party members don't read."

"The Party is mad about poetry, at certain times, on nationalist occasions. But they don't like literature, and if they read it, it's only in order to ban it." (Haddad 2008, 41)

Beyond an unrestrained jab at the absolute arbitrariness of the Party and its censorship regime, here is a critique of the ideological uses of poetry that strongly resonates with several moments in *Silence*. In a moment of foreshadowing, Fathi muses about the relationship between poetry and prose:

... we are a people that loves poetry, to the point that we love anything that even resembles poetry. We might even be satisfied with some occasionally rhyming speech, regardless of its content . . . Prose is oriented toward rational minds and individuals whereas poetry is directed at and directs the masses . . . Poetry inspires zealotry and melts away individual personality whereas prose molds the rational mind and individuality and personality . . . As for my works and prose writings, they are the imaginations of a traitor and a motherfucker, as the man in khaki was kind enough to remind me a little while ago. (Sirees 2004, 17)

Rather than portraying poetry, say, as the cultural patrimony of the Syrian citizenry, the Arab nation or the Muslim *umma*, both Haddad and Sirees take an ironic stance toward its production and circulation.

This point about the mechanics of poetry turns farcical when, at another point in *Silence*, an entire institutional apparatus is literally "discovered" beneath the Party headquarters, where poetry is instrumentalized in the service of state power, as an industrious underground hive of cultural workers slave away at sloganeering for the commemoration and reinforcement of Party authority, hegemony, and legitimation. One of those workers hopes that Fathi will join them in their endeavors, but Fathi, like many other protagonists in contemporary Syrian fiction, prefers to stay on the margins, out of the limelight, to observe the world around him and, in the process, to open a window for the reader onto some of the more absurd dimensions of these fictionalized Syrian landscapes. In their exchange, Fathi asks:

"But, I mean, who comes up with the sayings and the slogans that you put on the posters?"

Pointing toward another room, he said: "There's a special team whose members are specialists in psychology and education. Comrades, intellectuals and poets who work twelve hours a day coming up with slogans or writing poetry for the masses to recite at marches that are then printed on posters or published in the media and online."

"That is very special work."

"Indeed, it's tremendous educational and emotional labor as well, because the matter involves affection, that is, affection the masses have for the Leader. It's never easy work . . . The best poems and slogans are those that somebody can remember after only hearing it once."

"It's an important consideration for choosing slogans." (Sirees 2004, 148–149)

Fathi feigns indifference at the sight of this literalization of an entity he had actually theorized about earlier, and his deadpan response might be said to represent one way in which political criticism can be effectively launched through humor. Such representations of the banality of poetry might be read as critique of "traditional" forms of Arabic culture but also as critique of the cynical packaging and reinvention of the "traditional" by the progressive, secular Ba'thist regime.

Laughter is ultimately portrayed as an effective weapon in the arsenal of those fictional characters. "We would take revenge on our situation through laughter," Fathi declares, before equivocating, "but laughter is accursed chattering that only exposes us and gets us into uncomfortable situations" (Sirees 2004, 78). When a Party cadre asks for a moment of silence at a mourning session held in honor of a recently deceased intellectual friend, we soon learn that the moment is being dedicated by this functionary to the also recently deceased father of the Leader. In response, Lama fails to keep herself from bursting out laughing. Here is a case in which Lama is clearly laughing at the absurdity of an out-of-touch regime. Another moment where what might be thought of as "laughter out of place" successfully subverts the power of authoritarian repression comes when Fathi is temporarily thrown into solitary confinement underneath the Party headquarters for failing to accede to the demands that he work for the regime once again:

This was the first time I had even been imprisoned. I hadn't even been reprimanded once during my military service. I measured the length and width of the cell by my steps to calculate that it was three by six steps. Then I sat down against the wall, taking pleasure in the quiet and replacing the bandage around my wrist . . . I tried to figure out whether I was truly happy there or had deceived myself into believing I was. Coming to the conclusion that I was really quite comfortable, I laughed out loud, because the tranquility had calmed me and I didn't regret anything. (Sirees 2004, 168)

This is a far cry from the impassive or defiant prison literature so common in late-twentieth-century Arabic prose writing.

Silence concludes with Lama and Fathi falling asleep together at the end of his very long day. The final scene takes place in a dream sequence, insisting, perhaps, on the ultimate unreality and apparent irreconcilability of the situation in which Fathi finds himself. Within this dreamscape, Lama and Fathi bear witness to Mr. Ha'el and Fathi's mother in a violent climactic scene, but in response to this brutality they both fall down laughing. More space would be necessary to adequately chart some of the ethical implications and political effects of transforming authoritarianism and its violence into a joke. Nevertheless, by transforming the juggernaut of Syrian authoritarianism into sound, Sirees endows his characters with some measure of control over that infernal noise. The strategic deployment of laughter occasionally subverts the false choice between the silence and the roar. It is in this sense that Fathi, Lama, and, presumably, the reader can have the last laugh. "To this day, whenever we're together," Fathi says of his relationship with Lama, "we still laugh whenever the Party is mentioned" (Sirees 2004, 76).

BETWEEN ALLEGORY AND DISSENT

What are the symbolic, political, and emotional values of sound in literature? How might the production and reception of sound—of the senses more generally—intersect and interact with the social life of text and context in contemporary Syrian fiction? What has Sirees accomplished by transforming the juggernaut of Syrian authoritarianism into sound? How is sound rendered as repression, and how does the latter stack up against the very real repression that is all too often unleashed on uppity intellectuals such as Fathi Sheen? Is the sound of silence in *The Silence and the Roar* and *Solo Piano Music* revealing of other, perhaps (self-) imposed, silences? What might the stakes of political action be when the threat of silence becomes the least bad outcome imaginable alongside or against torture and arbitrary arrest, detention, and disappearing? An answer to these questions would require more space than this chapter will allow, but I would like to conclude with some preliminary speculations.

"Representation and verisimilitude are not, by their very nature, repressive and authoritarian," Susan Suleiman (1983, 293) notes in her elegant book on the French *roman à thèse,* and "neither is the novel." However, as the American writer John Gardner (1984, 85) points out, "Fiction has for centuries existed on a continuum running between authoritarian and existential." Fawwaz Haddad commented to me that the creative palette at his disposal for writing is no different than an actor working on an "open stage." And yet, somehow, the limits of that Syrian stage continue to be bounded and redefined by certain ideological, stylistic, and formal criteria, the definition and determination of which remain beyond the reach of literary artists, their palettes, or their brushes. The extent to which literary culture in Syria reflects openings in the political field that might transcend both the aesthetic tension between authoritarian and existential literature and the institutional political tensions between authoritarianism and democratization will surely depend on the complex outcome of myriad and ongoing political, social, and cultural processes and struggles. The gradual liberalization of politics and economy, of the Syrian regime as a whole, over the past ten years has begun to have noticeable effects in the realm of culture. The speakeasy condition in late-twentieth-century Syria described by Wedeen (1999) and Cooke (2007), in which writers, intellectuals, and cultural producers were obliged to speak in code for fear of potentially swift and automatic censorship or even more brutal tactics of repression was gradually disrupted; "straight talk" became more common over the course of the 2000s, a situation that has been effectively exploded since March 2011. Widespread corruption at all levels of government, the ruthlessly repressive nature of rule under President Hafiz al-Asad, the ideological and practical bankruptcy of the regime—these were no longer taboo topics in everyday Syrian talk, even if they remain subject to censorship and control in the approved public sphere. The fact that there are now ordinary people in the streets willing to call for the ouster of the president and even more violent forms of retribution is a testament to the possibility that was latent in even the most unlikely circumstances.

Meanwhile, the *mukhabarat,* the *shabbiḥa,* and other forms of repressive control continue to play a very real part in the lives of Syrian people. Fictionalized renditions of the *mukhabarat*—both its characterization and caricature, as it were—create at least some potential conditions for the critical distancing, objectification, and reimagining of the most ruthless and brutal arm of the state security apparatus. What seemed to persist, at least through the first decade of the twenty-first century, was an almost universal awareness of the fact that direct criticism of President Bashar al-Asad, his family, and coterie of advisers as well as a basket of other issues were highly sensitive topics, if not simply off limits. Be that as it may, the novel was one domain where Syrians were capable of debating politics with relative freedom.

Social scientists need to exercise caution when attempting to pronounce judgments on the process of transformation currently underway in Syria. Be that as it may, the patchy process of piecemeal liberalization—from the gradual "opening" of the economy to strategic political reforms guided from above—may have afforded Syrian writers certain liberties that would simply not have been possible ten years earlier. To be sure, it remains the case that there is no local independent press, and a robust if erratic and even incomprehensible censorship regime remains firmly in place. But authoritarian transformations in contemporary Syria may have anticipated consequences, and literary criticism may shed some light on the limited albeit expanding spaces of freedom—the "breathing room" so keenly identified by other scholars—that are both available to and claimed by Syrian writers and intellectuals. Robert Darnton (1995, 197) notes how the authors of forbidden books in ancien régime France

> had separated culture from power, or rather, they had directed a new cultural power against the orthodoxies of the old. So a contradiction opened up, separating an orthodox value system grounded in the absolutist state from a contestatory ethos rooted in literature. This contradiction defined the situation of the reader, whatever his or her social status. It demonstrated to everyone that times were out of joint, that cultural life no longer synchronized with political power.

The extent to which Syrian novels—the literary culture of authoritarianism in Syria, more broadly—can or will have had any feedback effect on the process of political transformation and to which they may help to expand spaces of freedom that might be claimed by Syrian writers and intellectuals remains to be determined.

Whatever the case, an ironic position permits political and imaginative acrobatics that would seem implausible in narratives of hard-boiled realism. But what are the ethical implications or political effects of literary or discursive transformations of authoritarianism into another sort of sound, into laughter, into a joke? Does this upended representation of authoritarianism in literature actually subvert the power of an autocratic regime or unwittingly contribute to its reinforcement in the cultural universe of writers and readers alike? Is there a danger that the truth of the regime, the wizard behind the curtain, will be exposed through such an exercise? On the other hand, is it possible that the exercise of imagination in such terms serves to further insulate the regime from legitimate political criticism in the real world? Is the simple naïveté of sloganeers and paid bureaucrats supposed to undermine the fearmongering of the regime or ensure that the true working of power remain unknown? In *The Silence and the Roar,* Fathi acquires a surfeit of eyewitness information that leads him to take the regime and its minions less and less seriously. By transforming the juggernaut of Syrian authoritarianism into sound, Sirees endows his characters in *Silence* with some measure of control over that infernal noise; in satirizing the ostensibly all-powerful regime, characters acquire power that would be more difficult to muster in reality. Fathi literally has the last laugh, even if the question remains of what the relationship between laughter—more broadly, humor—and politics is or might become. In *Solo Piano Music,* by contrast, despite the significance of music—Fateh is an amateur music connoisseur whose political entanglements complicate his enjoyment of music— outright laughter is relatively rare in the text. The reader is reminded that security "apparatuses" run the world and control the situation inside Syria. A paucity of reliable information sends Fateh further and further into paralyzing paranoia. One might argue that the plot reinforces Ba'thist rhetoric about how there are dangerous forces in the world—radical Islamists, international security networks, and powerful foreign governments—and that only an alert revolutionary regime is well positioned and bold enough to tackle those challenges. In this reading, it would appear that the last laugh returns to the regime, the powers that be—in short, the status quo.

But is laughter an adequate response to authoritarianism, censorship, and state repression in the first place? Slavoj Žižek (1989, 28) vigorously argues against the widespread "underlying belief in the liberating, anti-totalitarian force of laughter, of ironic distance." This is a fair point that needs to be taken seriously, but there is little value in ascribing a timeless and universal quality to any human endeavor—be it laughing, weeping, fighting, screaming, dancing, or whatever. Indeed, without slipping into the ideological trap of instrumentalizing laughter, one may identify how its potential multivalence can be put to a variety of uses. "He who has laughter on his side," Adorno (1974, 210) once mused, "has no need of proof." But whereas Adorno contends that laughter tends to accompany satire, which "preferred to side with the stronger party," irony "convicts its object by presenting it as what it purports to be; and without passing judgment, as if leaving a blank for the observing subject, measures it against its being-in-itself." Adorno, therefore, provides a slightly more nuanced approach to laughter as a social but also quintessentially political problem, one that might acquire a whole range of meanings and ultimately lead to a variety of social or cultural outcomes.

Even though characters in *The Silence and the Roar* laugh out loud in the face of Party bureaucrats, they might also be seen as contributing to the legitimation of an absurdist regime that depends on the apathetic resignation of its citizenry. Meanwhile, Fateh al-Qalaj in *Solo Piano Music* softly undermines the credibility of Islamists and—to a lesser extent—the cadres of the *mukhabarat*; the extent to which the quiet seriousness of Haddad's characters does or does not present an ideological threat to authoritarian rule may also be discussed and debated. In spite of the gritty realism of *Solo Piano Music,* and even if there are very real markers throughout *The Silence and the Roar* that index life in contemporary Syria, neither work presents an unambiguous challenge to the discourses and practices of Syrian authoritarianism. Regardless of whether literature can ever adequately channel discontent or dissent toward meaningful political change, both novels suggest the promise of literary transformations of Syrian authoritarianism even as they demarcate limits of such critique.

Part IV

CONTESTATION, GOVERNANCE, AND THE
QUEST FOR AUTHORITARIAN LEGITIMACY

8 PROSECUTING POLITICAL DISSENT

Courts and the Resilience of Authoritarianism in Syria

Reinoud Leenders

THIS CHAPTER AIMS to find answers to an outwardly simple, but on closer inspection surprisingly complex, question: to what extent, when, and why did the Syrian authoritarian regime judicialize its repression of political dissent, and why does this matter? Accordingly, this chapter analyzes the use of technologies of power in Syria since the Ba'th coup in 1963 until the uprising that started in March 2011 with regards to its judicial system. For this purpose, the main arguments critically engage with relevant observations and theories proposed in the study of authoritarian governance generally, principally in two ways.

First, many students of authoritarianism have rightly argued that the resilience of authoritarianism cannot be solely explained in reference to coercive mechanisms. Indeed, in this context it has become almost a truism to claim that authoritarian regimes rarely remain in power due to forceful repression of political dissent alone. This conviction also now dominates the analysis of Syria's "populist-authoritarian" regime and its striking resilience, at least up to 2011. While accepting this view, this chapter nonetheless contends that the coercive dynamics of authoritarianism matter a great deal and therefore need to be better understood for the ways in which they are organized, adjusted, and routinized with the effect of reproducing regime power vis-à-vis real or perceived challenges against a regime. As a modest step toward an analysis that aims to bring coercion back in, it will be argued that Syria's judiciary should be regarded as part and parcel of the regime's repressive apparatus and as such has played an important role in the resilience of authoritarian rule.

Second, this chapter engages with and hopes to contribute to a more specialized debate on the role of the judiciary in authoritarian regimes. A small but growing literature on this topic aims to correct analyses, still common both in academia and especially in liberal human rights discourses, that tend to conceptualize repressive authoritarian institutions and policies, including the judiciary, as a residual category standing at odds with consensual, liberal, and democratic principles and human rights. When dealing with the role of judiciaries in authoritarian regimes, such liberal approaches surely provide a service by denouncing the failure of courts under authoritarian rule to uphold key principles pertaining to a free, independent, and fair judiciary. Yet such condemnations rarely offer much insight into why authoritarian regimes bother to erect a "façade" of judicial process in the first place and why such false pretense is to be considered significant, if at all. An increasing number of critics have resisted the typically normative framework implied in these liberal approaches and concentrated instead on the role and use of courts under authoritarianism by trying to understand the rationales and motives of authoritarian rulers to extend some independence and powers to (parts of) the judiciary (Ginsburg and Moustafa 2008; Pereira 2005). In this context, an influential argument has been that in certain countries a range of "pathologies" of authoritarian rule prompted authoritarian regimes to rediscover the utility of courts, thereby generating a seeming paradox of relatively strong and independent judiciaries coexisting with unbridled personalized and discretionary rule. Yet where such a trend toward judicial empowerment has failed to emerge, or only so in a very limited sense—as in Syria— the judiciary remains foremost a tool at the service of the regime's coercive strategies to repress dissent. Consequently, the "rule of law" is replaced by the deeply authoritarian tendency to "rule by law." Yet in this context the question remains as to why authoritarian regimes bother at all to judicialize their repression of political dissent. This appears to be especially puzzling when such regimes may be assumed to be very well capable of resorting to alternative and perhaps much less cumbersome measures, such as "forced disappearances" or large-scale extrajudicial violence, to curb and deter opposition and dissent. In addition, when trials and judicial procedures fail to be viewed as credible by citizens generally, authoritarian regimes insisting on a judicial process merely seem to risk exposing and advertising the bogus nature of their institutions and related claims to uphold the rule of law.

Following a discussion of the main trends and variations in the judicialization of repression in Syria from the rise to power of the Ba'th regime in 1963 until the start of the upheaval in March 2011, this chapter investigates both the possible motives and the structural factors behind what appears as a zigzag pattern, alternating degrees of judicialization and outright extrajudicial repression. As for the *motives* for the regime's tangible if always hesitant efforts to judicialize its repression of political dissent, it is suggested that the regime's peculiar authoritarian conceptions of statehood and sovereignty, presented mainly vis-à-vis external audiences, appear to have greater explanatory weight than purported regime strategies to overcome its "authoritarian pathologies." However, such motivations alone cannot explain real levels of judicializing repression, if only because they always may be overtaken by other concerns and interests. In more *structural* and historical terms, the established but modest degree of Syria's judicialization of political dissent is elucidated in reference to the position and role of the legal profession in general and courts in particular within the wider matrix of the struggle for Syria's organization of its political economy. In short, Syria's legal profession has found itself on the losing side in the country's changing political and economic landscape since 1963. It is further argued that the regime's lapses into extrajudicial repression, whereby even the semblance of functioning courts has been abandoned, seem to strongly correlate with the regime's changing perceptions of the nature of major challenges to its power. Perceived links to foreign conspiracies have effectively stripped regime adversaries from their "rights" to be prosecuted as mere criminals; in the regime's view they had become warriors who were to be eradicated, not prosecuted. Finally, Syria's growing degree of modest judicialized repression, at least until March 2011, appears to have had the effect of helping to counter the perilous fallout of relying on direct violence and warlike measures. From this perspective, the use of courts seems to have helped in reducing or neutralizing the risk of specialized security agencies and paramilitary forces in charge of large-scale extrajudicial violence turning against the regime itself. In the conclusion, a few reflections will be offered with regards to the regime's massive relapse to extrajudicial repression in its response to the uprising in early 2011.

SYRIA'S JUDICIALIZATION OF REPRESSION
IN PERSPECTIVE

The meaning or definition of the "judicialization" of the repression of political dissent in authoritarian contexts may intuitively appear to be straightforward: it designates the prominence authoritarian regimes exhibit to courts and related judicial processes to persecute political views and actions that are considered undesirable, deviant, or oppositional and that are criminalized by law. Along these lines and depending on available data, one can sketch developments over time with regards to the judicialization of repression as, for example, Pereira (2005) does for the military juntas in Latin America in comparison to a variety of other authoritarian regimes. However, Syria's various courts differed in their adherence to judicial procedures, while extrajudicial procedures and measures coexisted with the ways in which courts operate and acquire significance. Before establishing broad trends and variations in Syria's record of judicialization since 1963 until 2011, such qualifications need to be understood to arrive at a meaningful scale of judicialization, conceived as a continuum contrasting full-blown extrajudicial repression and the predominance of judicial procedures via courts.

When full judicialization is understood to denote the use of formal and permanent civilian courts that are part of the regular judiciary, Syria's "state of emergency" laws and the Ba'th regime's heavy reliance on "exceptional" courts immediately puts the country at a lower score in terms of judicialization throughout the period under study.

Loosely based on Law 162 (September 1958) and Legislative Decree 51 (December 1962)—both stipulating the conditions for and powers engendered by declaring a state of emergency—Syria was in a state of emergency from March 9, 1963, the day after Ba'thist officers seized power in a coup, until April 21, 2011, when, urged by the uprising, a presidential decree abolished it. Next to granting the prime minister (acting as the martial law governor) and his deputy, the minister of interior, sweeping powers to arrest or delegate others to preventively arrest anyone suspected of endangering public security, the state of emergency laws cast a dark shadow on the judicial qualities of courts.

In 1968, the state of emergency allowed for the establishment of the Supreme State Security Court (SSSC), which in turn replaced the Extraordinary Military Court erected in 1965. The SSSC became the main court in charge of prosecuting political dissent in the country's "emergency situation." Although formally considered a "court," and indeed being named as such, the SSSC has put up only modest pretense of following or fulfilling a judicial status or to apply related procedures. By law (Legislative Decree 47 of March 1968), it was exempted from any controls by the country's Supreme Judiciary Council, which overlooked all other civilian courts, thereby suggesting that it was not part of the judiciary as such. Accordingly, the SSSC was also legally exempted from the judicial procedures formally adhered to by ordinary civilian courts pertaining to, inter alia, the right of defense and the gathering and presentation of evidence against defendants. Its decisions were to be ratified by the minister of interior, who acted as deputy martial law governor. Also by legal stipulation, the president of the republic, as head of the executive, could nullify SSSC verdicts, order a retrial, or reduce sentences. SSSC sentences could not be appealed at any other judicial institution, civilian or otherwise. Confirming the court's ambivalent judicial status and submission to the executive was the SSSC's housing, in its last years of operation, in the building of the Ministry of Justice in Mezzeh (Damascus), where it occupied a small classroomlike space. Any remaining pretense of a courtlike standing was further undermined by the fact that many of its sessions took place in the office of the chief judge, Fayez al-Nuri, who remained in his position from his appointment in 1968 until the court's elimination.[1] Yet, perhaps most importantly, actual experiences of the SSSC's trial sessions failed to register strict adherence to judicial procedures. Lawyers usually were not allowed to participate in court sessions; defendants were rarely questioned or even given the opportunity to speak. Witnesses rarely appeared. Lawyers could submit their defense only in writing, and court sessions routinely processed defendants in large groups, granting little time to each individual case.[2] On top of this, and according to several observers and former defendants, Judge Fayez al-Nuri, currently in his 70s, mumbled his way through the procedures, forgot to stick to the court's minimal protocol, occasionally cursed at defendants, and passed sentences that were often inaudible to those attending and that were not officially publicized.[3] As one Western diplomat who attended several trials at the SSSC put it, "The SSSC doesn't seem to be a court even by a far stretch of that word; it is more like a processing center for the emergency laws."[4] Human rights activists would undoubtedly agree with this assessment. Yet for our purposes and despite its apparent shortcomings in enjoying a clear judicial status and upholding minimal judicial procedures, it remains striking that the SSSC continued to be portrayed by the regime as a full-fledged court while it borrowed from judicial symbols and passed sentences in reference to the country's penal code.

Other "special" courts active since the rise of the Ba'th regime in the early 1960s include those formally under the supervision of the military and that have, both in practice and based on legal stipulations, tried civilians on a range of charges derived from military laws and the country's penal code. According to Law 51 (1962), military tribunals enjoy jurisdiction over civilians contravening the orders of the country's martial governor and may prosecute a range of vaguely worded crimes and violations related to public security.

Similarly, the Military Penal Code and Laws of Procedure, promulgated by Legislative Decree 61 (1950) and amended many times since, have given military tribunals jurisdiction beyond military servicemen in cases of civilian assaults on military property, treason and espionage, and other security-related charges (Ibrahim 2006). Similar to the SSSC, military tribunals fall outside the powers of the Supreme Judiciary Council, while its military judges are not required to have any legal qualifications or relevant education. Yet lawyers and observers to military court cases generally seem to be in agreement that the country's military tribunals follow a more elaborate set of judicial procedures, as they generally expect prosecutors to provide legal evidence and make case files available in advance of court sessions, allow defense lawyers to present their case, and permit judgments to be appealed by civilian defendants at the country's Court of Cassation, which for this purpose has a military chamber.

A sharply contrasting situation applies at the country's ad hoc military field courts (*mahakim 'askariyya midaniya*), tasked with applying summary justice to military servicemen found in contravention of the Military Penal Code during wartime. As legally stipulated by Legislative Decree 109 (August 1967), military field courts are exempted from all procedures applying to military tribunals, and defendants enjoy no right of appeal. Defense lawyers are not known to have attended any of their trials, which are reported to take less than a few minutes. Formally, the field courts require the attendance of a representative of the Ministry of Defense, a military officer as chief judge, and two other members, including a member of the military judiciary. Only death sentences are supposed to be countersigned by the president of the republic. Yet, in practice, trials at military field courts often involved only one officer sitting at a table proclaiming sentences without even informing the accused of the charges.[5] Their death sentences are reported to have been routinely approved by the minister of defense (Middle East Watch 1990, 35). Although their jurisdiction was originally restricted to "times of war," Legislative Decree 32 (July 1980) extended the authority of military field courts to situations wherein the country is proclaimed to suffer from "internal disturbances." In sum, even when compared to the minimal degree to which the SSSC adhered to judicial procedures, the military field courts scored even worse.

Just as Syria's "exceptional" tribunals put in perspective the manifestation of judiciality even where "courts" are nominally playing a role in the prosecution of political dissent, both the presentence and postsentence periods contain numerous extrajudicial practices. Forced disappearances or preventive detention affects virtually all arrested persons who may eventually be taken to a court for prosecution. Most arrests by the country's security agencies (*mukhabarat*) usually take place a considerable time before court proceedings commence, regardless of the involvement of ordinary civilian courts or any of the special courts, in some cases up to several months or even years. Nonlegal or indeed illegal detention may even be prolonged when the judicial process has started to look into individual cases. The average time span of a trial at the SSSC was around 2.5 years, while defendants often had to wait for an equal number of years to even appear before the court (Human Rights Watch 2009a, 13; Zeitouneh 2007). Constant deferrals by the SSSC, ostensibly deliberate in nature, kept defendants waiting in prison for years, thereby denying them access to any judicial process and thus effectively keeping them in extrajudicial detention. Furthermore, prison terms imposed by courts often are not respected, causing convicts to be detained long after their sentences expired. Even on their release from prison, convicted political dissidents are habitually confronted by extrajudicial punitive or restrictive measures, such as having to sign statements to give up on any political activities, by extensive surveillance and harassment by security agencies, by intrusive reporting obligations, and by travel bans. In sum, being convicted by a court does not mean that repression ends with judicial prosecution; in many cases the latter is only part of a wider assortment of measures, including extrajudicial ones, that have become attached to the functioning of courts and the sentences they hand out.

SYRIA'S JUDICIALIZATION OF REPRESSION: MAIN TRENDS

In light of the preceding discussion, we can now assess the period under study against a continuum along which the means of repression of political dissent ranged from, for Syrian standards, high levels of judicialization involving the country's ordinary civilian courts, to shades of lesser judicialization under the auspices of military tribunals and the SSSC, and culminating in the opposite extremes of marginal forms of judicialization signified by the military field courts and the abandonment of courts altogether. Based on available data, often impressionistic in nature but sufficient to establish trends, what emerges is a highly uneven or zigzag pattern, whereby degrees of judicialized repression vary and are interrupted by full-blown extrajudicial clampdowns on opposition groups and individuals.

Starting in 1963 until roughly the early 1970s, ordinary civilian courts in Syria seem to have coexisted with the newly created or empowered special courts in handling politically charged cases and indeed the repression of political dissent, with the important exception of the period between 1964 and 1965. During those years, military tribunals clearly took the lead in the judicial repression of merchants' and students' strikes and protests against the regime's nationalization policies, handing out dozens of death sentences (Middle East Watch 1990, 13, 34). Yet some protestors were referred to civilian courts on charges of "breaching public trust."[6] More striking, however, was the regime's resort to extrajudicial violence to deal with the strikes and protests as it sent military and paramilitary forces, which opened fire indiscriminately and committed other forms of violence against civilians (Heydemann 1999, 186; Lobmeyer 1995, 126–130)

Following the internal coup of 1970, or Hafiz al-Asad's "Corrective Movement," the judicialization of repression seemed to once again have moved away from ordinary civilian courts toward less judicialized procedures, this time embodied by the SSSC, which began prosecuting dissidents on a larger scale than before.[7] Such prosecutions primarily targeted Palestinians residing in Syria who protested against the events of "Black September" (1970) in Jordan (Middle East Watch 1990, 125). In addition, many rival Ba'thists associated with the preceding regime led by Salah Jadid similarly were tried by the SSSC (Mana' 2003).

In the mid-1970s, military tribunals experienced a frenzy of activity as they began to deal with protestors who took part in demonstrations in Hama and Aleppo against the regime's economic measures hitting these cities' small private entrepreneurs (Lobmeyer 1995, 145–146). Leaving no doubts about the regime's hardening position, Asad stated in January 1975 that "amnesties and mercy have their limits. From now on all opponents of the Revolution will be treated as criminals for who there is no mercy and no forgiveness" (cited in Lobmeyer 1995, 145). From 1976 onward in particular, military tribunals stepped up their prosecutions, targeting a broad range of political activists including members associated with the Iraqi branch of the Ba'th Party, communists, Nasserists, and lawyers who protested the regime's increasingly harsh measures in putting down demonstrations and breaking up strikes (Bonne 1997, 33). Yet when protests intensified following the regime's controversial military intervention in Lebanon in 1976, judicial or quasi-judicial repression began to be gradually overshadowed by extrajudicial violence.

Although by the end of the 1970s and early 1980s the country's special courts still prosecuted political dissidents and armed Islamists, paramilitary forces and state-supported militias besieged Islamist armed groups, thereby resorting to draconian violent measures. In one major incident following the assassination of eighty-three young officer cadets at a military academy in Aleppo in June 1979, security forces extrajudicially detained an estimated 6,000 people and killed scores of others (Middle East Watch 1990, 17). Extrajudicial violence escalated further in 1980 when army commandos pounded Jisr al-Shughur, a village between Aleppo and Lataqiya, with mortars and rockets and executed people on the spot in retaliation for riots and disturbances. The event also triggered the first reported mass persecution of suspected protestors by military field courts that ordered the execution of more than one hundred detainees (Middle East Watch 1990, 20). The violence was a forewarning of extrajudicial repression in Aleppo from April 1980 onward on a scale not witnessed before. Security troops used heavy armor against civilian targets, committed random killings, carried out on-the-spot executions, and detained large numbers of people without trial. The regime then turned on suspected Muslim Brothers who were kept (mostly without trial) in Tadmur prison, killing more than a thousand prisoners in one day (Middle East Watch 1990, 20). Extrajudicial violence peaked in Hama between April 1981 and March 1982 as army brigades, security forces, paramilitary groups, and state militias embarked on a campaign killing thousands and detaining many more. During the regime's onslaught on the city in February 1982, between 5,000 and 10,000 people were killed, although some estimates put the death toll as high as 40,000 (Lobmeyer 1995, 325; Middle East Watch 1990, 28).

By the early 1980s extrajudicial repression clearly had won out against any pretense of judicial process. On top of the extrajudicial mass killings, thousands of detainees were held in prisons and interrogation centers without trial or any judicial process, many of them for years. While the cases dealt with by special courts paled in comparison to the number of detained, military field courts throughout the 1980s summarily sentenced detainees to death or to long prison sentences.[8] In an interview with a German weekly, former Defense Minister Mustafa Tlass recalled that in the 1980s he signed 150 death sentences a week for the Damascus district alone (*Der Spiegel*, February 21, 2005).

In 1992 a modest improvement in the regime's judicialization of repression set in as hundreds of political activists, many of them detained without trial for over a decade, were brought to the SSSC (Human Rights Watch 1995). Many others were released in amnesties. The SSSC also began to process new cases, including prosecutions of activists from the Committees for the Defense of Democratic Freedoms and Human Rights in Syria, who had been arrested in late 1991 and early 1992. Forced disappearances and preventive detention continued, but more and more cases were brought before the SSSC and, to a lesser extent, military tribunals (Syrian Human Rights Committee 2001, 154). Military field courts, signifying the lowest form of judicialization, rarely processed cases during the 1990s, although some were reported. Full-blown extrajudicial campaigns like the ones witnessed in the early 1980s no longer occurred. Presidential pardons brought the release of many political prisoners detained since the 1980s, although thousands remained missing. Some prominent detainees remained in prison, including Communist Party leader and lawyer Riyyad al-Turk, who was released only in May 1998 after having been detained without trial since October 1980.

Following the succession of Hafiz al-Asad by his son Bashar in 2000, a more complex process of judicialization began to distinguish the regime's repression of political dissent. From 2002 onward, political activists increasingly began to be referred to civilian criminal courts. The year before, prodemocracy activists associated with the Damascus Spring, and arrested in August and September 2001, were mostly sent to the SSSC, where they received harsh prison sentences. Yet in April 2002 several activists, including MP Riad Seif and MP Ma'mun al-Homsi, for the first time found themselves in front of an ordinary criminal court. Although the court handed out equally harsh prison sentences, the cases of Seif and Homsi were significant in that now ordinary civilian courts had started to handle prominent political cases, for the first time in decades (Mana' 2003). The shift followed a statement by the regime in January 2001 announcing that the emergency law in force since 1963 was to be "frozen" and "not applied" (cited in Human Rights Watch 2003). Interestingly, from 2003 onward the official Bureau for Statistics began to issue data on the conviction by civilian courts of public security–related offenses and breaches of the Penal Code usually brought against political activists (Syrian Arab Republic 2004–2007). Syrian lawyers and human rights activists immediately noted the change in the ways in which the regime dealt with its opponents, but expectations that the regime would opt for a clear-cut judicialization of repressing political dissent in favor of ordinary civilian courts—let alone show more respect for the right on a fair trial—failed to materialize.

Aggregate data compiled by Syrian human rights activists on detentions and arrests between 2006 and 2009, however imperfect, may indicate some more recent trends until 2011 (Syrian Human Rights Information Link 2006 and subsequent years). The numbers of political cases brought to ordinary civilian courts and those brought to military tribunals in this period were about at an equal level, but both courts remained outperformed by the SSSC. For instance, of all estimated 973 political prisoners in 2008, the SSSC had sentenced 466 (Syrian Human Rights Information Link 2008). The estimates, although inconsistently organized and fragmented, suggest a tendency wherein the various courts seem to be specializing in certain political cases, with most suspected Kurdish, Islamist, or Salafist activists (together accounting for about 75 percent of all political prisoners) tried at the SSSC and to a lesser extent the military tribunals, and most secular political activists (around 25 percent), including cases widely reported in the West, transferred to civilian courts. However, up to 2011, exceptions to these trends remained as military courts, and the SSSC kept prosecuting some secular political activists. Also, extrajudicial repression briefly reared its head when in March 2004 security forces clamped down on Kurdish protestors in Qamishli, killing over forty and briefly detaining 2,000 without trial (Human Rights Watch 2009b, 14–15). Generally, however, variations in the repression of political dissent no longer occurred on the threshold of judicial and (extreme) extrajudicial repression. Since 2000 most political activists have received some sort of a trial and the civilian judiciary has been gradually more involved in processing their cases, especially after 2002. Of course, that does not mean that the sentences passed against them were "fair" by any reasonable standard nor that the judicialization of repression had reached very high levels. Yet, compared to the 1980s, courts seemed to be winning terrain from extrajudicial means in their designated task to punish, curb, or deter political dissent.

Although the Syrian regime seems to attach at least some importance to reaching and sustaining certain levels of judicialization, Syria's experience with judicialized and extrajudicial repression from 1963 to 2011 does not conform to the evolutionary pattern Pereira expects most authoritarian regimes to show over time (Pereira 2005, 178, 183). In this context, increased judicialization of repression over time is believed to signify efforts by authoritarian regimes to consolidate and routinize their rule. In contrast, in Syria modest levels of judicialization were repeatedly interrupted by significantly long periods of extrajudicial repression—primarily between 1964 and 1965 and between the late 1970s and early 1990s—while the judicialization of repression started to reach somewhat higher levels only from 2002 until 2011, when full-blown extrajudicial repression became the regime's response to the Syrian uprising. Against this backdrop, Syria's experience with varying degrees of judicialization seems to have zigzagged and to have been interrupted by significant intervals of outright extrajudicial repression. What explains these variations?

JUDICIAL STRATEGIES, PATHOLOGIES OF
AUTHORITARIAN RULE, AND REGIME NOTIONS
OF STATEHOOD

In their search for explanations as to why certain authoritarian regimes opt for a strategy in which courts are relatively empowered after being neglected or marginalized for years, Moustafa and Ginsburg propose to focus on sets of motivations to address or remedy common "pathologies of authoritarian rule" (Ginsburg and Moustafa 2008; Moustafa 2007). These pathologies include problems in creating credible property rights, pursuing controversial reforms, checking on state officials and the state bureaucracy at large, maintaining regime elite cohesion, and generating regime legitimacy. In this argument, courts can play a useful or even crucial role in addressing or overcoming such pathologies and consequently are likely to feature in authoritarian regimes' policies and choices of technologies of power in times of adjustment and reform. Although conceptualized for settings in which genuine empowerment of certain courts occurs, it may be tempting to analyze Syria's modest levels of judicialization of repression of political dissent accordingly. Indeed, similar arguments are sometimes made in Syria, especially in the context of economic reforms since the early 1990s and, even more frequently, since Bashar al-Asad took power in 2000. However, the use of courts in Syria does not fit well within Moustafa and Ginsburg's framework. For this reason, another motivating factor is suggested for the use of courts by the Syrian regime, one that is firmly embedded in the regime's discursive notions of modern statehood and state sovereignty.

Perhaps the most common argument to explain why authoritarian regimes make use of and grant some role to judiciaries is that the latter provide a sense of popular legitimacy in place of credible mechanisms of public accountability. Especially when the achievement of substantive or ideology-driven outcomes—such as equitable economic development broadly defined—pales against modest or indeed disastrous results, authoritarian regimes, and especially those of the populist variety, are argued to turn to courts to acquire some "procedural legitimacy" without allowing for genuine political participation (Moustafa 2007, 38). Likewise, Syrian lawyers and political activists almost unanimously replied to the author's question concerning why the regime bothered to have a judicial process at all by asserting that that it reflects the regime's interest in enhancing its legitimacy.[9] Yet for achieving popular legitimacy, or the generally perceived right to govern, what is required at a minimum is a domestic audience at whom such claims are directed. After all, "rights" generally, let alone the right to govern, cannot exist without some sort of receptive community, short of which legitimacy claims would constitute little more than lonesome expressions of self-righteousness.[10] Likewise, for judicial acts or processes to become instrumentalized as a way to muster legitimacy, it may be reasoned that they first require some sort of public involvement. Strikingly, Syria's judicial process in general and that pertaining to the prosecution of political dissent in particular is to a large extent hidden from the public. It is extremely rare for the regime to advertise court cases, with the notable exception of cases related to its anticorruption purges. Syria's heavily controlled state media seldom report on the prosecution of political activists or indeed on court cases generally, even when these are handled by the relatively more accessible ordinary civilian courts. Furthermore, the SSSC and, to a lesser extent, the military tribunals have banned or heavily restricted the attendance of audiences, even barring lawyers and family members of the defendants access to court sessions. Those who challenged the court's secrecy, as for example lawyer Muhannad al-Hassani did by regularly reporting on his trial observations at the SSSC in 2009, found themselves being prosecuted. Secrecy and information blackouts are common to the extent that, during trials held by military field courts, to mention an extreme example, the charges and even the sentences were kept secret from defendants.[11] Indeed, often such ad hoc field courts have been convened in remote prison complexes that are by their very nature hidden from the public. One former detainee of Tadmur's desert prison recalled in this context how twice a week officers from Damascus were flown in by helicopter for the sole purpose of conducting one-minute trials at the prison courtyard without anyone being able to witness the proceedings, not even the defendants who were dragged to the spot blindfolded (Khalifé 2007, 87–88; see also Naji 1993).

Evidently, this tendency to conceal the judicial process, and to nevertheless insist on judicial pomp even when audiences are lacking, stands in sharp contrast with the political show trials exhibited by some authoritarian regimes elsewhere, like in neighboring Iraq, especially during 1958 and 1960 (Tripp 2007). Audiences here are apparently deemed essential to the judicial process. Yet the Syrian Ba'th regime never resorted to such practices. Public and televised "confessions" were only rarely staged. On June 28, 1979, alleged members of the Muslim Brotherhood were paraded on Syrian state television to "confess" to their crimes, but the audience was granted no glimpse of any court proceedings (Syrian Arab Republic 1984b, 265–284).[12] Other such "confessions" were televised in 2005 and 2008, this time without even a passing reference to trials.[13] One may speculate that the Syrian regime lacks the ideological or indeed revolutionary self-confidence needed to resort to such extreme forms of judicial theater.[14] A similar argument may explain the concealment of Syria's judicial procedures involving political cases. An additional factor may be that the regime simply calculated that most ordinary Syrians would not find a celebration of judicial procedures to be credible—or equally likely, that it did not even expect ordinary Syrians to believe in the judicial process.[15] Yet the main point here is that an attempt to gain procedural legitimacy via courts does not seem to have been the reason why the Syrian regime bothered to have some sort of a judicial process, let alone that it provided incentives to genuinely empower courts.

A more convincing if less straightforward explanation for the Syrian regime's insistence on judicial procedures and institutions—even if these fail to meet liberal standards, enjoy little autonomy, and are often discarded—may perhaps be found in the regime's discursive and normative notions of statehood and, related to this, of state sovereignty. Any discussion of state affairs and politics with Syrian state representatives or Ba'th officials is bound to bring up legal and juridical dimensions. Syrian foreign policy discourses and presidential addresses on Syria's place in the world and the region are especially habitually riddled with references to international law, U.N. resolutions, and legal stipulations regarding noninterference in domestic affairs; in a simple phrase, juridical statehood. The emphasis on Syria's state sovereignty toward the outside world and within the international state system not only constitutes a remarkably consistent point of reference in regime discourse but is often posed in direct opposition to, or as a substitute for, individual human rights.

For instance, in April 1980 the regime dissolved the Bar Association for its relentless campaigns in favor of individual rights and against the emergency laws, and its journal, *al-Muhamun*, no longer contained legal analyses of individual human rights as it had throughout much of the 1970s. Instead, it devoted considerable attention to lengthy analyses, and sometimes diatribes, pertaining to "Arab rights," Israeli violations of international law, "the legitimate use of violence in resisting foreign occupation versus terrorism," the illegality of international sanctions, and "international terrorism" (Ashraf 1987; Qattan 1986; Rifa'at 1987). Correspondingly, articles in the journal emphasized external statehood and the sacrosanct imperative of national borders in meticulously detailed legal analyses of state measures to counter and penalize smuggling (*tahrib*) and customs fraud (Darkazalli 1987; Nabwani 1986).

One may dismiss such discourse merely as an attempt to clutter public space, but this would do injustice to the convictions and worldviews that inform them. As elsewhere in the Arab world, Syria's juridical statehood, legal sovereignty, and judicial autonomy were at the heart of its struggle for independence against (French) colonialism (Brown 1997, 236, 241; Reid 1981, 187). The so-called mixed courts under French colonialism particularly were the sites of Syria's struggle for independence. Consequently, in Syria as elsewhere in the Arab world, courts and state sovereignty came to be intimately associated with one another (Brown 1997, 241). Syria's postcolonial difficulties in asserting its standing as a nation-state—given its own multiple and often transnational identities and the regional permeability of its borders (Bacik 2008; Leenders 2010; Mufti 1996)—has given political elites' emphasis on juridical statehood additional urgency (Jackson 1990).

In this context, Syria's judicial institutions, or even a semblance of judicial procedure, began to connote and embody the state's claims, from the 1960s onward aggressively expressed by the Ba'th regime, concerning its external sovereignty. It is perhaps also in this context that some of the Ba'th regime's historians have claimed that judges played a key role in the 1963 revolution by granting full legality to the new regime and its capture of the state. (for example, Da'ud 1995, 183–184). The embodiment of the state's external sovereignty by the country's judicial institutions may also explain why Syrian courts generally do not so much address domestic audiences or even the regime's own core constituencies; rather, they are accentuated and displayed vis-à-vis other states as if to remind them of Syria's sovereign statehood.[16] Hence, the Syrian regime persistently chose international forums, such as the U.N. Human Rights Committee, to present its claimed achievements involving its judiciary in painstaking level of detail rarely offered to domestic audiences.[17]

These complex discursive processes can be further illustrated in reference to some recent developments involving Syria's courts in connection with its foreign policies. From 2004 onward, Western diplomats were given access to attend court sessions at the SSSC, which otherwise insisted on keeping spectators at bay. Indeed, at international forums Syrian state representatives explicitly invited their foreign counterparts to visit the court (for example, U.N. Office at Geneva 2010). This has prompted some mutual misunderstandings about diverging agendas. One foreign diplomat told the author that at one point he was puzzled when the SSSC chief judge Fayez al-Nuri approached him to boast about his court's respect for procedure and its legal underpinnings, exposing his obliviousness as to what this diplomat may himself have thought about what constituted fair judicial process.[18] One Syrian official said, "We let them [foreign diplomats] in [at the SSSC] because we want to say that we have our laws, we have our procedures. We are a sovereign state."[19] Similar arguments were raised in the context of the establishment of the special international court in March 2009 to try the suspected killers of former Lebanese Prime Minister Rafiq al-Hariri. Sensing an acute threat to Syria's state sovereignty, the regime hastily established a judicial committee, led by a civilian judge, to set up its own investigations and prepare litigation were any Syrian nationals to be implicated in Hariri's assassination. As one Syrian official pointed out, "Syria is not going to extradite any Syrians. Our judicial system can handle this perfectly. Our courts are fully competent."[20]

A penchant by the Syrian regime to sustain some sort of judicial process and mobilize courts in the repression of political dissent cannot be explained in direct reference to its assumed interests and concomitant motives to address or overcome certain pathologies of authoritarian rule. However, this should not necessarily be read as, and is certainly not intended to be, a critique of those who emphasized such authoritarian regime rationales and strategies in empowering courts elsewhere. In Syria, such considerations simply do not seem to have much relevance. The regime's discursive and normative notions of statehood and, more specifically, its preoccupation with displaying and preserving state sovereignty vis-à-vis outsiders perhaps better explain why courts matter to the regime. Yet as Brown (1997, 18) reminds us, "Intentions should not be confused with consequences (a point often forgotten in research on legal systems)." The study of legal practices and the evolution of legal systems, including the judicialization of repression, cannot be reduced to guessing at assumed interests, intentions, and deliberate designs divorced from their wider context. Such phenomena are "the outcome of intense political struggles rather than abstract reason" (Brown 2002, 105). It is to these struggles that I will turn next.

COURTS AND JUDICIALIZATION WITHIN
THE "STRUGGLE FOR SYRIA"

The view among Syrian regime elites that judicial institutions validated Syria's claim to state sovereignty had little impact on the degree of judicialization the regime deployed, especially with respect to the persecution of political dissent. Furthermore, Syrian history since 1963 witnessed repeated and sometimes lengthy lapses into extrajudicial repression during which the courts were ignored altogether. Such outcomes under military-led authoritarian regimes, Pereira argues, may be understood by an "historical-institutionalist" approach to legality and the use of courts (Pereira 2005, 200). Past conflicts and divergences between the military and the judiciary, he claims, can account for why judiciaries are marginalized when such military elites seize power, in extreme cases causing courts to be sidelined altogether to make way for extrajudicial repression. Nearly axiomatic in this context has become Argentinean courts' "failure" in 1973 to uphold the sentences passed on 300 political prisoners during military rule between 1966 and 1973, setting off their release when the Peronists returned to power (Pereira 2008, 31–32). This event caused the military junta, reinstalled in 1976, to be highly suspicious of and even hostile to the judiciary, to the extent that it took matters into its own hands by engaging in an all-out extrajudicial war against perceived opponents (the "dirty war" of the early 1980s).

Such a historical-institutional approach, I concur, is a fruitful starting point with which to analyze Syria's experience with limited and varying degrees of judicialization of repression since 1963. However, there are no blatant examples of comparable conflicts between Ba'thist military officers and Syria's judicial institutions prior to 1963 that would explain lasting hostile attitudes by the regime.[21] Instead I propose to place Syria's judiciary, the fate of its legal profession, and degrees of post-1963 judicialization firmly in the much wider context of what Seale famously called the "struggle for Syria" (Seale 1965). This struggle is to be understood in reference to the conflicts and instability generated by the intrigues of foreign powers and their penetration of the Syrian state and by foreign manipulation of the country's political elites (as Seale presented it). Yet the struggle for Syria at the same time had a key domestic dimension as elites, popular groups, and classes competed "to determine the organization of Syria's political economy and what role the state would play in its management" (Heydemann 1999, 31). Syria's legal profession was caught up and heavily involved in these struggles, which in turn had lasting repercussions for the levels of judicialization.

Popular mobilization prior to 1963 and the rise to power of a regime with primarily lower class and rural origins—and to some extent a particularly strong support base within marginalized communities including the Alawites—put the Ba'th regime from the onset on a collision course with a coalition of landed, commercial, and industrial elites. Consequently, class divisions, a rural–urban divide and, to varying degrees, sectarian identities have all been important factors in the Ba'th regime's strenuous efforts to build state institutions, expand the role of the state in the economy, favor popular socioeconomic strata over others, and ensure and consolidate its control over the state apparatus and society at large. In a nutshell, and from a historical perspective, Syria's legal profession—lawyers and judges—was caught up in the middle of these complex developments and confrontations.

First, on a political level the participation of lawyers in the "oligarchic" regimes preceding the 1963 Ba'thist military coup was markedly high. Between 1949 and 1958, and during the restoration of oligarchic rule between 1961 and 1963—scornfully labeled the "counterrevolutionary" period in Ba'thist parlance—lawyers were well represented among the country's political elite and in government (Reid 1981, 393). Indeed, lawyers often constituted a majority of cabinet members. For instance, every member of the government of Sa'id al-Ghazzi in 1954 had a law degree. Directly before the Ba'th takeover, Ma'mun Kuzbari, a prominent lawyer and former head of the Bar Association, served as prime minister, while Nazim al-Qudsi, another lawyer, was appointed president. Both in the cabinets of this period and in Parliament lawyers were represented in unusually high numbers (Heydemann 1999, 140).

Prior to 1963 Syria's legal profession was intimately tied up with the dominance of landed and merchant capital (Reid 1981, 229, 396–397). This is hardly surprising, as big landowners and merchants formed lawyers' most important clients. Many lawyers were also themselves heavily involved in business, most prominently Kuzbari and Qudsi, who could be counted among the country's most influential entrepreneurs at the time. Thanks to these lucrative connections and porous roles, the law profession boomed, attaining high social status and a strong association with the ruling oligarchy. Adding to the elitist nature of the law profession, trainee lawyers were expected to spend a long time in internships without getting paid, something only the affluent could afford.[22] Next to its distinct political inclinations and class affiliations, the legal profession was overwhelmingly urban based and, related to this, it appears to have drawn its members particularly from the Sunni community and urban-based minorities, primarily Christians.[23] By extension, largely because most judges had previously been active as lawyers, the Syrian judiciary was comprised predominantly of members who had a strong penchant toward business and landed interests, were well-connected to the oligarchic regime, had urban origins, and were mostly drawn from the Sunni and Christian communities (Qandaqji 2004).[24]

Most Ba'thist elites and Ba'th Party activists were drawn from very differ-ent socioeconomic strata in which legal professionals were far less well rep-resented. Some lawyers and judges surely played a leading role in the history of the Ba'th Party, particularly until the mid-1960s. Jalal al-Sayyid, one of the founding ideologues of the Party, was a judge from Deir al-Zur. Also, the first Ba'th Party congress in 1947 included some lawyers (Batatu 1999, 136). Yet the party and the post-1963 Ba'thist leadership became increasingly dominated by military officers while it shifted its support base decisively to rural and pri-marily Alawi constituencies. As a result, legal professionals found themselves more and more in the minority, among both Ba'th Party activists and regime strongmen. On top of this, when the Ba'th regime embarked on its ambitious efforts to build and expand the state bureaucracy throughout the 1960s, it at-tracted mostly rural and Alawite recruits who had historically failed to be fully incorporated into the legal profession; many of these opted instead for a vocational background in engineering (Batatu 1999, 160; Longuenesse 2007, 61–102). Between 1963 and 1966, Ba'thist lawyers still occupied some positions of political importance; about half of ministers serving in Ba'thist cabinets in this period were lawyers (Reid 1981, 228). Yet their numbers dwindled rapidly while they increasingly became excluded from positions of real influence. In the same period, the fifty-three-member Ba'th Regional Command counted only four lawyers; by 1970 only two were left (Batatu 1999, 165–167). This trend unfolded rapidly, illustrated by Batatu's data suggesting that between 1970 and 1997 only five out of the forty-eight-member Ba'th Regional Command were lawyers (Batatu 1999, 250). In the increasingly dominant and expanding mili-tary and security apparatus between 1970 and 1997, lawyers failed to be repre-sented in leading positions altogether (Batatu 1999, 218–224).

Lawyers and by extension civilian judges thus had few reasons to celebrate the 1963 "revolution." As Reid (1981, 229) points out, for both Syria and Egypt, leading lawyers had linked their fortunes to the landed elite and to business interests and thus lost ground when army officers destroyed the old regimes. Apart from the liberal-constitutionalist convictions some but not all of them may have held, many Syrian lawyers had lost their most important business clients due to the aggressive nationalization policies initiated after 1963 and increasingly stifling state intervention in and regulation of the economy, mea-sures that all prompted a massive flight of capital.[25] Established lawyers, many of them with urban and Sunni origins, also bitterly resented—and some do still resent—the massive influx of rural and Alawite migrants in urban areas who found employment in the state bureaucracy. In these lawyers' eyes, the regime's policies to emancipate long-marginalized sectors of society negatively affected the status of the law profession.[26] As the Law Faculty of Damascus University gradually opened its doors to ever-growing numbers of students, the quality of instruction suffered, a development that was exacerbated by regime restrictions on the curriculum, aggressive regime monitoring on campus, and corruption among lecturers.[27] Furthermore, new judges were no longer drawn from the affluent circles of society and had to survive on low state salaries. All these factors led to a situation wherein by the 1980s the law profession had lost significant prestige.

From the perspective of the Ba'thist ruling elite, law professionals were to be treated with extreme caution due to their association with the ancien régime and their traditional socioeconomic outlook. Yet very likely because the Ba'th Party and the regime failed to have a significant pool of confidents with the appropriate legal background, most judges remained in office after the 1963 coup.[28] No large-scale, Egyptian-style "massacre of the judges" occurred, although twenty-four judges known for their anti-Ba'thist affiliations or sympathies—including Haytham al-Maleh, Abd al-Kader al-Aswad, and Ali al-Tantawi—were fired in 1966 (Maleh 2005). Overall, however, the regime seems to have relied on the gradual expansion of the number of law students who, after graduation and strict political vetting, came to replace retiring judges and to dominate the judiciary (a phenomenon often called "court packing"). It is perhaps also in this context that the regime took the easier option in the short run of resorting to special courts, including the military tribunals, that could be expected to be more loyal and that often did not have to be staffed by a large number of judges with a lengthy background in law or even a legal education. In this respect it was also convenient that the ancien régime had done much of the groundwork, as most of the legal and institutional infrastructure for a state of emergency and the military courts was already in place. However, even among sitting military judges there were some who failed to please Ba'thist officers as, for example, a military judge who sentenced an officer, Muhammad Ibrahim al-Ali, to death for his role in an abortive coup attempt by Ba'thist officers in Aleppo in 1962 (Maleh 2002, 229–230). After Ba'thist officers seized power one year later, the judge was sacked, and Ali became commander of the National Guard and later of the People's Army (Van Dam 2009). The regime proceeded by establishing the SSSC, fully subject to its control, and by simultaneously granting the military tribunals and military field courts supplementary powers and exemptions from ordinary judicial procedural requirements.

Following Hafiz al-Asad's coup in 1970, some limited economic liberalization measures and the distribution of public procurement contracts to privileged sections of the business class, primarily in Damascus, improved relations between the regime and the country's entrepreneurs (Lobmeyer 1995, 223; Perthes 1995, 50–53). However, the regime still exhibited some anxiety vis-à-vis the civilian courts and the legal profession generally, despite their relative marginalization by the emergency law and associated special courts. The 1973 Constitution, which devoted a lengthy chapter to the judiciary's powers and organization, therefore clipped all of the remaining wings of ordinary civilian judges. Most strikingly, the role of the president of the republic (or his representative by way of the justice minister) in heading the Higher Judicial Council (already decreed in 1961 by Legislative Decree 81) now became enshrined in the Constitution (article 132). In effect, judges became vulnerable to immediate dismissal, demotions, or transfers if the executive so desired.

The regime's apprehensions vis-à-vis the legal profession were confirmed when, beginning in the mid-1970s, an increasing number of judges and former judges outside the courts started to challenge the regime's approach to the judiciary, some assertively (for example, former judge Haytham al-Maleh) and others more discreetly (for example, judge Nusrat Mulla Haydar, who later became chief judge of the Constitutional Court) (Haydar 1975a, 1975b, 1977, 1978; Maleh 1970).[29] Many more lawyers started to launch aggressive campaigns against the regime's dismal record of respect for the rule of law and the judiciary and indeed against regime policies more generally. Even in Damascus, where selective economic liberalization was designed to cultivate important elements of the business class, lawyers continued to fume against the regime. Significantly, their law practices had failed to benefit from the informal modus operandi of the crony capitalism that the "Corrective Movement" had brought, which further contributed to their impoverishment and loss of social status.[30] It is perhaps largely because of their shared professional misfortunes that the otherwise divided political opposition to the regime managed to build a remarkably cohesive platform within the bar association.

From 1976 onward, lawyers began to protest the regime's military intervention in Lebanon, its increasingly brutal repression of dissent, its emergency laws, and its special courts by sending petitions, calling for lawyers' strikes, refusing to appear before the special courts, and consistently criticizing the regime's policies in the bar's journal *al-Muhamun* ('Abbas 1979; Arslan 1978; Jayush 1978, 1979; Mustafa 1978; Shukri 1978; Syrian Bar Association 1978).

The regime responded with full force. Many lawyers were arrested, including Sabah al-Rikabi, the head of the bar. In April 1980 the regime dissolved the national and local bars and appointed regime loyalists, thankfully recruiting among the thousands of less politicized new law graduates (Bonne 1997, 35).[31] Yet despite this stiff repression and the regime's atrocities generally, lawyers sustained a measure of opposition throughout the 1980s, primarily by encouraging the Arab Lawyers Union to take critical positions on the Syrian regime's policies vis-à-vis the legal profession and human rights and by campaigning against the continued detention of prominent lawyers (Middle East Watch 1990, 105–106). These protests withered when the regime once again appointed a new board and adjusted the bar's internal regulations to ensure its complete submission to the regime's policies, a situation that has pretty much characterized the bar's status until today (Middle East Watch 1990, 106; Qandaqji 2004).[32]

The remarkably vocal and unified campaigns in the late 1970s raised by lawyers belonging to virtually all oppositional groups and parties illustrate the extent to which the legal profession had been caught up in the struggle for Syria.[33] The intensity of the regime's repressive measures—next to its draconian moves to curb the judiciary's independence and accumulative measures at its expense—can be viewed as the regime's recognition of its importance. It is this background that explains why the regime's confidence in the legal profession was never restored and why its approach to the judiciary remained extremely cautious at best. Within this wider context, the judicialization of the repression of political dissent achieved the modest levels prevailing only until early 2011. Evidently, this analysis corroborates Brown's warning that the study of legal practices and the evolution of legal systems cannot be reduced to exploring assumed regime interests and motivations. After all, in Syria structural and historical factors have proved to have put a cap on or constrained these motivations with the result that achieved levels of judicialization have been far less impressive than could have been predicted from the regime's motivations to showcase its judiciary in its claims on sovereignty in a world of states.

While modest levels of judicialization and the regime's suspicious and sometimes hostile attitudes toward the legal profession and the country's civilian courts can be explained in reference to the domestic political and socioeconomic frontlines of the struggle for Syria, this cannot adequately explain the regime's significant extrajudicial violence against its perceived opponents, particularly from 1976 onward. To clamp down on the opposition and prose-cute armed zealots as criminals, the regime could still have relied on its special courts—by then firmly established—and on the by then fully submissive civil-ian judiciary. It could have done so in reference to a large and steadily growing arsenal of emergency laws, articles in the Penal Code, new special laws (such as Law 49 of July 1980, imposing the death sentence on membership of the Muslim Brotherhood), and scores of legislative degrees. The regime's decision to instead wage an all-out war against the opposition and indeed against inno-cent civilians—while incarcerating them en masse without trial—originated in regime perceptions that the opposition and the attacks against it were insti-gated and supported by foreign governments. This, in the eyes of the regime, called for an iron fist approach and warlike measures, not the judicial subtle-ties designed to prosecute mere criminals.

Roughly from the mid-1970s onward the regime began to view its steadily radicalizing opponents, both on the left and armed Islamists, and gradually without discriminating between them, as puppets and agents instigated and supported by foreign governments, both in the region, including Israel, and by the United States. Evidently, its archrival and namesake, the Iraqi Ba'thist re-gime, was the Syrian regime's first and most prominent scapegoat for increas-ing unrest and violence in Syria (Lobmeyer 1995, 256). Saudi Arabia and Jordan were similarly singled out by aggressive statements blaming these and other countries for meddling in Syria's affairs and fueling domestic unrest. At home, the regime portrayed the Muslim Brotherhood as fifth columnists, supported by or even acting on behalf of reactionary foreign powers and having no local roots or popular standing (Syrian Arab Republic 1984a, 73–101; Tlass 1991).

Again, of course, regime rhetoric can be dismissed as propaganda de-signed to mislead and therefore of no analytic relevance. Yet the general em-phasis, at least, on foreign instigation and interference appears to have been genuine and indicative of dominant perceptions within the regime. First, the regime seems to have been taken aback by the magnitude of the challenges posed by opposition groups and their ability to strike at the regime with force, particularly the Islamists.[34] In view of this, the surge in antiregime violence and the increasingly radical opposition to the regime could only be explained by foreign instigation and support. Furthermore, the regime's own policies and actions had contributed to the blurring of domestic and foreign politics and conflict, also coloring the regime's perceptions of domestic opposition groups. The 1976 military invasion in Lebanon, Syria's alliance with Iran since the end of the 1970s and, going back to 1972, a series of (attempted) assassinations by Syrian security agents of Syrian opposition members, Lebanese journalists and politicians, and Jordanian politicians abroad is likely to have fostered the regime's anticipation that foreign powers would strike back inside Syria.[35] Memories among the regime's strongmen of the unremitting interference, intrigues, and support to various coups by foreign powers in Syria prior to 1963 was no less important in shaping such perceptions.[36] The struggle for Syria, in Seale's version, was the regime's prism through which it assessed its opponents, at home and abroad. Furthermore, such assessments were not just in the minds of regime strongmen; they were at least partly confirmed by credible information (Kienle 1990; Lobmeyer 1995, 268–270, 322; Mufti 1996; Seale 1990, 335–336). Iraq, Jordan, Saudi Arabia, and Egypt hosted and supported Syrian opposition members and helped in financing such groups in Syria. Lebanon became the site of Islamist opposition gatherings, and a coup attempt in January 1982 by pro-Iraqi Ba'thist officers was reasonably believed to have been masterminded by Iraq.

Between 1976 and 1982 the regime's discourse incorporated notions of criminality to denounce the armed attacks by Islamist groups, while in 1978 Hafiz al-Asad asserted that the unrest would be dealt with by imposing law and order (Middle East Watch 1990, 17). Yet the perceived foreign connection appears to have led the regime to believe that waging war, not judicial repression, was the appropriate answer.[37] The belligerent and warring language used by Rifa'at al-Asad, Hafiz's brother and head of the paramilitary Defense Brigades, although extreme even by the regime's standards, may be considered emblematic of the mood prevailing within the regime at the time.[38] Within this military and warmongering disposition, those who were seen has having sold themselves to foreign powers were no longer entitled to the few civil rights the regime still offered. To use Hannah Arendt's (1951, 294) well-known phrase, they had lost their "right to have rights." Decriminalized yet transformed into foreign combatants, all those who dared to oppose the regime became fair game for extreme extrajudicial repression.

If one accepts the argument that the regime's lapses into full-blown extrajudicial repression strongly correlate with the ways in which it perceived and portrayed its opponents as foreign agents, one is left with an apparent paradox. Exactly when perceived external or foreign forces formed an acute challenge to the regime, its desire to display the judicial processes as icons of state sovereignty toward the outside world failed to preserve the judicialization of repression at home. While this in itself can be viewed as proof of the disingenuousness of the regime's external discourse on the judiciary, it serves as yet another reminder that real levels of judicialization can never be fully explained in reference to the motivations and interests attributed to the regime solely with regard to its judicial strategies of repression. After all, in this instance it appears that such motivations and interests were clearly overshadowed by other considerations wherein the outside world purportedly had teamed up with domestic agents in a powerful alliance that, in the regime's view, could only be crushed by sheer force.

THE SIGNIFICANCE OF JUDICIALIZATION
AND THE RESILIENCE OF AUTHORITARIANISM

Does it matter that authoritarian regimes judicialize their repression of political dissent? Both strong normative considerations and, as emphasized here, a perspective on the resilience of the authoritarian regime in Syria suggest it does. One the one hand, human rights considerations overall render judicialization desirable. Yet judicialization is analytically significant because Syria's judiciary appears to have played a role in the "upgrading of authoritarianism," albeit in ways that may not be immediately expected or even be intended.

Courts matter for normative reasons derived from a human rights perspective. Even those who do not use liberal human rights perspectives to analyze courts in authoritarian settings emphasize that, in the end, it is preferable for political dissidents to be brought to court rather than being shot at, shelled, or made to disappear in extrajudicial dirty wars. Accordingly, Pereira notes that judicialization generally moderates the intensity of repression (Pereira 2005, 6, 13). This, the author argues, would also help explain why the common tendency of authoritarian regimes to judicialize repression over time coincides with a general decline in their reliance on violent coercion. This, one may add, may be because authoritarian judiciaries, despite their many flaws, have a tendency to counter the inclination of military authoritarian rulers to apply their trade in waging war against their own citizens. From this perspective, increasing judicialization also has the potential to set in motion changes toward less coercive authoritarianism. "Where repression is judicialized, regime opponents are likely to have a few more rights and a little more space in which to contest regime prerogatives" (Pereira 2005, 198). Furthermore, the potential of judicialization to push regimes to somewhat soften their authoritarianism—even when far from universal and unlikely to lead to full-blown and unremitted political liberalization—is a theme running through the work of Moustafa and Ginsburg (Ginsburg and Moustafa 2008; Moustafa, 2007).

Syrian human rights activists and lawyers have made some very similar arguments.[39] They, too, have campaigned against extrajudicial forced disappearances and preventive arrests and pressured the regime to bring political dissidents to court while knowing very well that this is unlikely to result in more just outcomes. Furthermore, Syrian defense lawyers and defendants' relatives and supporters systematically used the platform of courts to contest regime prerogatives.[40] Few lawyers, however, expected any tangible political changes to be initiated by the Syrian courts, given the modest levels of judicialization adhered to, primarily by the SSSC, and because of the regime's strong grip over all courts. Likewise, international human rights activists and Western governments calling for respect for human rights in Syria have stressed the desirability of courts and judicialization, even when Syria's courts do not meet their standards. This perspective, Western diplomats say, motivated them, sometimes at the level of ambassadors, regularly to observe politically charged trials, even if most of them felt that their presence failed to make a real difference either in the conduct of the proceedings or in the sentences imposed on defendants.[41]

However, the judicialization of repression in Syria had some important downsides, too, from a normative or human rights perspective, even if these paled in comparison with the excesses of outright extrajudicial repression. For instance, one former political prisoner lamented about his experience by arguing that instead of having been convicted by a court (the SSSC) he would have preferred to have been disappeared, as his brother was in the 1980s.[42] After all, the court sentence against him included penalties that stripped him of his civil rights. As a result, he was unable to obtain a passport, could not travel, could not get a job as a teacher, could not renew his driver's license, and could not register property that he inherited from his parents. His brother, who resurfaced in the early 1990s, faced no such obstacles. Such deprivations of citizen's rights were indeed commonly ordered as additional punishments against political defendants and thus judicially prolonged the repression of political dissent after release from prison (Saad and Zaitouneh 2006, 22).[43]

Former political convicts also have said that they had mixed feelings about having been tried by ordinary civilian courts as criminals and not by the SSSC or a military tribunal.[44] They felt that the special courts at least acknowledged the political nature of the alleged offense and as such bestowed those convicted with political status or even some legitimacy, something the criminal courts categorically did not. They sensed that this way their convictions at the civilian courts helped the regime's now common argument that there were no political prisoners in Syria but only convicted criminals.[45] Lawyers added that the increased judicialization by referrals to criminal courts also affected the prison conditions of political detainees. While political prisoners were commonly held together and often granted a few privileges such as being able to access reading materials, those convicted as "criminals" can "end up being detained among drug dealers, murderers and rapists and are given the same treatment."[46] Furthermore, an argument could be made that the referral of political cases to Syria's ordinary criminal courts negatively affected the integrity of such courts, which already was seriously compromised due to widespread judicial corruption and mismanagement. Interestingly in this context, Moustafa (2007) points out the reverse scenario, in which authoritarian regimes that are eager to bolster their civilian courts (for example, to help enforcing property rights), sometimes deliberately insulate such courts from the messy business of political persecution by sending political cases to special courts. On top of that, the criminalization of political dissent confronted at least some civilian judges with moral and professional dilemmas, as they were forced to be directly involved in the regime's repressive measures.[47] Those few civilian judges who put up some resistance were reportedly demoted and transferred to remote areas.[48] As such judges often enjoyed rare and long-standing reputations for integrity and professionalism, major civilian courts lost out. In sum, the use of courts certainly is to be preferred above extrajudicial repression, but within the boundaries of judicialization it also entails some costs.

The significance of the judicialization of repression can be approached by considering its broad implications for regime survival. Accordingly, the question as to "why judicialization matters" gets to be firmly placed in relation to what Heydemann calls "authoritarian upgrading" in the Arab world at large (Heydemann 2007b). In this view, Arab authoritarian regimes have achieved a marked degree of resilience by "reorganizing their strategies of governance" to face multiple challenges; "a product of trial and error more than intentional design" (Heydemann 2007b, 1).

However, it is suggested here that the significance of the judicialization of repression in Syria ought to qualify Heydemann's general propositions. First, while the judicialization of repression can indeed be viewed as one form in which strategies of governance have been adjusted, this does not mean that coercion has merely become one, let alone a less prominent, instrument within the regime's increasingly heterogeneous arsenal of technologies of power.[49] Instead, judicialization has been one instance of innovation but *within* the modes in which coercion and repression can be, are, and continue to be exercised; not in opposition to or supplementary to coercion and repression.

Secondly, and most importantly, the judicialization of repression—regarded as one domain of authoritarian upgrading—does not gain significance with respect to the challenges posed by pressures within society and by regimes' external environments to democratize, adjust to globalization, or reform the economy (Heydemann 2007b, 1, 3). Instead, in Syria the judicialization of repression through 2011, intentionally or inadvertently, appears to have helped counter the perilous fallout for the regime of reliance on extrajudicial full-scale violence and warlike measures. From this perspective, the use of courts seems to have helped neutralize or prevent repeated and—for the regime—likely fatal scenarios in which specialized security agencies and paramilitary forces turn onto the regime itself.[50] In this context it is no coincidence that, of all the attempted military coups and power grabs by paramilitary officers since 1963, many occurred during and directly after the use of significant levels of extrajudicial violence. In some cases, holding responsibility for extrajudicial violence made officers overconfident or determined to be rewarded, as for instance in the case of National Guard Commander Hamad 'Ubayd, who ordered tanks to fire against the Grand Mosque in Hama to put down the revolt there in 1964 (Seale 1990, 93). When these rewards did not come as expected, 'Ubayd rebelled in 1966 but was arrested. In September 1966, Druze Colonel Salim Hatum staged an abortive coup. He had been responsible for commandos who, using much violence, on February 23 of that year ousted President Amin al-Hafiz. Interestingly, Seale suggests that among the main motives behind Hatum's coup attempt was his frustration that he had not been sufficiently rewarded for having saved the regime (Seale 1990, 109).

However, the coup attempts during the peak of extrajudicial repression between 1976 and 1983 are especially instructive. In January 1982, Aleppine officers, led by Brigadier General Ibrahim Lutfi and mainly coming from the air force, staged a failed coup attempt allegedly in coordination with Islamist armed groups (Lobmeyer 1995, 322). This time, the main motive seems to have been resentment over their deployment in their hometown to violently put down protests and kill Islamist militants. Earlier, air force pilots had refused to carry out bombings in Aleppo and Hama. Of course, the most interesting and for the regime most challenging episode of (para)military forces responsible for extrajudicial repression turning against the regime was in 1984, when the Defense Brigades led by Rifa'at al-Asad entered Damascus to take over the regime but failed. According to Seale, Rifa'at viewed as one of his main credentials that he had taken a leading role in the violent clampdown on Islamists between 1980 and 1982, especially in Hama (Seale 1990, 425). When his brother Hafiz fell ill, he sensed the right moment to be rewarded for this role.

This is not to suggest that all coups or coup attempts were linked to motivations informed by prior extrajudicial violence or that coup attempts that did include such motivations can be reduced to such motives. Neither, for that matter, did all officers responsible for extrajudicial atrocities stage such coups. Yet it is clear that the use of extrajudicial violence can result in dangerous unintended consequences for the regime because security and military personnel may strongly resent their involvement or, on the contrary, may become overambitious in a bid to be rewarded. Against this background, a modest but still significant degree of judicialization of repression, or its gradual rejudicialization from the early 1990s until 2011, can be viewed as having helped to reduce such threats to the regime or, perhaps, as having helped to prevent their reoccurrence.[51] Syria's judiciary plays a key role in coercion and repression, but it does not control the means of violence that could be directed against the regime itself.

CONCLUSION

This paper hopes to have made a modest contribution toward bringing coercion back into the study of the technologies of power and the resilience of authoritarianism by a case study of Syria. It did so by studying the role of the judiciary which, in strongly authoritarian settings, turns "the rule by law" into a tool of repression. Accordingly, this chapter has presented some main arguments to elucidate the main reasons why Syria's authoritarian regime bothered to judicialize the repression of political dissent and why this matters. First, it was argued that the notion of judicialization should be approached critically because extrajudicial measures still coexist and are intermingled with the use of courts and indeed play an important role in how Syrian courts operate, especially due to the continued dominance of quasi-judicial "special" courts. Second, along a continuum contrasting judicialization and extrajudicial repression, Syria has shown a zigzag pattern since 1963, where modest and indeed inadequate levels of judicialization were interrupted by significant lapses into extrajudicial violence but improved until 2011. Third, in Syria the use of courts as such cannot be convincingly explained by reference to rational and deliberate regime motivations or strategies to address or overcome authoritarian pathologies. The main reason courts matter to the regime is related to its discursive and normative notions of statehood and, related to this, its preoccupations with claiming, displaying, and preserving state sovereignty embodied by courts. However, such intentions should not be confused with the factors driving real levels of judicialized repression. Instead, it was argued that the modest levels of judicialization of repression throughout the period under study originated in and are closely intertwined with the role of the legal profession and courts in the wider context of the "struggle for Syria." From the regime's perspective, lawyers and judges generally found themselves on the losing side in the domestic, political, and economic dimensions of this struggle, with lasting negative repercussions for the regime's trust in and reliance on judicial institutions.

In addition to this, it was argued that lapses into full-blown extrajudicial violence—reaching warlike proportions between 1976 and 1983—mainly originated in regime perceptions that the opposition and the attacks against it were instigated and supported by foreign powers. Perceived as foreign agents, political activists and armed militants were to be indiscriminately confronted with an iron first of armed force, not by the "rights to have rights" at least nominally granted by tribunals to mere criminals. Finally, the judicialization of repression in Syria matters principally in two ways: first, because courts, even when evidently failing to respect human rights and having their own downsides in this respect, on the whole moderate the intensity of regime repression; and, second, because the use of courts seems to have helped neutralize or prevent for the regime likely fatal scenarios wherein continued reliance on extrajudicial repression would have led security and paramilitary forces in charge of such violence to turn against the regime itself.

Following the start of the Syrian uprising in March 2011, the regime again has abandoned the judiciary in its attempt to quell protest. In a bid to appease criticisms, it abolished the state of emergency and the SSSC. Dramatic as these measures would have been a year earlier, they failed to have much significance in the country's revolutionary climate. Indeed, courts generally played no role whatsoever as security forces, combat troops, and thugs have been deployed to violently suppress the demonstrations that started in Dar'a, south of

Damascus and then quickly spread to the rest of the country. Echoing developments in the late 1970s and early 1980s, the regime's adversaries have been branded foreign agents and conspirators deserving no mercy and indeed no trials. The regime may or may not survive the challenge posed by its adversaries. Yet if our argument about the judiciary's contribution to regime resilience has any merit for analyzing the current crisis, the regime's reliance on raw extrajudicial repression may bring a serious backlash. Indeed, the regime's most notorious henchmen may want to be rewarded for defending it against the most serious challenge to its rule since at least the 1980s, or they may want to shield themselves from the regime's future attempts to get rid of its most unsavory elements who may stand in the way of "reforming" the regime. Those on the European Union's list of thirteen Syrian individuals who are believed to be leading Syria's current repressive campaign, drawn up to subject them to sanctions, should be carefully watched for their future moves.[52]

9 DEMOCRATIC STRUGGLES AND AUTHORITARIAN RESPONSES IN IRAN IN COMPARATIVE PERSPECTIVE

Güneş Murat Tezcür

THE ISLAMIC REPUBLIC OF IRAN has unique characteristics. Ultimate power is concentrated in the hands of a single individual, the supreme leader, who is not popularly elected, practically has life tenure, and controls a loyal security apparatus with a mission to repress internal dissent. Citizens who want to run in the elections for the parliament and presidency need their political credentials to be approved by an institution (the Guardians Council) whose members are not popularly accountable. The same institution can also strike down any parliamentary legislation or presidential bill on the grounds that it violates the constitution or Islam. At the same time, this very regime regularly holds elections that introduce a degree of uncertainty and competitiveness that is unprecedented in other Middle Eastern authoritarian regimes. Until recently, opposition candidates perceived the Iranian elections as means toward power and occasionally scored electoral victories, unlike their counterparts in authoritarian Arab regimes such as Syria. Furthermore, the main opposition group in Iran, the Green Movement, has strong and credible democratic commitments that have few counterparts among the Arab Islamists.

This chapter analyzes the dynamics of authoritarian resilience and struggles for the expansion of rights in contemporary Iran. Why did authoritarian rule recover from the rise of a prodemocratic reform movement in Iran after 2004? What explains the emergence of a powerful but ultimately unsuccessful mass movement in summer 2009? This chapter addresses these questions through a comparative framework that includes postcommunist and Arab authoritarian regimes. In the process, it makes two contributions to broader scholarly debates about authoritarianism. First, the capacities of a regime for repression, geopolitical conditions, and the distribution of economic endowments are important for the sustainability of authoritarian rule. Yet these structural and institutional factors by themselves do not explain the pace and direction of political change in authoritarian regimes. Equally important and relevant are the perceptions of predominant political actors and the strategies they pursue, especially during critical junctures such as electoral moments when uncertainty increases and opportunities for change abound.

These perceptions and strategies have an independent impact on democratic struggles and authoritarian resilience when uncertainty prevails. In these junctures, the vulnerabilities and strengths of authoritarian rule are exposed. Authoritarian regimes that are thought to be durable may suddenly collapse, as the swift victories of the Tunisian and Egyptian uprisings in early 2011 demonstrate. Similarly, structural factors provide a satisfactory explanation for neither authoritarian resilience nor democratic struggles in contemporary Iran. Structural and institutional explanations that are often based on a dichotomy between state and society need to be complemented by a perspective that recognizes the contingent nature of authoritarian rule and focuses on the interactive strategies pursued by the ruling elite and opposition (Capoccia and Ziblatt 2010, 937). While elections contribute to the sustainability of authoritarian rule in Iran, they also provide unique opportunities for opposition mobilization. The ability of the opposition to fully capitalize on these opportunities and develop new contentious repertoires (for example, street demonstrations, civic disobedience campaigns, and cyberspace networking) strongly contribute to the pace and scope of democratic struggles.

Second, the chapter eschews a dichotomous framework of authoritarian versus democratic rule in favor of a continuous framework that focuses on "episodes of democratization" that may take place even under the most authoritarian conditions. In this sense, it may be misleading to search for a single decisive threshold of democratic transition in every context (Ziblatt 2006, 335–337).

The next section offers conceptual perspectives that transcend the state–society dichotomy in studying political change in Iran. Following is a discussion that locates the dynamics of authoritarian resilience in Iran in a broader framework. The comparative analysis suggests that structural and institutional studies of authoritarian rule need to be complemented by perspectives that focus on the interaction between regime and opposition strategies. The penultimate section builds on these conceptual and theoretical perspectives to offer a narrative of political change in Iran between 1997 and 2009. The conclusion summarizes how the theoretical and comparative approach developed in this chapter informs the scholarly literature on authoritarianism. The data for the chapter come from a variety of original sources, including public opinion surveys conducted in Tehran; participant observation during the elections of 2005, 2008, and 2009; in-depth interviews; and written and electronic material in Persian.

CONCEPTUALIZING POLITICAL CHANGE IN IRAN

According to an influential perspective, a distinguishing characteristic of contemporary Iran is the emergence of civil society as the site of emancipatory ideas and practices. Changes in social values and preferences are perceived as the primary driving force of political change in the Islamic Republic of Iran (IRI). Ali Gheissari and Vali Nasr (2006, 8) are critical of perspectives that reduce conflict to an opposition between state and society: "This binary outlook does not adequately explain the complex ways in which state goals and social ideals converge in order to produce certain political outcomes." Yet their analytical framework still operates within the confines of this binary outlook. In their own words,

> Although state behavior in Iran does not normatively reflect democratic values, in many regards Iranian society has already turned the corner, passing through a more challenging threshold of democratization, by adopting the democratic ethos at the grassroots level and looking to civil society activism and elections to voice social and political demands. (vi)

Similarly, they argue that the goals of state building impeded the development of democracy (14, 148). They continue to treat the state as a monolithic actor and conceptualize it principally in terms of its repressive capacity. Society, which is also conceptualized as a homogenous entity, remains the source of democratic change.

Similar to Gheissari and Nasr, Ali Ansari (2000, 20) criticizes "the 'state versus society' model, which does not capture the highly integrated nature of state–society relations in Iran." Yet he does not disaggregate the state and identify the interactions among state and societal actors. He continues to argue that Iran may be "an example of a democratization process emphatically (though not exclusively) determined by society" (23). He interprets the victory of Khatami in the 1997 presidential elections as "the culmination of a decade of social and intellectual agitation which sought to define the legacy of the Islamic Revolution as distinct from the centralizing and autocratic tendencies of the 'state,' and refocus towards the needs, desires, and 'rights' of society" (2003, 250). While he recognizes that divisions among the political elite may generate and contribute to the process of change, he claims that elite power to restrain "the pace and scope of this change" has diminished (2000, 23). Fakhreddin Azimi (2008) traces the origins of democratic aspirations back to the 1906 Constitutional Revolution. Because these aspirations remain unfulfilled, "The Iranian regime continues to face the challenge of politically containing the growing rift separating the rulers from the ruled" (444). He also notes, "Iranian society should reveal far great attentiveness to social democratic values than have other societies in the region" (424). Postrevolutionary Iran has been characterized by a "tremendous rise in the appeal of democratic ideals and a resilient, albeit battered, civil society" (448).

The state–society dichotomy persists not only because it is appealing as a metanarrative of democratization. The development of civil society and the rise of democratically oriented social movements (for example, women's and student movements) in contemporary Iran provide some support for the notion of a progressive society confronting an increasingly reactionary state. However, this state-versus-society perspective offers an inadequate and narrow reading of political struggles in Iran for three reasons: (1) state and society are not very distinct entities in contemporary Iran; (2) the normative implications of the state–society dichotomy are not always justified; and (3) political preferences may be endogenous to political action. First and most obviously, the state and society are not monolithic entities with well-ordered preferences. Building on Joel Migdal's work, one can argue that these two entities are mutually constitutive of each other and have porous borders (2001). From its beginning, the Islamic regime has been characterized by the existence of multiple power centers controlled by prominent personalities who enter into loose coalitions, jockey for influence within the system, represent different social constituencies, and offer competing interpretations of the legacy of the revolution (Brumberg 2001, 3; Moslem 2002). Decisions are often made through informal channels; political allegiances are based on patronage as well as ideological affinity (Alamdari 2005; Buchta 2000, 6–7).

The conflict among state actors has been the main dynamic of political change in the IRI. The rise of the reformist movement in the late 1990s can be interpreted primarily as a process of elite defection facilitated by popular grievances. The troika that emerged as the leaders of the opposition later in 2009 was composed of a former president (Mohammad Khatami), a former prime minister (Mir Hossein Mousavi), and a former speaker of the parliament (Mehdi Karrubi). Their views have dramatically evolved since the establishment of the IRI. Mousavi was an ardent supporter of the Islamic revolution in the early 1980s. Karroubi espoused the formation of a Muslim alliance against the U.S. troops stationed in Saudi Arabia during the Saddam Hussein's invasion of Kuwait (Arjomand 2009, 134–135, 139). Moreover, another former president (Hashemi Rafsanjani) openly expressed his support to the opposition. While Rafsanjani initially supported the candidacy of Khatami in 1997, he became closer to Khatami's opponents a year later (Buchta 2000, 150–151). In the 2000 elections, Rafsanjani and Mahmoud Ahmadinejad were on the same candidate lists (Naji 2008, 43). They became bitter enemies when Ahmadinejad defeated Rafsanjani in the second round of the 2005 presidential elections.

The elections expanded the scope of societal participation in politics and increased the stakes of elite infighting within the IRI. They also facilitated the rise of a younger generation of hard-liners who successfully developed populist appeals (Ehteshami and Zweiri 2007, 34–45). Whereas the reformists were committed to a fundamental restructuring of political institutions and political pluralism, the hard-liners were content with the institutional status quo and had little tolerance for dissent (Rajaee 2007, 22). Ironically, both groups took advantage of electoral opportunities to appeal to their social constituencies, mobilize a broader base, and gain state power. The role played by local councils in political struggles is informative in this regard. The first local elections were held in February 1999 and resulted in sweeping reformist victories (Buchta 2000, 178–182). The Tehran council under the leadership of Saeed Hajjarian played an important role in the reformist victory in the 2000 parliamentary elections (Arjomand 2009, 132). Yet the same council that was central to the reformist strategy of expanding popular participation was also important in the rise of Ahmadinejad to the national prominence. Ahmadinejad, who failed to garner enough votes to win a seat on the council in 1999, was elected mayor of Tehran after a very low turnout in the February 2003 local council elections (Naji 2008, 48). Consequently, the expansion of political space may have very unintended consequences and does not simply signify the increasing power of society over the state.

Another factor that complicates the state–society dichotomy in Iran is that the reformists were deeply embedded in the state institutions they aimed to overhaul (Bayat 2007, 127–131). Not only had the leading reformist figures made their careers in state institutions, but they also perceived the state as the primary agent of progressive change. To their credit, they have achieved significant achievements, including an explicit ban on torture, greater rights to political prisoners, expansion of press freedoms, and limited reform of the judicial system (Abrahamian 2008, 190). In the words of a prominent human rights lawyer, courts were more sympathetic to proright litigation when Khatami and his allies were in charge of the government.[1] Similarly, the press had more freedom in discussing "politically sensitive issues" during the Khatami era than under its successor.[2] One can be critical of the reformists by claiming that they neglected "social dynamics and groups to instead concentrate all their efforts and energies on the state" (Kamrava 2008, 36). At the same time, the state-centric political strategy of the reformists is similar to social movements elsewhere. State power may be crucial to social movements' success in securing their gains and defending themselves against authoritarian backlash (for example, Sohrabi 1995). The Turkish Islamists, who are often described as a society-centric force, strived to use governmental authority to enforce Islamization whenever the electoral system presented opportunities blurring the boundaries between the state and society (Tuğal 2009). Recent works on contemporary Iran offer perspectives transcending the state–society dichotomy and demonstrate how interactions among state and societal actors are central to the dynamics of change in Iran (Keshavarzian 2007; Osanloo 2009, 110).

A second criticism of the state–society dichotomy concerns its normative implications. The state is not necessarily an obstacle to the expansion of rights, nor is civil society inherently a harbinger of democratic change. The Islamic state has contributed to the expansion of rights in several ways, notwithstanding its repressive character. First, rural areas saw significant increases in public investment and services that directly contributed to the well-being of peasants after the revolution (Harris, Chapter 3 in this volume; Salehi-Isfahani 2009, 19–22). Second, revolutionary success resulted in the formation of a more representative political elite with provincial backgrounds and contributed to social integration (Arjomand 2009, 115; 123–127; Ehsani 2009, 42–44, 65). Third, the mobilization of women during the revolution, the education and health care policies of the Islamic regime, and the ambiguities of regime's gender policies contributed to the formation of an autonomous, sustainable, and vibrant women's movement that directly challenged patriarchal practices and made considerable gains (Bayat 2007, 79–80; Haeri 2009; Keddie 2003, 286–289, 292; Osanloo, Chapter 6 in this volume; Sedghi 2007, 240–204).

Fourth, the Islamic regime exhibited more flexibility in dealing with ethnic grievances than many other regimes in the Middle East, including electoral democracies such as Israel and Turkey. In contrast to the Pahlavi monarchy, the IRI recognized the ethnic and religious pluralism and diversity inherent to Iranian society (with the significant exceptions of the Bahais, the Christian converts, and the Sufi sects), even if this recognition did not mean equal treatment of minorities (Sanasarian 2000, 6).

Nor has civil society inevitably been a site of democratic practices and ideas (for example, Berman 1997, 2003; Jamal 2007; but also Sadowski 1993). However, Iranian civil society is often portrayed as the agent of democratic change unlike any other in the region (for example, Bayat 2007, 204). This observation can be misleading. While the Iranian electoral system has many flaws, the popular vote for Ahmadinejad in the second round of the 2005 presidential elections was overwhelming. Why did a considerable segment of the Iranian electorate vote for a candidate who clearly represented the most authoritarian tendency in Iran's political spectrum? If Khatami's election "was a rejection of authoritarianism and a clear indication of the scale and strength of democratic aspirations in the country" (Azimi 2008, 381), did the election of Ahmadinejad signal popular support for authoritarianism in Iran? While a systematic analysis of voting behavior in Iran is beyond the scope of this chapter, voting habits of Iranians defy simplistic narratives. It was not untypical for an Iranian citizen to vote for Khatami in 1997, Ahmadinejad in 2005, and Mousavi in 2009. Hossein, a middle-aged art director, exhibited such a voting pattern. He voted for Khatami in 1997 because he supported his platform promising "freedom of speech." Yet he was completely disenchanted with Khatami by 2005 when he enthusiastically supported Ahmedinejad in both rounds of the presidential elections. He also persuaded his two "bad-hijab" daughters (a term applied to women who wear the compulsory headscarf in a liberal way), who were university students, to vote for him. For Hossein, Ahmedinejad was honest, modest, and an outsider to the corrupt political system. Many individuals who were in his social circle shared this positive conviction. Hossein would be deeply disappointed with his choice in several years. In 2009, he became an ardent supporter of Mousavi and took active role in his campaign. For Hossein, Iran became a despotic country under Ahmedinejad.

Voting behavior in the Iranian elections may reflect motivations other than commitment to democracy. According to a random sampling survey administered in Tehran in late 2007 and early 2008 ($n = 580$), 76 percent of the respondents think that no, a little, or limited democracy exists in Iran. Furthermore, an overwhelming majority of the respondents (83 percent) claim that the Iranian political system is not, a little, or to a limited extent accountable (Tezcür et al. 2012). Yet an extensive literature shows that patronage distribution and access to pecuniary incentives characterize voting behavior in authoritarian contexts where poorer and rural voters are more likely to vote and to vote for regime loyalists (for example, Gandhi and Lust-Okar 2009, 408–409; Lust-Okar 2009, 126–128).

A third and final criticism of the state–society dichotomy is related to the assumption that preferences are stable and unambiguous and directly inform political action. An extensive literature argues that preferences may be actually shaped by opportunities and action (for example, Elster 1989, 17; Kalyvas 2006, 101; Weingeist 2005, 181). In particular, political action may actually shape ambiguous and inconsistent preferences in certain historical periods, such as the Iranian Revolution. Only when people perceived the opposition to be viable did they participate in demonstrations in huge numbers, even if they did not necessarily share the ideology of the opposition (Kurzman 2004, 9–10; Parsa 2000, 9). The 2009 uprising in Iran can also be understood in similar terms. It was clear that a substantial segment of Iranians harbored widespread grievances against the ruling regime. Yet there was no automatic connection among grievances and electoral mobilization and uprising. Grievances might result in apathy in the absence of a well-organized and enthusiastic opposition movement. This was actually what happened in the 2005 presidential elections, when the main reformist candidate Moustafa Moin ended up fifth. In 2009, the reformists first coalesced around Mousavi's candidacy, built extensive cyber and physical networks, and engaged in extensive vote canvassing. They organized mass rallies, convinced many Iranians that Mousavi's candidacy was viable, and generated political momentum. In this sense, they not only built on preexisting preferences but also shaped popular preferences and beliefs about opportunities. For instance, Hadi, a journalist in his late twenties, was initially very pessimistic of Mousavi's chances. Yet his views rapidly changed in the days leading to the elections. After the elections, he overcame his fears and enthusiastically joined a huge march in Tehran. He felt emboldened when so many citizens openly challenged the regime. He left Iran for self-imposed exile a year later when it became clear that mass mobilization had lost its momentum.

These criticisms of the state–society dichotomy suggest that contemporary political struggles in Iran do not take place between two opposing and monolithic societal and statist sides with well-ordered preferences. Societal actors confront state authorities on certain issues and negotiate and collabo-rate on others. The reformists negotiated with and contested state authorities to expand the scope of civil rights and political liberties from 1997 to 2004. Their gains were rolled back by the hard-liners who also successfully pursued popular mobilization with their control of the key state institutions and access to substantial economic rents. Meanwhile, citizen preferences evolved consid-erably, reflecting changes in the political context. Consequently, democratiza-tion in Iran can be conceptualized as a dynamic but reversible struggle that involves cross-cutting alliances among state and societal actors (Tilly 2007).

ELECTORAL UPRISINGS AND AUTHORITARIAN
RESILIENCE IN COMPARATIVE PERSPECTIVE

It is informative to compare Iran with a set of nondemocratic regimes on the basis of these theoretical insights. This comparison shows the limits of struc-tural and institutional perspectives in explaining how authoritarian elites suc-cessfully manage electoral uncertainty in some instances but not in others. It supports the contention that elections can be both mechanisms of authoritar-ian resilience and facilitators of democratization. Elections are neither intrin-sically conducive to democratic progress nor only formal mechanisms that sustain authoritarian rule.

Since 2000, a number of postcommunist countries, such as Serbia, Geor-gia, Ukraine, and Kyrgyzstan, have had postelectoral protests that resulted in alternation in executive power. These competitive authoritarian regimes hold periodical and semifree elections, which opposition groups contest and perceive as the primary route to power even if they are subject to systematic repression and severely handicapped in access to resources (Levitsky and Way 2010). In this respect, the IRI is more like the postcommunist competitive authoritarian regimes than the authoritarian regimes of the Arab Middle East, where the victory of ruling groups was guaranteed. It would be tempt-ing to characterize the IRI as a sultanistic or neopatrimonial regime, where a single individual monopolizes decision making and has unlimited discre-tionary power (Arjomand 2009, 188–191; Ganji 2008, 49–50). Alternatively, the IRI can be described as a military regime given the increasing power of the Iranian Revolutionary Guard Corps. Such characterizations underplay the regime's ability to integrate and co-opt large segments of the society, its rela-tively broad channels of elite recruitment, and its strong ideological mobilization capacities. The IRI is not necessarily vulnerable to violent overthrows and succession crises, a key characteristic of sultanistic regimes (Chehabi and Linz 1998). Elections played a stabilizing role by expanding the scope of elite recruitment in the IRI at least until 2009 (Gandhi and Przeworski 2007, 1279). They also limited the willingness and capacity of elites to abandon institutional channels in favor of extraparliamentary strategies (for example, Magaloni 2008). Furthermore, the IRGC is not an ideologically and politically monolithic institution (Wehrey et al. 2009, 81). Its involvement in political affairs and economic business is likely to generate factionalism and dilute its professional identity (70).

Electoral uprisings in postcommunist countries have generated a prolific body of scholarship with competing claims. A primary source of disagreement concerns the role of opposition actors versus structural factors in sparking transitions. An earlier scholarship highlighted the role of uncertainty during regime transitions. Under conditions of extreme uncertainty that are characterized by insufficient information, malleable preferences, and unexpected events, structural factors have only very limited explanatory power (O'Donnell and Schmitter 1986, 5; Rustow 1970). This view was later challenged as ignoring the lasting legacy of persistent historical, economic, and institutional factors (Carothers 2002, 16; Linz and Stepan 1996, 57–60). The current debate on electoral uprisings follows these earlier debates. According to Lucan Way (2010, 230–234), the success of the uprisings was primarily a function of the strength of the ruling party, the robustness of its coercive apparatus, and the government's control over economic wealth; "Regime collapses had resulted more from authoritarian weakness than opposition strength" (Way 2008, 62). In contrast, other scholars highlight the importance of oppositional strategies in the success of electoral protests (McFaul 2010, 12–13). Opposition forces took advantage of the opportunities offered by fraudulent elections that generated popular outrage and aggravated existing grievances (Thompson and Kuntz 2004, 161). They employed a rich and diverse ensemble of tactics involving cooperation with similar movements and international NGOs, civil society activism, technology to coordinate actions and disseminate information, electoral monitoring, and rapid tabulation of votes (Beissinger 2007, 261–262; Birch 2002, 502; Bunce and Wolchik 2010b, 146–147; Muskhelishvili and Jorjoliani 2009; Wilson 2005, 111–133). These tactics were highly instrumental in overcoming voter apathy, mobilizing mass support, and translating grievances into collective political action (Howard and Roessler 2006, 317). Massive protests not only overwhelmed the security forces and made the incumbents reluctant to order violent crackdown but also led to shifts in the allegiance of security forces (McFaul 2007, 56) and generated informational cascades revealing widespread mass discontent (Lohmann 1994). In all cases, opposition had a limited time frame to be successful that ran "from the time when fraudulent results are announced to when fraudulently elected officials are formally sworn into office" (Beissinger 2007, 264).

In the light of this discussion, it is useful to compare Iran with competitive postcommunist authoritarian regimes and authoritarian Arab regimes. Following Valerie Bunce and Sharon Wolchik (2010a: 57), Table 9.1 shows key economic variables on the eve of twenty elections in fourteen countries, including Iran. Egypt (until 2011), Jordan, Morocco, and Syria have been noncompetitive Arab authoritarian regimes; Croatia, Georgia, Kyrgyzstan, Serbia, Slovakia, and Ukraine are competitive postcommunist authoritarian regimes that had successful electoral protests; Armenia, Azerbaijan, and Belarus are competitive postcommunist authoritarian regimes without successful protests. While Jordan and Morocco initiated changes to ease restrictions on political competition, elections continued to reinforce the political status quo in these countries (Heydemann 2007b, 10). A key difference between noncompetitive and competitive authoritarian regimes concerns turnout, which tends to be significantly lower in the former. With the exception of the 2000 parliamentary elections in Croatia and the 2005 parliamentary elections in Azerbaijan, competitive authoritarian regimes have consistently higher turnout rates than authoritarian Arab regimes. This observation supports the claim that opposition groups and voters perceive the elections as instruments of political change in the competitive authoritarian regimes. In this regard, the Iranian elections resemble the postcommunist elections.

Table 9.1 shows that economic factors are not good predictors of electoral change. It is difficult to discern any systematic relationship between the state of the economy, on the one hand, and the success of electoral uprisings, on the other hand. In particular, the connection between economic liberalization and political liberalization is tenuous (Heydemann 1993, 73). In terms of unemployment, economic freedom (EF), and economic inequality, all country–year pairs have similar statistics. The only significant exception is Serbia, which had exceptionally high rates of unemployment in 1999. In terms of economic development, authoritarian Arab countries tend to be poorer than both Iran and postcommunist regimes. This may lead to the conclusion that competi-

Table 9.1. Economic indicators on the eve of elections.

	Election year/type	Turnout	GDP per capita (in dollars)	GDP Growth (percentage)	Inflation (percentage)	Unemployment (percentage)	EF	Gini index
Morocco	2002 Par.	51.61	4781	0.8	0.78	12.46	63.9	0.40
Morocco	2007 Par.	37.00	5417	7.6	1.53	9.66	51.5	0.40
Jordan	2007 Par.	54.00	4939	9.0	7.92	12.4	63.7	0.39
Egypt	2005 Pre.	22.95	5002	4.1	11.68	10.74	55.5	0.35
Syria	2003 Par.	63.45	2506	5.2	4.56	11.62	36.6	n/a
Syria	2007 Par.	56.00	2596	4.5	9.06	10.27	46.3	n/a
Iran	1997 Pre.	88.00	7075	7.1	24.72	9.08	36.1	0.44
Iran	2005 Pre.	62.66	9029	5.1	20.59	10.30	42.8	0.39
Iran	2009 Pre.	85.0	10414	5.6	25.00	10.54	45.0	n/a
Croatia	2000 Par.	60.88	9555	-0.9	3.71	13.50	53.1	0.31
Georgia	2003 Par.	87.97	4616	5.5	5.92	12.59	56.7	0.42
Kyrgyzstan	2005 Par.	74.97	3775	7.0	5.11	8.53	58.0	0.36
Serbia	2000 Pre.	71.55	n/a	-1.8	n/a	25.5	n/a	0.38
Slovakia	1998 Par.	84.25	11374	4.6	4.87	11.89	55.5	0.24
Ukraine	2004 Pre.	77.28	7258	9.6	8.22	9.10	51.1	0.37
Armenia	2003 Par.	99.98	5412	13.2	2.37	10.78	68.0	0.41
Armenia	2008 Pre.	69.90	9556	13.4	4.26	9.6	68.6	0.39
Azerbaijan	2003 Pre.	71.23	4136	10.6	3.12	16.0	53.3	0.31
Azerbaijan	2005 Par.	40.47	4662	10.2	8.31	9.0	53.4	0.27
Belarus	2006 Pre.	92.94	18787	9.4	18.93	n/a	46.7	0.23

NOTES: All statistics except for turnout are from the years preceding the election years unless otherwise stated. Turnout statistics are obtained from IFES Election guide except for Jordan 2007 and Iran 2009, available at www.electionguide .org/voter-turnout.php. The Jordan data is obtained from the Interparliamentary Union, available at www.ipu.org/pdf/ publications/elections/2007-e.pdf. The Iran data is obtained from the Iranian Ministry of Interior, available at http://moi.ir/ Portal/Home/ShowPage.aspx?Object=News&CategoryID=832a711b-95fe-4505-8aa3-38f5e17309c9&LayoutID=dd8faff4-f71b-4c65-9aef-a1b6d0160be3&ID=5e30ab89-e376-434b-813f-8c22255158e1. Data for the Iranian elections in 2005 are for the first round. GDP per capita values (Constant Prices: Chain Series with 2005 as a base years in dollars) are from the PENN World Tables, available at http://pwt.econ.upenn.edu/php_site/pwt63/pwt63_form.php. GDP per capita for Iran-2009 is from 2007. GDP growth rates are obtained from the World Development Indicators, available at http://data.worldbank .org/indicator/NY.GDP.MKTP.KD.ZG. Inflation statistics are from the IMF, available at www.imf.org/external/datamapper/ index.php. Unemployment rates are from the World Development Indicators (online 2008 CD versions). Unemployment statistics for Jordan-2007 are from 2004, Syria-2007 from 2003, for Iran-2009 from 2007, for Armenia 2008 from 2004, for Azerbaijan 2003 from 1999, Azerbaijan-2005 from 2003. Unemployment statistic for Serbia 2000 comes from Bunce & Wolchik (2010a, 57). Economic Freedom (EF) statistics are from the Heritage Foundation, available at www.heritage.org/ index/Explore.aspx. Gini statistics are from the Standardized World Income Inequality Database, available at http://dvn .iq.harvard.edu/dvn/dv/fsolt/faces/study/StudyPage.xhtml?studyId=36908. Also see Solt (2009). Gini coefficient for Morocco is from 1999, for Jordan from 2003, for Iran-1997 from 1998, for Serbia 2000 from 2003, for Armenia-2008 from 2006.

tive authoritarian regimes are more likely to exist in wealthier countries. Yet Kyrgyzstan had an electoral revolution in 2005, even though its level of development in 2004 was lower than all country–year pairs other than Syria. Nor is GDP growth rate a good indicator of electoral protests and regime change. The presidential elections in Iran are instructive in this regard. Voters decisively rejected establishment candidates in favor of little-known candidates in

1997 and 2005. The elections in 2009 were highly disputed even if the incumbent, Ahmedinejad, was ultimately sworn in for a second term. Yet economic growth was high on the eve of all these three elections. Among the postcommunist countries, economic growth was not the decisive factor distinguishing between the countries with and without electoral protests or between the countries with and without successful electoral protests. Armenia had a very high growth rate in 2007 and huge and unsuccessful postelectoral protests in 2008. Ukraine had a similarly high growth rate in 2003 but experienced huge and successful postelectoral protests in 2004. Serbia had a negative growth rate in 1999 and huge and successful postelectoral protests in 2000. Finally, high inflation rates do not necessarily result in high levels of protests. Iran has consistently higher inflation rates than all country–year pairs in the sample. Yet there were mass protests only after the 2009 elections.

Table 9.2 shows a series of political indicators for the same sample, again following the practice of Bunce and Wolchik (2010a, 52, 55). Polity scores indicate that the competitive authoritarian regimes do not necessarily have higher scores of democracy than the noncompetitive regimes. For instance, Azerbaijan and Belarus have significantly lower polity scores than Jordan. At the same time, the competitive regimes with relatively higher polity scores are more likely to have successful electoral protests. While Iran has very low polity scores (–6) in years preceding the three presidential elections, its polity score (3) was significantly higher for a period of seven years between 1997 and 2003. The dramatic increase in Iran's score was due to the election of Khatami in 1997 and the dramatic decrease due to the mass disqualifications at the time of the 2004 parliamentary elections. Iran is the only country in the sample that has experienced significant dedemocratization in the last decade. What is also interesting about Iran is that democratization inaugurated by the Khatami's election took place when state-sponsored political terror was pervasive. In fact, Iran consistently has lower scores in physical integrity index (PIRI) than all cases in the sample with the exception of Egypt and Serbia. State-sponsored political terror was not sufficient to crush electoral protests. While Ukraine (2003) and Armenia (2002) had the same PIRI score, electoral protests were successful in the former but not in the latter. Media sustainability is very low for all observations, indicating the absence of a professional, objective, and independent media protected by legal and social norms.

Competitive authoritarian regimes with successful uprisings do not have higher scores in the rule of law dimension (measuring the quality of contract

Table 9.2. Political indicators on the eve of elections.

	Election year/type	Polity	PIRI	Media	Rule of law	Voice and accountability	Political protests	Power transfer
Morocco	2002 Par.	−6	5	n/a	−0.01	−0.34	None	No
Morocco	2007 Par.	−6	4	1.89	−0.11	−0.61	None	No
Jordan	2007 Par.	−2	4	1.86	0.47	−0.49	Low	No
Egypt	2005 Pre.	−6	2	1.88	0.05	−0.96	Low	No
Syria	2003 Par.	−7	4	n/a	−1.53	−1.53	None	No
Syria	2007 Par.	−7	3	1.08	−1.51	−1.51	None	No
Iran	1997 Pre.	−6	2	n/a	−1.03	−1.35	None	Yes
Iran	2005 Pre.	−6	2	1.57	−0.54	−1.27	Low	Yes
Iran	2009 Pre.	−6	1	1.16	−0.80	−1.48	High	No
Croatia	2000 Par.	1	7	n/a	−0.16	−0.29	Med.	Yes
Georgia	2003 Par.	5	5	1.71	−1.25	−0.58	Med.	Yes
Kyrgyzstan	2005 Par.	−3	5	1.74	−0.82	−0.96	Low	Yes
Serbia	2000 Pre.	n/a	0	n/a	−1.29	−1.11	High	Yes
Slovakia	1998 Par.	7	7	n/a	0.21	0.28	Low	Yes
Ukraine	2004 Pre.	6	3	1.96	−0.86	−0.66	Med.	Yes
Armenia	2003 Par.	5	3	1.71	−0.46	−0.52	Low	No
Armenia	2008 Pre.	5	2.5	1.60	−0.51	−0.59	High	No
Azerbaijan	2003 Pre.	−7	2.5	1.76	−0.88	−0.82	Med.	No
Azerbaijan	2005 Par.	−7	2.5	1.81	−0.83	−0.85	High	No
Belarus	2006 Pre.	−7	2.5	0.66	−1.09	−1.66	Low	No

NOTES: All statistics are from the years preceding the election years unless otherwise stated. Polity scores range from −10 (hereditary monarchy) to 10 (consolidated democracy). Available at www.systemicpeace.org/polity/polity4 .htm. Physical Integrity Index (PIRI) ranges between 0 (no government respect for rights and widespread torture, extrajudicial killings, political imprisonment, and disappearances) to 8 (full government respects for rights); available at http://ciri.binghamton.edu/index.asp. PIRI statistic for Serbia is for Serbia and Montenegro. PIRI statistic for Iran-2005 is from 2003, for Iran-2009 from 2005. Voice and accountability and rule of law scores are produced by the World Bank and range from −2.5 to 2.5. Higher score indicate better governance. These indexes are available at http:// info.worldbank.org/governance/wgi/index.asp. Scores for Syria-2003 is from 2000. Value and accountability score for Morocco-2002 is from 2000. Media sustainability Index ranges from 0 (unsustainable, unfree press) to 5 (sustainable press). Available at www.irex.org/msi/index.asp. Scores for Morocco-2007 and Jordan-2007 are from 2006/2007. The media sustainability index for the Middle East/North Africa begins in 2005.

enforcement, the police, and the courts, as well as the likelihood of crime and violence) than do the Arab authoritarian regimes. Jordan has the highest score, and Egypt and Morocco have significantly higher scores than Georgia, Kyrgyzstan, Serbia, and Ukraine. Although there was a decline in Iran's rule of law score between 2004 and 2008, its scores are still higher than the scores of the countries that had successful electoral uprisings. Perhaps the rule of law dimension stands for state capacity. Weak states may be less successful in preventing mass protests. Finally, no systematic relationship is observable between the patterns of electoral successes and voice and accountability scores measuring popular accountability of the government, freedom of expression, freedom of association, and free media. Slovakia has the highest score followed by Croatia, Morocco (2002), and Jordan (2007). Belarus, Syria, Iran, and Serbia have the lowest scores.

This brief analysis suggests that the structural and institutional factors, including economic indicators, prior level of democracy, state repression, and media development, are by themselves insufficient in explaining the dynamics of political change and authoritarian stability. Structural factors in Iran were not necessarily less conducive to successful oppositional mobilization than in postcommunist regimes. While the Iranian regime remains very robust in terms of its control over economic assets, security forces, and political institutions, it also experienced remarkably different electoral outcomes affecting the dynamics of political change between 1997 and 2009. This significant temporal variation calls for a more dynamic approach that focuses on the interactions among the elite and oppositional strategies between 1997 and 2009.

ELECTORAL DYNAMICS AND POLITICAL CHANGE IN IRAN (1997–2009)

Presidential and parliamentary elections in Iran since 1997 have often produced unexpected outcomes that fundamentally affected the balance of political power. In this sense, they did not just reveal political trends and ratify the power distribution (cf. Brownlee 2007, 9). While the 1997 presidential and 2000 parliamentary elections resulted in reformist victories, the 2004 parliamentary and 2005 presidential elections brought a newer generation of hardliners to power. The 2009 presidential elections triggered mass protests and signified that elections were no longer capable of regulating factional conflict. In all these five instances, the interaction among the elites and the strategies they pursued played a decisive role in shaping outcomes. While both judicial and violent state repression were important factors, they are not alone sufficient to explain variation in the electoral outcomes. Besides, neither the reformist nor the hardliner strategies can be made sense of in state versus society terms. Both political actors had extensive societal connections and have been strongly represented in state institutions.

The 1997 elections were the first really competitive presidential elections in Iran. Khatami pursued an energetic campaign with visits all around the country and made a systematic effort to appeal directly to voters. While this unprecedented electoral strategy ushered in an era of political liberalization in Iranian politics, its opponents soon responded with violence. Groups in the ministry of intelligence orchestrated a series of political murders to destabilize the Khatami government in late 1998. In July 1999, vigilante forces attacked students protesting the ban over a reformist newspaper. The ensuing riots in Tehran and other major cities resulted in dozens of casualties. Yet state terror was unable to halt the tide of the reformist movement that won sweeping victories in the 1999 local and 2000 parliamentary elections. That the Guardians Council did not bar many prominent reform figures from running in the parliamentary elections suggests that Khatami and his allies effectively negotiated with the supreme leader, Ali Khamenei'i, and the hardliners to minimize interference and fraud in the elections. It can be inferred that popular enthusiasm for the opposition gave the reformist movement important leverage over the hardliners, who were not electorally competitive.

However, the reformists soon lost this leverage as they could not effectively address salient socioeconomic and political issues. Public apathy replaced enthusiasm with the reformists, as reflected in extremely low turnout in the February 2003 local elections. A random sampling survey conducted in Tehran in August 2003 revealed that only 33 percent of the respondents thought that President Khatami, the reformist-controlled parliament, or the reformist movement had the ability to solve Iran's problems. When the reformists staged a parliamentary sit-in to protest the Guardians Council's mass disqualification of the reformist candidates from running in the 2004 parliamentary elections, they received no active support from the public. The Council acted with almost complete impunity as the reformists were isolated. It can be argued that the reformists became the victims of their very own electoral success. When his reform agendas were blocked, President Khatami repeatedly threatened to resign. Yet he never acted on his threats. In general, the reformist acts of defiance were uncoordinated, halfhearted, and too late to have credibility. They could not translate their popularity into a constant source of pressures over their hard-liner opponents. They could not establish durable coalitions with social movements and spent most of their energies in negotiating with well-entrenched elites rather than expanding the scope of their organizations (Tezcür 2010, 138–141). Once they lost the initiative, they were very vulnerable to an authoritarian backlash. Drawing from the experience of democratization in Europe, one can argue that the IRI's rulers would have been more willing to make concessions when confronted with the threat of massive social discontent and unrest (Acemoglu and Robinson 2006; Przeworski 2009, 310).

The reformists would have avoided complete defeat and limited authoritarian backlash had they been more consistent and decisive.

The developments following the 2004 parliamentary elections brought the complete political marginalization of the reformist movement. Ironically, this process of dedemocratization, which entailed significant reductions in the scope of human and political rights, was facilitated by the dynamics of electoral competition. Such an outcome would be incomprehensible from a perspective relying on the state–society dichotomy. Why would many Iranians willingly support an authoritarian backlash if they prefer democracy? The characterization of the hard-liners as an isolated group without social connections does not provide an answer to this question. As much as the reformists, the hard-liners had a significant social constituency. They prioritized the demands of urban poor, religious conservatives, and rural residents through themes of social justice and morality. The elections that had earlier served the reformists' goals of broadening the scope of liberties now became the primary mechanisms through which the ruling regime achieved resilience.

While the vote share of Ahmedinejad in the first round of the 2005 presidential elections was highly disputed, there was no question that he won a sweeping victory over Rafsanjani in the second round. As evident in the 2008 parliamentary elections, a new generation of hard-liners proved adept in the electoral game by using their superior financial and institutional resources. In response, the reformists, who were facing a very unequal playing field, could not develop a coherent and long-term strategy. While some reformists boycotted the 2004 elections, other reformist groups participated. In the 2005 presidential elections, the reformists could not field a strong candidate unifying different factions. In the 2008 parliamentary elections, the reformists decided to field candidates despite intervention by the Council that resulted in the disqualification of more than 90 percent of reformist candidates.[3] They were fearful that an electoral boycott would bring about their permanent exclusion from the institutional politics. In any case, many voters abstained, as the officially announced turnout was around 60 percent. The electoral strategy that was so successful between 1997 and 2003 had, by 2008, reached a dead end and revealed a fundamental weakness of the reformist movement. Despite its rhetoric of civil society, the movement had only limited success in establishing itself as a durable force among different societal groups such as teachers, workers, farmers, students, human rights advocates, women, and ethnic activists.[4] Its visibility and power ultimately depended on its ability to win elections and control state institutions. Once its ability to field candidates in the elections was several curtailed, its whole existence became tenuous. Consequently, neither the rise nor the equally spectacular fall of the reformist movement was inevitable and predetermined as a result of an institutional distribution of power, economic endowments, or geopolitical circumstances.

The events of the 2009 election showed that the dedemocratization of Iran starting with the 2004 parliamentary elections was not inevitable. The reformists learned from their past mistakes and rallied behind a single prominent candidate. Electoral mobilization started in late 2008 when various reformist groups established websites and networks and asked Khatami to run in the elections. Khatami announced his candidacy in early February 2009 but dropped out of the race in favor of Mousavi a month later. With an effective campaign supported by grassroots mobilization, the Mousavi clearly emerged as a *viable* alternative to the incumbent Ahmedinejad several weeks before the June 12 elections. The ability of the Mousavi campaign to organize mass rallies in many parts of Iran showed his popularity. Nonetheless, the reformist leaders did not develop an alternative plan in the case of electoral fraud. They did not even demand international election monitors who had prevented or reduced fraud in other contexts (Hyde 2007, 63). To make matters worse, the Mousavi campaign lost contact with its observers when its headquarters were stormed by plainclothes security forces, and the communication network was blocked on Election Day. In the absence of international observers, exit polls, or an independent electoral commission, there was no way empirically to back up allegations of widespread fraud. This difference with the postcommunist electoral uprisings proved to be crucial in Iran.

A popular slogan in the Mousavi electoral rallies was, "Hell will break loose if fraud occurs," which proved to be prophetic. Spontaneous demonstrations in many cities erupted on June 13, a day after the polling took place. The reformist leaders also called for mass demonstrations. The complete exclusion of the reformist movement from political institutions led to their radicalization and made them eager to pursue extrainstitutional channels to mobilize public support and call for street demonstrations (cf. Magaloni 2008, 738). The demonstrations grew exponentially but turned bloody on June 15 when paramilitary Basij forces opened fire on protestors in Tehran and several other cities. At least seven people were killed. Hundreds of thousands of people marched in Tehran on June 17 and 18 to protest the killings and electoral fraud. The following day, June 19, protests following Khamenei'i's Friday prayer sermon, in which he demanded an immediate end to the demonstrations, proved to be the deadliest yet. According to official figures, between a dozen and two dozen people were killed in the streets. Thousands of people, including the second-tier leaders of the reform movement, were arrested. The regime brought draconian restrictions against the press. At the same time, the ruling elite offered symbolic concessions. The Guardians Council announced that 10 percent of the votes would be recounted. Yet Mousavi and Karroubi, who also ran in the elections, remained defiant and did not attend the meeting called by the council. Their demands escalated from a rerun of elections to calls for a comprehensive reform of the Islamic Republic. Meanwhile, disunity among the ruling elite generated more uncertainty. Rafsanjani kept silent until his July 19 Friday prayer sermon, when he called for reconciliation and asked for the release of political prisoners. Ultimately the security forces managed to contain and suppress the demonstrations even though they continued sporadically until the end of 2009. Ahmedinejad was sworn on August 5. The regime proved to be resilient and survived the worst political crisis since its foundation in 1979.

It can be argued that the demonstrations failed simply because of state repression. After all, the security forces loyalty to the regime during confrontations were a decisive factor distinguishing between successful and unsuccessful nonviolent popular uprisings (Nepstad 2011). While the Iranian security forces suppressed protests with naked coercion, the level of repression in 2009 did not reach a point of mass terror, although it significantly increased the costs of oppositional activity. Reformist sources listed the deaths of 107 individuals as a result of political violence between June 15 and December 28, 2009. Additionally, two individuals were executed for their alleged role in postelection protests on January 28, 2010.[5] In comparison, 578 individuals were killed in street protests during the Iranian revolution from November 1977 to February 1979 (Abrahamian 2009, 32) and around 850 individuals during the 2011 uprising ending the Mubarak regime in Egypt.[6] In 2009, the regime did not need to employ mass terror simply because the opposition movement gradually lost its *viability*. If the protests had continued longer, the security forces would have been overwhelmed. Many Iranians were fence-sitters with ambivalent political positions, reluctant to take huge risks by participating in dwindling protests. Even people sympathetic to the movement found many excuses not to participate in demonstrations by February 2010.[7] Furthermore, many political elites who were not very enthusiastic about

Ahmedinejad, such as Speaker of the Parliament Ali Larijani, pursued a strategy of wait and see. They unambiguously committed themselves to the regime only when the opposition lost its momentum. The movement lost its power to shape political preferences through its actions.

Three reasons can be offered as to why the movement lost its viability. First, the opposition could not unambiguously demonstrate that the elections were actually rigged to fabricate an Ahmedinejad victory. This is not to downplay the irregularities characterizing the elections. The ways in which elections are conducted in Iran are very vulnerable to voter intimidation, vote buying, ballot stuffing, and altering the results. Yet there is no clear evidence showing that Ahmedinejad received less than 50 percent of the votes, a threshold below which he would have been required to stand in a run-off election. The reformists would have simply refused to participate in the elections without strict guarantees that no fraud would occur. Once they participated, however, the lack of information about the scope of fraud made it very difficult for them to coordinate against the regime and sway voters beyond their core supporters (Magaloni 2010, 761). Second, the reformist leadership could not establish coalitions transcending class, regional, and ethnic differences. The opposition had difficulties in appealing to social groups other than the urban middle classes. Many working- and lower-middle-class Iranians continued to perceive Ahmedinejad as uncorrupt and genuinely concerned with people's welfare. Furthermore, provinces populated by minorities such as the Kurds, Arabs, Baluchis, and Azeris were mostly silent during the postelectoral turmoil. The opposition movement did not incorporate demands for greater ethnic and cultural rights into its platform. Besides, the reformist movement had a limited presence outside of the large cities. In contrast, the 2011 uprisings in Syria and Tunisia erupted in small peripheral towns before spreading out to different parts of the country.

Finally, there were no signs that the regime was collapsing despite clear indications of elite disunity. In other words, the regime signaled that it was still *viable.* The ruling elite reacted to this unprecedented challenge by employing an ensemble of tactics ranging from sheer coercion to concessions, from forced confessions to cyber warfare. These tactics were vivid examples of authoritarian learning and showed the capacity of the regime to adapt itself to both domestic and international challenges (Heydemann 2007b). For instance, the regime came up with plans to increase the size of Basij forces and the scope of their activities in the greater Tehran area so that they would fight against foreign and subversive cultural and social influences.[8] It also identified and arrested cyber activists attacking and penetrating Iranian websites, fighting against the filtering of Facebook, and fabricating false news.[9] Additionally, the regime successfully sponsored pro-government mass demonstrations on December 30, 2009, and February 11, 2010, the anniversary of the return of Ruhollah Khomeini to Iran in 1979. These demonstrations, which signaled that large segments of the Iranian society appeared to support Ahmedinejad and were against the protests, brought an end to the opposition's street initiative.

CONCLUSION

This analysis of contemporary Iranian politics warrants three broader conclusions. First, the recent elections in Iran were characterized by a relatively high level of competition and uncertainty, similar to electoral dynamics in competitive authoritarian regimes and unlike those in Arab authoritarian regimes. An appreciation of the crucial importance of the elections under competitive authoritarian regimes requires explanatory frameworks that transcend the state–society dichotomy and complement structural analysis with a focus on the interaction among key political actors. In electoral moments of uncertainty, political preferences become more malleable, interaction between the rulers and the opposition becomes central for ultimate outcomes, and political opportunities expand. Authoritarian resilience depends on the ruling elite's management of this uncertainty and its ability to sustain its power without opting for total repression.

Second, this chapter demonstrates that authoritarian resilience in Iran cannot be exclusively explained by the regime's control over a vast security apparatus, economic endowments, economic performance, or prevailing geopolitical conditions. While these factors contribute to the strength of authoritarian rule, they are usually constant and do not explain variation in electoral outcomes. The ability of authoritarian actors to effectively respond to the opposition is equally important for understanding the dynamics of authoritarian resilience and regime reinforcing political change. The rise of a younger generation of authoritarian politicians with electoral skills since 2003 significantly contributed to the ability of the regime to sustain itself in the face of a popular opposition movement. Their trajectory suggests that authoritarian rulers may actually win elections using their superior forces to create a highly unequal playing field and developing populist appeals. In this sense, the assumption that their preferences are always further away from those of the majority may not be sustainable in all contexts (cf. Gandhi and Przeworski 2007, 1281). At the same time, oppositional forces can reduce the effects of structural and institutional disadvantages by taking advantage of relatively free and fair electoral competition. A perspective that prioritizes structural factors would not predict a strong challenge to President Ahmedinejad in 2009, given the robustness of the regime's coercive and welfare capacities. Spontaneous demonstrations in the immediate aftermath of the elections would not have been possible if not for effective electoral mobilization pursued by the opposition.

Finally, perspectives based on a simple threshold between democratic and authoritarian rule would overlook how electoral struggles taking place in an authoritarian regime may have major implications for the scope and pace of political change. There is no contradiction between simultaneously studying how authoritarianism sustains itself and how it generates opportunities for the expansion of rights. One can argue that electoral uprisings or opposition victories in competitive authoritarian regimes do not make a difference as authoritarian institutions persist (Hale 2006, 321; Kalandadze and Orenstein 2009; Tudoroiu 2007, 315). However, these events may also trigger changes beyond the replacement of one set of elites with another and contribute to increasing democratic performance (Bunce and Wolchik 2010a, 76; Cheterian 2008, 692, 701–3; Radnitz 2006, 132). In Iran, electoral moments significantly contributed either to the expansion or shrinking of human and political rights, depending on the outcome. Even if there were no institutional changes in the IRI, there were huge policy-based differences between the presidencies of Khatami and Ahmedinejad, which greatly influenced the well-being of rights activists, lawyers, journalists, political prisoners, civil society organizations, and ethnic and religious minorities.

10 AUTHORITARIAN RESILIENCE AND INTERNATIONAL LINKAGES IN IRAN AND SYRIA

Anoushiravan Ehteshami, Raymond Hinnebusch, Heidi Huuhtanen, Paola Raunio, Maaike Warnaar, and Tina Zintl

THIS CHAPTER EXAMINES the effect of external linkages on regime resilience in Syria and Iran. How do the Syrian and Iranian regimes try to exploit international resources and ward off threats, and how do such resources empower the regimes' survival strategies and thereby affect governance? Our focus is on the decade from 9/11 to 2010, a period that provides rich opportunities for analysis of this phenomenon. The external security environment for both regimes, marked by U.S. intervention on their borders, was seemingly most fraught, and two new leaders, Bashar al-Asad and Mahmoud Ahmadinejad, were being tested; but new external resources (the third oil boom and legitimacy windfalls from defying the United States) were also being made available.

THEORETICAL FRAMEWORK

External Factors, Authoritarian Power, and Regime Adaptation

Historical sociology (Hobden and Hobson 2002), in linking the international and internal, as in Tilly's (1992) analysis of the impact of war and capitalism on state formation in Europe, can profitably be extended to analysis of the impact of factors such as war and capital on authoritarian resilience in the Middle East.[1] Following Weberian approaches, power in Middle East North Africa (MENA) authoritarian regimes can be said to rest on a combination of: (1) ideology and identity, with legitimacy sought via discourses in which regime and opposition pose as defenders of the most widely held values, nationalism and Islam; (2) neopatrimonialism, a combination of authority to command from office and distribution of patronage to supporters; and (3) repression, which is more effective the more core supporters who undertake it are loyal and the fewer numbers of opponents can mobilize, both of which, in turn, are shaped by patronage and legitimacy. Power is measured not only by a regime's ability to suppress opposition but also by its ability to mobilize support and ensure compliance.

Authoritarian regimes' power depends on their management of participation pressures, which can be measured along Dahl's (1971) two dimensions: (1) level of elite contestation and (2) level of inclusion of social forces. MENA authoritarian republics typically issued from populist revolutions that sharply *contracted contestation* (among elites) *by expanding inclusion* (at mass levels) (Huntington 1968). The current era of neoliberal globalization is associated with limited political liberalization in which elite *contestation* is marginally expanded and mass *inclusion* contracted, with limited liberalization a substitute for rather than a step toward democratization. However, authoritarian adaptation could also mean a narrowing or widening on both dimensions, or sequences of widening and narrowing. A middle strategy typical of authoritarian regimes is *co-optation,* which at the elite level allows limited proregime contestation (for example, over co-optation to ministerial office) but little enhanced inclusion; because co-optation depends on patronage it requires resources often extracted less from within (which may require a social contract and power sharing) than from without.

Varieties of External Resources

Not just external threats, but externally accessed resources also have an impact on authoritarian resilience, although precisely *how* varies according to their type and source, as follows:

1. *Political capital* denotes the ability of regimes to use *foreign policy* to acquire *nationalist legitimacy* from *external threat.* Levitsky and Way (2006) note how Western pressures for democratization can shift the internal balance of power against authoritarian elites, but an alternative dynamic is authoritarian regimes' use of anti-Western nationalism to discredit democracy discourses. Where this happens, outside threats also become a resource, which may legitimize the *centralization* of power, securitize politics, and neutralize opposition democratization discourses (narrow contestation) yet *may* also widen inclusion if regimes can mobilize the population against the external threat.

2. *Financial capital:* If authoritarian regimes can extract state-to-state rent they become more autonomous of the inside (for example, of

the need for tax-raising bargains); can provide patronage to co-opt constituencies, hence are under less compulsion to democratize; and can even contract contestation while maintaining inclusion of popular constituencies. Conversely, declining rent has often forced economic liberalization to access foreign direct investment (FDI); this scenario, requiring some widening of contestation (incorporating investors) but often also contraction of mass inclusion (demobilization required by structural adjustment), has produced lopsided forms of limited political liberalization that empower the "haves" at the expense of the "have-nots." *Economic sanctions,* of which the two regimes have systematically been made targets, aim at reducing their governance resources, but authoritarian elites may be able to use privileged access to the resulting scarce resources to clientalize society, as Niblock (2001) shows, notably in the case of Saddam's Iraq.

3. *Social (human) capital:* In an age of globalization, authoritarian regimes are under pressure to open up, but they can facilitate *selective* liberalization by co-opting expatriate diasporas and returning migrants. Because returning migrants usually bring with them social capital—modern education, skills, and international contacts (sometimes accompanied by financial capital)—they can assist regime economic adaptation. Second, in some Islamic countries women constitute human capital that regimes, oppositions, and external powers compete to mobilize by invoking women's issues.

Omnibalancing, Regime Coalitions, and Participation Management

Regimes' survival strategies, including authoritarian upgrading (Heydemann 2007b), are usefully seen, following David (1991), as involving a complex *omnibalancing* shaped by whether the greatest threats are domestic or external and by the location of the greatest *resource opportunities.* Thus, many Middle East regimes seek to access *resources* from the United States global hegemon to balance against *threats* in their neighborhood or from domestic opposition; alternatively, however, as with Syria and Iran, they may balance against U.S. *threats* by mobilizing nationalist resistance (political capital) in the region and by accessing financial *resources* from other powers prepared to "soft balance" against the United States. However, civil society and the opposition inside authoritarian states can also be empowered by external factors, thereby affecting the internal power balance between them and the regime. Moreover, whatever choices regimes make there will be *trade-offs*: thus, maximizing political cal resources through militant nationalism carries risks of increased external threat and may sacrifice financial capital (if it invites sanctions and puts off investors); maximizing financial capital may cost legitimacy at home insofar as it requires favoring investors and reneging on the social contract. Indeed, every technique of authoritarian upgrading meant to access resources needed to "fix" one threat to regimes may sacrifice other resources or increase other threats. Omnibalancing strategies shape and are shaped by ruling coalitions. Following Solingen (1998), we distinguish internationalist coalitions (traders, investors, bankers) from nationalist-statist ones (military, public sector, populist constituencies). Not only will these favor different foreign policies (typically bandwagoning with versus balancing against the Western capitalist core, respectively), but the balance of power between rival potential ruling coalitions will also be affected by outside threats and resources. For example, the mobilization of external financial capital may require co-optation of internationalist elements into ruling coalitions while nationalist resistance to outside threats and high oil rents may shift power to nationalist-statist elements. In turn, coalitions affect regimes' management of participation pressures: thus, the internationalization of coalitions tends to widen contestation because newly co-opted private sector elements may compete with the military and bureaucracy, although the inclusion of new bourgeois constituencies is often accompanied by the exclusion of older and broader populist ones.

Comparing Syria and Iran

Comparing the impact of external factors on authoritarian resilience in Syria and Iran requires cognizance of their different "starting points." First, political contestation and inclusion have differed. The Syrian regime was the outcome of a "revolution from above" institutionalized in a single party-military regime under which there was a progressive contraction of elite contestation and some institutionalized inclusion of plebeian strata, which, however, also began to contract from the 1980s. The Iranian regime came out of a revolution from below that created mixed clerical-republican institutions, which, together with associated clerical networks, institutionalized factionalism, hence a measure of contestation that widened inclusion of a more active civil society. As such, Iran, especially under the Khatami-led reformists, started the period under review with a broader-based regime than in Syria.

Second, Iran enjoys much larger hydrocarbon resources than Syria, although it also has a bigger population. Given its limited domestic rent, Syria traditionally used its nationalist foreign policy to acquire foreign aid that allowed increased co-optation, but recently, as it became more dependent on attracting external capital, it had to contract inclusion and the potential costs of a nationalist foreign policy increased. The Iranian regime's greater resources allowed greater co-optation and inclusion and less vulnerability to outside pressures to temper its nationalist policies.

In comparing the cases, we will assess how foreign policies have affected external threats and resources and how these have shaped internal power balances, regime strategies of contestation and inclusion, and ultimately authoritarian adaptation.

SYRIA

The Syrian Ba'th regime has always depended on foreign policy for much of its capital: regime legitimation depended on Syria's nationalist defiance of Israel and its Western backers, with the struggle over Palestine and the Golan legitimizing the construction of a national security state. But co-optation and the social contract with the regime's constituency have also been dependent on the regime's ability to extract rent, either from foreign aid or its own modest hydrocarbon resources.

Hafiz al-Asad's regime was consolidated with the help of aid, mostly from Arab oil producers, given for its role as the main front line state with Israel: strategic rents in the 1970s and 1980s were estimated at $12.3 billion, 5 to 10 percent of GNP; oil revenues were equivalent to another 8 percent of GNP; and rent provided a varying 20 to 50 percent of government revenues. Rent enabled high spending on the military (for Soviet arms), a regime pillar essential to internal security and also the external deterrence needed to pursue a nationalist foreign policy, which absorbed around 35 percent of government revenue (Huuhtanen 2008; Perthes 2000, 158). However, in the 1990s, with the decline of Arab funding during the peace process and the withdrawal of Soviet patronage, Syria ceased to get significant strategic aid except for a windfall for siding against Iraq in the 1990 Gulf War. Rent had meanwhile fuelled the overdevelopment of the state relative to its economic base, and the public sector was exhausted as an engine of capital accumulation. The regime responded by new investment laws meant to entice private and foreign investment and by slashing military spending from about 18 percent of GNP in 1976 through 1988 to

7 percent in the 1990s. Fortuitously, Syria's own rising oil production soon filled the resource gap, with income from oil exports in the 1990s about 16 percent of GNP, covering half of state expenditures (Huuhtanen 2008). By 2000, however, it was clear that oil revenues would also decline and hence that new external resources had to be accessed through an opening to foreign and expatriate financial capital, with consequences for the reconstruction of the regime coalition.

In the age of bipolarity and Arab nationalism, Hafiz al-Asad's Arab nationalist foreign policy could serve both financial (Arab aid) and legitimacy needs. But in the contemporary period of U.S. hegemony, there may be trade-offs between them: A nationalist foreign policy may enhance domestic legitimacy but no longer commands Arab aid and can jeopardize access to alternative economic resources such as foreign investment. This was the situation faced by Bashar al-Asad on his accession to power.

Bashar's project was, as Perthes (2004b) argued, to "modernize authoritarianism" by opening up the Syrian economy and adapting his regime to the age of globalization. Initially, he had to share power with the "old guard" who were wary of change while also facing demands for political liberalization from democracy activists. His strategy was to co-opt moderate economic reformers into government and incrementally retire the old guard (Lesch 2005; Leverett 2005).

External Relations and Political Capital

Bashar's economic liberalization was initially to be matched by a tilt toward a West-centric foreign policy manifest in an opening to Western Europe to encourage financial capital. But the collapse of the peace process with Israel and the parallel souring of Syrian–U.S. relations dimmed prospects for foreign investment; to fill the gap, Syria pursued an opening to Iraq, which boosted its earnings from receipt of oil through the Syrian–Iraqi oil pipeline but also worsened relations with the United States. When Syria encouraged resistance to the 2003 U.S. occupation of Iraq, Washington began to talk of regime change in Syria as well. There were strong incentives for Asad to bandwagon with the United States in the Iraq war: his desire to reintegrate Syria into the international market, for which the U.S. hegemon was gatekeeper; the protection of Syria's economic interests in Iraq; and the chance of a share of postwar spoils. However, Syrian public opinion was so inflamed against the invasion that the regime would have had to sacrifice nationalist legitimacy if it bandwagoned, and defiance of the United States was made possible by Syria's persisting *relative* economic and security self-sufficiency (compared to other Arab states). The United States imposed economic sanctions and tried to deprive Syria of key foreign policy cards (and political capital), namely its hosting of militant Palestinian groups, its support of Hizbollah, and its position in Lebanon, all of which Syria refused to give up.

Indeed, while very risky, Asad's stand against the Iraq war won him a windfall of political capital that helped consolidate his regime. Some opposition activists initially believed the rapid collapse of the Iraqi Ba'th could be used to initiate change in Syria, but they were sharply constrained by public responsiveness to the regime's anti-(U.S.) imperialist discourse; unwilling to be associated with a deeply unpopular U.S. invasion, they urged on the regime the need for a democratic opening to mobilize national solidarity against the U.S. threat. They rejected democratization via American tanks and accused the United States of wanting to extract only those concessions from Syria that would benefit Israel. No opposition figure could advocate submission to U.S. demands to reduce support for Hizbollah or militant Palestinians. The fact that Washington targeted the regime for its support of Palestine, its association with Hizbollah, and its opposition to the invasion of Iraq generated a certain solidarity between regime and people. U.S. pressures on Syria undermined democracy activists and enabled the regime to justify continued emergency powers (*Financial Times,* August 26, 2003). The regime also used the Iraq war to strike a détente with the main opposition, Islamic militants, who were also aroused against the U.S. invasion. Additionally, the chaos and sectarian conflict in Iraq, underlined by the flight of refugees to Syria, together with the fear—ignited by the Kurdish riots of 2003 and the rise of Islamic militancy—that the "Iraqi disease" could spread to Syria generated for the regime what might be called "legitimacy because of a worse alternative."

However, the nationalist legitimacy of the regime must have suffered from several subsequent foreign policy reverses. Asad had to swallow several American and Israeli military provocations and Syria's forced evacuation of Lebanon after Rafiq al-Hariri's February 2005 assassination. Yet, at this juncture the regime used Syria's new cell phone system and its increased links to Islamist leaders to rally a wide spectrum of Syrian opinion against external threats (Pinto 2011; Shaery-Eisenlohr 2011). At the 2005 Ba'th party congress, the crisis was exploited to demand unity within the regime coalition, facilitating the removal of the old guard and consolidation of Asad's power. Some opposition militants thought the regime might be vulnerable to regime change through the Hariri tribunal indictments, leading them to join ranks with exiles, including the Muslim Brothers and purged former Vice President

Khaddam (once the senior Sunni Ba'thist in the regime) and with the opposition in Lebanon to promulgate the "Damascus Declaration." The opposition, however, petered out, having little resonance with the Syrian public at a time of external threats and being divided between those willing to be associated with the United States (who were discredited) and the majority that were not (Macaron 2008; Landis and Pace 2007). The regime's failure to pursue political reforms promised at the party conference and a crackdown on opposition were justified by the Mehlis report and continued external threats (Dunne 2008). Then the regime's nationalist legitimacy was replenished after its Hizbollah ally successfully resisted Israel's 2006 attack on Lebanon. With Syria's identity as a "confrontation state" in the conflict with Israel deeply ingrained in public thinking, Israeli attacks on Lebanon and Gaza shocked the Syrian population into rallying behind Asad, while the ability of resistance militants that Syria supported to withstand these assaults gave the regime some reflected political credit (Sottimano 2010). Hizbollah also turned the tables on pro-U.S. Lebanese factions in a 2008 showdown in Beirut, which restored much of Syria's position in Lebanon and obstructed efforts to make it a platform for regime change. This also broke the external siege of Damascus, with French President Sarkozy leading Syria's rehabilitation as the Bush administration departed office. The regime could credibly argue that it had successfully steered Syria through the crises that had enveloped its neighbors (Sottimano 2010). Yet, in both 2003 and again in 2005 the regime used its enhanced nationalist legitimacy for short-term gains—as an opportunity to repress dissent—rather than investing it in inclusion and broadening its support base.

At the same time, defiance of Washington had costs for Asad's economic reform drive: U.S.-imposed sanctions aimed to economically isolate Syria, in particular targeting Western high-tech exports (Tabler 2005). Two of the three main pillars of the Syrian economy, agriculture and the informal sector, were fairly invulnerable to the sanctions, but they did discourage Western investment and caused difficulties for the financial services and telecommunications industries by which the regime sought to propel the globalization of the Syrian economy. The third pillar of the economy, oil, was a mixed case: Western oil majors started withdrawing, but Syria found substitutes for them in independent oil companies or those from non-Western states, although these may lack sufficient advanced technology to fully develop Syria's declining oil fields.

Relations with Europe were another temporary casualty of the regime's policy. The European Union (EU) had become Syria's main trading partner in the 1990s after the end of the Soviet bloc. Asad had started negotiations for Syria's accession to the Euro–Med partnership as a means to shift the intraregime power balance against vested interests, gain access to resources to enable economic modernization, acquire legitimacy as a reformer, and, most important, as an urgent political buffer against rising U.S. hostility. However, the EU adopted a hard line in negotiations and finally suspended ratification of the agreement over the Hariri murder. Syria came to see the EU as a conduit of rather than buffer against U.S. pressures. Soured relations with Europe and also with Saudi Arabia over the Hariri issue deprived Syria of almost all of the limited foreign aid it had hitherto received. The increasingly united Western front against Syria underlined the political vulnerability of the country's West-centric trade concentration and accelerated regime efforts to diversify trade relations. During the height of political and military pressure around 2005, Syria's foreign trade actually increased significantly, shifted now toward China, Iran, and Turkey under bilateral trade agreements and to the Arab world under the Greater Arab Free Trade Association (GAFTA).

The regime's foreign policy aimed to situate Syria as pivotal to two rival coalitions: on the one hand, it still tried to shelter with Europe and Turkey against the United States and Israel while also appeasing or trying to bargain with the United States; on the other hand, it developed its links to Iran, Hizbollah and Hamas, Russia, and China, hence preserving the option to tilt one way or the other depending on whether its interests were acknowledged by the United States and the West. Its survival strategy was to diversify economic dependences while protecting legitimacy by selectively defying perceived threats to Arab national interests. This strategy gave the regime maneuvering room to adapt its economic policy and governance practices.

Financial and Human Capital and the Struggle for Economic Reform

Regime survival imperatives imparted new urgency to economic reform as petroleum exports began a seemingly inexorable decline while economic growth barely kept up with population growth, resulting in burgeoning youth unemployment. There was an intraregime consensus that private investment was the only solution to the exhaustion of Syria's statist economy, but the elite were divided over how far and how fast to proceed. Privatization of the public sector was excluded as likely to alienate the large part of the population that was state employed, many of them Alawis, as well as the mostly Sunni business class that benefited from state contracts and would, thus, not welcome a state withdrawal from the market. The political legitimacy of the regime rested on its provision of subsidized food and employment, and its co-optation capacity was based on state patronage. The Chinese model of spreading the private sector and the market while retaining a reformed public sector was in principle embraced, but in practice reform of the public sector was defeated by its exploitation for patronage and welfare purposes (Lust-Okar 2006).

A decisive factor in determining both the pace of economic reform and regime resilience was oil revenues. The regime was fortunate that the years of pressure from without were good years for oil exports, whose value doubled between 2000 and 2005 due to high prices and oil trade with Iraq, from which Syrian earned over $2 billion in 2001–2002 (ICG 2004, 16). Oil made up 70 percent of the value of exports, and annual revenues from fuel exports averaged 19.2 percent of GDP, an increase of 3 percent since the 1990s, rising close to a record high of $7 billion in 2005 and providing 40 to 50 percent of state revenues. At the same time, the regime built up a reserve of official foreign assets of around U.S.$17 billion, an economic security buffer that reached 68 percent of GDP in 2002 (Huuhtanen 2008). During the second half of the decade, however, oil revenues declined. The regime encouraged private investment in most fields to substitute for declining public investment and to extract a share of its profits for the treasury. New laws liberalized trade and foreign exchange, reduced tax rates, allowed capital repatriation, and relaxed labor protections (Abboud 2009; Leverett 2005, 86–87). The introduction of private banking and a stock market aimed to mobilize savings for investment, notably from expatriates. In fact, the proportion of GDP generated in the private sector steadily rose, and FDI climbed from a paltry $111 million in 2001 to $1.6 billion in 2006 (UNCTD 2007). Most of the latter was due to excess liquidity in the Gulf, including big investments from Qatar, ironically a result of the oil price boom precipitated by the U.S. invasion of Iraq and by Arab reluctance to invest in the United States given the political climate after September 11. In 2005, the year the regime appeared most vulnerable and experienced its most extreme isolation from the West, Syria was the fourth largest recipient of Arab investment. Investment inflows drove a boom in trade, housing, banking, construction, and tourism, satisfying the crony capitalists who were becoming the main constituency of the regime. The economy grew at a rate of 5 percent in 2006, 4 percent in 2007, and 4 percent in 2008, despite declining oil output. The currency, after absorbing a brief hit from international pressures, stabilized. The savings-investment gap did widen (2004–2009) as a percentage of GDP from 1.6 to 3.7 percent (IMF 2009, 21), and the budget deficit grew toward the end of the decade. Concerns about political stability and absence of rule of law still prevented the rapid return of Syria's enormous expatriate capital; hence, long-term investment in industry and significant job-creating enterprises were limited. However, improved tax collection enabled the regime to extract a share from the economic growth. From 2004 through 2009, oil revenues declined as a proportion of total state revenue by about 40 percent, and taxes increased by about 75 percent. The proportion of government revenue from oil decreased from a high of 55 percent in 2002 to about 20 percent in 2008 (IMF 2009). In parallel, reform discourse was used to cut the subsidies that drained the treasury but were part of the social contract with the masses left out of the new boom.

Parallel to this, the regime sought to tap human capital from the Syrian Diaspora. Syria already benefited from a large informal inflow of remittances from the roughly 15 million Syrians abroad (counting descendants of earlier migrants), with estimated holdings of up to $80 billion in capital.[2] To attract them back, the regime established a Ministry of Expatriates, and an NGO, the "Network of Syrian Scientists, Technologists, and Innovators Abroad" (NOSSTIA), was founded in 2001. Returned migrants helped to shift discourse in favor of the reformist camp, and their influence could, for example, also be traced in the licensing of several private universities, some founded in cooperation with foreign partners, that attracted home and employed foreign-educated Syrians. The modern education and global networking resources of the Syrian Diaspora were seen by the regime as reinforcing the discourse of meritocracy by which it justified cuts in state employment and political patronage. Several foreign-trained technocrats (some with experience in international institutions like the World Bank) were appointed to cabinet positions where they played a pivotal role in steering the regime's economic reforms.

Between Economic Liberalization and External Threat: Restructuring the Regime Coalition

The regime's reliance on a combination of external financial resources and nationalist foreign policy both deterred it from democratization and allowed it to contain societal pressures for it. Bashar al-Asad's experiment with political liberalization during the Damascus Spring of 2000–2001, aimed at strengthening his own reformist agenda against the old guard, did not survive the hard-line opposition's denial of the regime's legitimacy and the spotlight it put on the corrupt activities of regime barons, showing that rent-seeking crony capitalism would be exposed by a more open political system (George 2003). Asad tried to legitimize his shutdown of the experiment by arguing that Western democracy could not be imported and that democratization had to build on social and economic modernization rather than precede it. Then the external siege helped him to marginalize democracy pressures and also remove the last of his old-guard opponents, replaced by reforming technocrats and businessmen, who, however, also did not welcome democratization, which would have empowered the masses to block economic reform.

Indeed, rather than economic liberalization generating democratization pressures, the authoritarian state was *strengthened* by its replenishing of revenue sources, hence co-optative capabilities. The regime was assisted in marginalizing opposition by its co-optation of the bourgeoisie, which, being dependent on the state for business opportunities (contracts, licenses), for disciplining the working class and for rolling back populism, had no interest in leading a democratization movement. At the heart of the regime coalition was the new class of "crony capitalists"—the rent-seeking alliances of political brokers (led by Asad's mother's family, the Makhloufs)—and the regime-supportive bourgeoisie that thrived on the combination of limited economic liberalization and partnerships from the inflow of external investment. The regime aimed to survive the incremental transition to a (partial?) market economy by creating its "own" crony capitalists. Asad apparently hoped international trade agreements, notably the Euro-Mediterranean partnership, would eventually require cronies to become competitive capitalists. In the meantime, however, the cost was that more "productive capital" was discouraged.

Democratization was also incompatible with policies favoring investors with tax breaks while allowing public salaries to lag behind inflation, compromising the well-being of the middle class and cutting the subsidies on which the populist social contract was based. The main political innovations accompanying the liberalization of economic policy was the reversal of the former populist bias in the regime's corporatist system: investors now got increased access to policy makers while the popular syndicates that formerly represented workers and peasants were used to demobilize them. At the same time, the establishment of several development-promoting NGOs under the patronage of Syrian First Lady Asma al-Asad aimed to co-opt urban middle class civil society and create a favorable image with potential donors abroad; indeed the EU was accused of funding such regime-sponsored NGOs while abandoning support for the European Centre for Human Rights (Kawakibi 2009, 241f). State-led NGOs represented a benevolent authoritarianism offering inclusion to parts of civil society that did not challenge the regime (Donati, Chapter 2 in this volume); with the decline of regime patronage resources, co-optation was also being restructured in a more "efficient" way targeting entrepreneurs and professionals, especially those with international connections. Ultimately, this strategy aimed at co-opting secular segments of Syrian society to balance the increasing parallel empowerment of a moderate, nonpolitical Islamic civil society the regime also was sponsoring. Thus, the regime balanced above a divided society. In summary, economic liberalization was congruent with a simultaneous incremental *expansion of elite level contestation and shrinkage of popular inclusion* and, far from driving democratization, sustained authoritarian adaptation in the short run.

However, for longer-term durability, the regime would have had, at the very least, to adopt the authoritarian upgrading strategies pursued in other postpopulist Arab regimes, notably fostering a bourgeois party to support economic reform and some electoral contestation to satisfy, co-opt, and divide various opposition elements; in the period after 2008 when the Syrian regime had apparently defeated external pressures, it could have invested its nationalist legitimacy in such a move toward competitive authoritarianism. Preoccupied with the intraelite power struggle, economic reform, and foreign policy challenges and perhaps made complacent by his apparent successes on these fronts, Asad, moreover, neglected the costs and new vulnerabilities that had accompanied the shift in the regime's social base, namely, the contraction of popular inclusion.

IRAN

Like Syria's regime, the legitimacy of Iran's Islamic republic has derived from its foreign policy—its role in promotion of the Islamic cause—but also from its claim to constitute the only truly Islamic republic combining religious legitimacy with popular participation. However, its attempt to export its revolution, leading to the Iran–Iraq war, gave way, beginning with Rafsanjani's presidency (1989), to postwar reconstruction, which, in an era of low oil prices, required access to foreign capital through better relations with the West. The 1995 election of President Khatami signaled the rise of a reformist camp seeking a "dialogue of civilizations" with the West. Despite his wide popular support, Khatami was obstructed by hard-liners within and a hostile United States without. The growing challenge by hard-liners in the judiciary to his government was strengthened by the triumph of conservatives in the seventh *majlis* elections of 2004 and crowned by the victory of Mahmoud Ahmadinejad in the 2005 presidential election. This was followed by a narrowing of contestation and shift in the regime coalition away from internationalists facilitated by both external threats and rising oil rents; this, in turn, provoked a split in the ruling coalition that has narrowed the base of the regime.

External Threats and the Ideologization/
Militarization of Politics

Iran's hard-line "neoconservatives"[3] took advantage of the U.S. war on terror in the region to make their drive for power. The reelection of the reform-minded Mohammad Khatami in 2001 and the convergence of U.S. and Iranian interests in Afghanistan and Iraq after September 11 brought about opportunities for U.S.–Iranian rapprochement, but the Bush administration rebuffed the reformists' calls for dialogue (Poulson 2009). The neoconservatives used Iran's inclusion in Bush's "axis of evil" to attack the reformist foreign ministry's policy of détente with the West as "surrender to the enemy," forcing Khatami to aver that in such circumstances talks with the United States were against Iran's interest.[4]

In the 2005 presidential campaign, Ahmadinejad's populism gave voice to segments of society that had been ignored during Khatami's focus on democratic reforms, to the neglect of Iran's economic malaise, itself partly a function of low oil prices (Dorraj and Dodson 2009; Ehteshami 2002; Ehteshami and Zweiri 2007, 46). He also appealed to these segments by targeting the alleged corruption of the establishment, notably his pragmatic opponent, Rafsanjani. Though both candidates insisted on the country's right to a nuclear capability, Ahmadinejad was most successful in exploiting U.S. threats against Iran, and his election marked the revival of revolutionary ideology manifest in resistance to U.S. intervention in the region and an insistence on Iran's right to nuclear development.

Ahmadinejad was purportedly the candidate of the Revolutionary Guards (IRGC), whom his opponents claimed bankrolled his campaign. His victory was paralleled by an unprecedented role for the guards in politics at the expense of the business elite (represented by Rafsanjani) and cultural elite (represented by Khatami). The IRGC acquired a strong presence on the Supreme National Security Council and a dozen representatives in parliament, while fifteen members of the president's 2005 cabinet had military or security backgrounds. The IRPG increased its involvement in business and assumed a more overt political role against "internal enemies" (Wehrey et al. 2009, 33).

Political Capital through Foreign Policy

In the political discourse of President Ahmadinejad and of the supreme leader, Ayatollah Ali Khamenei'i, the United States and Israel were portrayed as a threat to Iran's security and the U.S. invasion of Iraq used to expose it as a power-hungry hegemon wrecking havoc on the region but unable to impose its will. The outcome of the 2006 war between Israel and Hizbollah was used to show that "Iranian steadfastness and defiance . . . could confront Israel and potentially defeat it" (Salem 2008, 20). The success of Hamas in the elections in Gaza was presented as a victory of Iran's revolutionary creed. Iran under Ahmadinejad established an apparently strong and radical role in the region, with an important presence in Iraq, Lebanon, and Palestine, and leader of resistance to a very unpopular United States under Bush, which became vulnerable to Iran in Iraq and Afghanistan. Opinion polls suggested public support for this foreign policy, at least as long as the Bush administration continued to demonize Iran.[5] Besides reaping political capital from apparent foreign policy successes, the regime used the struggle with the United States against internal opposition and the Bush administration's support for violent opposition groups such as the Mujahidin al-Khalq and Baluchi separatists to justify increased securitization.

The struggle over Iran's nuclear program had major implications for the internal power balance. Iran's right to nuclear power enjoyed widespread support, cutting across regime and opposition, although Iranians were more divided over acquisition of a nuclear weapon, given the high costs it could inflict on the country. U.S. saber rattling over the nuclear issue before 2009 led democracy activists to scale back their criticism of the regime lest they legitimize a U.S. attack, according to democracy activist Akbar Ganji.[6] Ahmadinejad tenaciously defended Iran's right to nuclear power and engaged in an active diplomacy with Third World states to evade isolation with some success: the Turkey–Brazil deal of 2010 that the West rejected enjoyed wide support in Iran.

Financial and Political Capital
and the Internal Balance of Power

Oil, accounting for around 80 percent of the value of Iran's exports and about half of government revenue, is a crucial regime capital. While Khatami's reformist administration came to power at a time of historically low oil prices ($11 a barrel), during Ahmadinejad's first term unprecedented high prices, peaking at over $140 a barrel in July 2008, enabled the country to amass U.S.$97 billion in foreign exchange reserves and sustain a gross net investment rate of 28 percent. For Khatami, low oil prices had made an economic opening to the West urgent and legitimized détente with Europe while also depriving him of the patronage resources to consolidate his power; by contrast, high prices gave Ahmadinejad's government financial autonomy on the inside and enabled him to defy the outside.

Newly enriched, the Ahmadinejad government went on a populist spending spree, initially winning considerable popularity among ordinary people and also investing a considerable amount in equipment for his military constituency. This dissipated much of the oil earnings, and he also raided the strategic reserve established by Khatami to guard against downturns in the price of oil, provoking criticism by ex-presidents, parliament, and the governor of the Central Bank. When oil prices softened from September 2008, Iran faced a growing budget deficit. Ahmadinejad sought to reduce Iran's vulnerability to outside pressures by increasing taxes and reducing subsidies, sparking riots in Tehran in June 2007 and forceful bazaari resistance to attempts to tax them (Kaussler 2008b).

Ahmadinejad's nuclear drive brought on Western sanctions, yet in the short run these actually appeared to strengthen regime cohesion and the hard-liners. The opposition was forced to reject them, and opposition leader Karrubi said they strengthened the regime. Well-connected regime insiders such as the Revolutionary Guard used their privileged import networks to profiteer on scarcities and exploited securitization from the external siege to get contracts without bidding. Even as Western companies reduced economic links with Iran, other states such as Russia and especially China, in spite of the nuclear issue, filled the vacuum, providing Iran with some political cover, arms, markets, technology, and industrial equipment, with many such deals agreed directly with the state sector, including the guards (Garver, Leverett, and Leverett 2010). The expansion of the guards' crony capitalist networks into every branch of the economy strengthened the nationalist/statist faction of the regime coalition at the expense of the business interests of the internationalist-minded elements around Rafsanjani.[7]

In the longer term, however, sanctions hurt Iran's ability to import Western technology needed to modernize its hydrocarbon industry and to develop its refining capability so as to reduce its dependence on imported gasoline; the government had, also, to phase out fuel subsidies to make Iran less vulnerable to sanctions, hurting its own popular constituency. Many merchants and contractors were squeezed between international sanctions and Ahmadinejad's allies; their disaffection carried dangers, given the intimate connection between the bazaar and the clergy.

Coalition Fracture

Ahmadinejad's promise in his 2005 presidential campaign to reduce the income gap between rich and poor and to fight corruption among the ruling elite had resonated with the poorest sections of the population, but, as the 2009 elections approached, many believed he had not addressed their concerns (according to one poll, nearly 63 percent of those who voted for him in 2005 said they would not vote for him again). In addition, for the middle class, cultural and political freedoms expanded under Khatami had been curbed. In December 2006, in a protest vote against the president, reformist candidates took 80 percent of all municipality councils (Kaussler 2008b). In the 2009 elections, Ahmadinejad was challenged from within the regime's own coalition by two popular reformist candidates, Mirhuseyn Musavi and Mehdi Karrubi. The hardliners claimed they were the candidates of the West, while Ahmadinejad took credit for having carried on Iran's nuclear program despite Western attempts to deny Iran nuclear energy.[8]

When Ahmadinejad claimed victory with an unlikely margin and reformist supporters poured into the streets in protests, his supporters branded them tools of the West. U.S. allocation of funds for regime change allowed the mullahs to accuse opposition activists of being on the CIA payroll. To justify the use of violence against the protestors Ayatollah Jannati accused the British of seeking to stage a velvet revolution.[9] In the postelection crisis, Western governments were careful not to show overt support for the Iranian opposition because there was widespread perception that this would damage it. Opposition leaders, enjoying the legitimacy of revolutionary veterans, were able to counterattack in claiming to be truer to the principles of the revolution and by charging that Ahmadinejad's reckless policies had given the West tools to isolate Iran. The regime was not able to discredit the opposition with large parts of the public, and its need to resort to violent repression confirms that it has lost much legitimacy, at least among the urban middle class. However, its nationalist discourse probably solidified its core support and fired the hardline ideological zeal of the militias used to repress the opposition. Moreover, the Revolutionary Guards leadership was empowered by eternal threats, and the recovery of oil prices in late 2009 allowed increased patronage resources to purchase the divided loyalties of the corps and new loyalists recruited in place of purged dissidents (Ansari 2010; Kaussler 2009).

Nevertheless, the contested election exposed and worsened intraelite conflicts within a regime that has factionalism built into its institutions. When Supreme Leader Ayatollah Khamenei, whose religious credentials to hold the post of Faqih had always been contested, sided with Ahmadinejad against the loyal opposition, he lost his remaining ability to stand above and mediate intraelite conflicts, and the unprecedented personal attacks on him by protestors were a blow to his prestige. The clerical establishment, the bedrock of the regime, was also fractured, with a substantial group of mullahs championing popular sectors alienated from the ruling core. However, as the postrevolutionary power elite in its entirety depends on the state for rent extraction and as members of the opposing camps are bound together by close business partnerships, one faction cannot be eliminated without seriously weakening the entire elite, and they are deterred from further pursuing their rivalry at a time when the entire regime is under external siege.

Civil Society and External Powers:
The Women's Movement and Iran's Diaspora

The case of the women's movement illustrates the varying impacts outside factors can have on the balance of power between regime and civil society (Osanloo, Chapter 6 in this volume). In 2002 the EU entered into a constructive dialogue with Iran meant to be paralleled by increased economic interdependence with the country and to empower civil society and strengthen the reformists' efforts to improve the human rights situation (Kaussler 2008a, 273). President Khatami sponsored roundtable meetings that brought together the EU delegation, international human rights NGOs, Iranian academics, civil society activists, and conservative clerics to discuss such issues as discrimination against women. This dialogue helped him and the Women's Faction in parliament to push through women's rights reforms, such as allowing single women to travel abroad on state scholarships, the introduction of adult education for rural women, raising the legal age of marriage for girls from nine to thirteen years, giving women greater rights to divorce their husbands and reforming child custody rights in their favor.[10]

When the conservatives began their backlash against the reformists after elections weakened the latter in parliament, the EU relation and President Khatami's political skills protected women's activism. When the women's press was constrained by the conservatives, magazines like *Zanan* went online, and thousands of weblogs emerged because the hard-liners were not in a position to regulate the internet. This dynamic is the familiar one identified by democratization analysts in which the West's influence, combined with the new technology of globalization, empowers civil society democratizers.

However, already in October 2001 U.S. President Bush had declared the fight against terrorism to be also a fight for the rights and dignity of women. Iranian women, with long experience of how foreign support could play in the hands of the conservatives, did not welcome this. Indeed, the regime stepped up its campaign against women's rights advocates, sometimes charging them with *moharebeh,* or waging war against God. After the election of the seventh *majles,* reform bills stalled, and the more relaxed dress code was targeted in 2007. Women's rights activists in the forefront of the Green Movement were accused of spreading propaganda against the Islamic state and acting against national security.

In contrast with Syria, where the regime actively sought to co-opt the Diaspora into its program of secular modernization, the Iranian regime had little attraction for the Iranian Diaspora, which had mostly fled the revolution. The brain drain, staunched under Khatami, was accelerated by the postelectoral conflict between Ahmadinejad and the Green Movement. The latter resonated strongly with Iranian expatriates via internet forums (Ghorashi and Boersma 2009, 678–682; Lotfalian 2009). While positive relations with the Diaspora strengthened the internationalist orientation of Syria's ruling coalition, negative relations with Iran's Diaspora deepened the anti-internationalist orientation of Ahmadinejad's coalition.

CONCLUSION

Authoritarianism resilience cannot be understood in isolation from external factors. To stay in power, authoritarian regimes need to ward off external and internal threats but also need to access *resources* to do so, including external ones. Both the Syrian and Iranian regimes faced participatory demands within that coincided with the U.S. reach for hegemony in the region through the export of neoliberal democratization, including coercive regime change in Iraq. To counter this grave national security threat, both regimes engaged in a reverse sort of omnibalancing, namely defying America's hegemonic project in the region to get the nationalist legitimacy (political capital) to contain or appease domestic opposition. The association of U.S. democracy discourse with the negative demonstration effects in Iraq and Lebanon diluted the extent to which this might otherwise have empowered civil society against authoritarianism. But, additionally, their joint sponsorship of Hizbollah and

Palestinian Hamas against Israel and their stalemating of U.S./Western projects in Lebanon and Iraq generated political capital internally and contributed
to U.S. imperial overreach, which diluted the external threat. Moreover, the
war in Iraq unleashed a new oil boom that gave both regimes crucial financial
resources at the time they were under high external pressure. This facilitated
a more classic sort of omnibalancing in which both regimes countered proxi-
mate (U.S., internal) threats by diversifying their economic resources via links
to states not under U.S. sway, such as Russia and China, but for Syria even
some within the U.S. orbit, such as Qatar, a sign of the gaps in U.S. hegemony.
Accessing such external financial resources enabled their nationalist defiance
of the West; one might even suggest that the parallel rise of oil prices and of
China emboldened both regimes to defy the United States.

Both the Asad and Ahmedinejad regimes were able to use externally derived resources to consolidate themselves but with *opposite consequences* for
the orientation of the ruling coalition. Bashar al-Asad used the external threat
to consolidate presidential power at the expense of his statist-nationalist old
guard rivals. He also appeased external investors to get the financial and
social capital needed to consolidate the new internationalist-leaning ruling
coalition: the co-optation of Western-educated technocrats, plus new private
banks mobilized expatriate and Arab financial capital, a share of which the
regime taxed, and which fostered supportive crony capitalists; this came at
the expense of the party apparatus and the regime's populist constituency,
shifting the ruling coalition in an internationalist direction. However, the
internationalists, satisfied by co-optation, did not favor widened democratic
inclusion that would have constrained economic liberalization. For a period
(2005–2010), Bashar al-Asad emerged on top, balancing nationalist and internationalist wings of his coalition.

In Iran, the U.S. threat weakened the West-leaning reformists under
Khatami and empowered the hardliners. While the reformists had suffered
from low oil prices, under Ahmadinejad a big oil price windfall, combined
with the diversification of relations toward Russia and Asia, gave the regime
confidence to pursue a nationalist foreign policy defying the West. Internally,
Ahmadinejad used a combination of nationalist militancy and rent windfalls
from the new oil boom to consolidate his core constituency, solidifying the
support of the Revolutionary Guards and marginalizing the reformers and
the pragmatic center. However, the 2008 dip in oil prices led to economic
troubles and reduced patronage that helped empower a challenge to him by a

more internationalist countercoalition in the 2009 elections. The struggle for power, with the warring factions each mobilizing a segment of society, ended with the hard-liners repressing their opponents, thereby excluding the urban middle class but only at a high cost in legitimacy. While in Syria the Diaspora and modern women provided social capital empowering the internationalists, in Iran both were used by opponents, inside and outside, to delegitimize the regime. Overall, external resources shifted the balance in Iran's ruling coalition toward the nationalist-statists and away from internationalists.

External financial and political resources initially had similar benefits for authoritarian resilience in both states. Financial resources gave both regimes greater autonomy and patronage capabilities that, together with political capital (nationalism), allowed them to solidify core neopatrimonial constituencies, which, in turn, made repression of opponents possible, narrowing contestation. Such resources gave both regimes considerable short-term resilience, even under intense external challenge, but also had longer-term costs for their capacity to partially satisfy, hence better manage, participatory pressures. Thus, resources allowed Ahmadinejad to repress the reformists at the expense of Iran's hitherto more flexible competitive semiauthoritarianism. In Syria the neoliberal policies needed to access FDI contracted the inclusionary capacity of the regime, and it failed to invest its nationalist legitimacy in any compensatory expansion of competitive practices at the elite level. Both regimes faced rebellions, but their locations in opposing sectors of society, Iran's in the urban middle class and Syria's in the deprived periphery, were reflective of the differential impact of external resources on the restructuring of their social bases. Iran's successful repression of the opposition owed much to the oil rent that allowed welfare expenditures to buy rural support while the Syrian regime's lack of such rent made it overdependent on urban-centered capital and cost it rural support, putting its very survival at risk. Authoritarian upgrading had "fixed" some problems and contributed to resilience in the shorter term while creating new longer-term vulnerabilities that would, themselves, need to be addressed if authoritarian governance was to remain resilient.

REFERENCE MATTER

NOTES

Chapter 1. Authoritarian Governance in Syria and Iran

1. Authors stressing the hybrid or semidemocratic features of authoritarian regimes tend to emphasize their static character as opposed to their dynamism and resilience. This seems to be the case because political change is solely defined in terms of democratic transitions, which were argued to be unforthcoming. See Levitsky and Way (2002) and Brownlee (2007).

2. As Stark (1996, 995) notes, "Recombinant property is a form of organizational hedging in which actors respond to uncertainty by diversifying assets, redefining and recombining resources." We view this general capacity—the ability to redefine and recombine organizational assets—as a core attribute of what we are labeling "recombinant authoritarian regimes."

3. However, important exceptions include Böttcher (1998) and *Maghreb-Machrek*'s special issue on "Islam in Syria" (2008), edited by Thomas Pierret.

Chapter 2. The Economics of Authoritarian Upgrading in Syria

1. Banking activity remains in the hands of the state, with state banks keeping a market share of 75 percent. The ratio of loans granted to the private sector only represents 21 percent of gross domestic product (GDP). Syria Economic Report, Bank Audit, "Building on Pent-up Economic Opportunities while Containing Persisting Challenges," March 2010, 11.

2. The president's uncle on his mother's side, Mohammed Makhlouf, controlled the National Tobacco Board and the Land Bank of Syria, which are now run by hired hands.

3. A law of January 4, 2010, allows foreign investors to acquire up to 60 percent of the capital of a private bank, up from 49 percent. Agence France Presse (AFP), January 13, 2010.

4. Furthermore, the four seats in the Board of Directors reserved for public sector representatives were attributed to private entrepreneurs.

5. Real estate prices ranked Damascus eighth among the ten most expensive cities in the world, according to research carried out by Cushman Wakefield, "Decision Makers Report," No. 26, April–4 May 2010, and Syria Economic Report, Bank Audit, op. cit.

6. "Market people" (meaning families that have widely invested in artisanship, industry, and agriculture over several generations) are above all the traditional souk merchants in large Syrian towns.

7. This body was created in the spring of 2007 and brings together the various NGOs sponsored by Asma al-Asad: FIRDOS, Shabab, Massar, Rawafed.

8. Khaled Yacoub Oweis, "Syria Launches Its First Electricity Privatization Tender," *Daily Star,* November 3, 2009.

9. As an example, FIRDOS is present in only sixty villages, unlike the Ba'ath Party, which is established all over the country.

10. The Party Congress, convened every five years, should have been held in June 2010.

11. In 2009 Ratib Challah was appointed honorary president of the Damascus Chamber of Commerce and president of the board of directors of the Stock Exchange.

12. Besides the fact that the Central Bank exercises its right to oversight by asking for an annual report, the minimum capital required of Islamic banks is higher than for conventional banks.

13. According to an Ipsos Syria study, commissioned by the Syrian Enterprise and Business Centre (SEBC), this category represents 20 to 25 percent of Syrian companies. According to The Syria Report, the same percentage also holds for the entirety of the population (Thépault 2010).

14. The tribes were fighting over two seats reserved for independent candidates, with confrontations lasting more than four days, compelling the regime to reestablish order by military force and impose its own candidates (Donati 2009).

15. The administration has 1.4 million employees and could function with a mere 40 percent of them.

16. Author interview with Aissam Zaïm, Damascus, April 2007.

17. In 2004, 10.36 percent of the population (two million Syrians) lived on less than two dollars a day. "Poverty in Syria: 1996–2004. Diagnosis and Pro-poor Policy Considerations." U.N. Development Program (June 2005).

18. Ibid.

19. That is why the regime is blocking the creation of new schools by religious authorities, permitting only the renovation of existing establishments.

Chapter 3. A Martyrs' Welfare State and Its Contradictions

Much of the research that informs this chapter was conducted by the author in multiple locations inside Iran from June 2009 to April 2010 and was assisted by a fellowship from the International Dissertation Research Fellowship Program of the Social Science Research Council, with funds provided by the Andrew W. Mellon Foundation.

1. The remarks are from summer 2010; available online at http://persian2english .com/?p=11421.

2. Interview in Tehran, July 2008.

3. Interview with consultant to the Ministry of Health and Medical Education, June 2011.

4. The Shah wrote, for example, "Moving against the bazaars was typical of the political and social risks I had to take in my drive for modernization" (Pahlavi 1980, 156).

5. Interview with IKRC officer, October 2009.

6. These statistics can be found on www.emdad.ir, though the frequency and accuracy of statistical collection in the IKRC are unverified. My purpose in citing these numbers is simply to give a picture of the breadth of the organization's activities and the target group—less than 10 percent of the population.

7. Interviews in Tehran at IKRC offices, October–November 2009.

8. There also exists the formal Social Welfare Organization that is more connected to the corporatist welfare regime. It is fully located within the state, was created by merging several Pahlavi-era programs together in 1980, and often competes with the IKRC via similar services. However, it has experienced budget problems and reaches fewer individuals, even though its orientation toward social problems such as disability and drug abuse are quite proactive.

9. Personal observations during field work in these three cities in 2009–2010.

10. The IKRC headquarters in Tehran boasted several signs stating that the payment of cash was moving to an ATM-based debit card system, which would mirror similar methods already in place in the Social Security Organization.

11. Conversely, if a village resident worked in a nearby factory, his or her insurance would be paid by the factory insurance (often through the Social Security Organization) and not the rural insurance.

12. The government is mandated to fully fund contributory pension schemes and as a result often falls into debt vis-à-vis organizations like the SSO. Instead of cash, the IRI has opted to hand over nationalized industrial assets to various pension funds, including the SSO, the armed forces, and the Revolutionary Guards. This is casually described in the opposition press as a "military takeover," but this is an exaggeration. In reality, several different processes are involved in the "pseudo privatization" of the Iranian economy, one of which is the attempt by the state to meet its welfare commitments by shifting state assets into the pension fund sector.

13. At least twenty pension plans exist in Iran based on occupation. The fragmented nature of the pension system is a result both of political divisions and also because beneficiaries in many of the plans enjoy substantial benefits and do not wish to merge. Of course, not all private sector business are enrolled in the SSO, especially the small family businesses of the petty bourgeoisie.

14. In addition, pensions are transferable to the families and widows of eligible male workers who are deceased.

15. July 2009.

16. February 2010.

Chapter 4. The State Management of Religion in Syria

1. *All4Syria,* September 16, 2010; retrieved on August 8, 2011, from http:// all4syria.info/content/view/32179/70/.

2. OFA refers to a biweekly survey of the Syrian press published between 1948 and 1997 by the Office Arabe d'Information. I consulted it at the library of the Institut Français du Proche-Orient (IFPO) in Damascus.

3. The Sharia institutes (*ma'ahid shar'iyya*), which until 2008 were exclusively private, are different from the Sharia secondary schools (*thanawiyyat shar'iyya*), which were either public or private. Until 2008, each of the former was allowed to teach its own almost exclusively religious curriculum, and their diplomas were not recognized by the state. As for the latter institution, they teach state-designed programs that include both secular and religious courses, and they deliver state-sanctioned literary baccalaureates.

4. I would like to thank Steffen Hertog for his help concerning the analysis of the quantitative data presented in this chapter.

5. *All4Syria,* August 19, 2009; retrieved on August 8, 2011, from http://all4syria .info/content/view/12811/113/.

6. *All4Syria,* August 19, 2009; retrieved on August 8, 2011, from http://all4syria .info/content/view/12811/113/.

7. See also, *Akhbar al-Sharq,* June 6, 2005. Dead link, retrieved on June 7, 2007. The Ministry of Religious Endowments is not responsible for charitable associations, which are supervised by the Ministry of Social Affairs.

8. Interview with a Syrian cleric, Damascus, September 23, 2006.

9. Interview with a Western diplomat, Damascus, May 11, 2008.

10. Ibid.

11. Personal communication from a Western diplomat, February 6, 2009.

12. *Cham Press.* September 6, 2008. Dead link, retrieved on September 7, 2008.

13. *Cham Press.* July 22, 2008, and August 28, 2008. Dead link, retrieved on September 7, 2008.

14. *Cham Press.* September 6, 2008. Dead link, retrieved on September 7, 2008.

15. Ibid.

16. Interview with a Syrian cleric, Brussels, October 15, 2008.

17. *Tishrin al-Iqtisadi.* Last updated September 1, 2009; retrieved on August 8, 2011, from www.mow.gov.sy/?pid=774.

18. Al-Fath Online, December 29, 2009, retrieved on August 8, 2011, from www .alfatihonline.com/news/ejtma3.htm.

19. Elaph, June 22, 2009, retrieved on August 8, 2011, from www.elaph.com/Web/ Politics/2009/6/453308.htm.

20. *All4Syria,* July 30, 2009, retrieved on August 8, 2011, from http://all4syria .info/content/view/11978/113/.

21. *All4Syria,* September 8, 2010, retrieved on August 8, 2011, from http://all4syria .info/content/view/31843/113/.

22. *All4Syria,* July 8, 2009, retrieved on August 8, 2011, from http://all4syria.info/ content/view/11194/96/.

23. *All4Syria,* July 9, 2009, retrieved on August 8, 2011, from http://all4syria.info/ content/view/11277/80/.

24. *All4Syria,* August 19, 2009, retrieved on August 8, 2011, from http://all4syria .info/content/view/12811/113/.

25. *All4Syria,* December 30, 2009, retrieved on August 8, 2011, from http://all4syria .info/content/view/19128/113/.

26. PBS. May 27, 2010. Retrieved on August 8, 2011, from www.charlierose.com/ view/interview/11029.

27. *Akhbar al-Sharq,* August 14, 2009. Retrieved on August 8, 2011, from www .thisissyria.net/2009/08/14/syriatoday/03.html.

28. *All4Syria,* June 3, 2010, retrieved on August 8, 2011, from http://all4syria.info/ content/view/27236/113/.

29. *All4Syria,* June 30, 2010, retrieved on August 8, 2011, from http://all4syria .info/content/view/28552/113/.

30. *All4Syria,* July 19, 2010, retrieved on August 8, 2011, from http://all4syria .info/content/view/29490/70/.

31. Ibid.

32. Also see *Tishrin al-Iqtisadi,* 2009, last updated September 1, retrieved on August 8, 2011, from www.mow.gov.sy/?pid=774 ; *All4Syria,* September 10, 2010, retrieved on August 8, 2011, from http://all4syria.info/content/view/31939/113/; and *Nahj al-Islam,* May 2009, 86.

33. *Al-Fath Online.* December 29, 2009; retrieved on August 8, 2011, from www .alfatihonline.com/news/ejtma3.htm.

34. Also see *All4Syria,* September 10, 2010; retrieved on August 8, 2011, from http://all4syria.info/content/view/31939/113/.

Chapter 5. Islamic Social Movements and the Syrian Authoritarian Regime

I would like to thank Thomas Pierret and the other participants of this volume for their insightful criticism on an earlier draft. Special thanks to Reinoud Leenders and Steven Heydemann for their encouragement, thorough critiques, and constructive comments at various stages of this project. Without their support this chapter would not have been possible. That said, any remaining mistakes are solely my own.

1. Political rights are defined by Freedom House as the extent to which people are enabled to "participate freely in the political process, including the right to vote freely for distinct alternatives in legitimate elections, compete for public office, join political parties and organizations, and elect representatives who have a decisive impact on public policies and are accountable to the electorate." Civil liberties are defined as the extent to which individuals are allowed "the freedoms of expression and belief, associational and organizational rights, rule of law, and personal autonomy without interference from the state." Retrieved from the Freedom House website at www.freedomhouse.org/printer_friendly.cfm?page=35&year=2006.

2. See Freedom House, *Freedom in the World*, "Syria" (2009); available at www.freedomhouse.org/inc/content/pubs/fiw/inc_country_detail.cfm?year=2009&country=7713&pf.

3. See Syrian Muslim Brotherhood, Al-Markaz al-'Ilami li Jama't al-Ikhwan al-Muslimin—Suria, 2009; available at www.ikhwansyria.com/ar/default.aspx. See also: The Democratic Islamic Current in Syria, "Risala al-tayar al-Islami al-dimocrati ila al-sha'ab al-Suri bimunasaba shahar ramadan al-mubarak," August 23, 2009; available at http://all4syria.info/content/view/13055/39/.

4. A sheikh is a person with some form of popular recognized religious authority. A mufti issues religious decrees (or *fatwas*) and an *'alim* (pl. *'ulama*) is a religious scholar.

5. The resulting analysis is mostly based on the situation as it was between 2000 and 2009. See also the conclusion of this chapter and Pierret's contribution in Chapter 4 of this volume. In addition, the specific research context renders it impossible to gather quantitative data on the topic of the analysis. In effect, this means that the analysis is based largely on interviews.

6. For example, the network and social movement debate; see for instance Diani (2003).

7. For example, resource mobilization theory; see for instance McCarthy and Zald (1977).

8. For example, the discussion on framing strategies; see Benford and Snow (2000).

9. For example, this implies a political processes approach; see Tarrow (1998) and Kriesi (2004).

10. Interview with a Syrian observer, Damascus, April 15, 2009.

11. Interview with a senior Damascus-based sheikh, July 15, 2010.

12. Interview with a senior Damascus-based sheikh, March 11, 2009.

13. Interview with an employee of the Ahmad Kiftaru Institute, July 16, 2010.

14. Interview with senior representative of the Ahmad Kiftaru Institute, April 4, 2009. See the website of the institute at http://abunour.net.

15. See his website at www.alfatihonline.com/.

16. Interview with secular activists, April 12, 2009.

17. See al-Buti's website at http://fikr.com/bouti/.

18. See his website at www.nabulsi.com.

19. Interview with senior sheikh, July 31, 2010.

20. See the website at www.altajdeed.org.

21. See *Levant News,* "Ba'ad nahwa arb'a ashur min tashkil majlas al-amin al-watani: Madha tarayr fi al-Siasa al-amin fi Suria?" October 27, 2009; available at www .thisissyria.net/2009/10/27/syriatoday/04.html.

22. Institutionally, political power is concentrated around the executive branches and specifically the intelligence services (*mukhabaraat*) and army.

23. Interview with senior Sunni religious actor, Damascus, March 9, 2009; interview with secular activists, Damascus, April 12, 2009; interview with a senior Sunni religious actor, Damascus, July 15, 2010.

24. This is not to imply that formal policies and institutional arrangements vis-à-vis the religious sphere are fixed. They have altered and developed with changing (formal) positions of the regime vis-à-vis religious activism, but the regime has never relented on its effective veto over Islamic initiatives.

25. The situation as of writing (October 2009).

26. This situation is a result of an historic trajectory in which the Ba'ath regime had insufficient financial and symbolic resources to reign in the strongly traditionally embedded religious movements present in Syrian society and found itself dependent on Islamic legitimacy (for a more elaborate description, see Pierret 2009).

27. Interview with Syrian Human Rights activists, April 8, 2009.

28. Syrian Human Rights Committee 2010, 30.

29. If interested, see the website and yearly reports of the SHRC at www.shrc.org.

30. Interview with Syrian Human Rights activists, April 8, 2009. Other examples of the unpredictability of state repression are provided by interviewees. First, about ten sheikhs are currently questioned per month according to a human rights activist. The selection is more or less at random. The main objective of these interrogations is "just to remind them" that the *mukhabaraat* are present (interview with Syrian Human Rights activist, May 1, 2009). Additionally, repression is also dependent on external influences. Policies versus religious movements between 2000 and 2010 have oscillated between a very hands-off approach (following the advent of Bashar's rule and the

American invasion of Iraq) and a much more active and restrictive one (following the end of international political isolation of the Syrian regime).

31. The phenomenon has extensively been studied, for example, for colonial Kenya (Tarrow, Tilly, and McAdam 2001, 102) and transnational global justice movements (Tarrow 2005).

32. See their information online: Mohammad Habash, "Lamha a'n al-duktur Muhammad Habash," 2007, available at altajdeed.org; Hassam al-Din al-Farfur, "al-Shaykh al-Duktur: Hassam Addin Farfur," 2010, available at www.alfatihonline .com/; Muhammad Ratib al-Nabulsi, "Long Biography of Dr. Muhammad Ratib al-Nabulsi," April 22, 2006, available at www.nabulsi.com/cv/cvlong_en.doc.

33. Interview with Sheikh Nabulsi, July 31, 2010.

34. Another (extreme) example is Mahmoud al-Aghasi, or Abu al-Qaqa. A controversial preacher from Aleppo, he rose to infamy throughout 2003 with highly inflammatory sermons against the American occupation in Iraq (Moubayed 2006a). On September 23, 2007, he was gunned down after leaving Friday prayer at his mosque (McGregor 2007). The facts that he was apparently allowed to send jihadis to Iraq throughout 2003, give highly inflammatory sermons, and have his own organization (*ghuraba al-sham*, Strangers of the Levant) led many to believe he had close contacts with the Syrian intelligence services, a suspicion that increased after he began to dress and live more expensively and, after 2006, issued a fatwa in favor of wearing Western dress (McGregor 2007). Who was behind the killing was never clarified. See also Moubayed (2006b).

35. Interview with an employee of the Ahmad Kiftaru Foundation, July 16, 2010.

36. Interview with board member of a Damascus Islamic association, April 16, 2009.

37. Interview with Damascus-based sheikh, March 23, 2009.

38. Interview with board member of Islamic association, April 16, 2009.

39. Interview with secular activists, April 12, 2009.

40. Interview with secular activist, July 15, 2010.

41. Interview with Syrian observer, April 18, 2009.

42. Interview with a follower of al-Buti, Damascus, July 29, 2010.

43. Interview with an employee of the Ahmad Kiftaru Foundation, Damascus, July 16, 2010.

44. Interview with Syrian observer, March 12, 2009; with secular activists, April 12, 2009; with Syrian secular activist, April 22, 2009; with Syrian human rights activist, May 1, 2009.

Chapter 6. Contesting Governance: Authority, Protest, and Rights Talk in Postrepublican Iran

1. I do not suggest that a binary division exists between civil and Islamic laws. To the contrary, in Iran, civil laws are based on religious texts, as others have sug-

gested with respect to civil laws in Europe (Merryman 1969). Instead, I suggest that religious state authorities grant themselves not only a monopoly over the domains of civil society and social relations, which in Islamic jurisprudence can be understood as *muamalat,* but also *ibadat,* domains of religious life, not previously under the purview of the state, because these are specific matters for religious guidance. Interestingly, family laws reside somewhere in between these two arenas. Only recently has the state guided family relations, once thought to be the unique province of the ulema. With the 1979 convergence of state governance and religious authority, Iranian leaders have justified legislating on matters of women and family when they denounced the same during the previous era. This is one of the reasons why the issue of control over women's status and roles is so significant for the legitimacy of the Islamic Republic today.

2. About 89 percent of Iranian Muslims are part of the Shi'i branch of Islam, as opposed to the Sunni branch, which is the predominant Muslim sect in the world. Shi'i Muslims, or partisans of Ali (Ali ibn Abu Talib), believe that Ali, the Prophet's son-in-law and cousin, should have been the Prophet's immediate successor.

3. Initially critics remained largely unnamed, with few notable exceptions, such as Khomeini's former successor, Ayatollah Montazeri, but today many critics have emerged, including Ayatollahs Sistani, Saanei, Shabestari, and Kadivar. State authorities have discredited, defrocked, imprisoned, forced them to flee, or otherwise neutralized dissenters.

4. When the Iranian government fell on February 14, 1979, parliament was immediately dissolved. The leaders of the revolution, who had formed the Council of the Revolution a month earlier, officially took control and dealt with all immediate transitional issues, including the legislative function of the state, until a new parliament could be elected. The Provisional Government was the executive branch of the Council of the Revolution and supervised the transformation of all political and legal institutions.

5. The constitution of the Islamic Republic of Iran was first enacted in 1979 and revised in 1989. Equal protection extends only to those citizens who are affiliated with a religion "of the book." Christians, Jews, and Zoroastrians have parliamentary representation, but members of the Baha'i faith do not. As it is an Islamic state, even members of recognized religions must abide by Islamic principles as interpreted and codified by the state leaders.

6. In some ways, the *Velayat-e Faqih* is a new position theorized by Khomeini in the 1960s, but in other ways it is an extension of a much longer debate going back to the constitutional revolution, and perhaps even the seventeenth-century Safavid consolidation of Shi'i Islam in state government. More specifically, a notion of limited guardianship can be traced back to the tenth century CE/fourth century AH when Sheikh Mofid introduced *ijtihad* (independent rule making) among Shi'i scholars. The more absolute version of guardianship was introduced in the Shi'i jurisprudence

through a famous text book, *Javaher-al-Kalem* (Philosophical Jewels). Later, the Iranian Ayatollah Molla Muhammad Mahdee Naraqi (1749 CE/1128 AH–1830 CE/1209 AH) published a paper advocating a modest level of political actions for Islamic leaders, or a limited version of *Velayat-e-Faqih*. Today among Shi'i ulema a debate exists as to the exact meaning of Velayat or guardianship. For current debates on this issue, see, Soroush (2000) and Salimi (2003).

7. Paidar (1995) details the confusion in choices of laws and courts in adjudicating divorce, and Zubaida (2005) discusses the disorder that ensued in drafting penal sanctions.

8. One example from the early 1990s was the need to control population growth. Khomeini's own justifications for authorizing legislation to allow for birth control were based on the interests of the Islamic state, not the Qur'an or the hadiths of the Prophet (Hoodfar 1994; Keddie 2000–2001).

9. *Zanan* was founded by prominent writer and journalist Shahla Sherkat. In February 2008, the government ordered its closure, after almost twenty years of publication.

10. *Hejab,* broadly speaking, means "modesty" but in colloquial language refers to women's modest dress.

11. The feast of duty or devotion, as it is called, is a public performance by the girls. Dressed in white veils with crowns of flowers on their heads, they recite the prayer they learned in school. Afterwards, school officials present each girl with gifts, which include copies of the Qur'an. Of these rituals, which are often televised, Adelkhah notes that individuation is "a mark of social recognition and the value accorded to the child, who is celebrated as a true individual . . . from the youngest age" (2000, 120).

12. The chador is a long, often black, tentlike dressing that covers a woman from head to toe, leaving only the eyes, hands, and feet visible. This was the preferred, but not mandated, dress of Islamic revolutionaries who wanted to show the world that Iran had changed (Taleghani 1982). Through this act, the revolution used the image of the veiled Iranian woman to comprise a political Irano-Islamic symbol of the country's revolution.

13. As marriage is a legal contract drawn up by the family of the bride and offered to the groom, the right to abrogate the contract rests with the groom under the theory that he has not received what he had agreed to under the contract. On the other hand, the bride has certain rights to dissolve the marriage, too, should she not receive her part of the bargain. Those rights are preserved both in the marriage contract and in the civil codes. Should the husband violate his specified obligations, the wife has rights to dissolve the marriage. In her case, however, she must present evidence to a judge who will evaluate it and then, technically, delegate the husband's right to abrogate the marriage contract to her.

14. One example of such meeting groups was the popular Wednesday night lectures held by religious scholar and intellectual, Dr. Abdolkarim Soroush, who had been an early supporter of Khomeini and participated in authoring parts of the 1979

constitution but who later fell out of favor with the establishment. Not long after, Soroush's talks were met with attacks by vigilante pro-government groups. Such pronouncements do not easily fit within dichotomous reformist and hard-liner agendas.

15. Since 1997, in some parts of Tehran, women wear makeup, nail polish, and shorter veils when they venture out of their homes. A seeming relaxation of restraints appeared when several men running for Tehran's first City Council race since the revolution posted their likeness around the city bearing neckties—formerly a symbol of Western support. None of the men wearing neckties won, however. Today, it appears, such an action could indeed disqualify them from running.

Chapter 7. Who Laughs Last

1. "Interview with Syrian President Bashar al-Assad," *Wall Street Journal,* January 31, 2011; retrieved on September 21, 2011, from http://online.wsj.com/article/SB10001424052748703833204576114712441122894.html.

2. Although this chapter is concerned exclusively with literary culture, there are important exceptions to this generalization, as in the case of cinema (Boëx, 2011).

3. On the idea of a "fierce" state, see Ayubi (1995, 449–450). On the Syrian state as a weak state, see Sluglett (2007, 93–108).

4. The only reference to Haddad that I am aware of in English is his brief cameo appearance in Salamandra (2004, 110).

5. All translations are my own.

6. Personal communication, October 26, 2009.

7. All translations are my own.

8. To my knowledge, there are only a handful of references in English to the work of Nihad Sirees. *The Peasant Comedy* is summarily discussed in Meyer (2001, 99–100) and cited briefly in Shannon (2006, 213ff6). *The Silence and the Roar* is discussed in Aghacy (2009, 123–129).

9. All translations are my own.

Chapter 8. Prosecuting Political Dissent

1. Al-Nuri formally retired in August 2000 but then remained in his position. It is not clear why, but one lawyer expressed a view shared by many: "They can't find anyone else who is prepared to take up this dirty role. Perhaps, too, al-Nuri fears being targeted by Islamists if he no longer enjoys formal protection as a high judge" (Interview in Damascus, February 4, 2010).

2. Interviews with Syrian lawyers and Western diplomats in Damascus, December 2009 and February 2010.

3. Ibid.

4. Interview in Damascus, February 7, 2010.

5. Interviews with former political prisoners and lawyers in Damascus, December 2009 and February 2010.

6. Interview with Syrian lawyer, Damascus, December 15, 2009.

7. Ibid.

8. The already negligible degree of judicialization involving military field courts often degenerated into unambiguous extrajudicial repression when those acquitted by field courts were kept in detention regardless. In the 1980s, Tadmur prison reportedly contained what prisoners and prison wards alike called "the dormitories of innocence" where acquitted individuals were kept in custody. Many are said to have died under torture (Dimashki 2002, 246; Khalifé 2007, 88–89). Others were executed even though military field courts had sentenced them to prison (Ziadeh 2010, 51).

9. Interviews in Damascus, December 2009 and February 2010.

10. My observations here are borrowed from Coicaud (2002, 12–13).

11. See, for example, the personal account of Heba Dabbagh (2007, 220) who was detained in a military prison between 1980 and 1989. She recalls that many of her prison inmates had completed their trials before military field courts but that "the rulings were classified." See also Khalifé (2007, 88).

12. The defendants were claimed to have also made their confessions at the SSSC a few days earlier. Yet the court was given no credit for having investigated or proven the charges. Interviews with Syrian Muslim Brother activists in London, March 2010.

13. These recantations were televised in November 2005 (by way of an interview with Husam Husam confessing to giving false testimony before the U.N. investigation into the assassination of former Lebanese Prime Minister Rafiq al-Hariri) and in November 2008 (when ten Islamist militants of Fatah al-Islam confessed to having blown up a security complex along the road to Damascus airport).

14. Interview with Syrian lawyer in Damascus, February 9, 2010.

15. Wedeen (1999) points to a similar paradox in her analysis, by observing that to most Syrians the claims made in state propaganda are not credible. She resolves this by attributing significance to a mechanism of "acting as if" and forced participation, which, she argues, generates power without popular legitimacy. I see no clear parallels to Syria's courts and judicial processes, as the regime's imposed messages are minimal or even deliberately concealed (as opposed to the rich content and public nature of state propaganda), while audiences are rarely allowed access to judicial procedures let alone expected to participate. Syria's judicial institutions, to follow Wedeen's borrowing from Foucault, on the whole do not serve as a stage for "public spectacles."

16. Interestingly in this context, Syria's moribund Constitutional Court was given an entire new building close to the U.S. ambassador's residence in Damascus in preparation for the city's status as "cultural capital of the Arab world" in 2008.

17. For a typical example, see Office of the High Commissioner for Human Rights (2001).

18. Interview in Damascus, December 17, 2009.

19. Author's interview in Damascus, March 2010.

20. Interview in Damascus, March 4, 2010.

21. In this period Syria's judiciary even may indirectly have contributed to the elimination of one of the Ba'th Party's main rivals, the SSNP (Syrian Socialist Nationalist Party). In 1955 a leading Ba'th military officer, Adnan al-Malki, was killed by a SSNP officer. The officer was later tried and found guilty. The "Malki affaire" is considered to have elevated the Ba'th's standing among the left-wing opposition (Lobmeyer 1995, 78).

22. Interview with former judge and MP in Damascus, December 15, 2009.

23. Interviews in Damascus with a former judge and lawyers, March 2010.

24. Interview with former judge in Damascus, February 9, 2010.

25. Reid (1981, 208) points out that prior to 1963 many Syrian lawyers had few qualms about the authoritarian measures and policies pursued by governments dominated by the oligarchy.

26. Interviews with former judge and lawyers in Damascus, December 2009 and February 2010.

27. Ibid.

28. Interview with former judge in Damascus, February 9, 2010.

29. Much later, in June 1993, Haydar (1993) argued with unprecedented candor that, in his view and given the absence of a real and serious threat to Syria's national security, the country's martial laws were to be considered null and void.

30. Interview with senior lawyer in Damascus, February 12, 2010.

31. Interviews with lawyers in Damascus, February 2010.

32. Ibid.

33. Author's interview with senior lawyer in Damascus, February 3, 2010. A 1985 Ba'th Party document alleged that, among the 2,538 lawyers in the country, 300 were Ba'thist, 99 were with the licensed Communist Party, 113 with other parties of the National Progressive Front, 12 with the illegal branch of the CP, 17 with the Muslim Brotherhood, 88 with the Syrian Nationalists, 9 with Kurdish nationalist parties, and 4 with a semilegal Nasserist group (Perthes 1995, 159). Prior to 1983, a significant number of lawyers also seem to have been involved in armed attacks against the regime, led by Islamist groups with or without ties to the Muslim Brotherhood. Exact estimates on lawyers' participation in such armed groups do not exist. Yet Lobmeyer (1995, 386–394) estimated on the basis of available data on the backgrounds of arrested suspected Islamist militants that nearly 26 percent of them were doctors, engineers, and lawyers, primarily from Aleppo, Hama, and Damascus.

34. In the early 1970s, Hafiz al-Asad reportedly said that "only 100 or 200 individuals at most" are involved in politics and would oppose the regime under any circumstances: "It is for them that the [military] Mezzeh prison was originally intended" (cited in Batatu 1999, 206).

35. For a list of such (attempted) assassinations abroad between 1972 and 1980, see Middle East Watch (1990, Appendix II, 182–185).

36. One Syrian former left-wing political activist and ex–political prisoner succinctly summed up what he believed was Hafiz al-Asad's main and lasting preoccupation:

He was sick and tired of foreign interventions by Syria's neighbors and other powers. For him it was unbearable that even ridiculous countries like Jordan had once managed to gain a foothold in Syria. For Asad Syria was a drifting ship in the region's troubled waters. He wanted it to make stable and strong again, with himself being the captain. (Interview in Damascus, December 12, 2009)

37. Accordingly, the regime's official indictment of the Muslim Brotherhood, published in 1984, brought about all sorts of "evidence" of its opponent's wickedness, but it did not detail the illegality of its conspiracies or argue that its members' guilt had been proven in front of a court of law (Syrian Arab Republic 1984a, 1984b).

38. In an oft-cited statement, Rifaat al-Asad said: "If necessary . . . we are ready to engage in a hundred battles, destroy a thousand citadels, and sacrifice a million martyrs to bring back peace and love, the glory of the country, and the honor of the citizens" (*Tishrin* July 1, 1989, cited in Seurat 1989, 62).

39. Interviews in Damascus, December 2009 and February 2010.

40. Syrian human rights lawyers often spent much of their written defense at the SSSC and military tribunals on legal arguments disputing the jurisdiction of these courts and the legality of the state of emergency. For instance, in April 2005 a detailed legal opinion challenging the legality of the SSSC was delivered by Anwar al-Bunni, then defense lawyer to human rights activist Akhtam Nu'aysah (Bunni 2005). Another lawyer added, "[During politically charged trials at criminal courts] we come with many lawyers to attend the court sessions. We shout, we clap, we boo, we make a lot of fuss. We use the court to raise our protest. This makes them [regime officials] go crazy; they fear a human rights circus" (interview with lawyer in Damascus, February 13, 2010). Defendants' relatives and supporters also repeatedly staged spontaneous protests and sit-ins in front of the SSSC.

41. Together with Canada and the United States, the members of the European Union have regularly attended court sessions in Syria since 2002, particularly when they involve prominent and mostly secular human rights and political activists including Riad Seif, Ma'mun al-Homsi, Riyyad al-Turk, Michel Kilo, Anwar al-Bunni, Haytham al-Maleh, Muhannad al-Hassani, and others. For a Dutch diplomat's personal account of these trial observations, see Stienen (2008, 266–278). More recently, Western diplomats also began to monitor lesser-known cases involving (Salafi) Islamists and Kurdish activists to address criticisms that they were using double standards by demonstrating concern about certain prosecutions and not others (interviews with Western diplomats in Damascus, December 2009 and February 2010).

42. Interview in Damascus, March 14, 2010.

43. However, others reported that relatives of those extrajudicially detained or "disappeared" were also denied their citizen rights, as they failed to obtain a security

clearance from the country's intelligence services needed for government employment (Ziadeh 2010, 54, 65).

44. Interviews in Damascus, February 2010.

45. See, for instance, the interview with Bashar al-Asad in *El País,* October 1, 2006.

46. Interview in Damascus, February 2010. Political prisoners do not seem to be protected against their criminal prison inmates either. For instance, in November 2006, detained human rights activist Kamal Labwani was badly beaten by a criminal prisoner (Amnesty International 2008).

47. This way the regime appears to have played civilian judges against the colleagues, friends, and relatives they have among human rights lawyers who were prosecuted in civilian courts. One civilian judge reportedly broke down in tears in front of defense lawyers because he was a friend of the accused, also a lawyer. He was subsequently demoted (interview with lawyer in Damascus, February 2, 2010). Another judge at Damascus's Criminal Court reportedly said to defendant Salah Kaftaru, the son of late Mufti Ahmad Kaftaru: "I could release you but your arrest has been ordered, and setting you free is not in my hands" (Kulluna Shuraka fi al-Watan, February 28, 2010). Kaftaru's prosecution was widely believed to be motivated by the regime's decreasing tolerance of Islamic activism.

48. One such reported case involved a female judge, Salwa Kadib, at the Court of Cassation in Damascus. At the end of 2009 she overturned a ruling by a lower court denying the customary release of a political prisoner (Michel Kilo) after serving two-thirds of his sentence. In a plenary session of all chief judges of the Court of Cassation, the ruling was revoked and removed from the court's files. Kadib was demoted and transferred to a lower court in the countryside (interviews with lawyers in Damascus, December 2009 and February 2010).

49. Heydemann (2007b, 3, 8) suggests that "authoritarian upgrading" consists of introducing noncoercive innovations *to supplement* continued coercion and repression as "tried-and-true strategies of the past" [emphasis added].

50. The suggested mechanism is similar to what Dankwart Rustow (1963, 11–12) observed in the early 1960s. The increased reliance of governments on military repression, Rustow argued, caused the army's skills in domestic coercion to be overdeveloped, which, in turn, made such governments a "more vulnerable and tempting target" for military coups.

51. Of course, other measures may be argued to have been important in this respect, including efforts to increase competition between security organizations, reduce the size of paramilitary forces suspected of adventurous inclinations, and grant influential officers extensive financial privileges and by establishing stronger central control over all security and intelligence agencies.

52. "Thirteen Named on Syrian Sanctions List," Al-Jazeera, May 10, 2011; available at http://english.aljazeera.net/news/middleeast/2011/05/20115109716137121.html.

Chapter 9. Democratic Struggles and Authoritarian Responses in Iran in Comparative Perspective

I would like to thank Steven Heydemann for his constructive criticisms, Reinoud Leenders for his useful comments, and Sara McKeever for her competent research.

1. Personal communication with Nasrin Sotoudeh, Tehran, June 13, 2009. Sotoudeh was arrested in September 2010 and sentenced to eleven years in prison in January 2011.

2. Personal communication with Badrosadat Mofidi, Tehran, March 10, 2008. She was sentenced to six years in prison in 2010.

3. Speech delivered by Dr. Abdollah Naseri in a reformist meeting in Tehran on March 9, 2008. He was sentenced to five years in prison in 2011.

4. Personal communication with Taghi Rahmani, Tehran, March 10, 2008.

5. The list of 107 individuals is available at www.pbs.org/wgbh/pages/frontline/ tehranbureau/2010/06/martyrs-of-the-green-movement.html (May 1, 2010). The executed individuals were actually arrested before the elections.

6. This number comes from a fact-finding commission established by the government. A copy of its report is available at www.ffnc-eg.org/assets/ffnc-eg_final.pdf (October 24, 2011).

7. For instance, see the articles written by journalists based in Tehran available at www.pbs.org/wgbh/pages/frontline/tehranbureau/2010/02/why-north-tehranis-dont -revolt.html (February 13, 2010); and http://mianeh.net/article/%E2%80%9Csilent -protesters%E2%80%9D-fear-foreign-intervention (April 6, 2010).

8. Reported by BBC Persian, February 26, 2010; available at www.bbc.co.uk/ persian/iran/2010/02/100226_lo6_basij_increase.shtml.

9. Reported by BBC Persian, March 13, 2010. Available at www.bbc.co.uk/ persian/iran/2010/03/100313_u03-cyber-war-prosecutor.shtml.

Chapter 10. Ehteshami, Hinnebusch, Huuhtanen, Raunio, Warnaar, and Zintl: Authoritarian Resilience and International Linkages in Iran and Syria

1. Previously, Heydemann (2000), Mufti (1996), and Huuhtanen (2008) looked at the impact of international factors, including war, on state formation in the Middle East.

2. See *Christian Science Monitor*, "Syrian Expatriates Return Home in Hopes of New Wealth," December 27, 1010, available at www.csmonitor.com; and "Syria: Educated Expatriates Resist the Call to Come Home," December 10, 2010, available at www.irinnews.org.

3. This term was applied to the hard-liners by Ehteshami and Zweiri (2007) to denote their combination of cultural and political conservatism with renewed ideological militancy.

4. Hossein Shariatmadari, "Radical Daily Says Reformists America's 'Fifth Column.'" *Kayhan,* May 19, 2002, in Persian. Translated text provided by BBC Worldwide Monitoring through LexisNexis; Norooz web site, "Activists Say 'Adventurists' Are Threatening Detente in Foreign Policy," in Persian. Translated text provided by BBC Worldwide Monitoring through LexisNexis, February 17, 2002; VIRI, "Radio Says No Talks with US as Long as It 'Threatens or Humiliates' Iran." *Voice of the Islamic Republic of Iran external service,* in English, May 31, 2002.[o]

5. Terror Free Tomorrow. (2009) *Ahmadinejad Front Runner in Upcoming Presidential Elections; Iranians Continue to Back Compromise and Better Relations with US and West. Results of a New Nationwide Public Opinion Survey of Iran Before the June 12, 2009 Presidential Elections.* Retrieved on March 1, 2010, from www.terrorfreetomorrow .org/.../TFT%20Iran%20Survey%20Report%200609.pdf.

6. *National Interest,* "Dealing with Iran," May 19, 2010.

7. BBC, "Expanding Business Empire of Iran's Revolutionary Guards," July 26, 2010; available at www.bbc.co.uk/news/world-middle-east-10743580.

8. Shariatmadari, Hossein, "Candidate Musavi Supports US, Israel viewpoints—Iran Daily." *Kayhan,* May 26, 2009, in Persian. Translated text provided by BBC Worldwide Monitoring through LexisNexis.

9. VIRI, "Ayatollah Jannati Delivers Tehran Friday Prayer Sermons 3 July." *Voice of the Islamic Republic of Iran,* July 3, 2009. in Persian. Translated text provided by BBC Worldwide Monitoring through LexisNexis.

10. BBC, "Iranian Women Get More Divorce Rights," December 2, 2002; retrieved on February 16, 2010, from http://news.bbc.co.uk/1/hi/world/middle_east/2534375.stm.

BIBLIOGRAPHY

'Abbas, 'Abdal H. 1979. "Al-Jihaz al-qada'i wa 'qzmat al-'idala," *Al-Muhamun* 4–5: 89–96.

Ababsa, Myriam. 2006. "Contre-réforme agraire et conflits fonciers en Jâzira syrienne (2000–2005)," in *La Syrie au quotidien, cultures et pratiques du changement*. ed. Sylvia Chiffoleau, 211–230. Aix-en-Provence: Editions Edisud, REMMM.

Abbasi-Shavazi, Mohammad, Peter McDonald, and Meimanat Hosseini-Chavoshi. 2009. *The Fertility Transition in Iran: Revolution and Reproduction*. New York: Springer.

Abboud, Samer. 2009. "The Transition Paradigm and the Case of Syria," in *Syria and the Transition Paradigm*. St Andrews, UK: St Andrews Papers on Contemporary Syria.

Abboud, Samer, and Ferdinand Arslanian. 2009. *Syria's Economy and the Transition Paradigm*. Fife, UK: University of St. Andrews Centre for Syrian Studies.

Abrahamian, Ervand. 1989. *The Iranian Mojahedin*. New Haven, CT: Yale University Press.

———. 2008. *A History of Modern Iran*. New York: Cambridge University Press.

———. 2009. "The Crowd in the Iranian Revolution." *Radical History Review* 105: 13–38.

Acemoglu, Daron, and James A. Robinson. 2006. *The Economic Origins of Dictatorship and Democracy*. New York: Cambridge University Press

Adelkhah, Fariba. 2000. *Being Modern in Iran*. New York: Columbia University Press.

Adorno, Theodor W. 1974. *Minima Moralia: Reflections from Damaged Life*. London: Verso.

Aghacy, Samira. 2009. *Masculine Identity in the Fiction of the Arab East since 1967*. Syracuse, NY: Syracuse University Press.

Aïta, Samir. 2007. "L'économie de la Syrie peut-elle devenir sociale?" in *La Syrie au présent, reflets d'une société*, ed. Baudoin Dupret, Zouhair Ghazzal, Youssef Courbage, and Mohammed al-Dbiyat, 541–581. Paris: Sindbad/Actes Sud.

Akhavi, Shahrough. 1992. "Shi'ism, Corporatism, and Rentierism in the Iranian Revolution," in *Comparing Muslim Societies: Knowledge and the State in a World Civilization*, ed. Juan Cole, 261–293. Ann Arbor: The University of Michigan Press.

Alamdari, K. 2005. "The Power Structure of the Islamic Republic of Iran: Transition from Populism to Clientelism, and Militarization of the Government." *Third World Quarterly* 26: 1285–1301.

Albrecht, Holger, and Schlumberger, Oliver. 2004. "Waiting for Godot: Regime Change without Democratization in the Middle East," *International Political Science Review*, 25 (4): 371–392.

Althusser, Louis. 1976. "Idéologie et appareils idéologiques d'etat (notes pour une recherche)," in *Positions (1964–1975)*, ed. Louis Althusser, 67–125. Paris: Les Editions sociales. Originally published in 1970 in *La Pensée* (151).

Amin, Shahid, and Marcel van der Linden, eds. 1997. *"Peripheral" Labour? Studies in the History of Partial Proletarianization*. Cambridge, UK: Cambridge University Press.

Amnesty International. 2008. "Syria." *Amnesty International Report 2007*. London: Amnesty International; available at www.amnesty.org/en/region/syria/report-2007.

Amouee, Bahman. 2003. *Political Economy of the Islamic Republic*. Tehran, Iran: Gam-e No Press [in Persian].

Ansari, Ali M. 2000. *Iran, Islam and Democracy: The Politics of Managing Change*. London: The Royal Institute of International Affairs.

———. 2003. *Modern Iran since 1921: The Pahlavis and After*. London: Longman.

———. 2010. "Moral Crisis Threatens Iran's Revolutionary Guards." *Guardian*, June 11.

Antoun, R. 2006. Fundamentalism, Bureaucratization and the State's Co-optation of Religion: A Jordanian Case Study. *International Journal of Middle East Studies* 38: 369–393.

Arjomand, Said Amir. 1988. *The Turban for the Crown: The Islamic Revolution in Iran*. Studies in Middle Eastern History. New York: Oxford University Press.

———. 2009. *After Khomeini*. New York: Oxford University Press.

Arendt, Hannah. 1951. *The Origins of Totalitarianism*. New York: Harcourt, Brace and Company.

Armstrong, Elizabeth A., and Mary Bernstein. 2008. "Culture, Power, and Institutions: A Multi-Institutional Politics Approach to Social Movements." *Sociological Theory* 26 (1): 74–99.

Arrighi, Giovanni. 1990. "The Developmental Illusion: A Reconceptualization of the Semiperiphery," in *Semiperipheral States in the World Economy*, ed. Bill Martin, 11–42. New York: Greenwood Press.

Arslan, Shahir. 1978. "Istiqlal al-qada'," *Al-Muhamun* (2–4): 61–71.

al-Ashraf, Usama. 1987. "Al-tafriq bayna al-irhab wa al-haqq al-mashru' li-al-muqawama al-wataniyya didd al-Ihtilal." *Al-Muhamun* 4: 386–391.

Aws (al), Yayha. 2010. *Wizarat al-awqaf, ila ayn? Majallat al-thara* 218; retrieved on August 8, 2011, from www.thara-sy.com/thara/modules/news/article.php?storyid =1342.

Ayubi, Nazih, N. M. 1995. *Over-Stating the Arab State: Politics and Society in the Middle East.* London: I. B. Tauris.

Azimi, Fakhreddin. 2008. *The Quest for Democracy in Iran.* Cambridge, MA: Harvard University Press.

Bacik, Gökhan. 2008. *Hybrid Sovereignty in the Arab Middle East: The Cases of Kuwait, Jordan and Iraq.* New York: Palgrave Macmillan.

Baden, Nancy T. 1999. *The Muffled Cries: The Writer and Literature in Authoritarian Brazil, 1964–1985.* Lanham, MD: University Press of America.

Batatu, Hanna. 1982. "Syria's Muslim Brethren." *MERIP Reports* 110: 12–20.

———. 1999. *Syria's Peasantry, the Descendants of Its Lesser Rural Notables, and Their Politics.* Princeton, NJ: Princeton University Press.

Bayat, Asef. 1997. *Street Politics: Poor People's Movements in Iran.* New York: Columbia University Press.

———. 2007. *Making Islam Democratic: Social Movements and the Post-Islamist Turn.* Palo Alto, CA: Stanford University Press.

Behdad, Sohrab and Farhad Nomani. 2009. "What a Revolution! Thirty Years of Social Class Reshuffling in Iran." *Comparative Studies of South Asia, Africa and the Middle East,* 29 (1): 84–104.

Beissinger, Mark R. 2007. "Structure and Example in Modular Political Phenomena: The Diffusion of Bulldozer/Rose/Orange/Tulip revolutions." *Perspectives on Politics* 5: 259– 276.

Benford, Robert D., and David A. Snow. 2000. "Framing Processes and Social Movements: An Overview and Assessment." *Annual Review of Sociology* 26 (1): 611–639.

Ben-Tzur, Avraham. 1968. The Neo-Ba'th Party of Syria. *Journal of Contemporary History* 3: 161–81.

Benjamin, Walter.1978. "On the Critique of Violence," in *Reflections,* ed. Peter Demetz, trans. Edmund Jephcott, 277–300. New York: Harcourt, Brace and Jovanovich.

Berman, Sheri. 1997. Civil Society and the Collapse of the Weimar Republic. *World Politics* 49: 401–429.

———. 2003. Islamism, Revolution, and Civil Society. *Perspectives on Politics* 1: 11–26.

Beydoun, Abbas. 2009. "Riwāyat 'al-mukhābarāt.'" *al-Safir,* August 12.

Birch, Sarah. 2002. "The 2000 Elections in Yugoslavia: The 'Bulldozer Revolution.'" *Electoral Studies* 21: 499–511.

Boëx, Cécile. 2011. "La contestation médiatisée par le monde de l'art en contexte autoritaire: l'Expérience cinématographique en syrie au sein de l'organisme général du cinéma 1964–2010." PhD Thesis, Université Paul Cézanne-Aix Marseille III.

Bonne, Emmanuel. 1997. "Justice: Institutions et contrôle politique." *Monde Arabe Maghreb Machrek* 158: 31–37.

Botiveau, Bernard. 1986. "La formation des oulémas en Syrie: La saculté de sharî'a de l'Université de Damas," in *Les Intellectuels et le Pouvoir: Syrie, Égypte, Tunisie, Algérie,* ed. G. Delanoue, 67–91. Cairo: CEDEJ.

Böttcher, Annabelle. 1998. *Syrische Religionspolitik unter Asad.* Freiburg im Breisgau: Arnold-Bergstraesser-Institut.

Brown, Nathan. J. 1997. *The Rule of Law in the Arab World. Courts in Egypt and the Gulf.* Cambridge, UK: Cambridge University Press.

———. 2002. *Constitutions in a Nonconstitutional World: Arab Basic Laws and the Prospects for Accountable Government.* Albany: State University of New York Press.

Brownlee, Jason. 2002. ". . . And Yet They Persist: Explaining Survival and Transition in Neopatrimonial Regimes." *Studies in Comparative International Development,* 37(3): 35–63.

———. 2007. *Authoritarianism in an Age of Democratization.* New York: Cambridge University Press.

Brumberg, Daniel. 2001. *Reinventing Khomeini: The Struggle for Reform in Iran.* Chicago: University of Chicago Press.

———. 2003. *Islam and Democracy in the Middle East.* Baltimore, MD: Johns Hopkins University Press.

Büchs, Annette. 2009. "The Resilience of Authoritarian Rule in Syria under Hafez and Bashar al-Asad." *GIGA Research Programme: Institute of Middle East Studies,* 97.

Buchta, Wilfried. 2000. *Who Rules Iran? The Structure of Power in the Islamic Republic.* Washington, DC: The Washington Institute for Near East Policy.

Bunce, Valerie J., and Sharon L. Wolchik. 2010a. "Defeating Dictators: Electoral Change and Stability in Competitive Authoritarian Regimes." *World Politics* 62: 43–86.

———. 2010b. "Defining and Domesticating the Electoral Market," in *Democracy and Authoritarianism in the Postcommunist World,* ed.Valerie Bunce, Michael McFaul, and Kathryn Stoner-Weiss, 134–154. New York: Cambridge University Press.

al-Bunni, Anwar. 2005. No title; Defense for Aktham Na'iseh (in Arabic). Damascus: unpublished.

al-Buti, Muhammad Sa'id Ramadan. 1973. *Ila kull fatat tu'min bi-allah.* Damascus: Dar al-Farabi.

Camau, Michel, and Geisser, Vincent. 2003. *Le syndrome autoritaire: Politique en Tunisie de Bourguiba à Ben Ali.* Paris: Presses de Sciences Po.

Capoccia, Giovanni, and Daniel Ziblatt. 2010. "The Historical Turn in Democratization Studies: A New Research Agenda for Europe and Beyond." *Comparative Political Studies* 43: 931–968.

Carothers, Thomas. 2002. "The End of the Transition Paradigm." *Journal of Democracy* 13: 5–21

Carré, Olivier. 1979. *La légitimation Islamique des socialismes Arabes: Analyse conceptuelle combinatoire des manuels scolaires Égyptiens, Syriens et Irakiens.* Paris: FNSP.

Castells, Manuel. 1992. "Four Asian Tigers with a Dragon Head: A Comparative Analysis of the State, Economy, and Society in the Asian Pacific Rim," in *States and Development in the Asian Pacific Rim,* ed. Richard Applebaum and Jeffrey Henderson, 33–70. Newbury Park, CA: Sage.

Catusse, Myriam. 2009. "Morocco's Political Economy: Ambiguous Privatization and the Emerging Social Question," in *The Arab State and Neo-Liberal Globalization: The Restructuring of State Power in the Middle East,* ed. Laura Guazzone and Daniela Pioppi, 185–216. New York: Ithaca Press.

Cavatorta, Francesco. 2008. "Civil Society, Democracy Promotion and Islamism on the Southern Shores of the Mediterranean." *Mediterranean Politics* 13 (1): 109–119.

Central Bureau of Statistics. 1962–2009. *Statistical Yearbook.* Damascus: CBS. Retrieved on September 7, 2008, from www.cbssyr.org/.

Chehabi, Houchang E., and Juan J. Linz, 1998. "A Theory of Sultanism 1: A Type of Nondemocratic Rule," in *Sultanistic Regimes,* ed. Houchang Chehabi and Juan Linz, 3–25. Baltimore, MD: Johns Hopkins University Press.

Chehayed, Jamal, and Heidi Toelle. 2001. *Al-riwāya al-sūriyya al-muʿasira: al-judhūr al-thaqāfiyya wa-l-tiqniyyāt al-riwāʾiyya al-jadida: Aʿmāl al-nadwa al-munʿaqida fī 26 waʾ-27 ayār 2000.* Damascus: al-Maʿhad al-Faransi li-l-Dirasat al-ʿArabiyya.

Cheterian, Vicken. 2008. "Georgia's Rose Revolution: Change or Repetition? Tension between State-Building and Modernization Projects?" *Nationalities Papers* 36: 689–712.

Clarke, John. 2004. *Changing Welfare, Changing States.* London: Sage.

Coicaud, Jean-Marc. 2002. *Legitimacy and Politics: A Contribution to the Study of Political Rights and Political Responsibility.* Cambridge, UK: Cambridge University Press.

Cooke, Miriam. 2007. *Dissident Syria: Making Oppositional Arts Official.* Durham, NC: Duke University Press.

Cottam, Richard W. 1986. "The Iranian Revolution," in *Shiʾism and Social Protest,* ed. Juan R. I. Cole and Nikki R. Keddie, 55–87. New Haven, CT: Yale University Press.

Cox, Robert. 1987. *Production, Power, and World Order: Social Forces in the Making of History.* New York: Columbia University Press.

Crystal, Jill. 1994. "Review: Authoritarianism and Its Adversaries in the Arab World." *World Politics* 46 (2): 262–289.

Dabbagh, Heba. 2007. *Just Five Minutes: Nine Years in the Prisons of Syria*. Toronto: Heba Dabbagh.

Dahl, Robert A. 1971. *Polyarchy: Participation and Opposition*. New Haven, CT: Yale University Press.

al-Darkazalli, Yasin. 1987. "Adwa' 'ala qanun al-'aqubat tahrib al-'amalat: Takhliyyat al-sabil fi al-jara'im al-iqtisadiyya." *Al-Muhamun* 9: 1083–1085.

Darnton Robert. 1995. *The Forbidden Best-Sellers of Pre-Revolutionary France*. New York: W. W. Norton & Co.

Da'ud, Danhu. 1995. *Al-marahil al-tarikhiyya wa al-saiyyasiyya li-tatawwur al-nizam al-idari fi Suriyya*. Damascus: Manshurat Dar 'Ilam al-Din.

David, Steven. 1991. "Explaining Third World Alignment." *World Politics* 43 (2): 233–256.

Della Porta, Donatella, and Mario Diani. 2006. *Social Movements: An Introduction*. Malden, MA: Blackwell Publishing.

Diani, Mario. 2003. "Networks and Social Movements: a Research Programme," in *Social Movements and Networks: Relational Approaches to Collective Action*, eds. Mario Diani and Doug McAdam, 299–319. Oxford, UK: Oxford University Press.

Dimashki, Mohammed Issam. I. 2002. "The Social and Psychological Effects of Detention and the Deprivation of Civil Rights," in *Democracy and Human Rights in Syria: A Collective Work with 18 Syrian Researchers*, ed. Violette Daguerre, 233–271. Paris: Arab Commission for Human Rights, Eurabe Publishers.

Donati, Caroline. 2009. *L'exception Syrienne, entre modernisation et résistance*. Paris: La Découverte.

Donker, Teije H. 2010. "Enduring Ambiguity: Sunni Community–Syrian Regime Dynamics." *Mediterranean Politics* 15 (3): 435–452.

Dorraj, Manochehr, and Michael Dodson. 2009. "Neo-Populism in Comparative Perspective: Iran and Venezuela." *Comparative Studies of South Asia, Africa and the Middle East* 29 (1): 137–151.

Dunne, Michelle. 2008. "Interview with Ayman Abd al-Nour." Carnegie Endowment: Arab Reform Project, August 14.

Dupret, Baudoin, Zouhair Ghazzal, Youssef Courbage, and Mohammed al-Dbiyat, eds. 2007. *La Syrie au présent, reflets d'une société*. Paris : Sindbad/Actes Sud.

Ehteshami, Anoushiravan. 2002. "Failure of Khatami Reformers, Not Reform Movement." *Journal of Iranian Research and Analysis* 18 (2): 69–72.

Ehsani, Kaveh. 2009. "The Urban Provincial Periphery in Iran: Revolution and War in Ramhormoz," in *Contemporary Iran: Economy, Society, Politics*, ed. Ali Gheissari, 38–76. New York: Oxford University Press.

Ehteshami, Anoushiravan, and Mahjoob Zweiri. 2007. *Iran and the Rise of Its Neoconservatives: The Politics of Tehran's Silent Revolution*. London and New York: I. B. Tauris.

Elster, Jon. 1989. *Nuts and Bolts for the Social Sciences*. New York: Cambridge University Press.

Erdem, Gazi 2008. "Religious Services in Turkey: From the Office of Şeyhülislâm to the Diyanet." *Muslim World* 98: 199–215.

Esping-Andersen, Gosta. 1990. *The Three Worlds of Welfare Capitalism*. Princeton, NJ: Princeton University Press.

Firat, Alexa. 2010. "Post-67 Discourse and the Syrian Novel: The Construction of an Autonomous Literary Field." PhD dissertation, University of Pennsylvania.

Fitzpatrick, Peter. 1992. *The Mythology of Modern Law*. London: Routledge.

Gaffney, Patrick D. 2004. "Conforming at a Distance: The Diffusion of Islamic Bureaucracy in Upper Egypt," in *Upper Egypt: Identity and Change*, ed. Nicholas S. Hopkins and Reem Saad, 119–140. Cairo: American University of Cairo.

Gandhi, Jennifer, and Ellen Lust-Okar. 2009. Elections under Authoritarianism. *Annual Review of Political Science* 12: 403–422.

Gandhi, Jennifer, and Adam Przeworski. 2007. "Authoritarian Institutions and the Survival of Autocrats." *Comparative Political Studies* 40: 1279–1301.

Ganji, Akbar. 2008. "The Latter-Day Sultan." *Foreign Affairs* 87: 45–66.

Gardner, John. 1984. *The Art of Fiction: Notes on Craft for Young Writers*. New York: A. Knopf.

Garver, John, Flynt Leverett, and Hillary M. Leverett. 2010. *Moving (Slightly) Closer to Iran: China's Shifting Calculus for Managing Its "Persian Gulf Dilemma."* Asia-Pacific Policy Papers Series. Washington DC: Johns Hopkins University School of Advanced International Studies.

George, Alan. 2003. *Syria: Neither Bread nor Freedom*. London and New York: Zed Books.

Ghadbian, Najib. 2001. "The New Asad: Dynamics of Continuity and Change in Syria." *Middle East Journal* 55 (4): 624–641.

———. 2006. *Al-Dawla al-asadiyya al-thaniyya: Bashar al-Asad wa-l-furads al-da'i'a*. Jeddah: Markaz al-Rayya.

Ghazzal, Zohair, Baudouin Dupret, and Souhail Belhadj. 2009. "Civil Law and the Omnipotence of the Syrian State," in *Demystifying Syria*, ed. Fred H. Lawson, 59–69. London: Saqi.

Ghessari, Ali, and Vali Nasr, 2006. *Democracy in Iran*. New York: Oxford University Press.

Ghorashi, Halleh, and Kees Boersma. 2009. "The 'Iranian Diaspora' and the New Media: From Political Action to Humanitarian Help." *Development and Change* 40 (4), 667–691.

Gillon, Jean-Yeves. 1993. "Anciennes fêtes de printemps à homs." *Bulletin d'etudes Orientales*: 69–71.

Gilman, Nils. 2003. *Mandarins of the Future: Modernization Theory in Cold War America*. Baltimore, MD: The Johns Hopkins University Press.

Ginsburg, Tom, and Tamir Moustafa. 2008. *Rule by Law: The Politics of Courts in Authoritarian Regimes*. Cambridge, UK, and New York: Cambridge University Press.

Goodell, Grace. 1986. *The Elementary Structures of Political Life: Rural Development in Pahlavi Iran*. New York: Oxford University Press.

Gough, Ian. 2004. "East Asia: The Limits of Productivist Regimes," in *Insecurity and Welfare Regimes in Asia, Africa and Latin America: Social Policy in Development Contexts*, ed. Ian Gough and Geoffrey Wood, 169–201. Cambridge, UK: Cambridge University Press.

Haddad, Fawwaz. 2008. *al-Mutarjim al-khā'in: riwāya*. Beirut: Riyad el-Rayyes.

———. 2009. *'Azf munfarid 'ala al-biyānū: riwāya*. Beirut: Riyad el-Rayyes.

———. 2011. *Junūd Allah: riwāya*. Beirut: Dar al-Adab.

Haeri, Shahla. 2009. "Women, Religion, and Political Agency in Iran," in *Contemporary Iran: Economy, Society, Politics*, ed. Ali Gheissari, 125–149. New York: Oxford University Press.

Haggard, Stephen, and Robert Kaufman. 2008. *Development, Democracy, and Welfare States: Latin America, East Asia, and Eastern Europe*. Princeton, NJ: Princeton University Press.

Hale, Henry E. 2006. "Democracy or Autocracy on the March? The Colored Revolutions as Normal Dynamics of Patronal Presidentialism." *Communist and Post-Communist Studies* 39: 305–329.

Halwani, Fadiya al-Mulayyih. 1998. *Al-Riwāya wa-l-idiyūlūjiyya fi suriya, 1958–1990*. Damascus: al-Ahali.

Hamidi, Ibrahim. 2006a. "Dimasq tasamuh li al-qubaysiyat bi nashat a'lani." *al-Hayat*, May 3.

———. 2006b. "Yuridin al-hijab aj-kahli wa yumalkin shabaka tadris wa nufuz wasa'... 'al-Nisat al-qubaysiyat yubashirun fi suria inkhirat al-nisa' fi "al-dawa' al-islami'... bi muwafaqa al-sulutat." *al-Hayat*. May 3.

Hamza, Husayn bin. 2009. "Nibrāt jadída fi al-riwāya al-sūriyya: al-tajríb ba'ídan 'an al-aydiyūlūjiyyā." *al-Akhbar*, April 30.

Hanlon, Joseph, Armando Barrientos, and David Hulme. 2010. *Just Give Money to the Poor: The Development Revolution from the Global South*. Sterling, VA: Kumarian Press.

Harris, Kevan. 2010. "The Politics of Subsidy Reform in Iran." *Middle East Report* 254: 36–39.

Haydar, Nasrat Munla. 1975a. "Lamha shamila 'an al-mahkama al-dusturiyya fi al-jumhuriyya al-'arabiyya al-suriyya," *Al-Muhamun* 1: 10–17.

———. 1975b. "Turuq al-riqaba 'ala dusturiyyat al-qawanin," *Al-Muhamun* 10–12: 275–280.

———. 1977. "Istiqlal al-sulta al-qada'iyya," *Al-Muhamun* 7–9: 95–140.

———. 1978. "Al- 'Athr al-raja'i li-qanun al-'aqubat al-iqtisadiyya yukhalif al-'ilan al-'alami li-huquq al-insan," *Al-Muhamun* 12: 353–354.

——.1993. "Mabda' al-musawa 'amam al-qada'," *Al-Muhamun* 1–2: 7–36.

Haysu, Ma'tz. 2010. "Difa'an a'n al-i'lmania." thara-sy.com. August 21, 2010; available at www.thara-sy.com/thara/modules/news/article.php?storyid=1724.

Heydemann, Steven. 1993. "Taxation without Representation: Authoritarianism and Economic Liberalization in Syria," in *Rules and Rights in the Middle East: Society, Law, and Democracy*, eds. Ellis Goldberg, Resat Kasaba, and Joel Migdal, 69–101. Seattle: University of Washington Press.

——. 1999. *Authoritarianism in Syria: Institutions and Social Conflict, 1946–1970.* Ithaca, NY: Cornell University Press.

——. ed. 2000. *War, Institutions, and Social Change in the Middle East.* Berkeley and Los Angeles: University of California Press.

——. 2007a. "Social Pacts and the Persistence of Authoritarianism in the Middle East." In *Debating Arab Authoritarianism*, ed. Oliver Schlumberger, 21–38. Stanford, CA: Stanford University Press.

——. 2007b. Upgrading Authoritarianism in the Arab World. Saban Center Analysis Paper, Brookings Institute, 13.

Heydemann, Steven, and Reinoud Leenders. 2011. "Authoritarian Learning and Authoritarian Resilience: Regime Responses to the 'Arab Awakening.'" *Globalizations* 8(5): 647–653.

Hibou, Béatrice. 1998. "Retrait ou redéploiement de l'etat." *Critique Internationale* 1 (1): 152–169.

——. 2004. *Privatising the State.* London: Hurst.

Hinnebusch, Raymond A. 1990. *Authoritarian Power and State Formation in Ba'thist Syria: Army, Party, and Peasant.* Boulder, CO: Westview Press.

——. 2002. *Syria. Revolution from Above.* London/New York: Routledge, Taylor and Francis Group.

Hinnebusch, Raymond A., and Søren Schmidt. 2009. *The State and the Political Economy of Reform in Syria.* Fife, UK: University of St. Andrews Centre for Syrian Studies.

Hobden Stephen, and John Hobson. 2002. *Historical Sociology of International Relations.* Cambridge, UK: Cambridge University Press.

Hoodfar, Homa. 1994. "Devices and Desires: Population Policy and Gender Roles in the Islamic Republic." *Middle East Report* 109: 11–17.

——. 2008. "Family Law and Family Planning Policy in Pre- and Post-Revolutionary Iran," in *Family in the Middle East: Ideational Change in Egypt, Iran, and Tunisia*, ed. Kathryn Yount and Hoda Rashad, 80–110. London: Routledge.

Howard, Marc M., and Phillip G. Roessler, 2006. "Liberalizing Electoral Outcomes in Competitive Authoritarian Regimes." *American Journal of Political Science* 50: 365–381.

Human Rights Watch. 1995. *Syria: The Price of Dissent.* New York: Human Rights Watch.

———. 2003. "Syria." *Human Rights Watch World Report 2002*. New York: Human Rights Watch.

———. 2009a. *Far From Justice: Syria's Supreme State Security Court*. New York: Human Rights Watch.

———. 2009b. *Group Denial. Repression of Kurdish Political and Cultural Rights in Syria*. New York: Human Rights Watch.

Huntington, Samuel. 1968. *Political Order in Changing Societies*. New Haven, CT: Yale University Press.

Huuhtanen, Heidi. 2008. *Building a Strong State: The Influence of External Security and Fiscal Environment on Syrian Authoritarianism*. PhD dissertation: University of Durham.

Hyde, Susan D. 2007. "The Observer Effect in International Politics: Evidence from a Natural Experiment." *World Politics* 60: 37–63.

Ibrahim, Nawar Bashir. 2006. *Sharh qanun usul al-mahakamat al-'askariyya*. Damascus: Al-Maktaba al-Qanuniyya.

Ilie, Paul. 1980. *Literature and Inner Exile: Authoritarian Spain, 1939–1975*. Baltimore: Johns Hopkins University Press.

International Crisis Group (ICG). 2004. "Syria under Asad (I): Foreign Policy Challenges." *Middle East Report* 23, February 11.

———. 2009. "Reshuffling the Cards? (I): Syria's Evolving Strategy." *Middle East Report* 92, December 14.

International Monetary Fund (IMF). 2009. "Syrian Arab Republic." *IMF Country Report 09/55*. Washington, DC.

Iqbal, Farrukh. 2006. *Sustaining Gains in Poverty Reduction and Human Development in the Middle East and North Africa*. Washington, DC: The World Bank.

Jackson, Robert. H. 1990. *Quasi-States: Sovereignty, International Relations and the Third World*. Cambridge, UK: Cambridge University Press.

Jamal, Amaney A. 2007. *Barriers to Democracy: The Other Side of Social Capital in Palestine and the Arab World*. Princeton, NJ: Princeton University Press.

al-Jayush, Mahmud. 1978. "Hawla mawdu'a al-huriyyat al-'ama wa siyyadat al-qanun," *Al-Muhamun* 9–11: 135–150.

———. 1979. "Anzimat al-tawari' wa quyudha 'ala huquq al-insan wa huriyyatihi al-asasiyya," *Al-Muhamun* 6–8: 88–93.

Johnson, Randal, and Nelson Vieira. 1989. *Literature, Culture and Authoritarianism in Brazil, 1930–1945*. Washington, DC: Latin American Program, The Wilson Center.

Kaftaru, Ahmad. 2010a. "Al-ijtima' al-nisa'i fi wizarat al-awqaf." *Majallat al-Thara* 215; retrieved on August 8, 2011, from www.tharasy.com/thara/modules/news/comment_new.php?com_itemid=1284&com_order=0&com_mode=flat.

———. 2010b. "Wayn manhaj al-i'tidal." *Majallat al-Thara* 217; retrieved on August 8, 2011, from www.thara-sy.com/thara/modules/news/article.php?storyid=1314.

Kahf, Mohja. 2001. "The Silences of Contemporary Syrian Literature." *World Literature Today* 75 (2): 224–236.

Kalandadze, Katya, and Mitchell A. Orenstein. 2009. "Electoral Protests and Democratization beyond the Color Revolutions." *Comparative Political Studies* 42: 1403–1425.

Kalyvas, Stathis N. 2006. *The Logic of Violence in Civil War.* New York: Cambridge University Press.

Kamrava, Mehran. 2008. *Iran's Intellectual Revolution.* New York: Cambridge University Press.

Karshenas, Massoud, and Valentine Moghadam. 2006. *Social Policy in the Middle East: Economic, Political, and Gender Dynamics.* New York: Palgrave Macmillan.

Kaussler, Bernd. 2008a. "European Union Constructive Engagement with Iran (2000–2004): An Exercise in Conditional Human Rights Diplomacy." *Iranian Studies* 41 (3): 269–295.

———. 2008b. "How the EU Could Resolve the US–Iran Crisis." *Europe's World,* Spring; available at www.europesworld.org.

———. 2009. "Ahmadinejad's Coup d'Etat." *Foreign Policy in Focus,* June 16; available at www.fpif.org/articles/ahmadinejads_coup_detat.

Kawakibi, Salam. 2009. "Syria's Mediterranean Policy," in *Mediterranean Politics from Above and Below,* ed. Isabel Schäfer and Jean-Robert Henry, 237–250. Baden-Baden: Nomos.

Keddie, Nikki R. 2000–2001. "The Study of Muslim Women in the Middle East: Achievements and Remaining Problems." *Harvard Middle Eastern and Islamic Review* 6: 26–52.

———. 2003. *Modern Iran: Roots and Results of Revolution.* New Haven, CT: Yale University Press.

Keshavarzian, Arang. 2007. *Bazaar and State in Iran.* New York: Cambridge University Press.

Khalifa, Khalid. 2008. *Madíh al-karāhiyya: riwāya.* Beirut: Dar al-Adab.

Khalifa, Mustafa. 2008. *Al-Qawqa'a: yawmiyyāt mutalaṣṣiṣ.* Beirut: Dar al-Adab.

Khomeini, Ruhollah. 1981. *Islam and Revolution: Writings and Declarations of Imam Khomeini,* trans. Hamid Algar. Berkeley, CA: Mizan Press.

Kienle, Eberhard. 1990. *Ba'th v. Ba'th: The Conflict between Syria and Iraq, 1968–1989.* London and New York: I. B. Tauris.

King, Stephen J. 2009. *The New Authoritarianism in the Middle East and North Africa.* Bloomington: Indiana University Press.

Klandermans, Bert. 1984. "Mobilization and Participation: Social-Psychological Expansisons of Resource Mobilization Theory." *American Sociological Review* 49 (5): 583–600.

Kriesi, Hanspeter. 1995. *New Social Movements in Western Europe: A Comparative Analysis.* Minneapolis: University of Minnesota Press.

———. 2004. "Political Context and Opportunity," in *The Blackwell Companion to Social Movements*, ed. David A Snow, Sarah A. Soule, and Hanspeter Kriesi, 67–90. Malden, MA: Blackwell Publishing.

Kurzman, Charles. 2004. *The Unthinkable Revolution in Iran*. Cambridge, MA: Harvard University Press.

Lawson, Fred, ed. 2009. *Demystifying Syria*. London: Saqi, in association with The London Middle East Institute.

Lee, Ching Kwan. 2008. "Rights Activism in China." *Contexts* 7 (3): 14–19.

Leenders, Reinoud. 2010. "Strong States in a Troubled Region: Anatomies of a Middle Eastern Regional Conflict Formation." *Comparative Social Research* 27: 171–196.

Lesch, David. 2005. *The New Lion of Damascus: Bashar al-Asad and Modern Syria*. New Haven, CT: Yale University Press.

Leverett, Flynt. 2005. *Inheriting Syria: Bashar's Trial by Fire*. Washington, DC: Brookings Institute Press.

Levitsky, Steven, and Lucan A. Way. 2002. "Elections without Democracy: The Rise of Competitive Authoritarianism," *Journal of Democracy* 13(2): 51–65.

———. 2006. "Linkage and Leverage: How Do International Factors Change Domestic Balances of Power?" in *Electoral Authoritarianism: The Dynamics of Unfree Competition*, ed. Andreas Schedler, 199–216. Boulder, CO, and London: Lynne Rienner Publishers.

———. 2010. *Competitive Authoritarianism: Hybrid Regimes after the Cold War*. New York: Cambridge University Press.

Linz, Juan J., and Alfred Stepan. 1996. *Problems of Democratic Transition and Consolidation*. Baltimore, MD: John Hopkins University Press.

Lobmeyer, Hans Gunter. 1995. *Opposition und Widerstand in Syrien*. Hamburg: Deutschen Orient-Instituts.

Lohmann, Susanne. 1994. "The Dynamics of Informational Cascades: The Monday Demonstrations in Leipzig, East Germany, 1989–91." *World Politics* 47: 42–101.

Lomnitz, Larissa. 1988. "Informal Exchange Networks in Formal Systems: A Theoretical Model." *American Anthropologist* 90 (1): 42–55.

Longuenesse, Élisabeth. 2007. *Professions et société au Proche-Orient: Déclin des élites, crise des classes moyennes*. Rennes: Presses universitaires de Rennes.

Lotfalian, Mazyar. 2009. "The Iranian Scientific Community and Its Diaspora after the Islamic Revolution." *Anthropological Quarterly* 82 (1): 229–250.

Lust-Okar, Ellen. 2005. *Structuring Conflict in the Arab World: Incumbents, Opponents, and Institutions*. New York: Cambridge University Press.

———. 2006. "Reform in Syria: Steering between the Chinese Model and Regime Change." *Carnegie Endowment Paper* 69, July.

———. 2009. "Competitive Clientelism in the Middle East." *Journal of Democracy* 20: 122–135.

Macaron, Joe. 2008. "The Opposition and Its Troubled Relationship with Washington." Retrieved on August 13, 2008, from www.carnegieendowment.org.

MacIntyre, Alisdair. 2008. *Alisdair MacIntyre's Engagement with Marxism: Selected Writings 1953-1974,* ed. Paul Blackedge and Neil Davidson. Leiden, The Netherlands: Brill.

Magaloni, B. 2008. "Credible Power-Sharing and the Longevity of Authoritarian Rule." *Comparative Political Studies* 41: 715–741.

———. 2010. "The Game of Electoral Fraud and the Ousting of Authoritarian Rule." *American Journal of Political Science* 54: 751–765.

Maghraoui, Driss. 2009. "The Strengths and Limits of Religious Reforms in Morocco." *Mediterranean Politics* 14: 195–211.

Mahmood, Saba. 2005. *Politics of Piety: The Islamic Revival and the Feminist Subject.* Princeton, NJ: Princeton University Press.

Majidyar, Ahmad, and Ali Alfoneh. 2010. "Iranian Influence in Afghanistan: Imam Khomeini Relief Committee." *Middle Eastern Outlook* 4. Washington, DC: American Enterprise Institute.

al-Maleh, Haitham. 1970. "Huquq al-nas bayna al-qada' wa al-muhama." *Al-Muhamun* 11: 531–541.

———. 2002. "The Judicial System," in *Democracy and Human Rights in Syria: A Collective Work with 18 Syrian Researchers,* ed. Violette Daguerre, 215–233. Paris: Arab Commission for Human Rights, Eurabe Publishers.

———. 2005. "Human Rights between Torture and the State of Emergency: Jurisdiction in Syria." Damascus: unpublished paper, July 16.

———. 2008. [Untitled report], accessed August 8, 2011, from www.dctcrs.org/s5178.htm.

Maloney, Suzanne. 2004. "Islamism and Iran's Postrevolutionary Economy: The Case of the Bonyads," in *Gods, Guns, and Globalization: Religious Radicalism and International Political Economy,* ed. Mary Ann Tetreault and Robert Denemark, 191–218. Boulder, CO: Lynne Rienner Publishers.

al-Mana', Haytham. 2003. "Istiqlal al-sulta al-qada'iyya fi suriyya." *Akhbar al-Sharq,* March 8.

Marcuse, Herbert. 2002 [1964]. *One Dimensional Man.* New York: Routledge Classics.

Marshall, Trevor H. 1964. *Citizenship and Social Class.* Cambridge, UK: Cambridge University Press.

Martín-Estudillo, Luis, and Roberto Ampuero. 2008. *Post-Authoritarian Cultures: Spain and Latin America's Southern Cone.* Nashville, TN: Vanderbilt University Press.

McAdam, Doug, John D. McCarthy, and Mayer N. Zald. 1996. *Comparative Perspectives on Social Movements: Political Opportunities, Mobilizing Structures, and Cultural Framings.* Cambridge, UK: Cambridge University Press.

McCarthy, John D., and Mayer N. Zald. 1977. "Resource Mobilization and Social Movements: A Partial Theory." *American Journal of Sociology* 82 (6): 1212–1241.

McFaul, Michael. 2007. "Ukraine Imports Democracy: External Influences on the Orange Revolution." *International Security* 32: 45–83.

———. 2010. "The Missing Variable: The 'International System' as the Link between Third and Fourth Wave Models of Democratization," in *Democracy and Authoritarianism in the Postcommunist World,* ed. Valerie Bunce, Michael McFaul, and Kathryn Stoner-Weiss, 3–29. New York: Cambridge University Press.

McGregor, Andrew. 2007. "Controversial Syrian Preacher Abu al-Qaqa Gunned Down in Aleppo." The Jamestown Foundation. *Terrorism Focus* 4 (33), October 16; available at www.jamestown.org/single/?no_cache=1&tx_ttnews%5Btt_news%5D =4481.

Mehryar, Amir. 2004. "Primary Health Care and the Rural Poor in the Islamic Republic of Iran." Paper presented at the World Bank Conference on Scaling Up Poverty Reduction, Shanghai, May 25–27.

Melucci, Alberto. 1996. *Challenging Codes: Collective Action in the Information Age.* Cambridge, UK: Cambridge University Press.

Merryman, John H. 1969. *The Civil Law Tradition: An Introduction to the Legal Systems of Western Europe and Latin America.* Stanford, CA: Stanford University Press.

Messkoub, Mahmood. 2006. "Social Policy in Iran in the Twentieth Century." *Iranian Studies,* 39 (2): 227–252.

Meyer, Stefan G. 2001. *The Experimental Arabic Novel: Postcolonial Literary Modernism in the Levant.* Albany: State University of New York Press.

Middle East Watch. 1990. *Human Rights in Syria.* New York: Middle East Watch.

Migdal, Joel S. 2001. *State in Society: Studying How States and Societies Transform and Constitute One Another.* Cambridge, UK: Cambridge University Press.

Mitchell, Timothy. 1999. "Economy, Society and the State Effect," in *State/Culture: State-Formation after the Cultural Turn,* ed. George Steinmetz, 76–97. Ithaca, NY: Cornell University Press.

Moore, Richard. 2007. "Family Planning in Iran, 1960–79," in *The Global Family Planning Revolution: Three Decades of Population Policies and Programs,* ed. Warren Robinson and John Ross, 33–57. Washington DC: The World Bank.

Moslem, Mehdi. 2002. *Factional Politics in Post-Khomeini Iran.* Syracuse, NY: Syracuse University Press.

Moubayed, Sami. 2006a. "Syria's Abu al-Qaqa: Authentic Jihadist or Imposter?" *Terrorism Focus* 3 (25), June 27.

———. 2006b. "Terror within Syria." *Al Ahram Weekly,* June 8; available at http:// weekly.ahram.org.eg/2006/798/re83.htm.

Moustafa, Tamir. 2007. *The Struggle For Constitutional Power: Law, Politics, and Economic Development in Egypt.* Cambridge, UK, and New York: Cambridge University Press.

Mufti, Malik. 1996. *Sovereign Creations: Pan-Arabism and Political Order in Syria and Iraq.* Ithaca, NY, and London: Cornell University Press.

Muskhelishvili, Marina, and Gia Jorjoliani. 2009. "Georgia's Ongoing Struggle for a Better Future Continued: Democracy Promotion through Civil Society Development." *Democratization* 16: 682–708.

Mustafa, Mahmud Mahmud. 1978. "Damanat al-huriyya al-shakhsiyya fi zil Al-qawanin al-istithna'iyya," *Al-Muhamun* 5–8: 125–137.

Mutahhari, Ayatollah Morteza. 1981. *The System of Women's Rights in Islam.* Qom: Entesharat Sadra.

al-Nabwani, F. 1986. "Buhuth fi al-qadaya al-jumrakiyya: al-Ad'a bi-al-tazwir fi-al-qadaya al-jumrakiyya." *Al-Muhamun* 2: 150–243.

al-Naji, 'Abdullah. 1993. *Hamamat al-dam fi Sijn Tadmur.* Syrian Human Rights Committee; available at www.shrc.org/data/aspx/012BOOKS.aspx.

Naji, Kasra. 2008. *Ahmedinejad: The Secret History of Iran's Radical Leader.* London: I. B. Tauris.

Nepstad, Sharon E. 2011. *Nonviolent Revolutions: Civil Resistance in the Late 20th Century.* New York: Oxford University Press.

Newell, Kenneth. 1975. *Health By the People.* Geneva: World Health Organization.

Niblock, Tim. 2001. *"Pariah States" and Sanctions in the Middle East: Iraq, Libya, Sudan.* Boulder, CO: Lynne Rienner Publishers.

O'Donnell, Guillermo A. 1999. *Counterpoints: Selected Essays on Authoritarianism and Democratization.* Notre Dame, IN: University of Notre Dame Press.

O'Donnell, Guillermo, and Philippe C. Schmitter. 1986. *Transitions from Authoritarian Rule: Tentative Conclusions and Uncertain Democracies.* Baltimore, MD: John Hopkins University Press.

Offe, Claus. 1984. *Contradictions of the Welfare State.* Cambridge, MA: MIT Press.

Office of the High Commissioner for Human Rights. 2001. *Comments by the Government of the Syrian Arab Republic on the Concluding Observations of the Human Rights Committee.* Geneva: UNOHCHR, May 28.

Osanloo, Arzoo. 2006. "Islamico-Civil Rights Talk: Women, Subjectivity and Law in Iranian Family Court." *American Ethnologist* 33 (2): 191–209.

———. 2009. *The Politics of Women's Rights in Iran.* Princeton, NJ: Princeton University Press.

Oweis, Khaled Y. 2009. "Syria Launches Its First Electricity Privatization Tender." *Daily Star,* November 3.

Pahlavi, Mohammad Reza. 1980. *Answer to History.* New York: Stein and Day.

Paidar, Parvin. 1995. *Women and the Political Process in Twentieth-Century Iran.* Cambridge, UK: Cambridge University Press.

Parsa, Misagh. 2000. *States, Ideologies, and Social Revolutions: A Comparative Analysis of Iran, Nicaragua, and the Philippines.* Cambridge, UK: Cambridge University Press.

Pereira, Anthony W. 2005. *Political (In)Justice. Authoritarianism and the Rule of Law in Brazil, Chile, and Argentina.* Pittsburgh: University of Pittsburgh Press.

———. 2008. "Of Judges and Generals: Security Courts under Authoritarian Regimes in Argentina, Brazil, and Chile," in *Rule by Law: The Politics of Courts in Authoritarian States,* ed. Tom Ginsburg and Tamir Moustafa, 23–58. Cambridge, UK: Cambridge University Press.

Perthes, Volker. 1995. *The Political Economy of Syria under Asad.* London: I. B. Tauris.

———. 1997. *The Political Economy of Syria under Asad.* London: I. B. Tauris.

———. 2000. "Si Vis Stabilitatem, Para Bellum: State Building, National Security and War Preparation in Syria," in *War, Institutions, and Social Change in the Middle East,* ed. Steven Heydemann, 149–173. Berkeley and LA: University of California Press.

———. 2004a. *Arab Elite: Negotiating the Politics of Change.* Boulder, CO: Lynne Rienner Publisher.

———. 2004b. *Syria under Bashar al-Asad: Modernisation and the Limits of Change.* Oxford, UK: Oxford University Press.

Petran, Tabitha. 1972. *Syria.* London: Ernest Benn Ltd.

Picard, Elizabeth. 2008. "Armée et sécurité au cœur de l'autoritarisme," in *Autoritarismes démocratiques et démocraties autoritaires au XXIe siècle,* ed. Olivier Dabène, Vincent Geisser, and Gilles Massardier, 303–329. Paris: La Découverte.

Pierret, Thomas. 2002. "Karbala in the Umayyad Mosque: Sunni Panic at the Shiitization of Syria in the 2000s," in *The Dynamics of Sunni-Shia Relationships: Doctrine, Transnationalism, Intellectuals and the Media,* ed. B. Maréchal and S. Zemni. London: Hurst.

———. ed. 2008. "L'Islam en Syrie." Special issue of *Maghreb-Machrek,* 198.

———. 2009. "Sunni Clergy Politics in the Cities of Ba'thi Syria," in *Demystifying Syria,* ed. Fred H. Lawson, 70–84. London: Saqi Books and The London Middle East Institute.

———. 2011a. *Baas et Islam en Syrie: La dynastie Assad face aux oulémas.* Paris: PUF.

———. 2011b. "Syrie: Les prêcheurs relaient la révolution malgré la répression." *Mediapart.* Retrieved on November 25, 2011, from http://blogs.mediapart.fr/blog/thomas-pierret/080911/syrie-les-precheurs-relaient-la-revolution-malgre-la-repression.

Pierret, Thomas, and Kjetil Selvik. 2009. "Limits of Authoritarian Upgrading in Syria: Private Welfare, Islamic Charities, and the Rise of the Zayd Movement." *International Journal of Middle East Studies* 41: 595–614.

Pinto, Paulo G. 2006. "Sufism, Moral Performance and the Public Shere in Syria." *Revue des mondes musulmans et de la Méditerrané* 115–116, December; available at http://remmm.revues.org/3026.

———. 2011. "'Oh Syria, God Protects You': Islam as Cultural Idiom under Bashar al-Asad." *Middle East Critique* 20 (2): 189–205.

Portes, Alejandro, and Kelly Hoffman. 2003. "Latin American Class Structures: Their Composition and Change During the Neoliberal Era." *Latin American Research Review* 38 (1): 41–82.

Posusney, Marsha Pripstein, and Michele P. Angrist, eds. 2005. *Authoritarianism in the Middle East: Regimes and Resistance.* Boulder, CO: Lynne Rienner Publishers.

Poulson, Stephen C. 2009. "Nested Institutions, Political Opportunity and the Decline of the Iranian Reform Movement Post 9/11." *American Behavioral Scientist* 53 (1): 27–43.

Pratt, Nicola Christine. 2007. *Democracy and Authoritarianism in the Arab World.* Boulder, CO: Lynne Rienner Publishers.

Przeworski, Adam. 2009. "Conquered or Granted? A History of Suffrage." *British Journal of Political Science* 39: 291–321.

Qaddur, 'Umar. 2009. "Al-Riwāya al-sūriyya al-jadída: zāhira ibdā'iyya am zāhira i'lāmiyya." *al-Adab* 9–10; retrieved on March 14, 2010, from www.adabmag.com/node/247.

Qandaqji, 'Amr Ibrahim. 2004. "Al-sulta al-tanfidhiyya wa niqabat al-muhamin—tashkil ha'iyya wataniyya 'ulya li-bahth al-wada' daman al-sulta al-qada'iyya," *Al-Nur* August 4.

Qattan, Fa'iz. 1986. "Hawla al-siyyasa al-sahyuniyya al-'isti'mariyya didd al-qutr al-'arabi al-suri," *Al-Muhamun* 12: 1325–1327.

Rabinovich, Itamar. 1972. *Syria under the Ba'th, 1963–66: The Army-Party Symbiosis.* Jerusalem: Israel Universities Press.

Rabo, Annika 2006. "Affective, Parochial or Innovative? Aleppo Traders on the Margin of Global Capitalism." *Revue des mondes musulmans et de la Méditerranée,* December, 115–116 ; available at http://remmm.revues.org/3013.

Radnitz, Scott. 2006. "What Really Happened in Kyrgyzstan?" *Journal of Democracy* 17: 132–146.

Reid, Donald M. 1981. *Lawyers and Politics in the Arab World, 1880–1960.* Chicago: Bibliotheca Islamica.

Rifa'at, Ahmad Mahmud. 1987. "Al-fawariq al-qanuniyya bayna al-kifah al-musalih al-murtabit bi-haqq taqrir al-masir wa al-irhab al-duwali," *Al-Muhamun* 6: 701–723.

Robalino, David. 2005. *Pensions in the Middle East and North Africa: Time for Change.* Washington, DC: The World Bank.

Rodrik, Dani. 2000. "What Drives Public Employment in Developing Countries?" *Review of Development Economics* 4 (3): 229–243.

Roy, Olivier. 1996. *The Failure of Political Islam*. Cambridge, MA: Harvard University Press.

———. 2006. *Globalized Islam: The Search for a New Ummah*. New York: Columbia University Press.

Rustow, Dankwart. A. 1963. "The Military in Middle Eastern Society and Politics," in *The Military in the Middle East: Problems in Society and Government,* ed. Sydney N. Fisher, 3–20. Columbus: Ohio State University Press.

———. 1970. "Transitions to Democracy: Toward a Dynamic Model." *Comparative Politics* 2: 337–363.

Al-Saad, Hossam, and Razan Zaitouneh. 2006. *Post-Prison Roads: The Situation of Political Prisoners and Prisoners of Conscience after Being Released from Custody.* Damascus: Damacus Center for Human Rights Studies, August.

Sabahi, Farian. 2002. *The Literacy Corps in Pahlavi Iran (1963–1979): Political, Social and Literary Implications*. Lugano, Italy: Sapiens.

Sadowski, Yahya. 1993. "The New Orientalism and the Democracy Debate." *Middle East Report* 183: 14–21, 40.

Saeidi, Ali. 2004. "The Accountability of Para-governmental Organizations (*bonyads*): The Case of Iranian Foundations." *Iranian Studies* 37 (3): 479–498.

Salamandra, Christa. 2004. *A New Old Damascus: Authenticity and Distinction in Urban Syria*. Bloomington: Indiana University Press.

Salehi-Isfahani, Djavad. 2009a. "Oil Wealth and Economic Growth in Iran," in *Contemporary Iran: Economy, Society, Politics,* ed. Ali Gheissari, 3–37. New York: Oxford University Press.

———. 2009b. "Poverty, Inequality, and Populist Politics in Iran." *Journal of Economic Inequality* 7: 5–28.

Salehi-Isfahani, Djavad, Mohammad Jalal Abbasi-Shavazi, and Meimanat Hosseini-Chavoshi. 2010. "Family Planning and Fertility Decline in Rural Iran: The Impact of Rural Health Clinics." *Health Economics* 19: 159–180.

Salem, Paul. 2008. "The Aftereffects of the Israeli–Hizbollah War." *Contemporary Arab Affairs* 1 (1): 15–24.

Salimi, Muhammad H., ed. 2003. *Islamic Views on Human Rights: Viewpoints of Iranian Scholars*. Organization for Islamic Culture and Communications, Directorate of Research and Education, Centre for Cultural-International Studies. New Delhi: Kanishka Publishers.

Saqr, Naomi. 1998. *Walls of Silence: Media and Censorship in Syria*. London: Article 19.

Schayegh, Cyrus. 2006. "The Development of Social Insurance in Iran: Technical-Financial Conditions and Political Rationales, 1941–1960." *Iranian Studies* 39 (4): 539–568.

Schlumberger, Oliver, ed. 2007. *Debating Arab Authoritarianism: Dynamics and Durability in Nondemocratic Regimes*. Stanford, CA: Stanford University Press.

Schmitter, Phillipe. 1974. "Still the Century of Corporatism?" *The Review of Politics* 36: 85–131.

Schneider, Anne, and Helen Ingram, eds. 2005. *Deserving and Entitled: Social Constructions and Public Policy.* Albany: State University of New York Press.

Seale, Patrick. 1965. *The Struggle for Syria: A Study of Post-war Arab Politics, 1945–1958.* London: Oxford University Press.

———. 1990. *Asad: The Struggle for the Middle East.* Berkeley: University of California Press.

Sedghi, Hamideh. 2007. *Women and Politics in Iran: Veiling, Unveiling, and Reveiling.* New York: Cambridge University Press.

Segura-Ubiergo, Alex. 2007. *The Political Economy of the Welfare State in Latin America: Globalization, Democracy, and Development.* Cambridge, UK: Cambridge University Press.

Selvik, Kjetil, and Thomas Pierret. 2009. "Limits to Upgrading Authoritarianism in Syria: Private Welfare, Islamic Charities, and the Rise of the Zayd movement." *International Journal for Middle East Studies* 41 (4): 595–614.

Seurat, Michel. 1989. *L'Etat de barberie.* Paris: Editions du seuil.

Shadpour, Kamel. 2000. "Primary Health Care Networks in the Islamic Republic of Iran." *Eastern Mediterranean Health Journal* 6 (4): 822–825.

Shaery-Eisenlohr, Roschanack. 2011. "From Citizens to Subjects? Civil Society and the Internet in Syria." *Middle East Critique* 20 (2): 127–138.

Shannon, Jonathan H. 2006. *Among the Jasmine Trees: Music and Modernity in Contemporary Syria.* Middletown, CT: Wesleyan University Press.

Shukri, Abdallah. 1978. "Huquq al-insan fi al-qutr al-'arabi al-suri," *Al-Muhamun* 2: 143–150.

Silver, Beverly. 1990. "The Contradictions of Semiperipheral Success: The Case of Israel," in *Semiperipheral States in the World Economy,* ed. William Martin, 161–181. New York: Greenwood Press.

Sirees, Nihad. 1996. *al-Kumidiyya al-fallahiyya.* Aleppo: Nihad Sirees.

———. 2004. *Al-samt wa-l-sakhab: Riwaya.* Beirut: Dar al-Adab.

Skocpol, Theda. 1992. *Protecting Soldiers and Mothers: The Political Origins of Social Policy in the United States.* Cambridge, MA: Harvard University Press.

Sluglett, Peter. 2007. "The Ozymandias Syndrome: Questioning the Stability of Middle Eastern Regimes," in *Debating Arab Authoritarianism: Dynamics and Durability in Nondemocratic Regimes,* ed. Oliver Schlumberger, 93–108. Stanford, CA: Stanford University Press.

Sohrabi, Nader. 1995. "Historicizing Revolutions: Constitutional Revolutions in the Ottoman Empire, Iran, and Russia, 1905–1908." *American Sociological Review* 100: 1383–1447.

Solingen, Etel. 1998. *Regional Orders at Century's Dawn: Global and Domestic Influence on Grand Strategy.* Princeton, NJ: Princeton University Press.

Soroush, Abdolkarim. 2000. In *Reason, Freedom, and Democracy in Islam: Essential Writings of Abdolkarim Soroush*, trans. and ed. Mahmoud Sadri and Ahmad Sadri. Oxford, UK: Oxford University Press.

Sottimano Aurora. 2010. "Package Politics: Antagonism, Resistance, and Peace in Syrian Political Discourse." University of Amsterdam, Civil Society in West Asia Working Paper Series: Working Paper 8; available at www.hivos.nl/english/ Hivos-Knowledge-Programme/Themes/Civil-Society-in-West-Asia/News/Package-Politics-Antagonism-Resistance-and-Peace-in-Syrian-Political-Discourse.

Sottimano, Aurora, and Kjetil Selvik. 2008. *Changing Regime Discourse and Reform in Syria*. Fife, UK: University of St. Andrews Centre for Syrian Studies.

Stark, David. 1996. "Recombinant Property in East European Capitalism." *American Journal of Sociology* 101(4): 993–1027.

Statistical Center of Iran (SCI). 2009. *Statistical Yearbook*. Tehran: Statistical Center of Iran.

Steinmetz, George. 1993. *Regulating the Social: The Welfare State and Local Politics in Imperial Germany*. Princeton, NJ: Princeton University Press.

Stepan, Alfred. 1978. *The State and Society: Peru in Comparative Perspective*. Princeton, NJ: Princeton University Press.

Stienen, Petra. 2008. *Dromen van een Arabische lente: Een Nederlandse diplomate in het Midden-Oosten*. Amsterdam: Nieuw Amsterdam Uitgevers.

Stinchcombe, Arthur. 1997. "Tilly on the Past as a Sequence of Futures," in *Roads from Past to Future*, by Charles Tilly. Lanham, MD: Rowman and Littlefield Publishers.

Suleiman, Susan. 1983. *Authoritarian Fictions: The Ideological Novel as a Literary Genre*. New York: Columbia University Press.

Syrian Arab Republic. 1984a. *Al-Ikhwan al-muslimun. nash'a mashbuha wa tarikh aswad (Vol. 3)*. Damascus: Syrian Arab Republic, Preparation Office.

———. 1984b. *Al-Ikhwan al-muslimun. nash'a mashbuha wa tarikh aswad (Vol. 4)*. Damascus: Syrian Arab Republic, Preparation Office.

———. 2004–2007. *al-majmu'a al-ihsa'iyya l-'Am 2003-6*. Damascus: Syrian Arab Republic.

Syrian Bar Association. 1978. "Mudhakirat niqabat al-muhamin 'ila al-mas'uliyyin hawla al-huriyyat al- 'ama wa siyyadat al-qanun wa da'm al-qada'." *Al-Muhamun* 5–8: 106–110.

Syrian Human Rights Committee. 2001. *Report on the Human Rights Situation in Syria over a 20-Year Period*. Damascus: SHRC; available at www.shrc.org/data/ pdf/1275.pdf.

———. 2010. *Ninth Annual Report on Human Rights in Syria 2010*. Damascus: SHRC.

Syrian Human Rights Information Link. 2006–2009. *List of Political Prisoners: 2006–2009*. Damascus: SHRIL; available at www.shril-sy.info/.

Tabler, Andrew. 2005. "Can Syria Afford United Nations Sanctions?" *The Daily Star*, December 6.

Taleghani, Mahmud. 1982. *Society and Economics in Islam: The Writings and Declarations of Ayatullah Sayyid Mahmud Taleghani,* trans. R. Campbell. Berkeley, CA: Mizan Press.

Tarrow, Sidney G. 1998. *Power in Movement: Social Movements and Contentious Politics.* Cambridge, UK: Cambridge University Press.

———. 2005. *The New Transnational Activism.* Cambridge, UK: Cambridge University Press.

Tarrow, Sidney G., Charles Tilly, and Doug McAdam. 2001. *Dynamics of Contention.* Cambridge, UK: Cambridge University Press.

Tezcür, Güneş M. 2010. *Muslim Reformers in Iran and Turkey: The Paradox of Moderation.* Austin: University of Texas Press.

Tezcür, Güneş M., Taghi Azadarmaki, Mehri Bahar, and Hooshang Nayebi. 2012. "Support for Democracy in Iran." *Political Research Quarterly* 65: 235–247.

Thaler, David, Alireza Nader, Shahram Chubin, Jerold Green, Charlotte Lynch, and Frederic Wehrey. 2010. *Mullahs, Guards, and* Bonyads: *An Exploration of Iranian Leadership Dynamics.* Santa Monica, CA: The RAND Corporation.

Thépault, Charles. 2010. "Le cas des banques islamiques dans la réforme du secteur bancaire syrien: introduction du référent religieux dans la libéralisation économique." Research dissertation supervised by Philippe Droz Vincent and d'Anne Bazin, I. E. P. Lille.

Thompson, Mark R., and Philipp Kuntz. 2004. "Stolen Elections: The Case of the Serbian October." *Journal of Democracy* 15: 159–172.

Tilly, Charles. 1992. *Coercion, Capital and European States, 1990–1992.* London: Blackwell Publishing.

———. 2006. *Regimes and Repertoires.* Chicago: University of Chicago Press.

———. 2007. *Democracy.* New York: Cambridge University Press.

Tlass, Mustafa. 1991. *Mar'at hayati.* Damascus: Dar Tlass. Excerpt available at www.moustafatlass.org/index.php?d=280&id=603.

Tripp, Charles. 2007. "In the Name of the People: The 'People's Court' and the Iraqi Revolution (1958–1960)," in *Staging Politics: Power and Performance in Asia and Africa,* ed. Julia C. Strauss and Donal B. Cruise O'Brien, 31–48. London and New York: I. B. Tauris.

Tudoroiu, Theodore. 2007. "Rose, Orange, and Tulip: The Failed Soviet Revolutions." *Communist and Post-Communist Studies* 40: 315–342.

Tuğal, Cihan. 2009. "Transforming Everyday Life: Islamism and Social Movement Theory." *Theory and Society* 38 (5): 423–458.

Underwood, Carol. 2004. "Islam and Social Policy: A Study of the Islamic Republic of Iran," in *Islam and Social Policy,* ed. Stephen Heynemann, 181–206. Nashville, TN: Vanderbilt University Press.

U.N. Conference on Trade and Development (UNCTD). 2007. *World Investment Report 2004–2006.* New York and Geneva: United Nations.

U.N. Development Program (UNDP). 2005. "Poverty in Syria: 1996–2004: Diagnosis and Pro-Poor Policy Considerations." Damascus: United Nations Development Programme, June.

U.N. Office at Geneva. 2010. *Committee against Torture Hears Response of Syria*. Geneva: UNOG, May 4; available at www.unog.ch/unog/website/news_media.nsf/ (httpNewsByYear_en)/6607744D0FA4106FC1257719004167DD?OpenDocument.

Valbjorn, Valbjørn, and André Bank. 2010. "Examining the 'Post' in Post-Democratization: The Future of Middle Eastern Political Rule through Lenses of the Past." *Middle East Critique*, 19(3): 183–200.

Van Dam, Nikolaos. 2009. "Syrian Ba'thist Memoirs," *Kulluna Shuraka fi al-Watan*, May 9–11; available at www.joshualandis.com/blog/?p=2988.

Vauthier, Elisabeth. 2007. *La création romanesque contemporaine en Syrie de 1967 à nos jours*. Damascus: IFPO.

Volpi, Frederic. 2010. *Political Islam Observed*. New York: Columbia University Press.

Wattar, Muhammad R. 2000. *Shakhsiyyat al-muthaqqaf fi al-riwaya al-'arabiyya al-suriyya: dirasa*. Damascus: Ittihad al-Kuttab al-'Arab.

Way, Lucan. 2008. "The Real Causes of the Color Revolutions." *Journal of Democracy* 19: 55–69.

——. 2010. "Resistance to Contagion: Sources of Authoritarian Stability in the Former Soviet Union," in *Democracy and Authoritarianism in the Postcommunist World*, ed. Valerie Bunce, Michael McFaul, and Kathryn Stoner-Weiss, 229–252. New York: Cambridge University Press.

Wedeen, Lisa. 1998. "Acting 'As If': Symbolic Politics and Social Control in Syria." *Comparative Studies in Society and History* 40 (3): 503–523.

——. 1999. *Ambiguities of Dominations: Politics, Rhetorics, and Symbols in Contemporary Syria*. Chicago: University of Chicago Press.

Wehrey, Frederic, Jerrold D. Green, Brian Nichiporuk, Alireza Nader, Lydia Hansell, Rasool Nafisi, and S. R. Bohandy. 2009. *The Rise of the Pasdaran: Assessing the Domestic Roles of Iran's Islamic Revolutionary Guards Corps*. Santa Monica, CA: RAND National Defense Research Institute.

Weingeist, Barry R.. 2005. "Persuasion, Preference Change, and Critical Junctures: The Microfoundations of a Macroscopic Concept," in *Preferences and Situations*, ed. Ira Katznelson and Barry R. Weingeist, 161–184. New York: Russell Sage Foundation.

Wiktorowicz, Quintan. 2004. *Islamic Activism: A Social Movement Approach*. Bloomington, IN: Indiana University Press.

Wilson, Andrew. 2005. *Ukraine's Orange Revolution*. New Haven, CT: Yale University Press.

Wood, Geoffrey, and Ian Gough. 2006. "A Comparative Welfare Regime Approach to Global Social Policy." *World Development* 34 (10): 1696–1712.

World Bank. 2011. *World Development Indicators.* Washington, DC: The World Bank.

Worth, Robert. 2008. "A Bloody Era of Syria's History Informs a Writer's Banned Novel." *The New York Times,* April 12.

Zeghal, Malika. 1996. *Gardiens de l'Islam: Les oulémas d'Al Azhar dans l'Egypte contemporaine.* Paris: FNSP.

Zeitouneh, Razan. 2007. *Can Extraordinary Courts Ensure Justice? The Supreme State Security Court.* Damascus: Damascus Center for Human Rights Studies, May; available at www.shril-sy.info/enshril/modules/news/article.php?storyid=174.

Ziadeh, Radwan. 2008. *al-Islam al-siyasi fi suriya.* Abu Dhabi: The Emirates Center for Strategic Studies and Research.

———. ed. 2010. *Years of Fear: The Enforced Disappeared in Syria.* Transitional Justice in the Arab World Project; available at www.shrilsy.info/enshril/modules/tinycontent/content/Years%20of%20Fear%20-%20English%20Draft.pdf.

Ziblatt, Daniel. 2006. "How Did Europe Democratize?" *World Politics* 58: 311–338.

Zisser, Eyal. 2005. "Syria, the Ba'th Regime and the Islamic Movement: Stepping on a New Path?" *The Muslim World* 95 (1): 43–65.

Žižek, Slavoj. 1989. *The Sublime Object of Ideology.* London: Verso.

Zubaida, Sami. 2005. *Law and Power in the Islamic World.* London: I. B. Tauris.

INDEX

Note: Page numbers in *italics* indicate figures; those with a *t* indicate tables.

Abdullah, King of Jordan, 1
'Abidin, 'Ala' al-Din, 102
Abrahamian, Ervand, 62, 68
Abu Nour Institute (Damascus), 112, 114, 116, 119
Adelkhah, Fariba, 135
Adorno, Theodor, 164–65
Aga Khan Development Network (AKDN), 56
al-Aghasi, Mahmoud, 252n34
Ahmadinejad, Mahmoud, 25; coalition of, 238–39; election of, 28, 204, 206, 216, 235; popularity of, 77; Rafsanjani and, 204; re-election of, 212, 217–21, 238–39; repression by, 128–29; resilience of, 217–21, 235–42. *See also* Green Movement
Alawites, 51–52, 96, 185, 187
Algeria, 25
al-Ali, Muhammad Ibrahim, 188
Ansari, Ali, 202–3
Anvari, Hossein, 70–71
Arab Lawyers Union, 190
Arab Writers' Union, 147
Arendt, Hannah, 192
Argentina, 185
Armenia, 210, 211t, 212, 213t
al-Asad, Asma, 23, 49; NGOs sponsored by, 45–46, 50, 233–34
al-Asad, Bashar, 3, 25; co-optation by, 119, 144, 148, 157, 208–9, 226–27, 231–34, 241; cultural movements under, 23–24, 48–49, *90*, 143–65; economic reforms

of, 12–14, 16, 35–60, 229–30; Islamic social movements and, 107–24, 149; judicialization of repression by, 26–27; political reforms of, 227, 230–32; religious policies of, 17–21, 83–84, 94–106; on U.S.-Iraq war, 227–29
al-Asad, Hafiz, 35; Corrective Movement of, 17, 89–90, 176, 189; corruption under, 162, 189; "cult" of, 144; economic policies of, 12, 14, 189, 226–27; on foreign interventions, 258n36; Islamic social movements and, 119
al-Asad, Maher, 40
al-Asad, Rifa'at, 192
al-Aswad, Abd al-Kader, 188
Ataturk, Kemal, 18, 64, 85–86
authoritarian regimes, 4–11, 24–31; literature on, 23–24, 143–45; notions of statehood of, 182–84; pathologies of, 170, 171, 180–83; "populist," 169; recombinant, 7–16, 58, 84, 245n2
authoritarian resilience, 21–23, 61–80, 200–202, 222–42; brokerage for, 108–9, 116–24; coalitions for, 224–25, 232–34; common factors of, 222–26; cultural policies for, 149–51; electoral uprisings and, 208–14, 211t, 213t; external resources for, 223–24; judicialization of repression and, 26–27, 169–99; religious affairs and, 17–21, 84
awqaf (religious endowments), 18, 68, 83, *88*, *90*, *92*, 114

287

Stanford Studies in Middle Eastern and Islamic Societies and Cultures

Jonathan Marshall, The Lebanese Connection: Corruption, Civil War, and the International Drug Traffic
2012

Joshua Stacher, Adaptable Autocrats: Regime Power in Egypt and Syria
2012

Bassam Haddad, Business Networks in Syria: The Political Economy of Authoritarian Resilience
2011

Noah Coburn, Bazaar Politics: Power and Pottery in an Afghan Market Town
2011

Laura Bier, Revolutionary Womanhood: Feminisms, Modernity, and the State in Nasser's Egypt
2011

Joel Beinin and Frédéric Vairel, editors, Social Movements, Mobilization, and Contestation in the Middle East and North Africa
2011

Samer Soliman, The Autumn of Dictatorship: Fiscal Crisis and Political Change in Egypt under Mubarak
2011

Rochelle A. Davis, Palestinian Village Histories: Geographies of the Displaced
2010

Haggai Ram, *Iranophobia: The Logic of an Israeli Obsession*
2009

John Chalcraft, *The Invisible Cage: Syrian Migrant Workers in Lebanon*
2008

Rhoda Kanaaneh, *Surrounded: Palestinian Soldiers in the Israeli Military*
2008

Asef Bayat, *Making Islam Democratic: Social Movements and the Post-Islamist Turn*
2007

Robert Vitalis, *America's Kingdom: Mythmaking on the Saudi Oil Frontier*
2006

Jessica Winegar, *Creative Reckonings: The Politics of Art and Culture in Contemporary Egypt*
2006

Joel Beinin and Rebecca L. Stein, editors, *The Struggle for Sovereignty: Palestine and Israel, 1993–2005*
2006